D0459680

THEORY OF
GROUND VEHICLES

THEORY OF
GROUND VEHICLES

J. Y. WONG, Ph.D.

Professor, Department of Mechanical and Aeronautical Engineering
Director, Transport Technology Research Laboratory
Carleton University
Ottawa, Ontario

A WILEY-INTERSCIENCE PUBLICATION

JOHN WILEY & SONS
New York • Chichester • Brisbane • Toronto • Singapore

Library of Congress Cataloging in Publication Data

Wong, Jo Yung.
   Theory of ground vehicles.

   "A Wiley-Interscience publication."
   Includes bibliographies and index.
     1. Motor vehicles—Design and construction.
2. Ground-effect machines—Design and construction.
I. Title.

TL240.W66   629.22   78-16714
ISBN 0-471-03470-3

Printed in the United States of America

10 9 8 7

PREFACE

Society's growing demand for better and safer transportation, environmental protection, and energy conservation has stimulated new interest in the development of the technology for transportation. Transport technology has now become an academic discipline in both graduate and undergraduate programs at an increasing number of engineering schools in North America and elsewhere. While preparing lecture notes for my two courses at Carleton on ground transportation technology, I found that although there was a wealth of information in research reports and in journals of learned societies, there was as yet no comprehensive account suitable as a text for university students. I hope this book will fill this gap.

Although this book is intended mainly to introduce senior undergraduate and beginning graduate students to the study of ground vehicles, it should also interest engineers and researchers in the vehicle industry. This book deals with the theory and engineering principles of nonguided ground vehicles, including road, off-road, and air-cushion vehicles. Analysis and evaluation of performance characteristics, handling behavior, and ride qualities are covered. The presentation emphasizes the fundamental principles underlying rational development and design of vehicle systems. A unified method of approach to the analysis of the characteristics of various types of ground vehicles is also stressed.

This book consists of eight chapters. Chapter 1 discusses the mechanics of pneumatic tires and provides a basis for the study of road vehicle characteristics. Chapter 2 examines the vehicle running gear-terrain interaction, which is essential to the evaluation of off-road vehicle performance. Understanding the interaction between the vehicle and the ground is important to the study of vehicle performance, handling, and ride, because, aside from aerodynamic inputs, almost all other forces and moments affecting the motion of a ground vehicle are applied through the running gear-ground contact. Chapter 3 deals with analysis and prediction of the performance of road vehicles. Included in the discussion are vehicle power plant and transmission characteristics, performance limits, acceleration characteristics, braking performance, and fuel economy. The performance of off-road vehicles is the subject of Chapter 4. Drawbar performance, tractive efficiency, operating fuel economy, transport productivity and efficiency, mobility map, and mobility profile are discussed. Chapter 5 examines handling behavior of road vehicles, including steady-state and transient responses, and directional stability. The steering of tracked vehicles is the subject of Chapter 6. Included in the discussion are the mechanics of skid-steering, steerability of tracked vehicles, and steering by articulation. Chapter 7 examines vehicle ride qualities. Human response to vibration, vehicle ride models, and the application of random process theory to the analysis of vehicle vibration are covered. In addition to conventional road and off-road vehicles, air-cushion vehicles have found applications in ground transport. The basic engineering principles of air-cushion systems and the unique features and characteristics of air-cushion vehicles are treated in Chapter 8.

A book of this scope limits detail. Since it is primarily intended for students, some topics have been given a simpler treatment than the latest developments would allow. Nevertheless, this book should provide the reader with a comprehensive background on the theory of ground vehicles.

I have used part of the material included in this book in my two engineering courses in ground transport technology at Carleton. It has also been used in two special professional programs. One is "Terrain-Vehicle Systems Analysis," given in Canada and Sweden jointly with Dr. M. G. Bekker, formerly with AC Electronics-Defense Research Laboratories, General Motors Corporation, Santa Barbara, California. The other is "Braking and Handling of Heavy Commercial Vehicles" given at Carleton jointly with Professor J. R. Ellis, School of Automotive Studies, Cranfield Institute of Technology, England, and Dr. R. R. Guntur, Transport Technology Research Laboratory, Carleton University.

In writing this book, I have drawn much on the knowledge and experience acquired from collaboration with many colleagues in industry, research organizations, and universities. I wish to express my deep appreciation to them. I am especially indebted to Dr. A. R. Reece, University of Newcastle upon Tyne, England, Dr. M. G. Bekker, and Professor J. R. Ellis for stimulation and encouragement.

I also acknowledge with gratitude the information and inspiration derived from the references listed at the end of the chapters and express my appreciation to many organizations and individuals for permission to reproduce illustrations and other copyrighted material.

Appreciation is due to Dr. R. R. Guntur for reviewing part of the manuscript and to Dean M. C. de Malherbe, Faculty of Engineering, Professor H. I. H. Saravanamuttoo, Chairman, Department of Mechanical and Aeronautical Engineering, and many colleagues at Carleton University for encouragement.

Jo Yung Wong

Ottawa, Canada
July 1978

CONTENTS

NOMENCLATURE

A	area, contact area
A_c	cushion area
A_f	frontal area
a	acceleration
a_x	acceleration component along the x axis
a_y	acceleration component along the y axis
a_z	acceleration component along the z axis
B	tread of the vehicle
B_a	barometric pressure
B_m	working width of machinery
B_0	barometric pressure under standard atmospheric conditions
B_v	vapor pressure
b	width
C_D	aerodynamic resistance coefficient
C_f	ratio of braking effort to normal load of vehicle front axle
C_i	longitudinal stiffness of tire
C_L	aerodynamic lift coefficient
C_{ld}	lift/drag ratio
C_M	aerodynamic pitching moment coefficient
C_r	ratio of braking effort to normal load of vehicle rear axle
C_{ro}	restoring moment coefficient

C_s	ratio of braking effort to normal load of semitrailer axle
C_{sk}	coefficient of skirt contact drag
C_{sp}	coefficient of spectral density function
C_{sr}	speed ratio of torque converter
C_{tr}	torque ratio of torque converter
C_α	cornering stiffness of tire
$C_{\alpha f}$	cornering stiffness of front tire
$C_{\alpha r}$	cornering stiffness of rear tire
C_γ	camber stiffness of tire
c	cohesion
c_a	adhesion
c_{eq}	equivalent damping coefficient
c_{sh}	damping coefficient of shock absorber
c_t	damping coefficient of tire
D	diameter
D_c	discharge coefficient
D_h	hydraulic diameter
E	energy
E_d	energy available at vehicle drawbar
F	force, thrust
F_b	braking force
F_{bf}	braking force of vehicle front axle
F_{br}	braking force of vehicle rear axle
F_{bs}	braking force of semitrailer axle
F_{cu}	lift generated by air cushion
F_d	drawbar pull
F_f	thrust of vehicle front axle
F_h	hydrodynamic force acting on a tire over flooded surfaces
F_{hi}	horizontal force acting at the hitch point of a tractor-semitrailer
F_i	thrust of the inside track of a tracked vehicle
F_l	lift generated by the change of momentum of an air jet
F_{net}	net thrust
F_o	thrust of the outside track of a tracked vehicle
F_p	resultant force due to passive earth pressure
F_{pn}	normal component of the resultant force due to passive earth pressure
F_r	thrust of vehicle rear axle
F_s	side force

F_x	force component along the x axis
F_y	force component along the y axis
F_{yf}	cornering force of front tire
F_{yr}	cornering force of rear tire
$F_{y\alpha}$	cornering force of tire
$F_{y\gamma}$	camber thrust of tire
F_z	force component along the z axis
f	frequency
f_c	center frequency
f_{eq}	equivalent coefficient of motion resistance
f_{n-s}	natural frequency of sprung mass
f_{n-us}	natural frequency of unsprung mass
f_r	coefficient of rolling resistance
G	grade
G_{acc}	lateral acceleration gain
G_{yaw}	yaw velocity gain
g	acceleration due to gravity
h	height of center of gravity of the vehicle
h_a	height of the point of application of aerodynamic resistance above ground level
h_b	depth
h_c	clearance height
h_d	height of drawbar
I	mass moment of inertia
I_w	mass moment of inertia of wheels
I_y	mass moment of inertia of the vehicle about the y axis
I_z	mass moment of inertia of the vehicle about the z axis
i	slip
i_f	slip of front wheel
i_i	slip of the inside track of a tracked vehicle
i_o	slip of the outside track of a tracked vehicle
i_r	slip of rear wheel
i_s	skid
J_j	momentum flux of an air jet
j	shear displacement
K	shear deformation modulus
K_a	augmentation factor

K_{bf}	proportion of total braking force placed on vehicle front axle
K_{br}	proportion of total braking force placed on vehicle rear axle
K_{bs}	proportion of total braking force placed on semitrailer axle
K_d	coefficient of thrust distribution
K_{di}	gear ratio of a controlled differential
K_e	engine capacity factor
K_p	passive earth pressure coefficient
K_s	ratio of the angular speed of the outside track sprocket to that of the inside track sprocket
K_{tc}	torque converter capacity factor
K_{us}	understeer coefficient
K_v	ratio of the theoretical speed of the front tire to that of the rear tire
K_w	weight utilization factor
k_c	cohesive modulus of terrain deformation
k_f	front suspension spring stiffness
k_r	rear suspension spring stiffness
k_s	stiffness of suspension spring
k_{tr}	equivalent spring stiffness of tire
k_ϕ	frictional modulus of terrain deformation
L	wheel base
L_c	characteristic length
l	length
l_{cu}	cushion perimeter
l_j	nozzle perimeter
l_o	distance between oscillation center and center of gravity of the vehicle
l_1	distance between front axle and center of gravity of the vehicle
l_2	distance between rear axle and center of gravity of the vehicle
M_a	aerodynamic pitching moment
M_b	braking torque
M_e	engine output torque
M_r	moment of turning resistance
M_{ro}	restoring moment in roll
M_{tc}	torque converter output torque

M_w	wheel torque
M_x	moment about the x axis
M_y	moment about the y axis
M_z	moment about the z axis
m	vehicle mass
m_s	sprung mass
m_{us}	unsprung mass
N	exponent of spectral density function
N_c, N_q, N_γ	bearing capacity factors
N_ϕ	flow value
n	exponent of terrain deformation
n_e	engine speed
n_g	number of speeds in a gearbox
n_{tc}	torque converter output speed
P	engine power
P_a	power required to sustain the air cushion
P_d	drawbar power
P_m	power required to overcome momentum drag
P_0	engine power under standard atmospheric conditions
P_{st}	power consumption of a tracked vehicle in straight line motion
P_t	power consumption of a tracked vehicle during a turn
p	pressure
p_c	pressure exerted by tire carcass
p_{cr}	critical pressure
p_{cu}	cushion pressure
p_d	dynamic pressure
p_g	ground pressure at the lowest point of contact
p_i	inflation pressure
p_j	total jet pressure
Q	volume flow
q	surcharge
R	turning radius
R_a	aerodynamic resistance
R_d	drawbar load
R_g	grade resistance
R_i	motion resistance of the inside track of a tracked vehicle
R_{in}	internal resistance of track system

R_L	aerodynamic lift
R_l	lateral resistance of track
R_m	momentum drag
R_o	motion resistance of the outside track of a tracked vehicle
R_r	rolling resistance
R_{rf}	rolling resistance of front wheel
R_{rr}	rolling resistance of rear wheel
R_{rs}	rolling resistance of semitrailer wheel
R_{sk}	skirt contact drag
R_{tot}	total motion resistance
R_w	wavemaking drag
R_{wave}	drag due to wave
R_{wet}	wetting drag
r	radius of wheel or sprocket
r_e	effective rolling radius of tire
r_y	radius of gyration of the vehicle about the y axis
S	distance
s	displacement
$S_g(\Omega)$	spectral density function of terrain profile (spatial frequency)
$S_g(f)$	spectral density function of terrain profile (temporal frequency)
$S_v(f)$	spectral density function of vehicle response (temporal frequency)
T	temperature
T_0	temperature under standard atmospheric conditions
t	time
t_j	thickness of air jet
t_p	pneumatic trail of tire
t_t	track pitch
U	energy dissipation
u_a	fuel consumed for work performed per unit area
u_e	energy obtained at the drawbar per unit volume of fuel spent
u_h	fuel consumed per hour
u_s	specific fuel consumption
u_t	fuel consumed during time t
u_{tr}	fuel consumed per unit payload for unit distance

V	speed
V_a	speed of wind relative to vehicle
V_c	speed of air escaping from cushion
V_i	speed of the inside track of a tracked vehicle
V_j	slip speed
V_{jc}	jet speed
V_m	average operating speed
V_o	speed of the outside track of a tracked vehicle
V_p	hydroplaning speed of tire
V_t	theoretical speed
V_{tf}	theoretical speed of front tire
V_{tr}	theoretical speed of rear tire
W	normal load, weight
W_a	load supported by air cushion
W_c	critical load
W_d	proportion of vehicle weight applied to driven wheels
W_f	load on vehicle front axle
W_{hi}	normal load at the hitch point of a tractor-semitrailer
W_p	payload
W_r	load on vehicle rear axle
W_s	load on semitrailer axle
α	slip angle of tire
α_a	angle of attack
α_{an}	angular acceleration
α_b	inclination angle
α_f	slip angle of front tire
α_r	slip angle of rear tire
β_b	inclination angle of blade
γ	camber angle of tire
γ_m	vehicle mass factor
γ_s	specific weight of terrain
δ	angle of interface friction
δ_f	steer angle of front wheel
δ_i	steer angle of inside front wheel
δ_o	steer angle of outside front wheel
δ_t	tire deflection

ε strain
ε_r road adhesion reduction factor

ζ damping ratio

η_b braking efficiency
η_c torque converter efficiency
η_{cu} cushion intake efficiency
η_d tractive efficiency, drawbar efficiency
η_m efficiency of motion
η_p propulsive efficiency
η_s slip efficiency
η_{st} structural efficiency
η_t transmission efficiency
η_{tr} transport efficiency

θ angular displacement
θ_c cushion wall angle
θ_j nozzle angle
θ_s slope angle
θ_t trim angle

μ coefficient of road adhesion
μ_c coefficient of cornering force
μ_0 nominal coefficient of road adhesion
μ_p peak value of coefficient of road adhesion
μ_s sliding value of coefficient of road adhesion
μ_t coefficient of lateral resistance
μ_{tr} coefficient of traction

ν concentration factor

ξ gear ratio
ξ_o overall reduction ratio
ξ_s steering gear ratio

ρ air density
ρ_f density of fluid
ρ_w density of water

σ normal stress
σ_a active earth pressure

σ_p	passive earth pressure
σ_r	radial stress
σ_z	vertical stress
τ	shear stress
τ_{max}	maximum shear stress
τ_r	residual shear stress
ϕ	angle of internal shearing resistance
Ω	spatial frequency
Ω_x	angular speed about the x axis
Ω_y	angular speed about the y axis
Ω_z	angular speed about the z axis
ω	angular speed
ω_i	angular speed of the sprocket of the inside track of a tracked vehicle
ω_n	circular natural frequency
ω_o	angular speed of the sprocket of the outside track of a tracked vehicle

INTRODUCTION

Ground vehicles are those vehicles that are supported by the ground, as contrasted with aircraft and marine craft that in operation are supported by fluid: air or water. Ground vehicles may be broadly classified as guided and nonguided. Guided ground vehicles are constrained to move along a fixed path (guideway), such as railway vehicles and tracked levitated vehicles. Nonguided ground vehicles can move, by choice, in various directions on the ground, such as road and off-road vehicles. The mechanics of nonguided ground vehicles is the subject of this book. The prime objective of the study of the mechanics of ground vehicles is to provide guiding principles for the rational development, design, evaluation, and selection of vehicles to meet various operational requirements.

In general, the characteristics of a ground vehicle may be described in terms of its performance, handling, and ride. Performance characteristics include the ability of the vehicle to accelerate, to develop drawbar pull, to overcome obstacles, and to decelerate. Handling qualities of interest are the response of the vehicle to the driver's commands and its ability to stabilize its motion against external disturbances. Ride characteristics are related to the vibration of the vehicle excited by surface irregularities and its effect on passengers and goods. The theory of ground vehicles is concerned with the study of the performance, handling, and ride and their relationships with the design of ground vehicles under various operational environments.

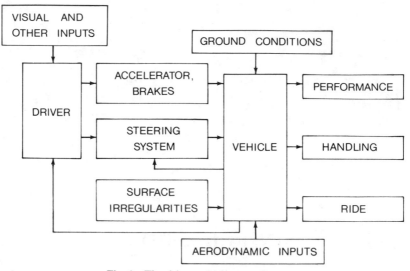

Fig. 1   The driver-vehicle-ground system.

The behavior of a ground vehicle represents the results of the interaction between the driver, the vehicle, and the environment as illustrated in Fig. 1. An understanding of the behavior of the human driver, the characteristics of the vehicle, and the physical and geometric properties of the ground is, therefore, essential to the design and evaluation of ground vehicle systems.

CHAPTER ONE

MECHANICS OF PNEUMATIC TIRES

Aside from aerodynamic and gravitational forces, almost all other forces and moments affecting the motion of a ground vehicle are applied through the running gear-ground contact. An understanding of the basic characteristics of the interaction between the running gear and the ground is, therefore, essential to the study of the performance characteristics, ride quality, and handling behavior of ground vehicles.

The running gear of a ground vehicle is generally required to fulfill the following functions:

1   to support the weight of the vehicle
2   to cushion the vehicle over surface irregularities
3   to provide sufficient traction for driving and braking
4   to provide adequate steering control and directional stability

Pneumatic tires can perform these functions efficiently, thus they are exclusively used in road vehicles and are also widely used in off-road vehicles. The study of the mechanics of pneumatic tires therefore is of fundamental importance to the understanding of the performance and characteristics of ground vehicles. Two basic types of problem in the mechanics of tires are of special interest to vehicle engineers. One is the mechanics of tires on hard surfaces, which is essential to the study of the characteristics of road vehicles. The other is the mechanics of tires on

3

deformable surfaces (unprepared terrain), which is of prime importance to the study of off-road vehicle performance.

The mechanics of tires on hard surfaces is discussed in this Chapter, whereas the behavior of tires over unprepared terrain will be discussed in Chapter 2.

A pneumatic tire is a structure of the shape of a toroid filled with air. The most important structural element of the tire is the carcass, which is made up of a number of layers of flexible cords of high modulus of elasticity encased in a matrix of low modulus rubber. The design and construction of the carcass determine, to a great extent, the characteristics of the tire. Among the various design parameters the direction of the cords plays a significant role in the behavior of the tire and is usually defined by the crown angle; the crown angle is the angle between the cord and the circumferential center line of the tire as shown in Fig. 1.1. When the cords have a low crown angle, the tire will have good cornering characteristics but a harsh ride. On the other hand, if the cords are at right angle to the tire periphery, the tire will be capable of providing a good ride but poor cornering characteristics.

A compromise is adopted in a conventional bias-ply tire, which is constructed with a crown angle of about 40° and has two or more layers of cord filaments. Normally alternate layers have cords at the opposite hand. Thus the cords overlap in a diamond-shaped pattern. In operation the diagonal plies flex and rub, thus elongating the diamond-shaped elements and the rubber filler. This flexing action produces a wiping motion between the tread and the road, which is one of the main causes of tire wear and of high rolling resistance [1.1, 1.2].*

Recently, radial-ply tires, which are constructed very differently from bias-ply tires, have been produced and successfully used in large quantities. The cords in the carcass of radial-ply tires are disposed in a radial direction giving a 90° crown angle as shown in Fig. 1.1. A belt of several plies of cords of high modulus of elasticity is fitted on top of the carcass under the tread and laid at a low crown angle of about 20° as shown in Fig. 1.1. The belt is essential to the proper functioning of the radial-ply tire. Without it, a radial-ply carcass can become unstable, since the tire periphery may develop into a series of buckles due to the irregularities in cord spacing when inflated. For the radial-ply tire, flexing of the carcass involves very little relative movement of the cords forming the belt. In the absence of wiping motion between the tire and the road, the power dissipation of radial-ply tires could be as low as 60% of that of bias-ply tires under similar conditions, and the life of radial-ply tires could be as

---

*Numbers in brackets designate references at end of chapter.

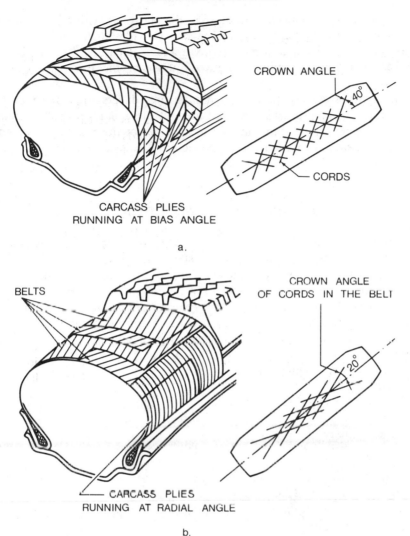

CROWN ANGLE

40°

CORDS

CARCASS PLIES
RUNNING AT BIAS ANGLE

a.

BELTS

CROWN ANGLE
OF CORDS IN THE BELT

20°

CARCASS PLIES
RUNNING AT RADIAL ANGLE

b.

Fig. 1.1 Tire construction. (*a*) Bias-ply tire; (*b*) radial-ply tire.

long as twice that of equivalent bias-ply tires [1.2]. For a radial-ply tire, there is a relatively uniform ground pressure over the whole contact area. In contrast with this, the ground pressure for a bias-ply tire varies greatly from point to point, as tread elements passing through the contact area undergo complex localized wiping motion.

Tires are also built with belts having a low crown angle on conventional bias-ply construction. Usually the cords in the belts are of materials with higher modulus of elasticity than those in the bias-plies. This type of tire is usually called the belted-bias tire. The belt provides high rigidity to the tread against distortion, and reduces tread wear. Generally, the belted-bias tire has characteristics midway between those of the bias-ply and the radial-ply tire.

Although the construction of pneumatic tires differs from one type to another, the basic problems involved are not dissimilar. In the following sections, the mechanics fundamental to all types of tire will be described. The characteristics peculiar to a particular kind of tire will also be discussed.

1.1 TIRE FORCES AND MOMENTS

To describe the characteristics of a tire and the forces and moments acting on it, it is necessary to define an axis system that serves as a reference for the definition of various parameters. One of the commonly used axis systems, recommended by the Society of Automotive Engineers, is shown in Fig. 1.2 [1.3]. The origin of the axis system is the center of tire contact. The x axis is the intersection of the wheel plane and the ground plane with a positive direction forward. The z axis is perpendicular to the ground plane with a positive direction downward. The y axis is in the ground plane, its direction being chosen to make the axis system orthogonal and right hand.

There are three forces and three moments acting on the tire from the ground. Tractive force (or longitudinal force) F_x is the component in the x direction of the resultant force acting on the tire by the road. Lateral force F_y is the component in the y direction, and normal force F_z is the component in the z direction of the resultant force acting on the tire by the road. Overturning moment M_x is the moment about the x axis acting on the tire by the road. Rolling resistance moment M_y is the moment about the y axis, and aligning torque M_z is the moment about the z axis acting on the tire by the road.

With this axis system many performance parameters of the tire can be conveniently defined. For instance, the longitudinal shift of the center of normal pressure is determined by the ratio of the rolling resistance moment to the normal load. The lateral shift of the center of normal pressure is defined by the ratio of the overturning moment to the normal load. The resultant of longitudinal shear stresses at the contact patch is measured by the tractive force. A driving torque about the axis of rotation of the tire produces a force tending to accelerate the vehicle, and a braking torque produces a force tending to decelerate the vehicle.

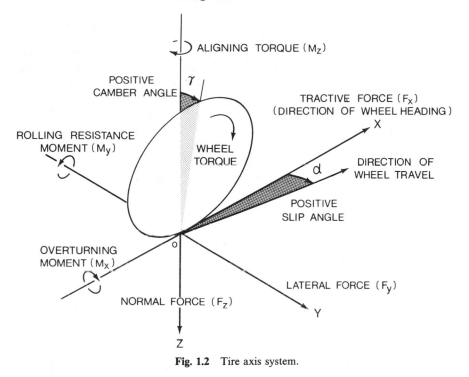

ALIGNING TORQUE (M_z)

POSITIVE
CAMBER ANGLE

γ

TRACTIVE FORCE (F_x)
(DIRECTION OF WHEEL HEADING)

X

ROLLING RESISTANCE
MOMENT (M_y)

WHEEL
TORQUE

DIRECTION OF
WHEEL TRAVEL

α

POSITIVE
SLIP ANGLE

OVERTURNING
MOMENT (M_x)

O

LATERAL FORCE (F_y)

NORMAL FORCE (F_z)

Y

Z

Fig. 1.2 Tire axis system.

There are two important angles associated with a rolling tire: the slip angle and the camber angle. Slip angle α is the angle formed between the direction of wheel travel and the line of intersection of the wheel plane with the road surface. Camber angle γ is the angle formed between the xz plane and the wheel plane. The lateral force at the tire-ground contact patch is a function of both the slip angle and the camber angle.

1.2 ROLLING RESISTANCE OF TIRES

The rolling resistance of tires on hard surfaces is primarily caused by the hysteresis in tire materials due to the deflection of the carcass while rolling. Friction between the tire and the road caused by sliding, the resistance due to air circulating inside the tire, and the fan effect of the rotating tire on the outside air also contribute to the rolling resistance of the tire, but they are of secondary importance. Available experimental results give a breakdown of tire losses in the speed range 128–152 km/h (80–95 mph) as

90–95% due to internal hysteresis, 2–10% due to friction between the tire and the ground, and 1.5–3.5% due to air resistance [1.4, 1.5].

When a tire is rolling, the carcass is deflected in the area of ground contact. As a result of tire distortion, the normal pressure in the leading half of the contact patch is higher than that in the trailing half. The center of normal pressure is shifted in the direction of rolling. This shift produces a moment about the axis of rotation of the tire, which is the rolling resistance moment. In a free rolling tire, the applied wheel torque is zero; therefore, a horizontal force at the tire-ground contact patch must exist to maintain equilibrium. This resultant horizontal force is generally known as the rolling resistance. The ratio of the rolling resistance to the normal load on the tire is defined as the coefficient of rolling resistance.

A number of factors affect the rolling resistance of a pneumatic tire. Tire construction has significant influence on its rolling resistance. Figure 1.3 shows the difference in rolling resistance between a conventional bias-ply tire and a radial-ply tire at various speeds [1.5]. Thicker treads and an increased number of carcass plies tend to increase the rolling resistance because of greater hysteresis losses. Tires made of synthetic rubber compounds generally have slightly higher rolling resistance than those made of

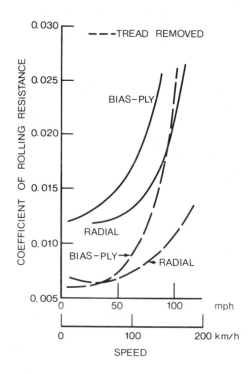

Fig. 1.3 Variation of the coefficient of rolling resistance with speed of a bias-ply and a radial-ply tire. (Reproduced, by permission, from *Mechanics of Pneumatic Tires*, edited by S. K. Clark, Monograph 122, National Bureau of Standards, 1971.)

natural rubber. Butyl rubber tires, which are shown to have better traction and road holding properties, have even higher rolling resistance than conventional synthetic rubber ones.

Surface conditions also affect the rolling resistance. On hard, smooth, dry surfaces, the rolling resistance is considerably lower than that on a worn out road. On wet surfaces, higher rolling resistance is usually observed.

Inflation pressure affects the flexibility of the tire. Depending on the deformability of the ground, the inflation pressure affects the rolling resistance of the tire in different manners. On hard surfaces, the rolling resistance decreases slightly with the increase of inflation pressure as shown in Fig. 1.4 [1.6]. On deformable surfaces, such as sand, high inflation pressure results in increased ground penetration work and therefore higher rolling resistance. Conversely, lower inflation pressure, while decreasing ground penetration, increases the deflection of the tire and hence hysteresis losses. Therefore, an optimum pressure exists for a particular surface condition [1.6].

Rolling resistance is also affected by driving speed, because of the increase of work in deforming the tread and of vibration in the tire carcass with the increase of speed. The influence of speed on the rolling resistance of a conventional bias-ply tire and a radial-ply tire is illustrated in Fig. 1.3.

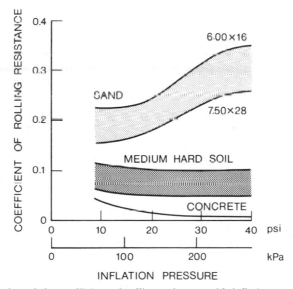

Fig. 1.4 Variation of the coefficient of rolling resistance with inflation pressure of tires on various surfaces. (Reproduced, by permission, from reference 1.6.)

For a given tire under a particular operating condition, there exists a threshold speed above which the phenomenon popularly known as standing waves will be observed as shown in Fig. 1.5. The approximate value of the threshold speed V_{th} may be determined by the expression $V_{th} = \sqrt{F_t/\rho_t}$, where F_t is the circumferential tension per unit area in the tire and ρ_t is the density of tread material [1.7]. Standing waves are formed because, owing to high speed, the tire tread does not recover immediately from distortion originating from tire deflection after it leaves the contact surface, and the residual deformation intiates a wave. The amplitude of the wave is the greatest immediately on leaving the ground and is damped out in an exponential manner around the circumference of the tire. The formation of the standing wave greatly increases energy losses, which in turn cause considerable heat generation that can lead to tire failure. This places an upper limit to the safe operating speed of tires.

Operating temperature, tire diameter, and tractive force also have effects on the rolling resistance of a tire. Figure 1.6 shows the dependence of the rolling resistance on the internal tire temperature for an automobile tire [1.4]. The effect of tire diameter on the coefficient of rolling resistance is shown in Fig. 1.7 [1.6]. It can be seen that the effect of tire diameter is negligible on hard surfaces (concrete) but is considerable on deformable or soft ground. Figure 1.8 shows the effect of the braking and tractive effort on the rolling resistance [1.5].

When considering the effect of material, construction, and design parameters of tires on the rolling resistance, it is necessary to have proper perspective of the relationship between the energy losses in the tire and the characteristics of the tire-vehicle system as a whole. Although it is desirable to keep the rolling resistance as low as possible, it should be judged against other performance parameters such as tire endurance and life, traction, cornering properties, cushioning effect, etc. For instance, from the standpoint of rolling resistance synthetic rubber compounds are less favorable than natural rubber compounds, yet because of significant advantages

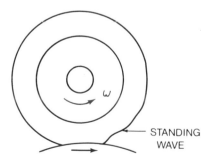

STANDING WAVE

Fig. 1.5 Formation of standing waves of a tire at high speeds.

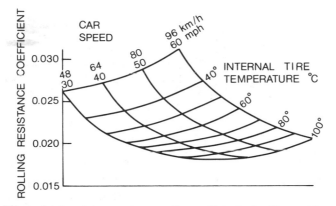

Fig. 1.6 Effect of internal temperature on the coefficient of rolling resistance of a tire. (Reproduced by permission of the Council of the Institution of Mechanical Engineers, from reference 1.4.)

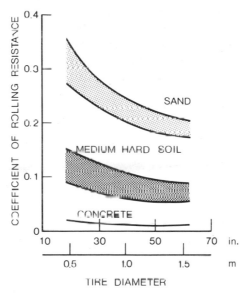

Fig. 1.7 Effect of tire diameter on the coefficient of rolling resistance on various surfaces. (Reproduced, by permission, from reference 1.6.)

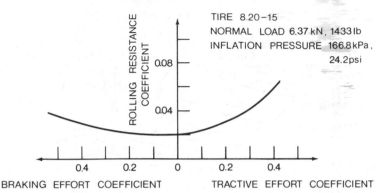

Fig. 1.8 Effect of tractive and braking effort on the coefficient of rolling resistance of a tire. (Reproduced, by permission, from *Mechanics of Pneumatic Tires*, edited by S. K. Clark, Monograph 122, National Bureau of Standards, 1971.)

in tread life, wet-road grip, and tire squeal they have virtually displaced natural rubber compounds from automobile tires, particularly for treads. For high-performance vehicles there may be some advantages for using butyl rubber tires because of the marked gains in traction, road holding, silence, and comfort, in spite of their poor hysteresis characteristics [1.4].

The complex relationships between the design and operational parameters of the tire and its rolling resistance make it extremely difficult, if not impossible, to develop an analytic method for predicting the rolling resistance of tires. The determination of the rolling resistance, therefore, relies almost entirely on experiments. Based on experimental results, many

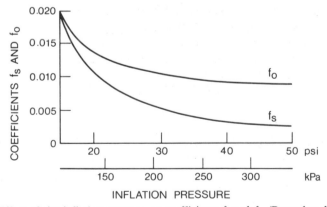

Fig. 1.9 Effect of tire inflation pressure on coefficients f_s and f_o. (Reproduced, by permission, from reference 1.6.)

Table 1.1   Coefficient of Rolling Resistance

Vehicle Type	Surface		
	Concrete	Medium Hard Soil	Sand
Passenger cars	0.015	0.08	0.30
Trucks	0.012	0.06	0.25
Tractors	0.02	0.04	0.20

Source.   Reference 1.6.

empirical formulas have been proposed for calculating the rolling resistance of tires on hard surfaces. For instance, the values of the coefficient of rolling resistance f_r for passenger car tires on concrete pavement may be calculated from the following equation [1.6]:

$$f_r = f_o + f_s \left(\frac{V}{100} \right)^{2.5} \tag{1.1}$$

where V is speed in km/h, and coefficients f_o and f_s depend on the inflation pressure and may be taken from Fig. 1.9 [1.6].

In many performance calculations, it is often sufficient to consider the coefficient of rolling resistance as a linear function of speed. For the most common range of inflation pressure (around 179 kPa or 26 psi), the following equation gives values of f_r for passenger car tires on concrete surfaces [1.6]:

$$f_r = 0.01 \left(1 + \frac{V}{160} \right) \tag{1.2}$$

This equation predicts the values of f_r with acceptable accuracy for speeds up to 128 km/h (80 mph).

In many cases, even the effect of speed may be ignored, and the average value of f_r for a particular application may be used in performance calculations. The average values of f_r for various types of tire over different surfaces are summarized in Table 1.1 [1.6].

1.3   RELATIONSHIP BETWEEN TRACTIVE (OR BRAKING) EFFORT AND LONGITUDINAL SLIP OF TIRES

When a driving torque is applied to a pneumatic tire, a tractive force is developed at the tire-ground contact patch as shown in Fig. 1.10 [1.5]. At the same time, the tire tread in front of and within the contact patch is

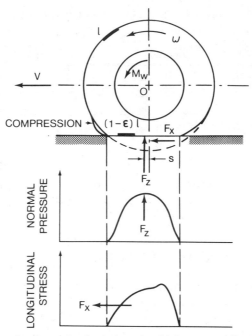

Fig. 1.10 Behavior of a tire under the action of a driving torque. (Reproduced, by permission, from *Mechanics of Pneumatic Tires*, edited by S. K. Clark, Monograph 122, National Bureau of Standards, 1971.)

subjected to compression. A corresponding shear deformation of the side wall of the tire is also developed.

As tread elements are compressed before entering the contact region, the distance that the tire travels when subject to a driving torque will be less than that in free rolling. This phenomenon is usually referred to as deformation slip. The slip of the vehicle running gear, when a driving torque is applied, is usually defined by

$$i = \left(1 - \frac{V}{r\omega}\right) \times 100\% = \left(1 - \frac{r_e}{r}\right) \times 100\% \qquad (1.3)$$

where V is the translatory speed of the tire center, ω is angular speed of the tire, r is the rolling radius of the free-rolling tire, and r_e is the effective rolling radius of the tire, which is the ratio of the translatory speed of the tire center to the angular speed of the tire. When a driving torque is applied, the tire rotates without the equivalent translatory progression; therefore, $r\omega > V$.

As the tractive force developed by a tire is proportional to the applied wheel torque under steady-state conditions, slip is a function of tractive effort. Generally speaking, at first the wheel torque and tractive force increase linearly with slip, because initially slip is mainly due to elastic deformation of the tire tread. This corresponds to section OA of the curve shown in Fig. 1.11. Further increase of wheel torque and tractive force results in part of the tire tread sliding on the ground. Under these circumstances, the relationship between the tractive force and the slip is nonlinear. This corresponds to section AB of the curve shown in Fig. 1.11. Based on available experimental data, the maximum tractive force of a pneumatic tire on hard surfaces is usually reached somewhere between 15 and 20% of slip. Any further increase of slip beyond that results in an unstable condition, with the tractive effort coefficient, which is the ratio of the tractive effort to the vertical load of a tire, falling rapidly from the peak value μ_p to the pure sliding value μ_s as shown in Fig. 1.11.

A general theory that can accurately predict the relationship between the tractive effort and the longitudinal slip of pneumatic tires on hard surfaces has yet to be evolved. However, several theories have been proposed that could provide a basic understanding of the physical nature of the processes involved. One of the earliest and the simplest theoretical treatments on the relationship between the tractive effort and the longitudinal slip of pneumatic tires was made by Julien [1.8].

In Julien's theory, it is assumed that the tire tread can be regarded as an elastic band, and that the contact patch is rectangular and the normal

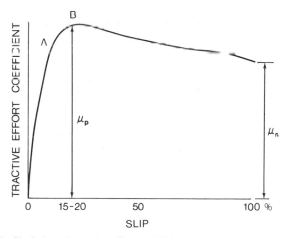

Fig. 1.11 Variation of tractive effort coefficient with longitudinal slip of a tire.

pressure is uniformly distributed [1.8]. Consider that a driving torque is applied to a tire. In the region in front of the contact patch, the driving torque produces a longitudinal strain ε (in compression) in the tread. It remains constant in the adhesion region of the contact patch, where no sliding between the tire tread and the ground takes place. Let e_0 be the longitudinal deformation of the tire tread in front of the contact patch, and let e be the longitudinal deformation of the tread at a point at a distance of x behind the front contact edge

$$e = e_0 + x\varepsilon \tag{1.4}$$

Assume that e_0 is proportional to ε, and $e_0 = \lambda\varepsilon$. Then

$$e = (\lambda + x)\varepsilon \tag{1.5}$$

It is further assumed that within the adhesion region, where no sliding between the tire tread and the ground occurs, the tractive force per unit contact length is proportional to the deformation of the tread. Thus

$$\frac{dF_x}{dx} = k_t e = k_t(\lambda + x)\varepsilon \tag{1.6}$$

where k_t is the tangential stiffness of the tire tread and F_x is the tractive force.

The tractive force developed between o and x is then given by

$$F_x = \int_0^x k_t(\lambda + x)\varepsilon\, dx = k_t\lambda x\varepsilon\left(1 + \frac{x}{2\lambda}\right) \tag{1.7}$$

Let p be the normal pressure, b be the width of the contact patch, and μ_p be the peak value of the coefficient of road adhesion. Then the condition for adhesion, that is, no sliding occurs between the tread and the ground, is

$$\frac{dF_x}{dx} = k_t(\lambda + x)\varepsilon < pb\mu_p \tag{1.8}$$

This implies that if a point at a distance of x behind the front edge is in the adhesion region, then x must be less than a characteristic length l_c, which defines the length of the region where no sliding between the tire tread and the ground takes place, that is

$$x \leqslant l_c = \frac{pb\mu_p}{k_t\varepsilon} - \lambda = \frac{\mu_p W}{l_t k_t\varepsilon} - \lambda \tag{1.9}$$

where W is the normal load on the tire and l_t is the contact length of the tire.

If $l_t < l_c$, then the entire contact area is an adhesion region. Putting $x = l_t$ in Eq. 1.7, the tractive force becomes

$$F_x = k_t \lambda l_t \varepsilon \left(1 + \frac{l_t}{2\lambda} \right) = K_t \varepsilon \tag{1.10}$$

where $K_t = k_t \lambda l_t [1 + (l_t / 2\lambda)]$.

Since the longitudinal strain ε is a measure of the deformation slip of the tire, it is concluded that if the entire contact patch is an adhesion region, the relationship between tractive force F_x and slip i is linear. This corresponds to the region between points O and A on the tractive effort coefficient-slip curve shown in Fig. 1.11.

The condition for sliding at the rear edge of the contact area is given by

$$l_t = l_c = \frac{\mu_p W}{l_t k_t \varepsilon} - \lambda \tag{1.11}$$

This means that, if the slip and tractive force reach the critical values i_c and F_{xc} given below, sliding in the trailing part of the contact patch begins:

$$i_c = \frac{\mu_p W}{l_t k_t (l_t + \lambda)} \tag{1.12}$$

$$F_{xc} = \frac{\mu_p W [1 + (l_t / 2\lambda)]}{1 + (l_t / \lambda)} \tag{1.13}$$

A further increase of slip or tractive force above the respective critical values results in the spread of the sliding region from the trailing edge toward the leading part of the contact patch. The tractive force developed at the sliding region F_{xs} is given by

$$F_{xs} = \mu_p W (1 - l_c / l_t) \tag{1.14}$$

and the tractive force at the adhesion region F_{xa} is given by

$$F_{xa} = k_t \lambda l_c \varepsilon \left(1 + \frac{l_c}{2\lambda} \right) \tag{1.15}$$

where l_c is determined by Eq. 1.9.

Hence the relationship between the total tractive force and slip when part of the tire tread sliding on the ground is expressed by

$$F_x = F_{xs} + F_{xa} = \mu_p W - \frac{\lambda(\mu_p W - K'\varepsilon)^2}{2l_t K'\varepsilon}$$

$$= \mu_p W - \frac{\lambda(\mu_p W - K'i)^2}{2l_t K'i} \tag{1.16}$$

where $K' = k_t \lambda l_t$.

This equation clearly indicates the nonlinear behavior of the tractive effort coefficient-longitudinal slip relationship when sliding occurs in part of the contact area. This corresponds to the region between A and B of the curve shown in Fig. 1.11.

When sliding extends over the entire contact patch, the tractive force F_x is equal to $\mu_p W$. Under this condition the slip i is obtained by setting l_c

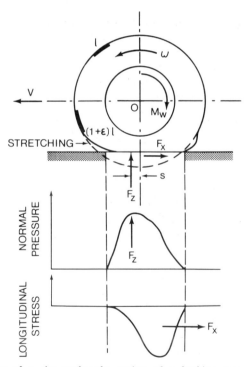

Fig. 1.12 Behavior of a tire under the action of a braking torque. (Reproduced, by permission, from *Mechanics of Pneumatic Tires*, edited by S. K. Clark, Monograph 122, National Bureau of Standards, 1971.)

equal to zero in Eq. 1.11. The value of the maximum deformation slip i_m is equal to $\mu_p W / l_t k_t \lambda$ and corresponds to point B shown in Fig. 1.11. A further increase of tire slip results in an unstable situation with the value of the coefficient of road adhesion falling rapidly from the peak value μ_p to the pure sliding value μ_s.

In practice, the normal pressure distribution over the tire-ground contact patch is not uniform. There is a gradual drop of pressure near the edges. It is expected, therefore, that a small sliding region will be developed in the trailing part of the contact area even at extremely low tractive effort.

When a braking torque is applied to the tire, the stretching of the tread elements occurs prior to entering the contact area as shown in Fig. 1.12, in contrast with the compression effect for a driven tire. The distance that the tire travels when a braking torque is applied, therefore, will be greater than that in free rolling. The severity of braking is often measured by the skid of the tire i_s, which is defined as

$$i_s = \left(1 - \frac{r\omega}{V}\right) \times 100\%$$

$$= \left(1 - \frac{r}{r_e}\right) \times 100\% \tag{1.17}$$

For a locked wheel, the angular speed ω of the tire is zero, whereas the translatory speed of the tire center is not zero. Under this condition, the skid is denoted 100%. Usually the relationship between the braking effort coefficient, which is defined as the ratio of the braking effort to the normal

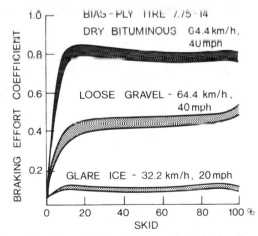

Fig. 1.13 Variation of braking effort coefficient with skid of a tire on various surfaces. (Reproduced by permission of the Society of Automotive Engineers from reference 1.9.)

Table 1.2   Average Values of Coefficient of Road Adhesion

Surface	Peak Value μ_p	Sliding Value μ_s
Asphalt and concrete (dry)	0.8–0.9	0.75
Asphalt (wet)	0.5–0.7	0.45–0.6
Concrete (wet)	0.8	0.7
Gravel	0.6	0.55
Earth road (dry)	0.68	0.65
Earth road (wet)	0.55	0.4–0.5
Snow (hard-packed)	0.2	0.15
Ice	0.1	0.07

Source.   Reference 1.6.

load of the tire, and skid exhibits similar characteristics to that between the tractive effort coefficient and slip discussed previously. Figure 1.13 shows the variation of the braking effort coefficient with skid for a bias-ply passenger car tire over various surfaces [1.9].

Surface conditions as well as tire design and construction are the most important factors affecting the coefficient of road adhesion. The average peak and sliding values of the coefficient of road adhesion μ_p and μ_s on various surfaces are given in Table 1.2 [1.6].

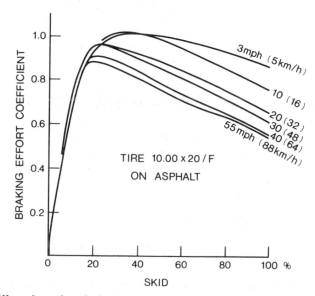

Fig. 1.14   Effect of speed on the braking performance of a truck tire 10.00×20/F on asphalt. (Reproduced, by permission, from reference 1.10.)

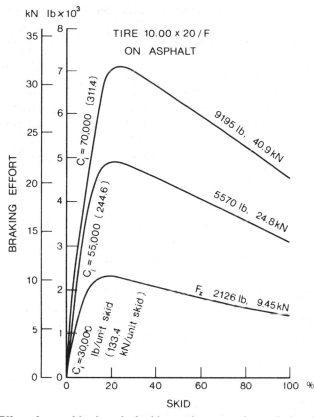

Fig. 1.15 Effect of normal load on the braking performance of a truck tire $10.00 \times 20/F$ on asphalt. (Reproduced, by permission, from reference 1.10.)

Among the operational parameters speed and vertical load have noticeable effects on the tractive (braking) effort-slip (skid) characteristics. Figure 1.14 shows the influence of speed on the braking effort coefficient-skid characteristics of a truck tire on asphalt [1.10]. The effect of vertical load on the braking effort-skid relationship is shown in Fig. 1.15 [1.10].

1.4   CORNERING PROPERTIES OF TIRES

1.4.1   Slip Angle and Cornering Force

When a pneumatic tire is not subject to any force perpendicular to the wheel plane (i.e., side force), it will roll in a direction coinciding with the wheel plane. If, however, a side force F_s is applied to a tire, a lateral force is developed at the contact patch, and the tire will move along a path at an angle α with the wheel plane, as OA shown in Fig. 1.16. The angle α is the slip angle, and the phenomenon of side slip is mainly due to the lateral elasticity of the tire.

The lateral force developed at the tire-ground contact patch is usually called the cornering force $F_{y\alpha}$ when the camber angle of the wheel is zero. The relationship between the cornering force and the slip angle is of fundamental importance to the directional control and stability of road vehicles.

When the tire is moving at a uniform speed in the direction of OA, the side force F_s applied at the wheel center and the cornering force $F_{y\alpha}$ in the ground plane are usually not colinear as shown in Fig. 1.16. At small slip angles, the cornering force in the ground plane is normally behind the applied side force giving rise to a torque (or couple), which tends to align

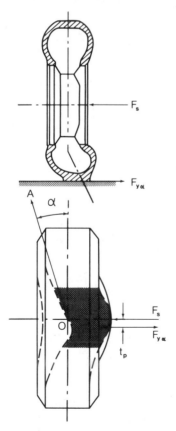

Fig. 1.16 Behavior of a tire subjected to a side force. (Reproduced, by permission, from *Mechanics of Pneumatic Tires*, edited by S. K. Clark, Monograph 122, National Bureau of Standards, 1971.)

the wheel plane with the direction of motion. This torque is called the self-aligning torque and is one of the primary restoring moments which help the steered tires return to the original position after negotiating a turn. The distance t_p between the side force and cornering force is called the pneumatic trail, and the product of cornering force and pneumatic trail determines the self-aliging torque.

The relationships between the slip angle and the cornering force of various types of tire under a variety of operating conditions have been investigated quite extensively. Typical plots of the cornering force as a function of the slip angle for a bias-ply tire and a radial-ply tire are shown in Fig. 1.17 [1.5]. It can be seen that for slip angles below a certain value, such as the 4° angle shown in Fig. 1.17, the cornering force is approximately proportional to the slip angle. Beyond that the cornering force increases at a lower rate with the increase of slip angle and reaches a maximum value where the tire begins sliding laterally. To provide a common basis for comparing the cornering behavior of different tires, a parameter called cornering stiffness C_α is used, which is defined as the derivative of the cornering force $F_{y\alpha}$ with respect to slip angle [1.3].

$$C_\alpha = \frac{\partial F_{y\alpha}}{\partial \alpha} \tag{1.18}$$

A number of factors affect the cornering behavior of pneumatic tires. The vertical load on the tire strongly influences the cornering characteristics. Some typical results are shown in Fig. 1.18 [1.5]. It can be seen that

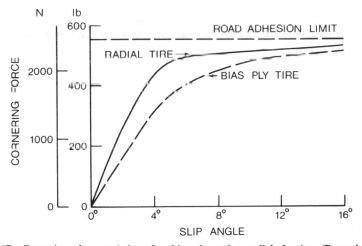

Fig. 1.17 Cornering characteristics of a bias-ply and a radial-ply tire. (Reproduced, by permission, from *Mechanics of Pneumatic Tires*, edited by S. K. Clark, Monograph 122, National Bureau of Standards, 1971.)

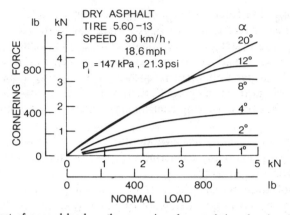

Fig. 1.18 Effect of normal load on the cornering characteristics of a tire. (Reproduced, by permission, from *Mechanics of Pneumatic Tires*, edited by S. K. Clark, Monograph 122, National Bureau of Standards, 1971.)

for a given slip angle, the cornering force generally increases with the increase of vertical load. However, the relationship between the cornering force and the vertical load is nonlinear. Thus the transfer of load from the inside to the outside tire during a turning maneuver will reduce the total cornering force that a pair of tires can develop. Consider a pair of tires on a beam axle, each with vertical load F_z as shown in Fig. 1.19. The cornering force per tire with normal load F_z is F_y for a given slip angle. If the vehicle is undergoing a steady-state turn, owing to lateral load transfer, the normal load on the inside tire will be reduced to F_{zi} and that on the outside tire will be increased to F_{zo}. As a result, the total cornering force of the two tires will be $F_{yi} + F_{yo}$, which is less than $2F_y$, as shown in Fig. 1.19. This implies that for a pair of tires on a beam axle to develop the required

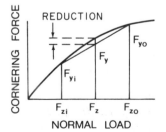

Fig. 1.19 Effect of lateral load transfer on the cornering capability of a pair of tires on an axle.

amount of cornering force to balance a given centrifugal force, the lateral load transfer results in the increase of the slip angle of the tires.

To evaluate the effect of the vertical load on the cornering ability of tires, a parameter called cornering coefficient, which is defined as the cornering stiffness per unit vertical load, is often used. Figure 1.20 shows the variation of the cornering coefficient with the vertical load of a tire [1.6]. It shows that the cornering coefficient decreases as the increase of the vertical load.

Inflation pressure usually has a moderate effect on the cornering properties of a tire. In general the cornering stiffness of tires increases with the increase of inflation pressure.

A number of attempts have been made to develop mathematical models for describing the cornering behavior of pneumatic tires. There are two basic types of model. One is based on the assumption that the tread band of the tire is equivalent to a stretched string restrained by lateral springs, representative of the tire wall, with the wheel rim acting as the base of the springs, as shown in Fig. 1.21. In the other model, the tread band is considered equivalent to an elastic beam with continuous lateral elastic support [1.8, 1.11].

In both models, it is assumed that the cornering characteristics of a tire can be deduced from the behavior of the equatorial line of the tire, which is the intersection of the undeformed tire surface with the wheel plane. The portion of the equatorial line in the contact area is called the contact line.

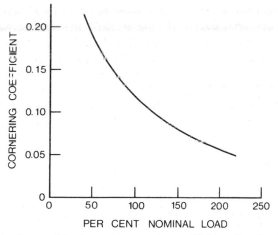

Fig. 1.20 Effect of normal load on the cornering coefficient of a tire. (Reproduced, by permission, from reference 1.6.)

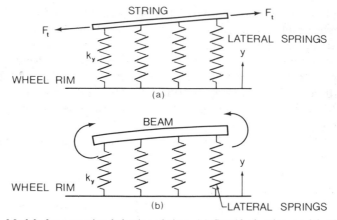

Fig. 1.21 Models for cornering behavior of tires. (*a*) Stretched string model; (*b*) beam on elastic foundation model. (From *Vehicle Dynamics* by J. R. Ellis, Business Books, 1969. Reproduced by permission of the author.)

One of the major differences in these two basic models is that in the stretched-string model discontinuities of slope of the equatorial line are permissible, whereas for the beam model it is not the case. It has been shown that for small slip angles, the stretched-string model can provide a basic understanding of the lateral behavior of a pneumatic tire [1.11]. In the following, the stretched-string model as proposed by Temple and von Schlippe will be discussed [1.8].

Consider a tire in a steady-state motion with a fixed slip angle. The shape of the equatorial line *BC* in the contact area in Fig. 1.22 is the path of the tire, and is immobile relative to the ground if no sliding takes place. Let the dotted line *AB* in the figure represent the projection of the portion of the equatorial line outside and in front of the contact patch. As the tire rolls forward, points of *AB* become points of *BC*. This indicates that *AB* and *BC* must have a common tangent at point *B*. At the rear of the contact patch, such conditions do not hold, and a kink may be present at

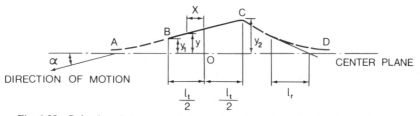

Fig. 1.22 Behavior of the equatorial line of a rolling tire subjected to a side force.

point C. Thus, it can be stated that for a rolling tire, the slope of the equatorial line is continuous at the front edge of the contact area but not necessarily at the rear.

Consider an element of the distorted equatorial line shown in Fig. 1.22. Let the lateral deflection from the wheel plane be y and the distance measured along the undistorted equatorial line be x with origin at the center of the contact patch. It is assumed that the lateral force applied to the rim by the element due to lateral deflection y is given, in differential form, by

$$dF_{y1} = k_y y\, dx \qquad (1.19)$$

where k_y is the lateral stiffness of the tire. This equation applies at all points of the periphery.

In an element of the equatorial line, there is another force component acting in the lateral direction, which is due to the tension in the string. This component is proportional to the curvature of the equatorial line, and for small deflection is given, in differential form, by

$$dF_{y2} = -F_t \frac{d^2y}{dx^2}\, dx \qquad (1.20)$$

where F_t represents the tension in the string. It is usually convenient to write $F_t = k_y l_r^2$, where l_r is termed "relaxation length," in which the lateral deflection, described by an exponential function, decreases to $1/2.718$ of its prior value as shown in Fig. 1.22.

Let l_t be the contact length with the origin for x at the center, and y_1 and y_2 be the deflections of the equatorial line at the front and rear ends of the contact patch, as shown in Fig. 1.22. Over that part of the tire not in contact with the ground (i.e., free region) having total length l_h, the tire is not loaded by external means and therefore from Eqs. 1.19 and 1.20

$$k_y \left(y - l_r^2 \frac{d^2y}{dx^2} \right) = 0 \qquad (1.21)$$

The solution of this differential equation will yield the deflected shape of the equatorial line in the free region, which is given by

$$y = \frac{y_2 \sinh\left[(x - l_t/2)/l_r\right] + y_1 \sinh\left[(l_t/2 + l_h - x)/l_r\right]}{\sinh(l_h/l_r)} \qquad (1.22)$$

If r is the tire radius, under normal conditions l_h lies between $4.5r$ and $6r$, whereas l_r is approximately equal to r [1.8]. Hence, Eq. 1.22 may be approximated by an exponential function.

For the free region near the front of the contact area (i.e., $x > l_t/2$)

$$y = y_1 \exp\left[\frac{-(x - l_t/2)}{l_r} \right] \qquad (1.23)$$

For the free region near the rear of the contact area (i.e., $x < l_t/2 + l_h$)

$$y = y_2 \exp\left[\frac{-(l_t/2 + l_h - x)}{l_r} \right] \qquad (1.24)$$

Thus in the free region not in contact with the ground but near either end of the contact patch, the shape of the equatorial line is an exponential curve.

The expressions for the lateral deflection and the lateral forces acting on an element of the tread band described above permit the determination of the cornering force and the aligning torque in terms of constants k_y and l_r, and contact length l_t. This can be achieved in two ways:

1 Integrating the lateral force exerted on the tire by the ground over the contact length, but including an infinitesimal length of the equatorial line in the free region at each end, as proposed by Temple;
2 Integrating the lateral force exerted on the rim by the tire over the entire circumference including the contact length, as proposed by von Schlippe. The essence of these two methods is illustrated in Fig. 1.23.

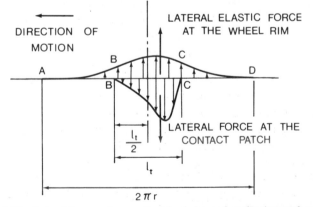

Fig. 1.23 Lateral force acting on the wheel rim and at the tire-road contact patch.

Following Temple's method, and assuming that the equatorial line in the contact region is a straight line, one can obtain the total lateral force F_y by integration

$$
F_y = k_y \int_{-l_t/2}^{l_t/2} \left(y - l_r^2 \frac{d^2 y}{dx^2} \right) dx
$$

$$
= k_y \int_{-l_t/2}^{l_t/2} y \, dx - k_y l_r^2 \left(\frac{dy}{dx} \right) \bigg]_{-l_t/2}^{l_t/2}
$$

$$
= \frac{k_y (y_1 + y_2) l_t}{2} + k_y l_r (y_1 + y_2)
$$

$$
= k_y (y_1 + y_2) \left(l_t + \frac{l_t}{2} \right) \tag{1.25}
$$

For a nonrolling tire subjected to a pure side force,

$$
y_1 = y_2 = y_o, \quad \text{and} \quad F_y = 2 k_y y_o \left(l_r + \frac{l_t}{2} \right) \tag{1.26}
$$

The moment of lateral force about a vertical axis through the center of contact (i.e., the aligning torque) is given by

$$
M_z = k_y \int_{-l_t/2}^{l_t/2} x \left(y - l_r^2 \frac{d^2 y}{dx^2} \right) dx
$$

$$
= k_y \int_{-l_t/2}^{l_t/2} xy \, dx - k_y l_r^2 \left(x \frac{dy}{dx} - y \right) \bigg]_{-l_t/2}^{l_t/2}
$$

$$
= k_y \frac{(l_t/2)^2}{3} (y_1 - y_2) + k_y l_r \left(l_r + \frac{l_t}{2} \right)(y_1 - y_2)
$$

$$
= k_y (y_1 - y_2) \left[\frac{(l_t/2)^2}{3} + l_r \left(l_r + \frac{l_t}{2} \right) \right] \tag{1.27}
$$

Following von Schlippe's approach, one can obtain the same expressions.

For a tire rolling at a slip angle α, the slope of the equatorial line in the contact area will be equal to $\tan \alpha$, if the tread band in the contact patch is not sliding. Thus

$$
\alpha \cong \tan \alpha = \frac{y_2 - y_1}{l_t} = \frac{y_1}{l_r} \tag{1.28}
$$

Substituting the above expression into Eqs. 1.25 and 1.27, the relationships between the lateral force, self-aligning torque and slip angle become

$$\frac{F_y}{\alpha} = 2k_y \left(l_r + \frac{l_t}{2} \right)^2 \tag{1.29}$$

$$\frac{M_z}{\alpha} = k_y l_t \left[\frac{(l_t/2)^2}{3} + l_r \left(l_r + \frac{l_t}{2} \right) \right] \tag{1.30}$$

The pneumatic trail t_p is given by

$$t_p = \frac{M_z}{F_y} = \frac{(l_t/2)\left[(l_t/2)^2/3 + l_r(l_r + l_t/2) \right]}{(l_r + l_t/2)^2} \tag{1.31}$$

The two basic parameters k_y and l_r, which specify the characteristics of the lateral elasticity of the pneumatic tire, can be measured by suitable tests. It is noted that the ratio of F_y/α to M_z/α is independent of k_y, and therefore l_r can be determined from the measured values of F_y/α and M_z/α (l_t being known). On the other hand, the ratio of $(F_y/y_0)^2$ of a nonrolling tire to F_y/α is independent of l_r and therefore k_y can be determined from the measured values of $(F_y/y_0)^2$ and F_y/α. Measurements of k_y and l_r have been carried out by several investigators. Values of l_r for a family of aircraft tires of different sizes but with similar proportion were found by von Schlippe to vary from $0.6r$ to $0.9r$ approximately. Values of k_y measured by von Schlippe were about 90% of the inflation pressure [1.8].

Equations 1.29 and 1.30 indicate that, if no sliding between the tread band and the ground occurs, the lateral force and the aligning torque increase linearly with the slip angle. This is the case for small slip angles as shown in Fig. 1.17. As the slip angle increases, sliding between the tread and the ground occurs. The assumption that the equatorial line in the contact patch is a straight line is no longer valid. Thus, the theory proposed by Temple and von Schlippe is restricted to small slip angles.

In the discussion of the cornering behavior of pneumatic tires described above, the effect of the longitudinal force has not been considered. However, quite often both the side force and the longitudinal force are present. In general, tractive (or braking) effort will reduce the cornering force that can be generated for a given slip angle, as illustrated in Fig. 1.24 [1.5]. It can be seen that for a given slip angle, the lateral force decreases gradually with the increase of the tractive or braking effort. At low values of tractive (or braking) effort, the decrease of the cornering force is mainly

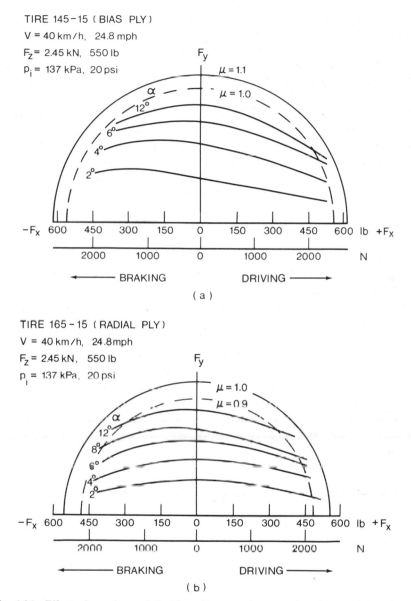

TIRE 145-15 (BIAS PLY)

V = 40 km/h, 24.8 mph

F_z = 2.45 kN, 550 lb

p_i = 137 kPa, 20 psi

F_y

μ = 1.1

μ = 1.0

α

12°

6°

4°

2°

−F_x 600   450   300   150   0   150   300   450   600 lb +F_x

2000   1000   0   1000   2000   N

←———— BRAKING   DRIVING ————→

(a)

TIRE 165-15 (RADIAL PLY)

V = 40 km/h, 24.8 mph

F_z = 2.45 kN, 550 lb

p_i = 137 kPa, 20 psi

F_y

μ = 1.0

μ = 0.9

α

12°

8°

6°

4°

2°

−F_x 600   450   300   150   0   150   300   450   600 lb +F_x

2000   1000   0   1000   2000   N

←———— BRAKING   DRIVING ————→

(b)

Fig. 1.24 Effect of tractive and braking effort on the cornering characteristics of (*a*) a bias-ply tire and (*b*) a radial-ply tire. (Reproduced, by permission, from *Mechanics of Pneumatic Tires*, edited by S. K. Clark, Monograph 122, National Bureau of Standards, 1971.)

caused by the reduction of the cornering stiffness of the tire. A further increase of the tractive (or braking) force results in a pronounced decrease of the cornering force for a given slip angle. This is due to the utilization of the available local adhesion by the tractive (or braking) effort, which reduces the amount of adhesion available in the lateral direction. The tire approaches sliding when the resultant of the tractive (or braking) effort and cornering force reaches the maximum value determined by the coefficient of road adhesion and the vertical load of the tire.

The difference in behavior between a bias-ply and a radial-ply tire is shown in Fig. 1.24 [1.5]. It is interesting to note that a radial-ply tire produces a more or less symmetric curve for both braking and driving conditions. For a bias-ply tire, however, braking gives a higher obtainable cornering force than when the tire is driven. The fact that the presence of the tractive (or braking) effort requires a higher slip angle to generate the same cornering force is also illustrated in Fig. 1.24.

It is interesting to point out that if an envelope around each family of curves in Fig. 1.24 is drawn, a curve approximately semielliptical in shape may be obtained. This enveloping curve is often referred to as the friction ellipse. It defines the maximum values of the resultant of the tractive (or braking) effort and the cornering force that can be obtained under a particular operating condition.

Based on experimental data, attempts have been made to formulate an analytic expression for the relationships between the tractive (or braking) effort, cornering force, longitudinal slip (or skid), slip angle, and other design and operational parameters of pneumatic tires. Dugoff et al. proposed the following expressions for predicting the longitudinal and lateral forces of a tire, F_x and F_y, as functions of longitudinal skid i_s and slip angle α [1.12].

For the longitudinal force

$$F_x = \frac{C_i i_s}{1 - i_s} f(s) \tag{1.32}$$

and for the cornering force

$$F_y = \frac{C_\alpha \tan \alpha}{1 - i_s} f(s) \tag{1.33}$$

where

$$f(s) = \begin{cases} s(2 - s) & s < 1 \\ 1 & s > 1 \end{cases}$$

$$s = \frac{\mu_0 W \left[1 - \varepsilon_r V \sqrt{i_s^2 + \tan^2 \alpha} \right](1 - i_s)}{2\sqrt{C_i^2 i_s^2 + C_\alpha^2 \tan^2 \alpha}}$$

C_i = longitudinal stiffness of the tire, i.e., $\left.\dfrac{\partial F_x}{\partial i_s}\right|_{i_s=0}$

C_α = cornering stiffness of the tire

μ_0 = nominal coefficient of road adhesion, which is equivalent to that obtained at low speeds

V = vehicle speed

ε_r = adhesion reduction coefficient representing the effect of speed

Example 1.1 A truck tire $10 \times 20/F$ with vertical load of 24.15 kN (5430 lb) is moving on a dry asphalt pavement with nominal coefficient of road adhesion $\mu_0 = 0.85$. The cornering stiffness of the tire C_α is 133.3 kN/rad (523 lb/degree) and the longitudinal stiffness C_i is 186.82 kN/unit skid (42,000 lb/unit skid) at an inflation pressure of 586 kPa (85 psi).

A Estimate the cornering force that the tire can develop at a side slip angle $\alpha = 4°$ at low forward speeds.

B Calculate the braking force and the cornering force that the tire can develop with a side slip angle $\alpha = 4°$ and longitudinal skid $i_s = 10\%$, at a forward speed of 80 km/h (60 mph). From experiments the adhesion reduction coefficient ε_r representing the effect of speed on road adhesion is found to be 0.0031.

Solution.

A At low forward speeds, the effect of speed on road adhesion may be neglected. From Eq. 1.33

$$s = \frac{\mu_0 W}{2 C_\alpha \tan \alpha} = 1.10$$

Since $s > 1$

$$f(s) = 1$$

The cornering force, $F_y = C_\alpha \tan \alpha \, f(s) = 9.32$ kN (2096 lb). The value of the lateral force measured using a flatbed tire test machine at the Highway Safety Research Institute, University of Michigan, is 8.14 kN (1830 lb) (see "A computer based mathematical method for predicting the directional response of trucks and tractor-trailers, Phase II Technical Report" by J. E. Bernard, C. B. Winkler and P. S. Fancher, Highway Safety Research Institute Report UM-HSRI-PF-73-1, June 1, 1973). The difference between the measured and the predicted value is approximately 14%.

B   At a speed of 80 km/h, the effect of speed on road adhesion can no
longer be neglected. From Eqs. 1.32 and 1.33

$$s = \frac{\mu_0 W \left[1 - \varepsilon_r V \sqrt{i_s^2 + \tan^2 \alpha} \right](1 - i_s)}{2\sqrt{C_i^2 i_s^2 + C_\alpha^2 \tan^2 \alpha}}$$

$$= \frac{0.85 \times 24.15 \left(1 - 0.0031 \times 80 \sqrt{0.1^2 + 0.07^2} \right)(1 - 0.1)}{2\sqrt{186.82^2 \times 0.1^2 + 133.3^2 \times 0.07^2}}$$

$$= 0.429$$

Since $s < 1$

$$f(s) = s(2 - s) = 0.674$$

The braking force

$$F_x = \frac{C_i i_s}{1 - i_s} f(s) = 13.99 \text{ kN } (3145 \text{ lb})$$

The cornering force

$$F_y = \frac{C_\alpha \tan \alpha}{1 - i_s} f(s) = 6.98 \text{ kN } (1569 \text{ lb})$$

1.4.2   Camber and Camber Thrust

Camber is the inclination of the wheel plane from a plane perpendicular to
the road surface when viewed from the fore and aft direction of the vehicle
as shown in Fig. 1.25. Its main purpose is to achieve axial bearing pressure
and to decrease the king pin offset distance. Camber on passenger cars is
between $\frac{1}{2}$ and 1 degree. High camber angles promote excessive tire wear
[1.6].

Camber causes a lateral force developed on the contact patch. This
lateral force is usually referred to as camber thrust $F_{y\gamma}$, and the development of this thrust may be explained in the following way. A free rolling
tire with a camber angle would revolve about point 0 as shown in Fig. 1.25.
However, the cambered tire in a vehicle is constrained to move in a
straight line. A lateral force in the direction of the camber is, therefore,
developed in the ground plane. It is interesting to note that camber thrust
acts ahead of the wheel center and therefore forms a small camber torque.

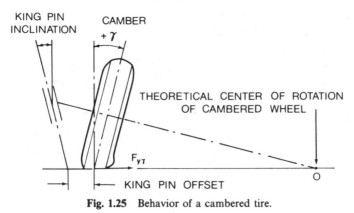

Fig. 1.25 Behavior of a cambered tire.

The relationship between camber thrust and camber angle (at zero slip angle) is illustrated in Fig. 1.26 [1.13]. It has been shown that the camber thrust is approximately one-fifth the value of the lateral force obtained from an equivalent angle of sideslip for a bias-ply tire and somewhat less for a radial-ply tire. To provide a common basis for the comparison of the camber characteristics of different tires, a parameter called camber stiffness is often used. It is defined as the derivative of the camber thrust with respect to the camber angle [1.3].

$$C_\gamma = \frac{\partial F_{y\gamma}}{\partial \gamma} \tag{1.34}$$

Similar to the cornering stiffness, vertical load and inflation pressure have influence on the camber stiffness.

The total lateral force of a cambered tire operating at a slip angle is the sum of the cornering force $F_{y\alpha}$ and the camber thrust $F_{y\gamma}$

$$F_y = F_{y\alpha} \pm F_{y\gamma} \tag{1.35}$$

If the cornering force and the camber thrust are in the same direction, the positive sign should be used in the above equation. For small slip and camber angles, the relationship between the cornering force and the slip angle and that between the camber thrust and the camber angle are essentially linear, the total lateral force of a cambered tire at a slip angle can, therefore, be determined by

$$F_y = C_\alpha \alpha \pm C_\gamma \gamma \tag{1.36}$$

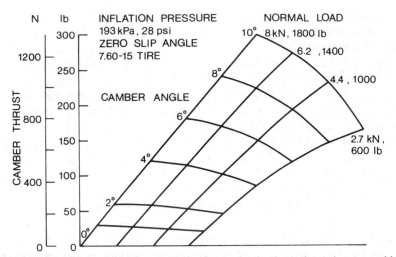

Fig. 1.26 Variation of camber thrust with camber angle of a tire under various normal loads. (Reproduced by permission of the Society of Automotive Engineers from reference 1.13.)

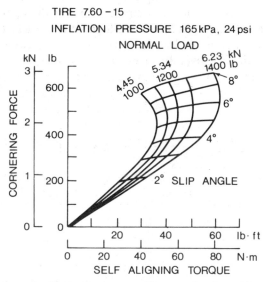

Fig. 1.27 Variation of self-aligning torque with cornering force of a tire 7.60–15 under various normal loads. (Reproduced by permission of the Society of Automotive Engineers from reference 1.14.)

As discussed previously, the lateral forces due to slip angle and camber produce an aligning torque. The aligning torque due to side slip, however, is usually much greater.

Figure 1.27 shows a plot of cornering force versus aligning torque for several vertical loads and slip angles [1.14]. It is interesting to note that with a constant vertical load, the aligning torque first increases with the increase of cornering force and slip angle. It reaches a maximum at a particular slip angle and then decreases with the further increase of slip angle. This is mainly caused by the skidding of the tread in the trailing part of the contact patch at high slip angles, which results in shifting the point of application of the cornering force forward.

Tractive effort affects the aligning torque significantly. Generally speaking, the effect of a driving torque is to increase the aligning torque for a given slip angle, while a braking torque has the opposite effect. Inflation pressure and vertical load also have effects on the self-aligning torque because they affect the size of the contact area. Higher loads and lower inflation pressures enlarge the contact area and increase the pneumatic trail. This results in the increase of self-aligning torque.

1.5 PERFORMANCE OF TIRES ON WET SURFACES

The behavior of tires on wet surfaces is of considerable interest from a vehicle-safety point of view, as many accidents occur on slippery roads. The performance of tires on wet surfaces depends on the surface texture, water depth, tread pattern, and operating mode of the tire (i.e., free rolling, braking, accelerating, or cornering). To achieve acceptable performance on wet surfaces, maintaining effective contact between the tire tread and the road is of importance, and there is no doubt about the necessity of removing water from the contact area as much as possible.

To maintain effective contact between the tire and the road, the tire tread should have suitable pattern to facilitate the flow of fluid from the contact area, and the surface of the pavement should have appropriate texture to facilitate drainage as well. To provide good skid resistance, road surfaces must fulfill two requirements: an open macrotexture to facilitate gross drainage, and microharshness of the asperities to produce subdivision of the surface into sharp points that can penetrate the remaining water film [1.15].

Effects of tread pattern and speed on the braking performance of tires on various wet surfaces have been studied experimentally by a number of investigators. Figures 1.28 and 1.29 show the variation of the peak values and the sliding values of the coefficient of road adhesion, μ_p and μ_s, with

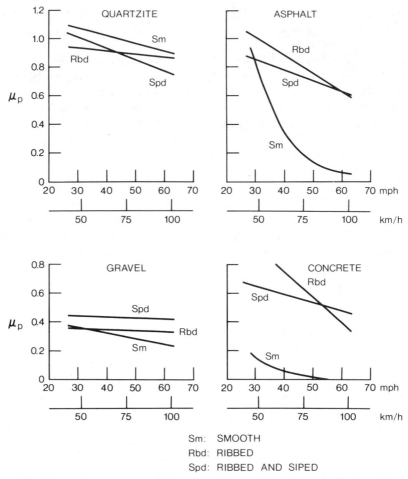

Fig. 1.28   Effect of tread design on the peak value of coefficient of road adhesion μ_p over wet surfaces. (Reproduced, by permission, from *Mechanics of Pneumatic Tires*, edited by S. K. Clark, Monograph 122, National Bureau of Standards, 1971.)

speed for a smooth tire, a tire with ribs, and a tire with ribs and sipes on wet quartzite, asphalt, gravel, and concrete [1.15]. It can be seen that there is a marked difference in the coefficient of road adhesion between patterned tires, including the ribbed and siped tires, and smooth tires on wet asphalt and concrete surfaces. The tread pattern increases the value of coefficient of road adhesion and reduces its speed dependence. In contrast, there is little pattern effect on wet quartzite surfaces and a high level of friction is maintained over the whole speed range. Thus, it can be concluded that the advantages of a patterned tire over a smooth tire are pronounced only on badly drained surfaces.

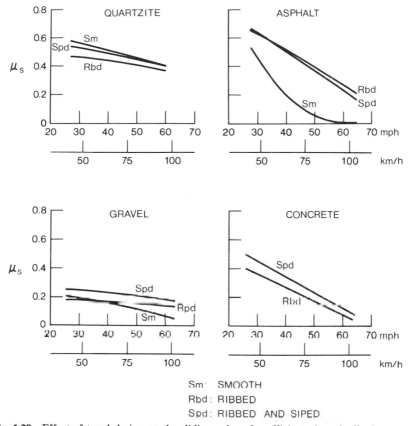

Sm: SMOOTH
Rbd: RIBBED
Spd: RIBBED AND SIPED

Fig. 1.29 Effect of tread design on the sliding value of coefficient of road adhesion μ_s over wet surfaces. (Reproduced, by permission, from *Mechanics of Pneumatic Tires*, edited by S. K. Clark, Monograph 122, National Bureau of Standards, 1971.)

It should be pointed out that tread pattern can function satisfactorily on a wet road only when grooves and sipes constitute a reservoir of sufficient capacity and that its effectiveness decreases with the wear of the tread. The decline in value of the coefficient of road adhesion with the decrease of tread depth is more pronounced on smooth than on rough roads, as rough roads can provide better drainage.

When a pneumatic tire is braked over a flooded surface, the motion of the tire creates hydrodynamic pressure in the fluid. The hydrodynamic pressure acting on the tire builds up as the square of speed of the tire and tends to separate the tire from the ground. At low speeds, the front part of the tire rides on a wedge or a film of fluid. This fluid film extends backward into the contact area as the speed of the tire increases. At a particular speed, the hydrodynamic lift developed under the tire equals the

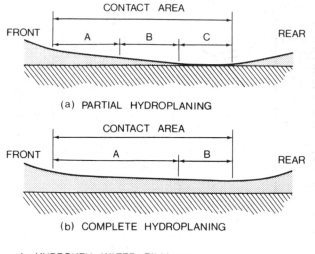

CONTACT AREA

FRONT | A | B | C | REAR

(a) PARTIAL HYDROPLANING

CONTACT AREA

FRONT | A | B | REAR

(b) COMPLETE HYDROPLANING

A – UNBROKEN WATER FILM
B – REGION OF PARTIAL BREAKDOWN OF WATER FILM
C – CONTACT ZONE

Fig. 1.30 Hydroplaning of tires on flooded surfaces. (Reproduced, by permission, from *Mechanics of Pneumatic Tires*, edited by S. K. Clark, Monograph 122, National Bureau of Standards, 1971.)

vertical load, the tire rides completely on the fluid and all contact with the ground is lost. This phenomenon is usually referred to as hydroplaning and is illustrated in Fig. 1.30 [1.16].

For smooth or close-patterned tires that do not allow escape paths for water and for patterned tires on flooded surfaces with fluid depth exceeding the groove depth in the tread, the speed at which hydroplaning occurs may be determined based on the theory of hydrodynamics. It can be assumed that the lift component of the hydrodynamic force F_h is proportional to the tire-ground contact area A, fluid density ρ_f, and the square of the vehicle speed V [1.17, 1.18].

$$F_h \propto \rho_f A V^2 \qquad (1.37)$$

When hydroplaning occurs, the lift component of the hydrodynamic force is equal to the vertical load acting on the tire. The speed at which hydroplaning begins, therefore, is proportional to the square root of the nominal ground contact pressure W/A, which is proportional to the inflation pressure of the tire p_i. Based on this reasoning and on experimental data shown in Fig. 1.31 [1.18], the following formula was proposed by

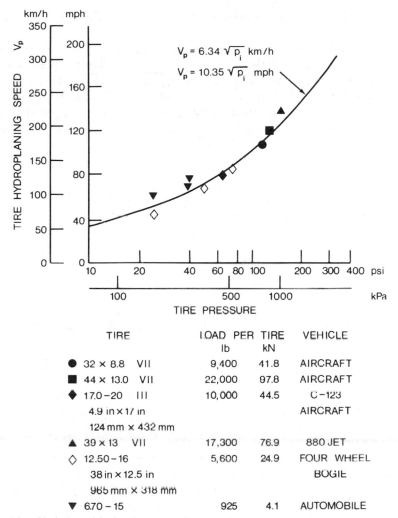

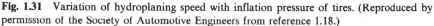

Fig. 1.31 Variation of hydroplaning speed with inflation pressure of tires. (Reproduced by permission of the Society of Automotive Engineers from reference 1.18.)

Horne et al. for predicting the hydroplaning speed V_p

$$V_p = 10.35\sqrt{p_i} \text{ mph} \tag{1.38}$$

or

$$V_p = 6.34\sqrt{p_i} \text{ km/h} \tag{1.39}$$

where p_i is the inflation pressure of the tire in psi for Eq. 1.38 and in kPa for Eq. 1.39.

For patterned tires on wet surfaces where the fluid depth is less than the groove depth of the tread, the prediction of the hydroplaning speed is more complex and a generally accepted theory has yet to be evolved. The parameters found to be of significance to hydroplaning are pavement surface texture, pavement fluid depth, fluid viscosity, fluid density, tire inflation pressure, tire vertical load, tire tread pattern, and tire tread wear.

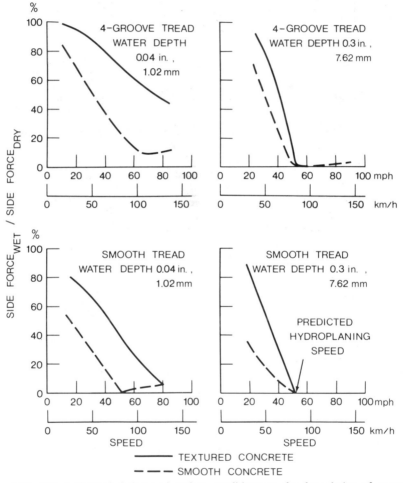

Fig. 1.32 Effect of tread design and surface conditions on the degradation of cornering ability of tires on wet surfaces. (Reproduced by permission of the Society of Automotive Engineers from reference 1.18.)

The most important effect of hydroplaning is the reduction in the coefficient of road adhesion between the tire and the ground. This affects braking, steering control, and directional stability. Figure 1.32 shows the degradation of the cornering force of passenger car tires on two different wet surfaces at various speeds [1.18].

1.6 RIDE PROPERTIES OF TIRES

Supporting the weight of the vehicle and cushioning it over surface irregularities are two of the basic functions of a pneumatic tire. When a vertical load is applied to an inflated tire, the tire progressively deflects as the load increases. Figure 1.33 shows the static load-deflection relationship for a 5.60 × 13 bias-ply tire at various inflation pressures [1.19]. The type of diagram shown in Fig. 1.33 is usually referred to as lattice plot in which the origin of each load-deflection curve is displaced along the deflection axis by an amount proportional to inflation pressure. The relationship

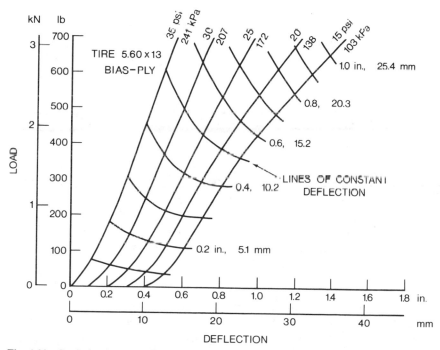

Fig. 1.33 Static load-deflection curves of a 5.60 × 13 bias-ply tire. (Reproduced by permission of the Council of the Institution of Mechanical Engineers from reference 1.19.)

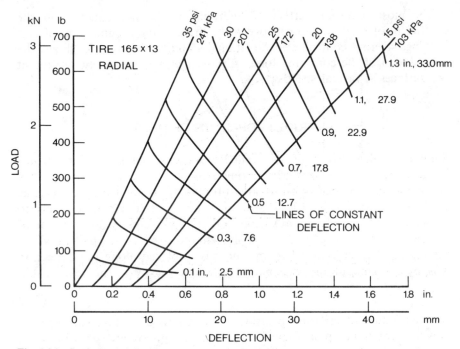

Fig. 1.34 Static load-deflection curves of a 165×13 radial-ply tire. (Reproduced by permission of the Council of the Institution of Mechanical Engineers from reference 1.19.)

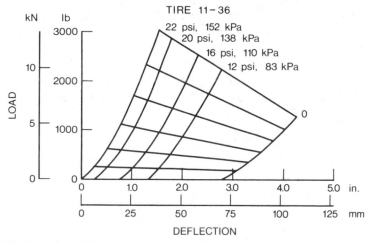

Fig. 1.35 Static load-deflection curves of a 11–36 tractor tire. (Reproduced by permission of the *Journal of Agricultural Engineering Research* from reference 1.20.)

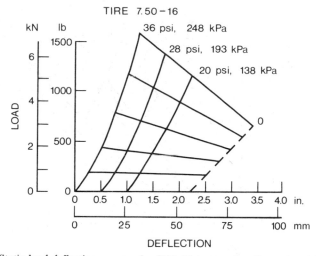

TIRE 7.50 – 16

Fig. 1.36 Static load-deflection curves of a 7.50–16 tractor tire. (Reproduced by permission of the *Journal of Agricultural Engineering Research* from reference 1.20.)

between load and inflation pressure for constant deflection can also be shown in the lattice plot. Figure 1.34 shows the interrelationship between static load, inflation pressure, and deflection for a 165×13 radial-ply tire [1.19]. The lattice plots of load-deflection data at various inflation pressures for tractor tires 11–36 and 7.50–16 are shown in Figs. 1.35 and 1.36, respectively [1.20]. The load-deflection curves at various inflation pressures for a terra tire 26×12.00–12 are shown in Fig. 1.37. The vertical load-deflection curves are useful in estimating the static stiffness of tires in relation to the evaluation of vehicle vibration and ride qualities.

The vertical load of a tire is supported by both the pressurized air and the tire carcass. Depending on the type of tire, the proportion of the load carried by the pressurized air and that carried by the tire carcass vary. It has been found that for aircraft tires the carcass carries 3 to 8% of the vertical load, whereas for automobile tires it may carry up to 15% of the load [1.5]. For tractor tires, it has been reported that the tire carcass may carry up to 60% of the load under certain operating conditions [1.20]. This is mainly due to the fact that the inflation pressure of tractor tires is usually lower than that of aircraft and automobile tires.

In vehicle vibration analysis and ride simulation, the cushioning characteristics of a pneumatic tire may be represented by various mathematical models. The most widely used and the simplest model representing the fundamental mode of vibration of the pneumatic tire consists of a mass element and a linear spring in parallel with a viscous damping element.

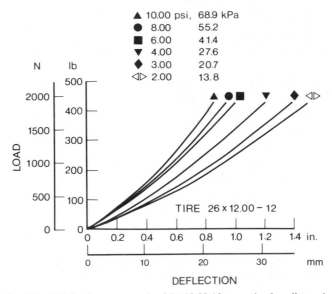

Fig. 1.37   Static load-deflection curves of a 26×12.00-12 terra tire for all terrain vehicles.

Other models, such as the so-called "viscoelastic" model shown in Fig. 1.38, have also been proposed.

Depending upon the test conditions, three distinct types of tire stiffness may be defined: static, nonrolling dynamic, and rolling dynamic stiffness.

Static Stiffness

The static stiffness of a tire is determined by the slope of the static load-deflection curves shown in Figs. 1.33–1.37. It has been found that for a given inflation pressure, the load-deflection characteristics for both radial- and bias-ply tires are more or less linear except at relatively low values of load. Consequently, it can be assumed that tire stiffness is

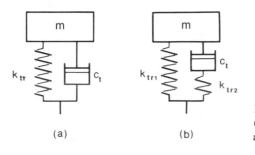

Fig. 1.38   (a) Simple linear model and (b) viscoelastic model proposed for analysis of tire vibration.

independent of load in the range of practical interest. Figure 1.39 shows the variation of the stiffness with inflation pressure for a 165×13 radial-ply tire. The values of stiffness shown are derived from the load-deflection curves shown in Fig. 1.34 [1.19]. The values of the static stiffness of tractor tires 11–36 and 7.5-16, and those of a terra tire 26×12.00–12 at various inflation pressures are given in Table 1.3.

Nonrolling Dynamic Stiffness

The dynamic stiffness of a nonrolling tire may be obtained using various methods. One of the simplest is the so-called "drop test." In this test, the tire with a certain load is allowed to fall freely from a height at which the tire is just in contact with the ground. Consequently the tire remains in contact with the ground throughout the test. The transient response of the tire is recorded. A typical amplitude decay trace is shown in Fig. 1.40. The values of the tire dynamic stiffness as well as the equivalent viscous damping coefficient can then be determined from the decay trace using the well-established theory of free vibration of a single-degree-of-freedom system. Table 1.3 shows the values of the nonrolling dynamic stiffness and

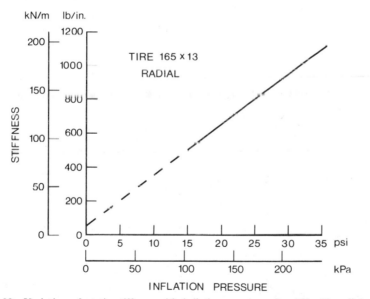

Fig. 1.39 Variation of static stiffness with inflation pressure of a 165×13 radial-ply tire. (Reproduced by permission of the Council of the Institution of Mechanical Engineers from reference 1.19.)

Table 1.3 Vertical Stiffness of Tires

Tire	Inflation Pressure	Load	Static Stiffness	Nonrolling Dynamic Stiffness (Average)	Damping Coefficient
11–36[a] (4-ply)	82.7 kPa (12 psi)	6.67 kN (1500 lb)	357.5 kN/m (24,500 lb/ft)	379.4 kN/m (26,000 lb/ft)	2.4 kN·s/m (165 lb·s/ft)
		8.0 kN (1800 lb)	357.5 kN/m (24,500 lb/ft)	394.0 kN/m (27,000 lb/ft)	2.6 kN·s/m (180 lb·s/ft)
		9.34 kN (2100 lb)	—	423.2 kN/m (29,000 lb/ft)	3.4 kN·s/m (230 lb·s/ft)
	110.3 kPa (16 psi)	6.67 kN (1500 lb)	379.4 kN/m (26,000 lb/ft)	394.0 kN/m (27,000 lb/ft)	2.1 kN·s/m (145 lb·s/ft)
		8.0 kN (1800 lb)	386.7 kN/m (26,500 lb/ft)	437.8 kN/m (30,000 lb/ft)	2.5 kN·s/m (175 lb·s/ft)
		9.34 kN (2100 lb)	394.0 kN/m (27,000 lb/ft)	423.2 kN/m (29,000 lb/ft)	2.5 kN·s/m (175 lb·s/ft)
7.5-16 (6-ply)	138 kPa (20 psi)	3.56 kN (800 lb)	175.1 kN/m (12,000 lb/ft)	218.9 kN/m (15,000 lb/ft)	0.58 kN·s/m (40 lb·s/ft)
		4.45 kN (1000 lb)	175.1 kN/m (12,000 lb/ft)	233.5 kN/m (16,000 lb/ft)	0.66 kN·s/m (45 lb·s/ft)
		4.89 kN (1100 lb)	182.4 kN/m (12,500 lb/ft)	248.1 kN/m (17,000 lb/ft)	0.80 kN·s/m (55 lb·s/ft)
	193 kPa (28 psi)	3.56 kN (800 lb)	218.9 kN/m (15,000 lb/ft)	233.5 kN/m (16,000 lb/ft)	0.36 kN·s/m (25 lb·s/ft)
		4.45 kN (1100 lb)	226.2 kN/m (15,500 lb/ft)	262.7 kN/m (18,000 lb/ft)	0.66 kN·s/m (45 lb·s/ft)
		4.89 kN (1300 lb)	255.4 kN/m (17,500 lb/ft)	277.3 kN/m (19,000 lb/ft)	0.73 kN·s/m (50 lb·s/ft)
26 x 12.00-12	15.5 kPa (2.25 psi)	1.78 kN (400 lb)	51.1 kN/m (3500 lb/ft)	—	0.47 kN·s/m (32 lb·s/ft)
(2-ply)	27.6 kPa (4 psi)	1.78 kN (400 lb)	68.6 kN/m (4700 lb/ft)	—	0.49 kN·s/m (34 lb·s/ft)

[a]Source. Reference 1.20.

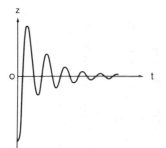

Fig. 1.40 An amplitude decay record of a nonrolling tire obtained from a "drop test."

the damping coefficient for tractor tires 11–36 and 7.5-16 [1.20], and the damping coefficient for a terra tire 26×12.00-12. The values of the damping coefficient for a 5.60×13 bias-ply and a 165×13 radial-ply car tire are given in Table 1.4 [1.19].

Rolling Dynamic Stiffness

The rolling dynamic stiffness is usually determined by measuring the response of a rolling tire to a known harmonic excitation. The response is normally measured at the hub and the excitation is given at the tread band. By examing the ratio of output to input and the phase angle, it is possible to determine the dynamic stiffness and the damping coefficient of a rolling tire.

An alternative method for determining the dynamic stiffness of a tire is to measure its resonant frequency when rolling on a drum or belt. Figure 1.41 shows the values of the dynamic stiffness for various types of car tire

Table 1.4   Damping Coefficient of Tires

Tire	Inflation Pressure	Damping Coefficient
Bias-ply	103.4 kPa (15 psi)	4.59 kN·s/m (315 lb·s/ft)
5.60×13	137.9 kPa (20 psi)	4.89 kN·s/m (335 lb·s/ft)
	172.4 kPa (25 psi)	4.52 kN·s/m (310 lb·s/ft)
	206.9 kPa (30 psi)	4.09 kN·s/m (280 lb·s/ft)
	241.3 kPa (35 psi)	4.09 kN·s/m (280 lb·s/ft)
Radial-ply	103.4 kPa (15 psi)	4.45 kN·s/m (305 lb·s/ft)
165×13	137.9 kPa (20 psi)	3.68 kN·s/m (252 lb·s/ft)
	172.4 kPa (25 psi)	3.44 kN·s/m (236 lb·s/ft)
	206.9 kPa (30 psi)	3.43 kN·s/m (235 lb·s/ft)
	241.3 kPa (35 psi)	2.86 kN·s/m (196 lb·s/ft)

Source.   Reference 1.19.

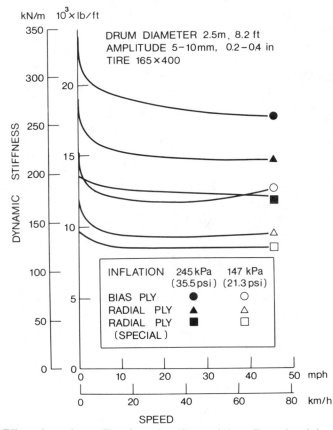

Fig. 1.41 Effect of speed on rolling dynamic stiffness of tires. (Reproduced, by permission, from *Mechanics of Pneumatic Tires*, edited by S. K. Clark, Monograph 122, National Bureau of Standards, 1971.)

obtained using this method [1.5]. It is shown that the dynamic stiffness of car tires decreases sharply as soon as the tire is rolling. However, beyond a speed of approximately 20 km/h (12 mph), the influence of speed becomes less important. In simulation studies of vehicle ride characteristics, the use of rolling dynamic stiffness is usually preferred.

Attempts to determine the relationship between the static and dynamic stiffness of tires have been made. However, no general conclusions have been reached. Some reports indicate that for automobile tires the rolling dynamic stiffness may be 10–15% less than the stiffness obtained from static load-deflection curves. For tractor tires, it has been reported that the dynamic stiffness may exceed the static value by approximately 10% [1.20].

As pointed out by Gough [1.21], the difference between the static and dynamic stiffness reported in the literature is not necessarily due to dynamic effects. The difference may well be due to the use of linear analysis in obtaining the dynamic stiffness of a tire that is essentially a nonlinear system.

It has been shown that among various operational parameters, inflation pressure, speed, and vertical load have noticeable influence on tire stiffness. Tire design parameters, such as the crown angle of the cords, tread width, number of plies, and tire material, also affect the stiffness.

The damping of a pneumatic tire is mainly due to the hysteresis of tire materials. Generally speaking, it is neither Coulomb-type nor viscous-type damping, and it appears to be a combination of both. However, an equivalent viscous damping coefficient can usually be derived from dynamic tests mentioned previously. Its value is subject to variation, depending on the design and construction of the tire as well as operating conditions. It has been shown that the damping of pneumatic tires made of synthetic rubber compounds is considerably less than that provided by a shock absorber.

To evaluate the overall vibrational characteristics of tires, tests may be carried out on a variable-speed rotating drum. The profile of the drum may be random, sinusoidal, square, or triangular. Experience has shown that the use of a periodic type of excitation enables rapid assessments to be made. Figure 1.42 shows the wheel hub acceleration as a function of

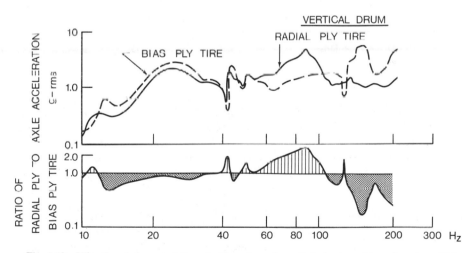

Fig. 1.42 Vibrational characteristics of a bias-ply and a radial-ply tire subjected to sinusoidal excitation. (Reproduced by permission of the Council of the Institution of Mechanical Engineers from reference 1.22.)

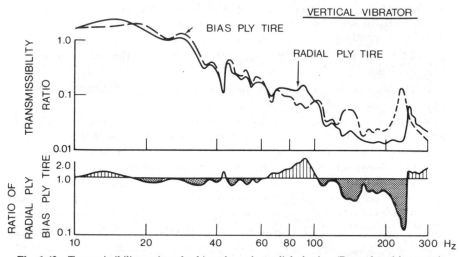

Fig. 1.43 Transmissibility ratios of a bias-ply and a radial-ply tire. (Reproduced by permission of the Council of the Institution of Mechanical Engineers from reference 1.22.)

frequency for a radial-ply and a bias-ply tire over a sinusoidal profile with 133 mm (5.25 in.) pitch and 6 mm ($\frac{1}{4}$ in.) peak to peak amplitude [1.22]. The transmissibility ratios in the vertical direction over a wide frequency range of a radial-ply and a bias-ply tire are shown in Fig. 1.43 [1.22]. This set of results has been obtained using a vibration exciter. The vibration input is imparted to the tread of a nonrolling tire through a platform mounted on the vibration exciter.

REFERENCES

1.1 V. E. Gough, Structure of the Tire, in S. K. Clark, Ed., *Mechanics of Pneumatic Tires*, Monograph 122, National Bureau of Standards, Washington, DC, 1971, Chap. 3.

1.2 D. F. Moore, *The Friction of Pneumatic Tyres*, Elsevier, Amsterdam, 1975.

1.3 Vehicle Dynamics Terminology, SAE J670 a, Society of Automotive Engineers, 1965.

1.4 T. French, Construction and Behavior Characteristics of Tyres, *Proceedings of the Institution of Mechanical Engineers, Automobile Division*, AD 14/59, 1959.

1.5 H. C. A. van Eldik Thieme and H. B. Pacejka, The Tire as a Vehicle Component, in S. K. Clark, Ed., *Mechanics of Pneumatic Tires*, Monograph 122, National Bureau of Standards, Washington, DC, 1971, Chap. 7.

1.6 J. J. Taborek, Mechanics of Vehicles, *Machine Design*, May 30–December 26, 1957.

1.7 J. D. C. Hartley and D. M. Turner, Tires for High-Performance Cars, *SAE Transactions*, Vol. 64, 1956.

1.8 R. Hadekel, The Mechanical Characteristics of Pneumatic Tyres, S. & T. Memo No. 10/52, Ministry of Supply, London, 1952.

1.9 J. L. Harned, L. E. Johnston, and G. Sharpf, Measurement of Tire Brake Force Characteristics as Related to Wheel Slip (Antilock) Control System Design, *SAE Transactions*, Vol. 78, 690214, 1969.

1.10 R. D. Ervin, Mobile Measurement of Truck Tire Traction, *Proceedings of a Symposium on Commercial Vehicle Braking and Handling*, Highway Safety Research Institute, University of Michigan, MI, 1975.

1.11 J. R. Ellis, *Vehicle Dynamics*, Business Books, London, England, 1969.

1.12 H. Dugoff, P. S. Fancher, and L. Segel, *Tire Performance Characteristics Affecting Vehicle Response to Steering and Braking Control Inputs*, Final Report for Contract No. CST-460, Office of Vehicle Systems Research, National Bureau of Standards, Washington, DC, August 1969.

1.13 D. L. Nordeen and A. D. Cortese, Force and Moment Characteristics of Rolling Tires, Society of Automotive Engineers, paper 713A, 1963.

1.14 V. E. Gough, Practical Tire Research, *SAE Transactions*, Vol. 64, pp. 310–318, 1956.

1.15 A. Schallamach, Skid Resistance and Directional Control, in S. K. Clark, Ed., *Mechanics of Pneumatic Tires*, Monograph 122, National Bureau of Standards, Washington, DC, 1971, Chap. 6.

1.16 S. K. Clark, The Contact Between Tire and Roadway, in S. K. Clark, Ed., *Mechanics of Pneumatic Tires*, Monograph 122, National Bureau of Standards, Washington, DC, 1971, Chap. 5.

1.17 W. B. Horne and R. C. Dreher, Phenomenon of Pneumatic Tire Hydroplaning, NASA TND-2056, November, 1963.

1.18 W. B. Horne and U. T. Joyner, Pneumatic Tire Hydroplaning and Some Effects on Vehicle Performance, Society of Automotive Engineers, paper 650145, 1965.

1.19 J. A. Overton, B. Mills, and C. Ashley, The Vertical Response Characteristics of the Non-Rolling Tire, *Proceedings of the Institution of Mechanical Engineers*, Vol. 184, Part 2A, No. 2, 1969-1970.

1.20 J. Matthews and J. D. C. Talamo, Ride Comfort for Tractor Operators, III. Investigation of Tractor Dynamics by Analogue Computer Simulation, *Journal of Agricultural Engineering Research*, Vol. 10, No. 2, 1965.

1.21 V. E. Gough, Tyres and Air Suspension, *Advances in Automobile Engineering (Symposium on Vehicle Ride Problem)*, Pergamon Press, Oxford, England, 1963.

1.22 C. W. Barson, D. H. James, and A. W. Morcombe, Some Aspects of Tire and Vehicle Vibration Testing, *Proceedings of the Institution of Mechanical Engineers*, Vol. 182, Part 3B, 1967-1968.

PROBLEMS

1.1 Compare the power required to overcome the rolling resistance of a passenger car weighing 15.57 kN (3500 lb) and having bias-ply tires with that of the same vehicle but with radial-ply tires in the speed range 40–100 km/h (25–62 mph). The variation of the coefficient of rolling resistance of the bias-ply and radial-ply tire with speed is shown in Fig. 1.3.

1.2 A truck tire with vertical load of 24.78 kN (5570 lb) travels on a dry concrete pavement with nominal coefficient of road adhesion $\mu_0 = 0.80$.

The longitudinal stiffness of the tire C_i is 224.64 kN/unit skid (55,000 lb/unit skid). Using the empirical formulas given in Section 1.4, plot the relationship between the braking force and skid of the tire at low speeds.

1.3 Using the empirical method described in Section 1.4, determine the relationship between the cornering force and slip angle in the range 0-16° of the truck tire described in Problem 1.2. The cornering stiffness of the tire C_α is 132.53 kN/rad (520 lb/degree). Assume that there is no braking torque applied to the tire and that it travels at low speeds.

1.4 Evaluate the effect of longitudinal skid on cornering force of the truck tire described in Problems 1.2 and 1.3 at a slip angle of 4°, using the empirical method described in Section 1.4. Plot the cornering force of the tire versus skid in the range of 0-100%.

1.5 A passenger car travels over a flooded pavement. The inflation pressure of the tires is 179.27 kPa (26 psi). If the initial speed of the car is 100 km/h (62 mph) and brakes are then applied, determine whether or not the vehicle will be hydroplaning.

1.6 An all-terrain vehicle weighs 3.56 kN (800 lb) and has four terra tires each of which has a vertical stiffness of 52.54 kN/m (300 lb/in.) at an inflation pressure of 27.6 kPa (4 psi), and a stiffness of 96.32 kN/m (550 lb/in.) at a pressure of 68.9 kPa (10 psi). Estimate the variation of the fundamental natural frequency of the vehicle in the vertical direction over the range of inflation pressure given. The vehicle has no spring suspension.

CHAPTER TWO

MECHANICS OF VEHICLE-TERRAIN INTERACTION—TERRAMECHANICS

In cross-country operations, various types of terrain with differing characteristics, ranging from desert sand through deep mud to snow, may be encountered. The mechanical properties of the terrain quite often impose severe limitations to the mobility and performance of cross-country vehicles. An adequate knowledge of the mechanical properties of the terrain and an understanding of the mechanics of vehicle-terrain interaction are therefore essential for the proper design, selection, and operation of off-road vehicles. The study of the relationship between the performance of an off-road vehicle and its physical environment (terrain) has now become known as "Terramechanics."

In this chapter a brief review of the theories of elastic and plastic behavior of the terrain that covers most of the trafficable earth surface will be presented. Applications of these theories to the solutions of some of the problems in terramechanics will be discussed. These theories provide a basis for the understanding of the physical nature of vehicle-terrain interaction. However, they have not yet been developed to the point that will permit vehicle-terrain relationships to be accurately defined in the field. To provide a practical engineering approach to the evaluation and prediction of off-road vehicle performance, various semiempirical methods have been proposed. To develop these methods successfully, the mechanical behavior of the terrain must be measured under loading conditions similar to those exerted by the vehicle. Among the various techniques for measuring terrain values, the Bevameter method developed by Bekker is one of the widely used and will be briefly described [2.1–2.3]. Later in the chapter, the relationships between the mechanical properties of terrain and vehicle performance based on the Bevameter technique will be discussed, and methods for predicting motion resistance, sinkage, tractive effort, and slip of off-road vehicles will be presented. It should be noted that methods for evaluating off-road vehicle performance are being continuously refined and improved. When better mathematical models and terrain inputs are available, they could fit into the methodological framework presented here to make a more comprehensive picture.

2.1 DISTRIBUTION OF STRESSES IN THE TERRAIN UNDER VEHICULAR LOADS

Certain types of terrain, such as saturated clay and compact sand, which cover part of the trafficable earth surface, may be compared to an ideal elasto-plastic material with stress-strain relationship shown in Fig. 2.1. When the stress level in the terrain does not exceed a certain limit, such as that denoted by "a" in Fig. 2.1, the terrain may exhibit elastic behavior. The idealization of the terrain as an elastic medium has found applications in the prediction of stress distribution in the soil, in connection with the study of soil compaction due to vehicular loads [2.4].

The prediction of stress distribution in an elastic medium when subjected to any specific load may be based on the analysis of the distribution of stresses under a point load. The method for calculating the stress distribution in a semi-infinite, homogeneous, isotropic, elastic medium subjected to a vertical point load was first developed by Boussinesq. His solutions give the following expressions for the vertical stress σ_z acting upon various points on a horizontal surface situated at depth z (see Fig. 2.2):

$$\sigma_z = \frac{3W}{2\pi} z^3 (x^2 + y^2 + z^2)^{-5/2} = \frac{3}{2\pi} \frac{1}{\left[1 + (r/z)^2\right]^{5/2}} \frac{W}{z^2}$$

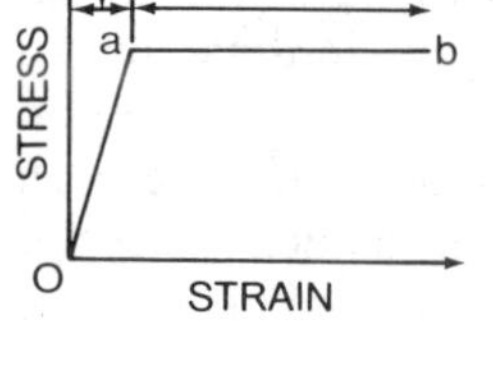

Fig. 2.1 Behavior of an idealized elasto-plastic material.

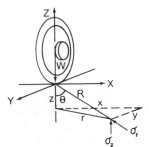

Fig. 2.2 Stresses at a point in a semi-infinite elastic medium subjected to a point load. (From *Theory of Land Locomotion* by M. G. Bekker, copyright © by the University of Michigan 1956, reproduced by permission of the University of Michigan Press.)

or

$$\sigma_z = \frac{3W}{2\pi R^2}\left(\frac{z}{R}\right)^3 = \frac{3W}{2\pi R^2}\cos^3\theta \qquad (2.1)$$

where

$$r = \sqrt{x^2 + y^2} \quad \text{and} \quad R = \sqrt{z^2 + r^2}$$

When polar coordinates are used, the radial stress σ_r (Fig. 2.2) is given by

$$\sigma_r = \frac{3W}{2\pi R^2}\cos\theta \qquad (2.2)$$

It is interesting to note that the stresses are independent of the modulus of elasticity of the material and that they are only functions of the load applied and the distance from the point of application of the load. It should be mentioned that Eqs. 2.1 and 2.2 are only valid for calculating stresses at points not too close to the point of application of the load. The material in the immediate vicinity of the point load does not behave elastically.

Based on the analysis of stress distribution beneath a point load, the distribution of stresses in an elastic medium under a variety of loading conditions may be predicted using the principle of superposition. For instance, for a circular contact area having radius r_0 and with a uniform pressure p_0 (Fig. 2.3), the vertical stress at depth z below the center of the contact area may be determined in the following way [2.1]. The load acting upon the contact area is first divided into a number of discrete point loads, $dW = p_0 dA = p_0 r dr d\theta$. Hence, in accordance with Eq. 2.1,

$$d\sigma_z = \frac{3}{2\pi}\frac{p_0 r dr d\theta}{\left[1 + (r/z)^2\right]^{5/2} z^2} \qquad (2.3)$$

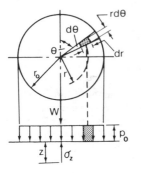

Fig. 2.3 Vertical stresses in a semi-infinite elastic medium below the center of a circular loading area. (From *Theory of Land Locomotion* by M. G. Bekker, copyright © by the University of Michigan 1956, reproduced by permission of the University of Michigan Press.)

The resultant vertical stress σ_z at depth z below the center of contact area is then equal to the sum of the stresses produced by point loads of $p_0 r \, dr \, d\theta$, and can be computed by a double integration [2.1].

$$\sigma_z = \frac{3}{2\pi} p_0 \int_0^{r_0} \int_0^{2\pi} \frac{r \, dr \, d\theta}{\left[1+(r/z)^2\right]^{5/2} z^2} = 3 p_0 \int_0^{r_0} \frac{r \, dr}{\left[1+(r/z)^2\right]^{5/2} z^2}$$

By substituting $(r/z)^2 = u^2$, it is found that

$$\sigma_z = 3 p_0 \int_0^{r_0/z} \frac{u \, du}{\left[1+u^2\right]^{5/2}} = p_0 \left[1 - \frac{z^3}{\left(z^2+r_0^2\right)^{3/2}}\right] \tag{2.4}$$

The computation of the stresses at points other than those below the center of contact area is rather involved and cannot be generalized by a simple set of equations. The stress distribution in an elastic medium under distributed loads over an elliptic area, similar to that applied by a tire, can be determined in a similar way.

Another case of interest from the vehicle viewpoint is the distribution of stresses under the action of a strip load (Fig. 2.4). Such a strip load may be considered as an idealization of that applied by a tracked vehicle. It can be shown that the stresses in an elastic medium due to a uniform pressure p_0 over a strip of infinite length and of constant width b (Fig. 2.5) can be computed by the following equations [2.1]:

$$\sigma_x = \frac{p_0}{\pi} \left[\theta_2 - \theta_1 + \sin\theta_1 \cos\theta_1 - \sin\theta_2 \cos\theta_2\right] \tag{2.5}$$

$$\sigma_z = \frac{p_0}{\pi} \left[\theta_2 - \theta_1 - \sin\theta_1 \cos\theta_1 + \sin\theta_2 \cos\theta_2\right] \tag{2.6}$$

$$\tau_{xz} = \frac{p_0}{\pi} \left(\sin^2\theta_2 - \sin^2\theta_1\right) \tag{2.7}$$

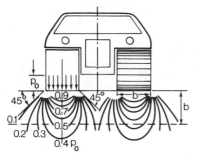

Fig. 2.4 Distribution of vertical stresses in a semi-infinite elastic medium under a tracked vehicle. (From *Theory of Land Locomotion* by M. G. Bekker, copyright © by the University of Michigan 1956, reproduced by permission of the University of Michigan Press.)

The points in the medium that experience the same level of stress form a family of iso-stress surfaces commonly known as pressure bulbs. The general characteristics of the bulbs of vertical pressure under a uniform strip load are illustrated in Fig. 2.4. It is interesting to note that at a depth equal to the width of the strip, the vertical stress under the center of the loading area is approximately 50% of the applied pressure, and practically vanishes at a depth twice the width of the strip. The boundary of the bulbs of vertical pressure, for all practical purposes, may be assumed as being sloped at an angle of 45° [2.1].

It should be pointed out that the use of the theory of elasticity for predicting stresses in a real soil produces approximate results only. Measurements have shown that the stress distribution in a real soil deviates from that computed using Boussinesq's equations [2.4]. There is a tendency for the compressive stress in the soil to concentrate around the loading axis. This tendency becomes greater when the soil becomes more plastic due to increased moisture content or when the soil is less cohesive such as sand. In view of this, various semiempirical stress equations have been developed to comply better with real situations. Fröhlich introduced a concentration factor ν to Boussinesq's equations. The factor ν could be adapted to changing soil conditions. Introducing the concentration factor, the expressions for the vertical and radial stress in the soil subjected to a

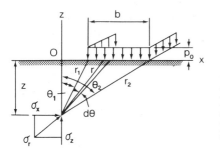

Fig. 2.5 Stresses at a point in a semi-infinite elastic medium subjected to a uniform strip load. (From *Theory of Land Locomotion* by M. G. Bekker, copyright © by the University of Michigan 1956, reproduced by permission of the University of Michigan Press.)

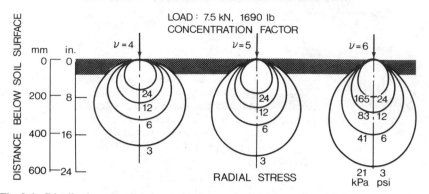

Fig. 2.6 Distribution of radial stresses under a point load in media with different concentration factors. (Reproduced, by permission, from reference 2.4.)

point load take the following forms

$$\sigma_z = \frac{\nu W}{2\pi R^2} \cos^\nu \theta = \frac{\nu W}{2\pi z^2} \cos^{\nu+2} \theta \tag{2.8}$$

and

$$\sigma_r = \frac{\nu W}{2\pi R^2} \cos^{\nu-2} \theta = \frac{\nu W}{2\pi z^2} \cos^\nu \theta \tag{2.9}$$

Equations 2.8 and 2.9 are identical with Eqs. 2.1 and 2.2, respectively, if ν is equal to 3. The value of the concentration factor depends on the type of soil and its moisture content. Figure 2.6 shows the bulbs of radial stress σ_r under a point load in soils with different concentration factors [2.4].

A tire transfers its load to the soil usually not at one point but through a finite area of contact. To determine the actual stress distribution in the soil due to tire loading, the actual size of the contact area and the pressure distribution over the contact patch must be known. Figure 2.7 shows the measured contact areas of a tire under different soil conditions [2.4]. The rut becomes deeper with increasing porosity and moisture content. An approximately uniform pressure over the entire contact area may be assumed for tires without lugs in hard, dry soil. In soft soils the pressure over the contact area varies with the depth of the rut. Usually the contact pressure decreases toward the outside of the contact area and is more concentrated toward the center of the loading area. Representative pressure distributions over the contact area in hard, dry soil, in fairly moist, relatively dense soil, and in wet soil are shown in Fig. 2.8(a), (b) and (c), respectively [2.4].

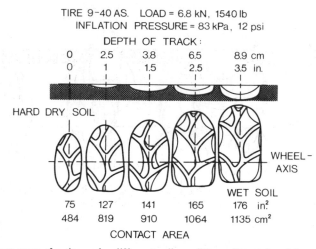

TIRE 9-40 AS.   LOAD = 6.8 kN, 1540 lb
INFLATION PRESSURE = 83 kPa, 12 psi

DEPTH OF TRACK:

| 0 | 2.5 | 3.8 | 6.5 | 8.9 cm |
| 0 | 1 | 1.5 | 2.5 | 3.5 in. |

HARD DRY SOIL

WHEEL-AXIS

WET SOIL

| 75 | 127 | 141 | 165 | 176 in² |
| 484 | 819 | 910 | 1064 | 1135 cm² |

CONTACT AREA

Fig. 2.7 Contact areas of a tire under different soil conditions. (Reproduced, by permission, from reference 2.4.)

Knowing the shape of the contact area and pressure distribution over the contact patch, it is possible to predict the distribution of stresses in a real soil by employing Eqs. 2.8 and 2.9 as proposed by Fröhlich. It has been reported by Söhne that the difference between the measured values and calculated ones obtained using Fröhlich's equations is approximately 25%, which may be regarded as reasonable for this type of problem [2.5]. Figure 2.9 shows the distribution of the major principal stress under various tire loads in a soil having normal field density and moisture [2.4]. In the calculations, it is assumed that the concentration factor ν is 5 and

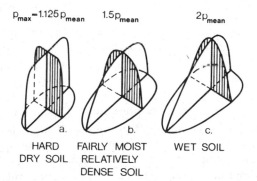

$p_{max} = 1.125\, p_{mean}$ $1.5\, p_{mean}$ $2\, p_{mean}$

| a. | b. | c. |
| HARD DRY SOIL | FAIRLY MOIST RELATIVELY DENSE SOIL | WET SOIL |

Fig. 2.8 Pressure distribution over the contact area under various soil conditions. (Reproduced, by permission, from reference 2.4.)

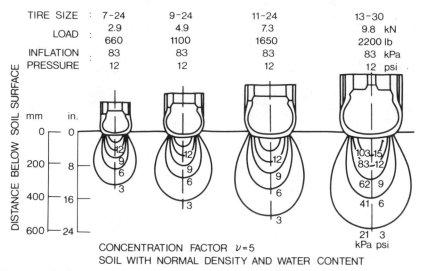

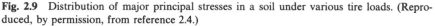

Fig. 2.9 Distribution of major principal stresses in a soil under various tire loads. (Reproduced, by permission, from reference 2.4.)

that the pressure distribution over the contact area is similar to that shown in Fig. 2.8(b). It has been found that for soil compaction the major principal stress is a more pertinent parameter than the vertical stress. Figure 2.9 shows that the stress can penetrate much deeper with higher loads for the same tire inflation pressure.

Figure 2.10 shows the effects of soil conditions on the shape of the pressure bulbs [2.4]. In hard, dry, and dense soil, the lines of equal major principal stress are approximately circular. The softer the soil, the narrower the pressure bulbs become. This is because in soft soil, the soil can flow sideways so that the stress is more concentrated toward the center of the loading area.

For tires with lugs, such as tractor tires, the pressure distribution over the contact area differs from that shown in Fig. 2.8. In hard, dry soil, the lugs of the tire carry the entire load. The pressure over the contact area of the lugs is three to four times higher than that of an equivalent tire without lugs. In a wet soil, because of the sinkage of the tire, there may be hardly any difference between the contact pressure under the lugs and that under the grooves. In this case, the distribution of contact pressure may be similar to that shown in Fig. 2.8(c). In principle, the stress distribution in the soil under tires with lugs may be estimated following an approach similar to that described above. However, the computation will be more involved.

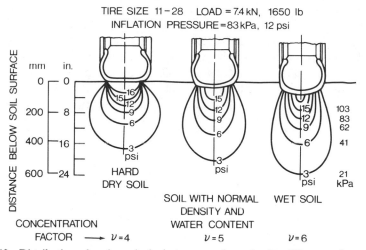

Fig. 2.10 Distribution of major principal stresses under a tire for different soil conditions. (Reproduced, by permission, from reference 2.4.)

2.2 APPLICATIONS OF THE THEORY OF PLASTIC EQUILIBRIUM TO THE MECHANICS OF VEHICLE-TERRAIN INTERACTION

When the vehicular load applied to the terrain exceeds a certain limit, the stress level within a certain boundary of the terrain may reach that denoted by "a" on the idealized stress-strain curve shown in Fig. 2.1. An infinitely small increase of stress beyond point "a" produces a rapid increase of strain, which constitutes plastic flow. The state that precedes plastic flow is usually referred to as plastic equilibrium. The transition from the state of plastic equilibrium to that of plastic flow represents the failure of the mass.

There are a number of criteria proposed for the failure of soils and other similar materials. One of the widely used and the simplest criteria is that due to Mohr-Coulomb. It postulates that the material at a point will fail if the shear stress at that point in the medium satisfies the following condition:

$$\tau = c + \sigma \tan \phi \tag{2.10}$$

where τ is the shear strength of the material, c is the apparent cohesion of the material, σ is the normal stress on the sheared surface, and ϕ is the angle of internal shearing resistance of the material.

Cohesion of the material is the bond that cements particles irrespective of the normal pressure exerted by one particle upon the other. On the other hand, particles of frictional masses can be held together only when a normal pressure is exercised between them. Thus, theoretically the shear strength of saturated clay and the like does not depend on the normal load, whereas the shear strength of dry sand increases with the increase of normal load. For dry sand, therefore, the shear strength may be expressed as

$$\tau = \sigma \tan \phi \tag{2.11}$$

and for saturated clay and the like, it may take the form

$$\tau = c \tag{2.12}$$

Granular masses that cover most of the trafficable earth surface, however, usually have both cohesive and frictional properties.

The meaning of the Mohr-Coulomb criterion may be illustrated with the aid of the Mohr circle of stress. If test specimens of a soil are subjected to different states of stress, for each mode of failure a Mohr circle can be constructed (Fig. 2.11). If a straight line envelope is drawn to the set of Mohr circles so obtained, it will be of the form of Eq. 2.10 with the cohesion of the soil being given by the intercept of the envelope with the shear stress axis, and the angle of internal shearing resistance being determined by its slope. The Mohr-Coulomb criterion is simply that if a Mohr circle representing the state of stress at a point in the soil touches the envelope, failure will take place at that point.

The shear strength parameters c and ϕ in Eq. 2.10 may be measured by a variety of instruments [2.6]. The triaxial apparatus and the translational shear box are the most commonly used in civil engineering. For the vehicle mobility study, however, rectangular or annular shear plates shown in Fig.

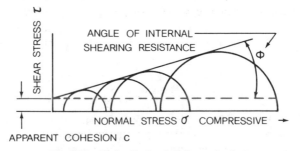

Fig. 2.11 Mohr-Coulomb failure criterion.

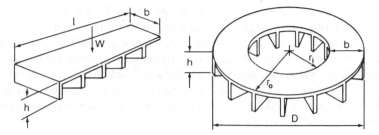

Fig. 2.12 Rectangular and annular shear plates used in vehicle mobility studies. (From *Introduction to Terrain-Vehicle Systems,* by M. G. Bekker, copyright © by the University of Michigan 1956, reproduced by permission of the University of Michigan Press.)

2.12 are usually employed to simulate the shearing action of the vehicle running gear and to obtain the shear strength parameters of the terrain.

To illustrate the application of the Mohr-Coulomb criterion, let us consider the problem of plastic equilibrium of a prism in a semi-infinite mass (Fig. 2.13). The prism of soil with unit weight γ_s, having depth z and width equal to unity, is in a state of incipient plastic failure due to lateral pressure as shown in Fig. 2.13. There are no shear stresses on the vertical sides of the prism, the normal stress on the base of the prism and that on

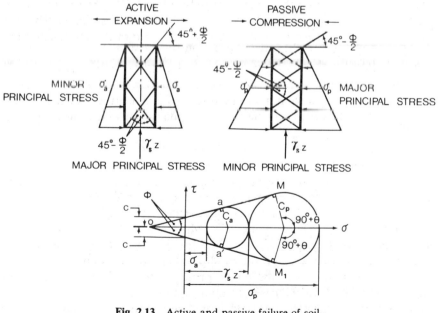

Fig. 2.13 Active and passive failure of soil.

the vertical sides are therefore the principal stresses. The prism may be set into a state of plastic equilibrium by two different operations: one is to stretch it; the other is to compress it in the horizontal direction. If the prism is stretched, the normal stress on the vertical sides decreases until the conditions for plastic equilibrium are satisfied, while the normal stress on the bottom remains unchanged. Any further expansion merely causes a plastic flow without changing the state of stress. In this case, the weight of the soil assists in producing an expansion and this type of failure is called the active failure. On the other hand, if the soil is compressed, the normal stress on the vertical sides of the prism increases, while the normal stress on the bottom remains unchanged. In this case, lateral compression of the soil is resisted by its own weight, and the resulting failure is called the passive failure. The two states of stress prior to plastic flow caused by compression and expansion of the soil are often referred to as the Rankine passive and active state, respectively [2.7].

Both types of soil failure may be analyzed quantitatively by means of the Mohr circle, as shown in Fig. 2.13. In the case of active failure, the normal stress on the base of the element at depth z, $\sigma = \gamma_s z$, is the major principal stress. Circle C_a therefore can be traced to represent the state of stress at that point. This circle is tangent to the lines OM and OM_1, which represent the Mohr-Coulomb failure criterion. The point of intersection between the circle and the horizontal axis of the Mohr diagram determines the minor principal stress, which is the normal stress on the vertical sides required to bring the mass at that point into active failure. This normal stress is called the active earth pressure σ_a. From the geometry of the Mohr diagram shown in Fig. 2.13, the expression for the active earth pressure σ_a can be obtained.

$$\sigma_a = \gamma_s z \frac{1}{N_\phi} - 2c \frac{1}{\sqrt{N_\phi}} \tag{2.13}$$

where N_ϕ is equal to $\tan^2 (45° + \phi/2)$ and is called the flow value.

It is interesting to point out that circle C_a touches the lines of failure, OM and OM_1, at a and a', as shown in Fig. 2.13. This indicates that there are two planes sloped to the major principal stress plane on either side at an angle of $45° + \phi/2$, on which the shear stress satisfies the Mohr-Coulomb criterion. These planes are called surfaces of sliding, and the intersection between a surface of sliding and the plane of drawing is usually referred to as a shear line or slip line. It follows that there are two sets of slip lines sloped to the major principal stress on either side at an angle of $45° - \phi/2$. In the case of active failure, since the major principal stress is vertical, the slip line field comprises parallel lines sloped to the horizontal at $45° + \phi/2$ as shown in Fig. 2.13.

As passive failure is caused by lateral compression, the normal stress acting on the bottom of the element, $\sigma = \gamma_s z$, is the minor principal stress. Circle C_p can, therefore, be drawn to represent the stress conditions of a point in the state of incipient passive failure as shown in Fig. 2.13. The point of intersection between the circle and the horizontal axis of the Mohr diagram determines the major principal stress, which is also the required lateral, compressive stress on the vertical sides to set the mass at that point into passive failure. This normal stress is referred to as the passive earth pressure σ_p. From the geometric relationships shown in Fig. 2.13, the following expression for the passive earth pressure σ_p can be obtained:

$$\sigma_p = \gamma_s z N_\phi + 2c\sqrt{N_\phi} \qquad (2.14)$$

For passive failure, since the major principal stress is horizontal, the slip line field is composed of parallel lines sloped to the horizontal at $45° - \phi/2$, as shown in Fig. 2.13.

If load q, usually referred to as the surcharge, is applied to the soil surface, then the normal stress on the base of an element at depth z is

$$\sigma = \gamma_s z + q \qquad (2.15)$$

Accordingly, the active and passive pressures are given by

$$\sigma_a = \gamma_s z \frac{1}{N_\phi} + q \frac{1}{N_\phi} - 2c \frac{1}{\sqrt{N_\phi}} \qquad (2.16)$$

$$\sigma_p = \gamma_s z N_\phi + q N_\phi + 2c\sqrt{N_\phi} \qquad (2.17)$$

The action of the vehicle running gear and other soil-engaging devices generally causes passive failure of the terrain.

The theory of passive earth pressure has found applications in the prediction of the force acting on a soil cutting blade and in the estimation of the tractive effort developed by a lug (grouser) of a wheel, as shown in Fig. 2.14.

Consider a vertical cutting blade, such as a bulldozer blade, being pushed against the soil. The soil in front of the blade will be brought into a state of passive failure. If the ratio of the width of the blade to the cutting depth is large, the problem may be considered as two dimensional. Furthermore, if the blade is vertical and its surface is relatively smooth, then the normal pressure exerted by the blade on the soil will be the major principal stress and will be equal to the passive earth pressure σ_p. If there is no surcharge, the resultant force acting on the blade per unit width F_p may be calculated by integrating the passive earth pressure σ_p over the cutting

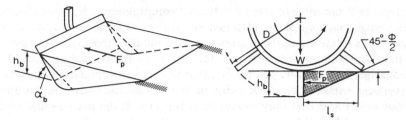

Fig. 2.14   Interaction of a soil cutting blade and of a grouser of a wheel with soil.

depth h_b. From Eq. 2.14,

$$F_p = \int_0^{h_b} \sigma_p \, dz = \int_0^{h_b} \left(\gamma_s z N_\phi + 2c \sqrt{N_\phi} \right) dz$$

$$= \tfrac{1}{2} \gamma_s h_b^2 N_\phi + 2c h_b \sqrt{N_\phi} \qquad (2.18)$$

If there is a surcharge q acting on the soil surface in front of the blade, the resultant force acting on the blade per unit width F_p may be determined by

$$F_p = \int_0^{h_b} \sigma_p \, dz = \int_0^{h_b} \left(\gamma_s z N_\phi + q N_\phi + 2c \sqrt{N_\phi} \right) dz$$

$$= \tfrac{1}{2} \gamma_s h_b^2 N_\phi + q h_b N_\phi + 2c h_b \sqrt{N_\phi} \qquad (2.19)$$

It should be mentioned that for a blade of finite width, end effects would increase the total force acting on the blade.

A similar approach may be followed to estimate the tractive effort developed by the lug of a wheel, such as that used in paddy fields or that attached to a tire as a traction-aid device under wet soil conditions, as shown in Fig. 2.14. In general, the lug may behave in one of two ways. If the spacing between the lugs is too small, the space between them may be filled up with soil, and shearing will occur across the lug tips. Under these conditions, the main effect of the lugs would be the increase of the effective diameter of the wheel. On the other hand, if the spacing between the lugs is large so that the soil fails in front of each lug as shown in Fig. 2.14, then the behavior of the lug will be similar to that of the soil cutting blade. When the ratio of the width to the depth of the lug is large and the lug surface is relatively smooth, the tractive effort per unit width developed by the lug in the vertical position can be estimated by Eq. 2.18. If the wheel rim and the lugs are of the same width, there will be a surcharge acting on the soil surface in front of the lug due to the vertical load applied through the wheel rim. In this case, Eq. 2.19 is applicable. For some lugged steel wheels, such as those attached to tires as traction-aid devices, the wheel rim is relatively narrow, and the vertical load is mainly supported by the tire. Under these circumstances, the benefit of the surcharge would not be obtained. It should be pointed out that the shearing forces developed on the vertical surfaces on both sides of the lug would increase the total tractive effort and that they should be taken into account when the depth of the lug is relatively large.

Example 2.1   A traction-aid device with 20 lugs on a narrow rim is to be attached to a wheeled vehicle to increase its traction. The outside diameter of the device measured from the lug tips is 1.72 m (5.6 ft). The lugs are 25 cm (10 in.) wide and penetrate 15 cm (6 in.) into the ground at the vertical position. Estimate the tractive effort that a lug can develop at the vertical position in a clayey soil with $c = 20$ kPa (2.9 psi), $\phi = 6°$, and $\gamma_s = 15.7$ kN/m³ (100 lb/ft³). The surface of the lug is relatively smooth, and the friction and adhesion between the lug and the soil may be neglected.

Solution.   The spacing between two lugs at the tip is 27 cm (10.6 in.). The rupture distance l_s shown in Fig. 2.14 with penetration $h_b = 15$ cm (6 in.) is

$$l_s = \frac{h_b}{\tan(45° - \phi/2)} = 16.7 \text{ cm (6.6 in.)}$$

It indicates that the spacing between two lugs is large enough to allow the soil to fail in accordance with the Rankine passive state. Since the rim of the device is narrow, the effect of surcharge may be ignored. The horizontal force acting on a lug in the vertical position owing to passive failure of the soil is given by

$$F_p = b\left(\tfrac{1}{2}\gamma_s h_b^2 N_\phi + 2 c h_b \sqrt{N_\phi}\right)$$

where b is the width of the lug.
    Substituting the given data into the above expression, the value of the tractive effort that the lug in the vertical position can develop is

$$F_p = 1.9 \text{ kN (427 lb)}$$

As the wheel rotates, the inclination as well as penetration of the lug vary. Thus the tractive effort developed by the lug varies with its angular position. Since more than one lug is in contact with the terrain, the total tractive effort that the device can develop is the sum of the horizontal forces acting on all the lugs in contact with the ground.

There are limitations to the application of the simple earth pressure theory described above to the solutions of practical problems. For instance, the surface of bulldozer blades or lugs is usually not smooth as assumed in the simple theory. It has been found that the angle of soil-metal friction δ may vary from $11°$ for a highly polished, chromium plated steel with dry sand to almost equal to the angle of internal shearing resistance of the soil for very rough steel surfaces [2.6]. Because of the existence of friction and/or adhesion between the soil and the blade (or lug) surface, there will be shear stresses on the soil-blade interface when the soil adjoining the blade is brought into a state of plastic equilibrium. Consequently, the normal pressure on the contact surface will no longer be the principal stress, and the failure pattern of the soil mass will be as that shown in Fig. 2.15(a). The soil mass in zone ABC is in the Rankine passive state, which is characterized by straight slip lines inclined to the horizontal at an angle of $45° - \phi/2$. Zone ABD adjacent to the blade is characterized by curved and radial slip lines and is usually called the radial shear zone. The shape of the curved slip lines, such as DB in Fig. 2.15(a), can be considered, with sufficient accuracy, being either a logarithmic spiral (for materials with frictional property) or an arc of a circle (for cohesive

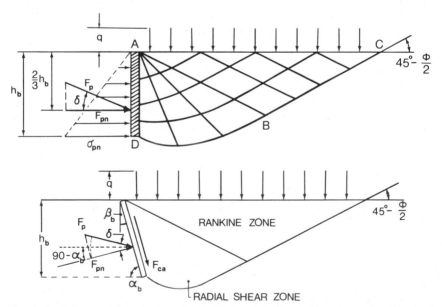

Fig. 2.15 Failure patterns of soil in front of (a) a vertical and (b) an inclined cutting blade with rough surface. (From *Theory of Land Locomotion* by M. G. Bekker, copyright © by the University of Michigan 1956, reproduced by permission of the University of Michigan Press.)

materials). In the presence of friction and/or adhesion between the blade and the soil, Eq. 2.14 can no longer be used to predict the passive earth pressure.

Referring to Fig. 2.15(a), the normal component σ_{pn} of the passive earth pressure acting on a vertical rough blade at a depth z below A can be approximately expressed by a linear equation

$$\sigma_{pn} = \gamma_s z K_{p\gamma} + q K_{pq} + c K_{pc} \tag{2.20}$$

where q is the surcharge, and $K_{p\gamma}$, K_{pq}, and K_{pc} are constants whose values are functions of the angle of internal shearing resistance of the soil and of the friction between the soil and the blade, but do not depend on z and γ_s. They may be computed by various methods including the logarithmic spiral method and friction circle method [2.7]. The resultant force F_p will be sloped to the normal of the blade at the angle of soil-metal friction δ as shown in Fig. 2.15(a).

In practice, bulldozer blades are usually not vertical, and the inclination of the lug of a wheel varies as the wheel rotates. If the blade or the lug is sloped to the horizontal at an angle α_b (or to the vertical at an angle $\beta_b = 90° - \alpha_b$) as shown in Fig. 2.15(b), then the resultant force F_{pn} normal to the blade will be

$$F_{pn} = \frac{1}{\sin \alpha_b} \int_0^{h_b} (\gamma_s z K_{p\gamma} + q K_{pq} + c K_{pc}) \, dz$$

$$= \frac{1}{2} \gamma_s h_b^2 \frac{K_{p\gamma}}{\sin \alpha_b} + \frac{h_b}{\sin \alpha_b} (q K_{pq} + c K_{pc})$$

or

$$F_{pn} = \frac{1}{2} \gamma_s h_b^2 \frac{K_{p\gamma}}{\cos \beta_b} + \frac{h_b}{\cos \beta_b} (q K_{pq} + c K_{pc}) \tag{2.21}$$

Combining the normal component F_{pn} with the frictional component $F_{pn} \tan \delta$, the resultant force F_p, which acts at an angle δ to the normal on the contact surface, becomes

$$F_p = \frac{F_{pn}}{\cos \delta} = \frac{1}{2} \gamma_s h_b^2 \frac{K_{p\gamma}}{\sin \alpha_b \cos \delta} + \frac{h_b}{\sin \alpha_b \cos \delta} (q K_{pq} + c K_{pc})$$

or

$$F_p = \frac{1}{2} \gamma_s h_b^2 \frac{K_{p\gamma}}{\cos \beta_b \cos \delta} + \frac{h_b}{\cos \beta_b \cos \delta} (q K_{pq} + c K_{pc}) \tag{2.22}$$

In addition to the soil-metal friction, there may be adhesion c_a between the soil and the surface of the working element. The adhesion force F_{ca}

$$F_{ca} = \frac{h_b}{\sin \alpha_b} c_a = \frac{h_b}{\cos \beta_b} c_a \qquad (2.23)$$

For a cohesionless soil without surcharge, the resultant force is given by

$$F_p = \tfrac{1}{2} \gamma_s h_b^2 \frac{K_{p\gamma}}{\sin \alpha_b \cos \delta} = \tfrac{1}{2} \gamma_s h_b^2 \frac{K_{p\gamma}}{\cos \beta_b \cos \delta}$$

$$= \tfrac{1}{2} \gamma_s h_b^2 K_p \qquad (2.24)$$

Figure 2.16 reproduces a graph by Caquot and Kerisel for the values of K_p for $\phi = \delta = 30°$ at various values of blade inclination β_b and soil surface inclination θ_s [2.8]. Additional graphs for values of K_p are given in reference [2.9]. Recently, a method for the rapid calculation of passive pressure based on a more rigorous application of the theory of plastic equilibrium has been developed by Hettiaratchi and Reece [2.10].

The theory of passive earth pressure described above also finds application in the prediction of the maximum load of a tracked vehicle that can be supported by a particular type of soil or terrain. The vertical load applied to a rigid track may be idealized as a strip load. When the load applied to the track is light, the soil beneath it may be in a state of elastic

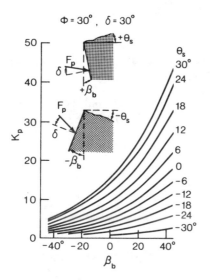

Fig. 2.16 Variation of the values of K_p with inclination angle β_b and slope angle θ_s for $\phi = \delta = 30°$. (From *Foundation Engineering*, edited by G. A. Leonards., copyright © by McGraw-Hill, Inc. 1962, reproduced by permission of McGraw-Hill Book Co.)

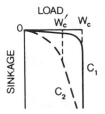

Fig. 2.17 Load-sinkage relationships of a footing under different soil conditions.

equilibrium as mentioned previously. However, when the load on the track is increased to a certain level, the soil beneath the track will pass into a state of plastic flow and the sinkage of the track will increase abruptly. This may be illustrated by the load-sinkage curve C_1 shown in Fig. 2.17. The initial part of the curve represents the elastic deformation and compression of the soil. The failure of the soil beneath the track may be identified by the transition of the curve into a steep tangent, such as at W_c of curve C_1 in Fig. 2.17. For an ideal elasto-plastic material, the curve passes into a vertical tangent. The load per unit contact area that produces the failure is usually called the bearing capacity of the soil [2.7].

At the moment of failure the soil beneath the track can be divided into three different zones as shown in Fig. 2.18(a). When the base of the track is relatively rough, which is usually the case, the existence of friction and adhesion limits the lateral movement of the soil immediately beneath the track. The soil in AA_1D is in a state of elastic equilibrium and behaves as if it were rigidly attached to the track. Both boundaries of the wedge-shaped soil body, AD and A_1D, may therefore be identified with the inclined blades discussed previously. However, in this case the friction angle between the blade and the soil will be equal to the angle of internal shearing resistance of the soil, and the adhesion between the blade and the soil will be the same as the cohesion of the soil. ABD in Fig. 2.18(a) is a radial shear zone, whereas ABC is the Rankine passive zone. As the track sinks, the wedge-shaped soil body AA_1D moves vertically downward. This requires that the slip line DB at point D should have a vertical tangent. As mentioned previously, potential slip lines in the soil mass intersect each other at an angle of $90° - \psi$. AD and A_1D must therefore be sloped to the horizontal at an angle of ϕ as shown in Fig. 2.18(b). In other words, both boundaries AD and A_1D of the wedge-shaped soil body can be considered as inclined blades with a slope angle $\alpha_b = 180° - \phi$. The problem of determining the bearing capacity of the soil for supporting strip loads can then be solved using the passive earth pressure theory discussed previously [2.7].

The passive load F_p which acts at an angle ϕ to the normal on AD and A_1D will be vertical, as the base angle of the wedge-shaped body AA_1D is

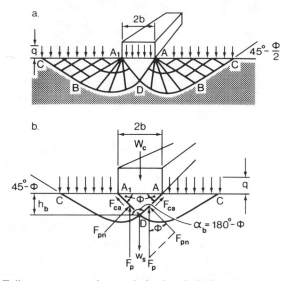

Fig. 2.18 (*a*) Failure patterns under a strip load and (*b*) forces acting on a footing. (From *Theory of Land Locomotion* by M. G. Bekker, copyright © by the University of Michigan 1956, reproduced by permission of the University of Michigan Press.)

equal to ϕ [Fig. 2.18(b)]. From Eq. 2.22 and with $\alpha_b = 180 - \phi$, $\delta = \phi$, and $h_b = b \tan \phi$, F_p is expressed by

$$F_p = \tfrac{1}{2} \gamma_s b^2 K_{p\gamma} \frac{\tan \phi}{\cos^2 \phi} + \frac{b}{\cos^2 \phi} (q K_{pq} + c K_{pc}) \qquad (2.25)$$

The adhesion force F_{ca} acting along AD and $A_1 D$ is

$$F_{ca} = \frac{b}{\cos \phi} c \qquad (2.26)$$

The weight per unit length of the soil in zone $AA_1 D$ is

$$w_s = \gamma_s b^2 \tan \phi \qquad (2.27)$$

The equilibrium of the mass of soil in zone $AA_1 D$ requires that the sum of the vertical forces be equal to zero.

$$W_c + w_s - 2F_p + 2F_{ca} \sin \phi = 0 \qquad (2.28)$$

where W_c is the critical load per unit length of the track, which produces the failure of the soil beneath it.

Substituting Eqs. 2.25, 2.26, and 2.27 into Eq. 2.28, the expression for W_c becomes [2.7]

$$W_c = \gamma_s b^2 K_{p\gamma} \frac{\tan\phi}{\cos^2\phi} + \frac{2b}{\cos^2\phi}(qK_{pq} + cK_{pc}) + 2bc\tan\phi - \gamma_s b^2 \tan\phi$$

$$= \gamma_s b^2 \tan\phi\left(\frac{K_{p\gamma}}{\cos^2\phi} - 1\right) + 2bq\frac{K_{pq}}{\cos^2\phi} + 2bc\left(\frac{K_{pc}}{\cos^2\phi} + \tan\phi\right) \quad (2.29)$$

if it is denoted that

$$\tfrac{1}{2}\tan\phi\left(\frac{K_{p\gamma}}{\cos^2\phi} - 1\right) = N_\gamma$$

$$\frac{K_{pq}}{\cos^2\phi} = N_q$$

and

$$\frac{K_{pc}}{\cos^2\phi} + \tan\phi = N_c$$

then

$$W_c = 2\gamma_s b^2 N_\gamma + 2bq N_q + 2bc N_c \quad (2.30)$$

The values of coefficients N_γ, N_q, and N_c, which are usually referred to as Terzaghi's bearing capacity factors, can be determined from $K_{p\gamma}$, K_{pq}, and K_{pc} and the angle of internal shearing resistance ϕ. Since $K_{p\gamma}$, K_{pq}, and K_{pc} in this case are functions of ϕ, the bearing capacity factors N_γ, N_q, and N_c are dependent on ϕ. The variation of bearing capacity factors with ϕ is shown in Fig. 2.19 [2.7]. It should be pointed out that Eq. 2.30 and the values of N_γ, N_q, and N_c given in Fig. 2.19 are only applicable to dense soils whose deformation preceding failure is very small. There is no noticeable sinkage of the track until a state of plastic equilibrium is reached. This kind of failure is called general shear failure [2.7]. For loose soils, failure is preceded by considerable deformation, and the relationship between sinkage and load is shown by curve C_2 in Fig. 2.17. In this case the critical load that produces the failure of the soil is identified, somewhat arbitrarily, by the point where the curve passes into a steep and fairly straight tangent, as point W_c' in Fig. 2.17. This type of failure is usually referred to as local shear failure [2.7]. Because of the compressibility of the

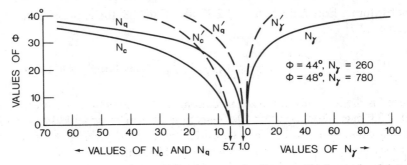

Fig. 2.19 Variation of the Terzaghi bearing capacity factors with the angle of internal shearing resistance. (From *Theoretical Soil Mechanics*, by K. Terzaghi, 1966, reproduced by permission of John Wiley and Sons, Inc.)

loose soil, the critical load W_c' per unit length for local shear failure is different from that for general shear failure. In the calculation of the critical load for local shear failure, the shear strength parameters c' and ϕ' of the soil are assumed to be smaller than those for general shear failure [2.7].

$$c' = \tfrac{2}{3}c$$

and

$$\tan\phi' = \tfrac{2}{3}\tan\phi$$

Accordingly, the critical load W_c' per unit length of the track for local shear failure is given by

$$W_c' = 2\gamma_s b^2 N_\gamma' + 2bqN_\gamma' + \tfrac{4}{3}bcN_c' \tag{2.31}$$

The values of N_γ', N_q', and N_c' are smaller than those of N_γ, N_q, and N_c, as can be seen from Fig. 2.19.

Based on the theory of bearing capacity, the critical load of a tracked vehicle W_{ct} that may be supported by two tracks without causing failure of the soil can then be estimated by the following equations:

For general shear failure,

$$W_{ct} = 2lW_c$$

$$= 4bl(\gamma_s bN_\gamma + qN_q + cN_c) \tag{2.32}$$

and for local shear failure

$$W'_{ct} = 2lW'_c$$

$$= 4bl\left(\gamma_s bN'_\gamma + qN'_q + \tfrac{2}{3}cN'_c\right) \tag{2.33}$$

where l is the length of the track in contact with the terrain. Equations 2.32 and 2.33 may shed light on the selection of track configurations from bearing capacity point of view. Consider the case of general shear failure and assume that there is no surcharge q. Then in a dry sand (cohesion $c = 0$), the critical load of the vehicle W_{ct} is given by

$$W_{ct} = 4b^2 l\gamma_s N_\gamma \tag{2.34}$$

This indicates that the load capacity of a track in a frictional soil increases with the square of track width. To increase the load that the vehicle can carry, it is, therefore, preferable to increase the track width than to increase the track length. This concept may be illustrated by the following example. Consider two tracked vehicles having the same ground contact area, but the track width of one vehicle is twice that of the other, that is, $b_1 = 2b_2$. Consequently, the contact length of the vehicle with the wider track will be half of that of the other, that is $l_1 = 0.5l_2$. According to Eq. 2.34, the ratio of the critical loads that the two vehicles can carry is given by

$$\frac{W_{ct_1}}{W_{ct_2}} = \frac{4b_1^2 l_1 \gamma_s N_\gamma}{4(0.5b_1)^2 2l_1 \gamma_s N_\gamma} = 2$$

This indicates that the critical load that the vehicle with the wider track can support is higher than that of the other, although both vehicles have the same ground contact area.

In cohesive soils, such as saturated clay ($\phi = 0$), the critical vehicle load W_{ct} is given by

$$W_{ct} = 4blcN_c \tag{2.35}$$

This indicates that under these circumstances the critical load merely depends on the contact area of the track.

It should be emphasized that the use of the bearing capacity theory to predict the critical load that a tracked vehicle can carry without excessive sinkage produces, at best, only approximate results. This is because a number of simplifying assumptions have been made. For instance, the effects of pressure distribution and the flexibility of the track have not

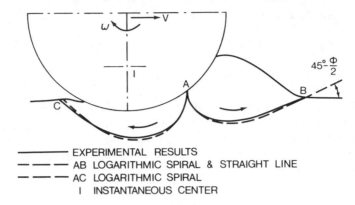
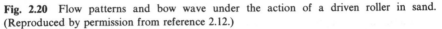

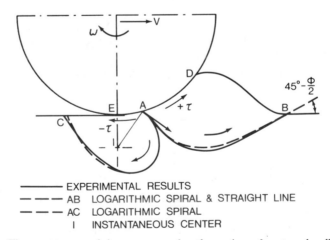

Fig. 2.20 Flow patterns and bow wave under the action of a driven roller in sand. (Reproduced by permission from reference 2.12.)

been taken into consideration. Perhaps, the most significant point is that the theory does not deal quantitatively with the deformation of the terrain produced by the load. The knowledge of the relationship between the vertical load applied to the vehicle running gear and the resulting deformation of the terrain (sinkage) is, however, essential for predicting vehicle performance.

In practice, the actual interaction between the vehicle running gear and the terrain is much more complex than that discussed above. Figures 2.20–2.23 show the flow patterns of sand beneath a wide rigid wheel under

Fig. 2.21 Flow patterns and bow wave under the action of a towed roller in sand. (Reproduced by permission from reference 2.12.)

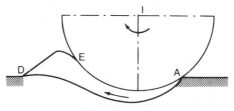

Fig. 2.22 Flow patterns beneath a driven roller at 100% slip in sand. (Reproduced by permission from reference 2.12.)

various operating conditions obtained by Wong and Reece [2.11, 2.12]. It can be seen that the flow patterns beneath a rigid wheel in the longitudinal plane depend on a number of factors including slip. There are normally two zones of soil flow beneath a rolling wheel. In one zone, the soil flows forward, and in the other the soil flows backward. These degenerate into a single backward flow zone at 100% slip (Fig. 2.22) and a single forward zone for a locked wheel (Fig. 2.23). It is interesting to note that in front of a locked wheel, there is a wedge-shaped soil body that behaves as if it were part of the wheel. Figure 2.24 shows the trajectories of clay particles beneath a wide rigid wheel under various operating conditions [2.12]. The characteristics of the trajectories indicate that the soil is at first in the Rankine passive state when it is in front of an oncoming wheel. As the wheel is advancing, the soil beneath it is driven backward. The characteristics of the trajectories further verify the existence of the two flow zones beneath a moving wheel. The problem of wheel-soil interaction is complex in that the wheel rim represents a curved boundary, and that the stress conditions on the boundary are influenced by a variety of operational and design parameters, such as the vertical load and torque applied to the wheel, and the resulting slip.

The complex nature of many vehicle-terrain interaction problems indicates that a more general approach to the prediction of the interacting

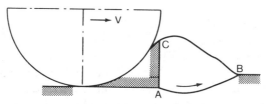

Fig. 2.23 Flow patterns and soil wedge formed in front of a locked wheel with 100% skid in sand. (Reproduced by permission from reference 2.12.)

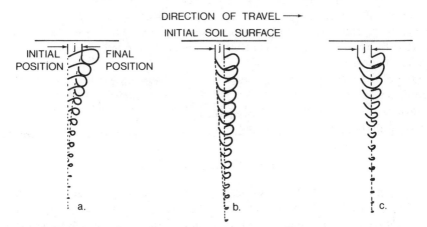

Fig. 2.24   Trajectories of clay particles under the action of a roller. (*a*) Towed, (*b*) driven at 37% slip, and (*c*) driven at 63% slip. (Reproduced by permission from reference 2.12.)

forces is required. Attempts to apply the theory of plastic equilibrium, visio-plasticity technique, and the finite element method to the study of wheel-soil interaction have been made [2.13–2.15].

2.3   TECHNIQUES FOR MEASURING TERRAIN VALUES

The theories of elasticity and plastic equilibrium described in preceding sections can only offer solutions to a limited range of problems in terra-mechanics. This is because the theories are based on the assumption that the terrain behaves like a perfect, elasto-plastic material. In practice, the terrain encountered in cross-country operations usually does not exhibit the idealized elasto-plastic behavior. Furthermore, the bearing capacity theory, for instance, is only concerned with the estimation of the maximum load that the vehicle can exert on the terrain without causing failure. Consequently, the load-deformation relationship of the terrain, which is of importance to the evaluation of vehicle performance, cannot be predicted by the theory.

Owing to the limitations of existing theories, a number of semi-empirical methods for predicting off-road vehicle performance have been proposed. A ground vehicle applies horizontal load to the terrain surface through the running gear, and this results in the development of thrust and associated slip. Similarly, the vertical load that the vehicle exerts on the terrain results in sinkage giving rise to motion resistance. The measurement of both the horizontal and vertical load-deformation characteristics of the terrain is, therefore, of prime importance in the evaluation and prediction of off-road vehicle performance. To obtain meaningful results, the loading conditions exerted by the measuring apparatus and those by the vehicle should be as similar as possible.

One of the well-known techniques for measuring load-deformation characteristics of terrain for purposes of predicting off-road vehicle performance is that proposed by Bekker [2.2, 2.3]. The method is based on a series of plate penetration and shear tests.

2.3.1   Load-Sinkage Relationship

In the penetration test, a plate simulating the contact area of a track or a tire is forced vertically into the ground. The pressure p and sinkage z are measured. The test procedure is shown schematically in Fig. 2.25 [2.3]. A family of pressure-sinkage curves obtained from penetration tests in various homogeneous soils are shown in Fig. 2.26 [2.3]. Since the normal pressure of commonly used off-road vehicles does not exceed 103 kPa (15 psi), and sinkage higher than normal ground clearance of 25–50 cm (10–20 in.) will immobilize the vehicle, instrumentation for measuring pressure-sinkage relationships is usually calibrated for pressures and sinkages up to 103 kPa (15 psi) and 50 cm (20 in.), respectively [2.3]. Based on experimental data, Bekker proposed the following pressure-sinkage

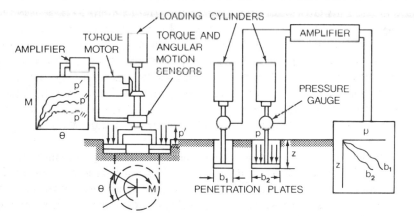

Fig. 2.25 Schematic view of a bevameter for measuring terrain properties. (From *Introduction to Terrain-Vehicle Systems*, by M. G. Bekker, copyright © by the University of Michigan 1969, reproduced by permission of the University of Michigan Press.)

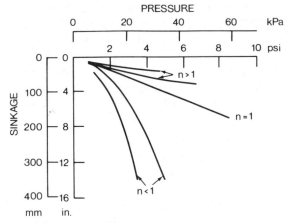

Fig. 2.26 Pressure-sinkage curves of various homogeneous soils. (From *Introduction to Terrain-Vechicle Systems*, by M. G. Bekker, coppyright © by the University of Michigan 1969, reproduced by permission of the University of Michigan Press.)

relationship for homogeneous soils

$$p = \left(\frac{k_c}{b} + k_\phi \right) z^n \tag{2.36}$$

where n is the exponent of deformation, b is the smaller dimension of the loading area (or the width of a rectangular plate), and k_c and k_ϕ are cohesive and frictional moduli of deformation, respectively. It has been shown by Bekker that in this formula, moduli k_c and k_ϕ are insensitive to plate width, for plates with large aspect ratios (larger than 5–7) in homogeneous soils. In view of the possible localized nonhomogeneity of soil in the field, however, the width of the plate designed for field measurements should not be less than 5 cm (2 in.) and preferably not less than 10 cm (4 in.). A number of tests have been performed to determine the degree of independence of the values of k_c, k_ϕ, and n on the form of the test plate. Experimental results reported by Bekker indicate that there is little difference between the values of k_c, k_ϕ, and n obtained with a set of rectangular plates of high aspect ratios (larger than 5–7) and those obtained with a set of circular plates having radii equal to the widths of the rectangular plates. Because of this, circular plates are used in some of the instruments, since they require less total load than the corresponding rectangular plates to produce the same ground pressure. The rate of penetration used in existing instruments normally varies from 2.5 to 5 cm/s (1–2 in./s) [2.3].

The values of k_c, k_ϕ, and n can be obtained by a minimum of two tests with two sizes of plates having different widths (or radii). The tests

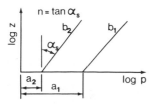

Fig. 2.27 Method for determining sinkage moduli and exponent.

produce two curves

$$p_1 = \left(\frac{k_c}{b_1} + k_\phi \right) z^n$$

$$p_2 = \left(\frac{k_c}{b_2} + k_\phi \right) z^n$$

(2.37)

On the logarithmic scale, the above equations can be rewritten as follows:

$$\log p_1 = \log\left(\frac{k_c}{b_1} + k_\phi \right) + n\log z$$

$$\log p_2 = \log\left(\frac{k_c}{b_2} + k_\phi \right) + n\log z$$

(2.38)

They represent two parallel straight lines of the same slope on log-log scale as shown in Fig. 2.27. It is evident that $\tan\alpha_s = n$ (Fig. 2.27). Thus the exponent of deformation n can be determined from the slope of the straight lines. At sinkage $z = 1$, the values of the normal pressure for the two sizes of plates are

$$(p_1)_{z=1} = \frac{k_c}{b_1} + k_\phi = a_1$$

$$(p_2)_{z=1} = \frac{k_c}{b_2} + k_\phi = a_2$$

(2.39)

In the above equations, $(p_1)_{z=1}$ and $(p_2)_{z=1}$ are measured values, and the only unknowns are k_c and k_ϕ. Thus, the moduli of deformation k_c and k_ϕ can be determined by the following equations

$$k_\phi = \frac{a_2 b_2 - a_1 b_1}{b_2 - b_1}$$

$$k_c = \frac{(a_1 - a_2) b_1 b_2}{b_2 - b_1}$$

(2.40)

Table 2.1 Terrain Values

Terrain	Moisture Content (%)	n	k_c		k_ϕ		c		ϕ
			lb/in.$^{n+1}$	kN/m^{n+1}	lb/in.$^{n+2}$	kN/m^{n+2}	lb/in.^{2}	kPa	
Dry Sand (Land Locomotion Lab., LLL)	0	1.1	0.1	0.95	3.9	1528.43	0.15	1.04	28°
Sandy Loam (LLL)	15	0.7	2.3	5.27	16.8	1515.04	0.25	1.72	29°
	22	0.2	7	2.56	3	43.12	0.2	1.38	38°
Sandy Loam Michigan (Strong, Buchele)	11	0.9	11	52.53	6	1127.97	0.7	4.83	20°
	23	0.4	15	11.42	27	808.96	1.4	9.65	35°
Sandy Loam (Hanamoto)	26	0.3	5.3	2.79	6.8	141.11	2.0	13.79	22°
	32	0.5	0.7	0.77	1.2	51.91	0.75	5.17	11°
Clayey soil (Thailand)	38	0.5	12	13.19	16	692.15	0.6	4.14	13°
	55	0.7	7	16.03	14	1262.53	0.3	2.07	10°
Heavy Clay (Waterways Experiment Stn., WES)	25	0.13	45	12.70	140	1555.95	10	68.95	34°
	40	0.11	7	1.84	10	103.27	3	20.69	6°
Lean Clay (WES)	22	0.2	45	16.43	120	1724.69	10	68.95	20°
	32	0.15	5	1.52	10	119.61	2	13.79	11°
Snow (Harrison)		1.6	0.07	4.37	0.08	196.72	0.15	1.03	19.7°
		1.6	0.04	2.49	0.10	245.90	0.09	0.62	23.2°

Source. References 2.3 and 2.16.

Owing to the nonhomogeneity of soil and experimental errors, the pressure sinkage lines may not be quite parallel on the log-log scale in some cases. Thus, two values of the exponent of deformation may be produced. Under these circumstances, the value of n is usually taken as the mean of the two values obtained.

The values of k_c, k_ϕ, and n for various types of soil are given in Table 2.1 [2.3, 2.16]. More terrain data can be found in reference 2.3.

It should be emphasized that Eq. 2.36 is essentially an empirical equation. Furthermore, the moduli of deformation k_c and k_ϕ have variable dimensions depending on the value of the exponent n. Influenced by the work of a more fundamental nature in soil mechanics and by experimental evidence, Reece proposed a new equation for the pressure-sinkage relationship [2.17],

$$p = (ck'_c + \gamma_s bk'_\phi)\left(\frac{z}{b}\right)^n \tag{2.41}$$

where k'_c and k'_ϕ are cohesive and frictional moduli of deformation, n is the exponent of deformation, γ_s is weight density of the terrain, c is cohesion, and b is the smaller dimension of the loading area. A series of penetration tests were carried out by Reece to verify the validity of the principal features of the above equation. Plates with various widths and with an aspect ratio of at least 4.5 were used. The test results are shown in Fig. 2.28. For a frictionless clay, the term k'_ϕ should be negligible. The results shown in Fig. 2.28 indicate that this is true, the curves for clay collapsing to almost a single line for all plates regardless of their width when plotted against z/b. For dry cohesionless sand, the term k'_c should be negligible. The equation thus suggests that pressure increases linearly with the width of the plate for a given value of z/b. Wetting the sand would not alter its value of ϕ but would add a cohesion component. This would be expected to add a pressure term independent of width representing the first term of Eq. 2.41 to the dry sand, similar to that for the clay. This again seems to be well borne out by test results.

Reece pointed out that although Eq. 2.41 only differs from Eq. 2.36 in the effect of the width, this is sufficient to mark a radical improvement. The soil values k'_c and k'_ϕ in Eq. 2.41 are dimensionless, whereas k_c and k_ϕ in Eq. 2.36 have dimensions dependent on n. Furthermore, Eq. 2.41 seems to allow itself to fit in with the conceivable theoretical approach. For instance, Eq. 2.41 and Terzaghi's bearing capacity equation (Eq. 2.30), have similar form. In cohesionless dry sand, both equations show that increasing width can cause a linear increase in pressure. On the other hand, in frictionless clay, both equations show that the increase of width has no effect on pressure.

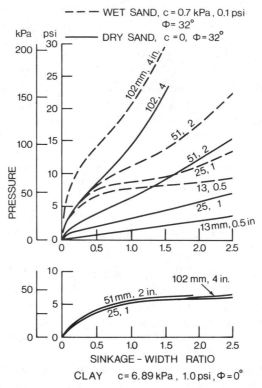

Fig. 2.28 Pressure-sinkage curves obtained from various sizes of rectangular plates in three soils. (Reproduced by permission of the Council of the Institution of Mechanical Engineers from reference 2.17.)

2.3.2   Shear Stress-Displacement Relationship

When a track or a tire is driven, it produces shearing action at the ground contact area as shown in Fig. 2.29. To predict vehicle thrust and slip, the relationship between the shear stress and shear deformation of the terrain is required, and this can be determined by a shear test. In the test, the shearing of soil by the vehicle running gear is simulated by a shear plate. For purposes of vehicle performance prediction, rectangular or annular shear plates, as shown previously in Fig. 2.12, are usually used.

When a rectangular shear plate is used, it is placed on the terrain surface and normal load is applied. The plate is then pulled horizontally, and the pulling force and the horizontal displacement of the plate are measured. From the measurements, the relationship between the shear stress and shear displacement at a given normal pressure can be established as shown

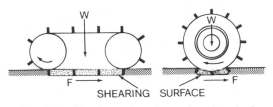

Fig. 2.29   Shearing action of a track and a wheel.

in Fig. 2.30 [2.18]. If the maximum shear stress of the terrain is plotted against the corresponding normal pressure, a straight line may be obtained as shown in Fig. 2.31. The slope of the straight line determines the angle of internal shearing resistance of the terrain, and the intercept of the straight line with the shear stress axis determines the apparent cohesion of the terrain as discussed previously. For rectangular shear plates, to minimize the nonuniform shear stress distribution and the bulldozing resistance due to soil piling up in front of the plate, a minimum length of 75 cm (30 in.) is recommended. One of the possible methods to eliminate the bulldozing resistance (or frontal drag) is to use a two-plate tandem arrangement. The first plate clears the way for the second one, which is used for measurements. Shear plates with width varying from 5 to 17.5 cm (2 to 7 in.) have been used. It has been found that within this range the effect of plate width on the shearing characteristics is insignificant. To ensure soil-to-soil shearing on the contact area, shear plates are usually equipped with grousers as shown in Fig. 2.12. Shear tests are performed with normal pressures and shear rates corresponding to those found in actual vehicle operations. Shear rates in the range 2.5–25 cm/s (1 to 10 in./s) are typical in off-road locomotion [2.3].

Annular shear plates are also used, particularly in field work. During the test, the torque and angular displacement of the annular plate are measured. The relationship between the shear stress and shear displacement at a given normal pressure can then be derived. In existing devices, the outside diameter of the annular shear plate varies from 17.5 to 30 cm (7 to 12 in.), and the ratio of the outside diameter to inside diameter of the annulus varies from 1.2 to 1.5.

The results shown in Fig. 2.31 indicate that rectangular and annular shear plates give practically the same results of soil strength. The choice of the form of shear plate, therefore, mainly depends upon its convenience and practical utility.

The shear stress-displacement characteristics of terrain commonly encountered in off-road operations may be seen in two patterns. One displays a hump of maximum shear stress τ_{max} and a flattened portion of residual

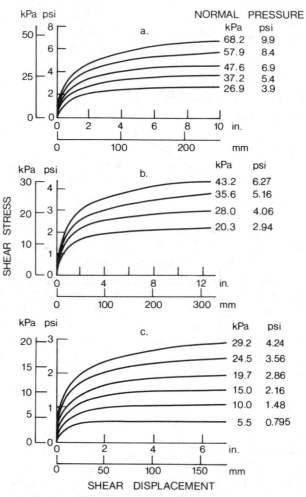

Fig. 2.30 Shear stress-shear displacement curves obtained from (*a*) a shear ring with 22.2 cm (8.75 in.) outside diameter, (*b*) a shear ring with 29.8 cm (11.75 in.) outside diameter, and (*c*) a rigid track of 13.2×71.1 cm (5.18×28 in.) in sand. (Reproduced by permission of the *Journal of Agricultural Engineering Research* from reference 2.18.)

shear stress τ_r after yielding, as shown by curve 1 in Fig. 2.32 [2.3]. Undisturbed firm soils, such as compacted sand, silt, and loam, and frozen snow may exhibit these characteristics. It is seen that a certain shear deformation is developed before the maximum shear stress is reached. The relationship between the shear stress τ and shear displacement j in this case may be expressed by an equation similar to that for defining an aperiodic

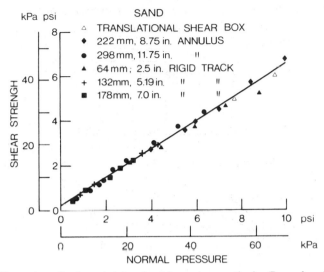

Fig. 2.31 Shear strength of sand determined by various methods. (Reproduced by permission of the *Journal of Agricultural Engineering Research* from reference 2.18.)

damped vibration [2.2],

$$\tau = \frac{(c + \sigma \tan \phi)}{y_{max}} \left\{ \exp\left(-K_2 + \sqrt{K_2^2 - 1} \right) K_1 j \right.$$

$$\left. - \exp\left(-K_2 - \sqrt{K_2^2 - 1} \right) K_1 j \right\} \tag{2.42}$$

where K_2 and K_1 are coefficients and y_{max} is the maximum value of the function enclosed between brackets{ }.

Another type of terrain exhibits a smooth shear stress displacement characteristic, and the shear stress does not fall off after the maximum, as shown by curve 2 in Fig. 2.32. Loose soils, such as loose sand and

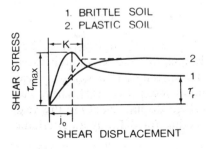

Fig. 2.32 Two types of shear stress-shear displacement curve. (From *Introduction to Terrain-Vehicle Systems*, by M. G. Bekker, copyright © by the University of Michigan 1969, reproduced by permission of the University of Michigan Press.)

saturated clay, dry snow, and most of the disturbed soils are of this type. For this kind of terrain, the following shear stress-displacement relationship may be used [2.3]:

$$\tau = (c + \sigma \tan\phi)(1 - e^{-j/K})$$

$$= \tau_{max}(1 - e^{-j/K}) \qquad (2.43)$$

where K is the horizontal shear deformation modulus.

K may be considered as a measure of the magnitude of the deformation required to develop the maximum shear stress. The value of K is determined by the distance between the vertical axis and the point of intersection of the straight line tangent to the shear curve 2 at the origin and the extension of the horizontal portion of the curve as shown in Fig. 2.32. The slope of the shear curve at the origin can be obtained by differentiating τ with respect to j. From Eq. 2.43,

$$\left.\frac{d\tau}{dj}\right|_{j=0} = \left.\frac{\tau_{max}}{K} e^{-j/K}\right|_{j=0} = \frac{\tau_{max}}{K} \qquad (2.44)$$

Thus the value of K can be determined from the slope of the shear curve at the origin and τ_{max} as shown.

The value of K depends on the compressibility of soils. According to Reece [2.17], the value of K is approximately 2.5 cm (1 in.) for loose sand and about 0.6 cm (1/4 in.) for frictionless clay at maximum compaction. Experimental data suggest that the value of K is also a function of normal pressure [2.18]. However, their precise relationship is yet to be determined.

Bekker pointed out that the hump of the shear curve (curve 1 in Fig. 2.32) has little practical meaning, as far as the prediction of vehicle thrust under normal operating conditions is concerned [2.3]. It is therefore suggested that the smoothing of the "humped" shear curve is desirable, whenever τ_{max} is not too great in comparison with τ_r. After smoothing, the shear stress-displacement relationship can be expressed by Eq. 2.43.

It should be mentioned that the pressure-sinkage relationship (Eq. 2.26 or Eq. 2.41) discussed previously is for the prediction of the sinkage of a loading surface with uniform normal pressure and without horizontal load. Strictly speaking, it can only be used to estimate the static sinkage of a motionless vehicle. In practice, when a vehicle moves, horizontal thrust with resulting shear deformation will be developed at the contact area. Experimental evidence has shown that shear deformation causes the increase of sinkage under a given normal pressure. Figure 2.33 shows the relationships between sinkage and shear deformation under constant normal pressure for various types of terrain [2.17]. The additional sinkage due

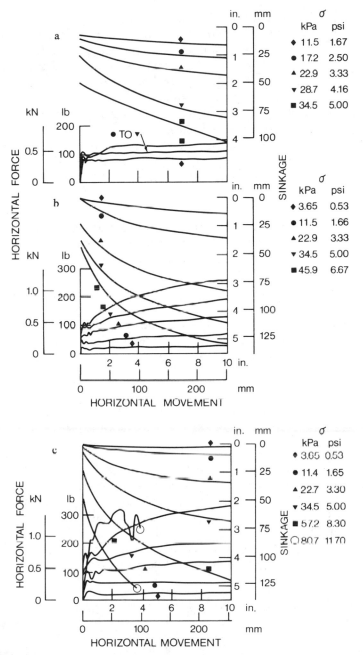

Fig. 2.33 Slip-sinkage phenomenon in three types of soil. (*a*) Clay, $\phi=0$, $c=6.9$ kPa (1.0 psi); (*b*) dry sand, $\phi=32°$, $c=0$; (*c*) wet sand, $\phi=32°$, $c=0.69$ kPa (0.1 psi). (Reproduced by permission of the Council of the Institution of Mechanical Engineers from reference 2.17.)

to shear deformation (or horizontal load) is usually referred to as slip sinkage. It appears that to predict the total sinkage of a vehicle in motion, the effect of shear deformation on slip sinkage should be taken into consideration. Reece has proposed a tentative theoretical explanation of the slip-sinkage phenomenon [2.17]. However, a generally accepted theory for predicting slip sinkage is still lacking.

It should also be pointed out that the methods for characterizing the load-sinkage and shear stress-displacement relationships described above are mainly for homogeneous terrain. For nonhomogeneous or stratified terrain, the procedures for characterizing terrain properties are more complex, and the reader is referred to references 2.3 and 2.23.

2.4 SEMIEMPIRICAL METHODS FOR PREDICTING THE PERFORMANCE OF VEHICLE RUNNING GEAR OVER UNPREPARED TERRAIN

The wheel and the track constitute two basic forms of running gear for off-road vehicles. The study of the mechanics of the wheel and of the track on unprepared terrain is, therefore, of fundamental inportance. One of the basic objectives in the study of vehicle-terrain interaction is to provide reliable methods for predicting the tractive effort and the motion resistance of various forms of running gear.

2.4.1 Motion Resistance of a Rigid Wheel

Although pneumatic tires have long replaced rigid wheels in off-road vehicles, the mechanics of rigid wheels over unprepared terrain is still of interest, as pneumatic tires may behave like a rigid rim in soft terrain even at low inflation pressure. One of the well-known semiempirical methods for predicting the motion resistance of a rigid wheel is that proposed by Bekker [2.1–2.3]. In developing the method, it is assumed that the terrain reaction at all points is purely radial and is equal to the normal pressure beneath a horizontal plate at the same depth. The equilibrium equations of a towed rigid wheel can be written as (Fig. 2.34)

$$R_c = b \int_0^{\theta_0} \sigma r \sin \theta \, d\theta \qquad (2.45)$$

$$W = b \int_0^{\theta_0} \sigma r \cos \theta \, d\theta \qquad (2.46)$$

where R_c is the motion resistance, W is the vertical load, σ is the normal

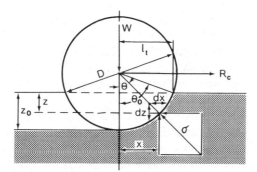

Fig. 2.34 Simplified wheel-soil interaction model. (From *Theory of Land Locomotion* by M. G. Bekker, copyright © by the University of Michigan 1956, reproduced by permission of the University of Michigan Press.)

stress, and b is the width of the wheel. Since it is assumed that the radial pressure σ acting on the wheel rim is equal to the normal pressure p beneath a plate at the same depth z, $\sigma r \sin\theta \, d\theta = p dz$ and $\sigma r \cos\theta \, d\theta = p dx$. Using the pressure sinkage relationship defined by Eq. 2.36, Eq. 2.45 becomes

$$R_c = b \int_0^{z_0} \left(\frac{k_c}{b} + k_\phi \right) z^n \, dz$$

$$= b \left[\frac{z_0^{n+1}}{n+1} \right] \left(\frac{k_c}{b} + k_\phi \right) \tag{2.47}$$

The value of R_c calculated by Eq. 2.47 is equivalent to the vertical work done per unit length in pressing a plate of width b into the ground to a depth of z_0. The assumption for the stress distribution made by Bekker implies that the motion resistance of a rigid wheel is due to the vertical work done in making a rut of depth z_0. The motion resistance so determined is usually referred to as the compaction resistance.

Using Eq. 2.47 to calculate the compaction resistance, the sinkage z_0 expressed in terms of wheel parameters and terrain properties has to be determined first. From Eq. 2.46

$$W = - b \int_0^{z_0} p \, dx = - b \int_0^{z_0} \left(\frac{k_c}{b} + k_\phi \right) z^n \, dx \tag{2.48}$$

From the geometry shown in Fig. 2.34

$$x^2 = [D - (z_0 - z)](z_0 - z) \tag{2.49}$$

where D is wheel diameter.

For small sinkages,

$$x^2 = D(z_0 - z) \tag{2.50}$$

and

$$2x\,dx = -D\,dz \tag{2.51}$$

Substituting Eq. 2.51 into Eq. 2.48, one obtains

$$W = b\left(\frac{k_c}{b} + k_\phi\right)\int_0^{z_0} \frac{z^n\sqrt{D}}{2\sqrt{z_0 - z}}\,dz \tag{2.52}$$

Let $z_0 - z = t^2$, then $dz = -2t\,dt$ and

$$W = b\left(\frac{k_c}{b} + k_\phi\right)\sqrt{D}\int_0^{\sqrt{z_0}} (z_0 - t^2)^n\,dt \tag{2.53}$$

Expanding $(z_0 - t^2)^n$ and only taking the first two terms of the series $(z_0^n - nz_0^{n-1}t^2 + \ldots)$, one obtains

$$W = \frac{b(k_c/b + k_\phi)\sqrt{z_0 D}}{3}\,z_0^n(3 - n) \tag{2.54}$$

Rearranging Eq. 2.54, it becomes

$$z_0^{(2n+1)/2} = \frac{3W}{b(k_c/b + k_\phi)\sqrt{D}\,(3 - n)}$$

or

$$z_0 = \left[\frac{3W}{b(3 - n)(k_c/b + k_\phi)\sqrt{D}}\right]^{2/(2n+1)} \tag{2.55}$$

Substituting Eq. 2.55 into Eq. 2.47, the compaction resistance R_c becomes

$$R_c = \frac{1}{(3 - n)^{(2n+2)/(2n+1)}(n + 1)b^{1/(2n+1)}(k_c/b + k_\phi)^{1/(2n+1)}}$$

$$\times \left[\frac{3W}{\sqrt{D}}\right]^{(2n+2)/(2n+1)} \tag{2.56}$$

It can be seen from Eq. 2.56 that to reduce the compaction resistance it seems more effective to increase wheel diameter D than wheel width b, as D enters the equation in higher power than b.

Bekker pointed out that acceptable predictions may be obtained using Eq. 2.56 for moderate sinkage (i.e., $z_0 \leqslant D/6$), and that the larger the wheel diameter and the smaller the sinkage, the more accurate the predictions are [2.3]. He also mentioned that predictions based on Eq. 2.56 for wheels smaller than 50 cm (20 in.) in diameter become less accurate, and that predictions of sinkage based on Eq. 2.55 in dry, sandy soil are not accurate if there is slip sinkage [2.3]. Recent experimental evidence shows that the actual normal pressure distribution beneath a rigid wheel is different from that assumed in the theory described above (Fig. 2.35) [2.12, 2.19]. According to the theory, the maximum normal pressure should occur at the lowest point of contact (bottom-dead-center) where the sinkage is a maximum. Experimental results, however, show that the maximum normal pressure occurs in front of the bottom-dead-center, and that its location varies with slip as shown in Fig. 2.35. It has been found by Wong and Reece that the maximum normal pressure occurs at the junction of the two flow zones as shown in Fig. 2.20 [2.12, 2.20]. The variation of normal pressure distribution with slip implies that the motion resistance should be expected as a function of slip. This indicates that the actual interaction between the wheel and the terrain is much more complicated than that assumed in the semiempirical method described above. To take into account the effect of slip on normal pressure distribution over the contact area, a refined method for predicting the sinkage and motion resistance of rigid wheels has been proposed by Wong and Reece [2.20, 2.21].

Equation 2.56 is intended for predicting the compaction resistance of rigid wheels in both frictional and cohesive soils. In clay, Uffelmann proposed another theory for predicting the compaction resistance [2.22].

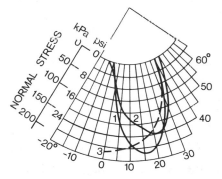

Fig. 2.35 Comparison of the measured normal stress distribution on a rigid wheel with calculated one using the simplified soil-wheel interaction model. Curve 1, measured at 3.1% slip; curve 2, measured at 35.1% slip; and curve 3, calculated. (Reproduced by permission from reference 2.12.)

As in Bekker's theory, Uffelmann's theory assumes that the soil reaction is purely radial, thereby equating compaction resistance to the vertical work done in making a rut per unit length. However, in this theory, the normal (or radial) stress is assumed to be constant over the entire contact area and equal to the theoretical surface bearing capacity of a perfectly rough strip footing, that is $\sigma = 5.7c$. This can be considered as a particular case of Bekker's pressure-sinkage equation with $n = 0$ and $k_c/b + k_\phi = 5.7c$. Substituting $n = 0$ and $k_c/b + k_\phi = 5.7c$ into Eqs. 2.55 and 2.56, the expressions for sinkage and compaction resistance of rigid wheels in clay become

$$z_0 = \frac{W^2}{(5.7c)^2 b^2 D} \tag{2.57}$$

$$R_c = \frac{W^2}{5.7cbD} \tag{2.58}$$

It is found that the above theory works well for small sinkages [2.22].

It should be pointed out that in off-road operations, the sinkage of the running gear is usually considerable, and that a so-called "bow wave" is formed in front of the wheel. This can be seen from Figs. 2.20, 2.21, and 2.23. In addition to the compaction resistance, the resistance offered by the "bow wave", which is usually referred to as the bulldozing resistance, should therefore be taken into consideration when estimating the total resistance of a wheel. Because of the similarity between the flow patterns of the "bow wave" in front of the wheel and that in front of a soil cutting blade shown in Fig. 2.15, the bulldozing resistance can, in principle, be estimated using the passive earth pressure theory discussed previously.

In predicting the bulldozing resistance R_b, Bekker assumed that it is equivalent to the horizontal force acting on a vertical blade, which can be calculated using Eq. 2.21 with $h_b = z_0$, $q = 0$, $\alpha_b = 90°$, or $\beta_b = 0$ [2.23]

$$R_b = b\left(cz_0 K_{pc} + 0.5z_0^2 \gamma_s K_{p\gamma}\right), \tag{2.59}$$

where z_0 is sinkage, and

$$K_{pc} = (N_c - \tan\phi)\cos^2\phi$$

and

$$K_{p\gamma} = \left(\frac{2N_\gamma}{\tan\phi} + 1\right)\cos^2\phi$$

N_c and N_γ are bearing capacity factors shown in Fig. 2.19, and ϕ is the angle of internal shearing resistance of the soil. In soft terrain or loose soils, local shear failure in front of the wheel may be assumed, and the bulldozing resistance may be estimated using the following equation:

$$R'_b = b\left(0.67 cz_0 K'_{pc} + 0.5 z_0^2 \gamma_s K'_{p\gamma}\right) \tag{2.60}$$

where

$$K'_{pc} = (N'_c - \tan\phi') \cos^2\phi'$$

$$K'_{p\gamma} = \left(\frac{2N'_\gamma}{\tan\phi'} + 1\right) \cos^2\phi'$$

N'_c and N'_γ are bearing capacity factors for local shear failure shown in Fig. 2.19, and $\tan\phi' = \frac{2}{3}\tan\phi$.

2.4.2 Motion Resistance of a Pneumatic Tire

The motion resistance of a pneumatic tire depends on its mode of operation. If the ground is sufficiently soft and the sum of the inflation pressure p_i and the pressure produced by the stiffness of the carcass p_c is greater than the maximum pressure that the ground can support at the lowest point of the tire circumference, the tire will remain round like a rigid rim, as shown in Fig. 2.36. On the other hand, if the ground is firm enough, a portion of the circumference of the tire will be flattened. When predicting the motion resistance of a tire, it is necessary, first of all, to determine whether the pneumatic tire behaves like a rigid rim or an elastic wheel under the given operating condition. If the tire behaves like a rigid rim, using Bekker's pressure sinkage relationship, the normal pressure at the lowest point of contact (bottom-dead-center) p_g is

$$p_g = \left[\frac{k_c}{b} + k_\phi\right] z_0^n \tag{2.61}$$

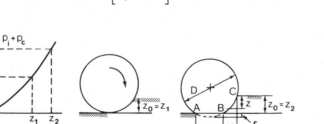

Fig. 2.36 Behavior of a pneumatic tire under different soil conditions. (Reproduced by permission of the Council of the Institution of Mechanical Engineers from reference 2.24.)

Substituting Eq. 2.55 into the above equation, the expression for p_g becomes [2.24]

$$p_g = \left[\frac{k_c}{b} + k_\phi\right]^{1/(2n+1)} \left[\frac{3W}{(3-n)b\sqrt{D}}\right]^{2n/(2n+1)} \tag{2.62}$$

If the sum of the inflation pressure p_i and the pressure due to carcass stiffness p_c is greater than p_g, which may be called the critical pressure p_{cr}, the tire will remain round like a rigid wheel [2.24]. Under this condition, the motion resistance due to compacting the terrain can be predicted using Eq. 2.56. On the other hand, if the sum of p_i and p_c is less than p_{cr} calculated from Eq. 2.62, a portion of the circumference of the tire will be flattened and the contact pressure on the flat portion will be equal to $p_i + p_c$. In this case, the sinkage of the tire z_0 can be determined by the following equation, using Bekker's pressure-sinkage relationship,

$$z_0 = \left(\frac{p_i + p_c}{k_c/b + k_\phi}\right)^{1/n} \tag{2.63}$$

Substituting Eq. 2.63 into Eq. 2.47, the expression for the motion resistance of an elastic wheel due to compacting the terrain becomes

$$R_c = b\left(\frac{z_0^{n+1}}{n+1}\right)\left(\frac{k_c}{b} + k_\phi\right)$$

$$= \frac{b(p_i + p_c)^{(n+1)/n}}{(n+1)(k_c/b + k_\phi)^{1/n}} \tag{2.64}$$

For tires that are wide in comparison with the diameter, such as terra tires and rolligons, care must be taken in using Eqs. 2.63 and 2.64 to predict the sinkage and compaction resistance. For this type of tire, the smaller dimension of the loading area (i.e., b in the pressure sinkage equation, Eq. 2.36 or Eq. 2.41) is not necessarily the width of the tire, and the contact length l_t shown in Fig. 2.36 may well be the smaller dimension, as pointed out by Bekker [2.23]. This indicates that to predict the performance of this type of tire, the contact length l_t has to be estimated first. An approximate method for analyzing the performance of this type of tire is given below.

In a first approximation, it may be assumed that the contact length l_t is a function of tire deflection δ_t shown in Fig. 2.36,

$$l_t = 2\sqrt{D\delta_t - \delta_t^2} \tag{2.65}$$

When l_t is less than the width of the tire, its value should be used as the denominator of k_c in calculating the sinkage z_0

$$z_0 = \left(\frac{p_i + p_c}{k_c / l_t + k_\phi} \right)^{1/n} \tag{2.66}$$

The vertical load W on the tire is supported by the ground pressure $p_g = p_c + p_i$ on the flat portion AB as well as by the reaction on the curved portion BC shown in Fig. 2.36. In a first approximation, BC may be assumed to be a circular arc with radius $r = D/2$. The vertical load W_{cu} supported by BC may be determined following an approach similar to that for a rigid wheel described in the previous section,

$$W_{cu} = -b \int_0^{z_0} p\, dx = -b \left(\frac{k_c}{l_t} + k_\phi \right) \int_0^{z_0} \frac{z^n \sqrt{D}\, dz}{2\sqrt{z_0 + \delta_t - z}}$$

Denote $z_0 + \delta_t - z = t^2$, then $dz = -2t\, dt$ and

$$W_{cu} = b \left(\frac{k_c}{l_t} + k_\phi \right) \sqrt{D} \int_{\sqrt{\delta_t}}^{\sqrt{z_0 + \delta_t}} (z_0 - t^2)^n\, dt \tag{2.67}$$

Expanding $(z_0 - t^2)^n$ and only taking the first two terms of the series, one obtains

$$W_{cu} = \frac{b(k_c / l_t + k_\phi)\sqrt{D}\,(z_0 + \delta_t)^{n-1}\left(\sqrt{z_0 + \delta_t} - \sqrt{\delta_t} \right)}{3}$$

$$\times \left[z_0(3 - n) + \delta_t(3 - 2n) - n\sqrt{\delta_t(z_0 + \delta_t)} \right] \tag{2.68}$$

The vertical load on the tire therefore is equal to

$$W = b(p_i + p_c)l_t + W_{cu} \tag{2.69}$$

It can be seen that the vertical load W of a given tire determines δ_t, l_t, and z_0, and that the relationships between l_t, z_0, and δ_t are governed by Eqs. 2.65 and 2.66. This indicates that for a given tire with known vertical load, there is a particular value of tire deflection δ_t that satisfies Eq. 2.69 over a specific terrain. In principle, the tire deflection δ_t, therefore, can be determined by solving Eqs. 2.65, 2.66, 2.68, and 2.69 simultaneously. In practice, however, it is more convenient to follow an iteration procedure to determine the value of tire deflection. In the iteration process, a value of δ_t is first assumed and is substituted into Eq. 2.65 to calculate the contact length l_t. Then use is made of Eq. 2.66 to calculate the sinkage z_0. With the values of δ_t, l_t, and z_0 known, the vertical load W that the tire can support for the assumed value of δ_t can be determined. If the assumed value of δ_t is a correct one, the calculated value of W should be equal to the given vertical load. If not, a new value of δ_t should be assumed and the whole process should be repeated until convergence is achieved. After the correct value of δ_t is obtained, the appropriate contact length l_t and sinkage z_0 can be calculated using Eqs. 2.65 and 2.66. The compaction resistance can then be determined by

$$R_c = \frac{b(k_c/l_t + k_\phi)z_0^{n+1}}{n+1} \tag{2.70}$$

The bulldozing resistance of a pneumatic tire can be determined in the same way as that for a rigid wheel using Eq. 2.59 or Eq. 2.60. For pneumatic tires, in addition to the compaction and bulldozing resistance, energy is dissipated in the hysteresis of tire material, which appears as a resisting force acting on the tire. The resistance due to tire flexing motion depends on tire design, construction, and material and on operating conditions. The value of this resistance is usually determined experimentally. Recently, Bekker and Semonin have proposed a semiempirical method for predicting the tire flexing motion resistance [2.25].

In summary, the motion resistance of a rigid wheel has two basic components: compaction resistance and bulldozing resistance. For a pneumatic tire, in addition to the compaction resistance and bulldozing resistance, the tire flexing resistance should also be taken into consideration. It has been shown that this methodology yields reasonable predictions of wheel performance [2.23].

It should be mentioned that the methods described above are for the prediction of the compaction and bulldozing resistance of a single wheel or tire. In practice, quite often the rear wheels of a vehicle travel in the ruts formed by the front wheels. The properties of the terrain in contact with the consecutive wheels may, therefore, be different from those of the original terrain. If the terrain changes its properties under load, terrain values measured in the ruts should be used for the prediction of the performance of the consecutive wheels. It has been found that in loose sand, consecutive passes will cause some increase in the value of soil deformation modulus k_ϕ and a slight decrease in the value of the exponent of deformation n [2.3]. In frictional soils with certain original structure, the value of k_ϕ usually decreases after the first loading, whereas the value of n either remains unchanged or decreases slightly. For a certain type of clay, its shear strength may decrease noticeably after consecutive vehicular loads. In general, changes in the properties of the terrain due to the passage of the vehicle running gear mainly depend on the initial state and the structure of the terrain, and the load applied.

Example 2.2   A 38×20–16 tire with diameter $D = 0.975$ m (3.2 ft) and width 0.47 m (1.54 ft) is to operate over a sandy loam with $n = 0.44$, $k_c = 8.93$ kN/m$^{1.44}$ (10.1 lb/in.$^{1.44}$), and $k_\phi = 230.69$ kN/m$^{2.44}$ (6.7 lb/in.$^{2.44}$). Estimate the compaction resistance of the tire with vertical load of 5886 N (1323 lb) at an inflation pressure of 49 kPa (7.1 psi). The pressure due to carcass stiffness is 19.6 kPa (2.8 psi).

Solution.   It is necessary, first of all, to determine whether the tire behaves like a rigid rim or an elastic wheel under the given operating conditions. Assume that the tire behaves like a rigid rim and that the contact length l_t shown in Fig. 2.34 is the smaller dimension of the contact area. From the geometry shown in Fig. 2.34,

$$l_t = \sqrt{2rz_0 - z_0^2} = \sqrt{Dz_0 - z_0^2}$$

The sinkage of a rigid rim z_0 under a given vertical load can be determined by solving the following equation that is based on Eq. 2.54 with l_t as the smaller dimension of the loading area.

$$W = \frac{b\sqrt{D}}{3} z_0^{(2n+1)/2}(3-n)\left[\frac{k_c}{\sqrt{Dz_0 - z_0^2}} + k_\phi\right]$$

In practice, it is more convenient to follow an iteration procedure to determine z_0 from the above equation. With the given data, the value of z_0 is found to be 0.045 m. The contact length l_t can then be calculated

$$l_t = \sqrt{0.975 \times 0.045 - 0.045^2} = 0.205 \text{ m (8 in.)}$$

Since the tire width $b = 0.47$ m (1.54 ft) and $l_t < b$, the contact length l_t is indeed the smaller dimension of the loading area. The critical pressure p_{cr} is determined by Eq. 2.61

$$P_{cr} = \left(\frac{k_c}{l_t} + k_\phi\right)z_0^n = \left(\frac{8.93}{0.205} + 230.69\right)0.045^{0.44}$$

$$= 70.1 \text{ kPa (10.2 psi)}$$

The sum of inflation pressure p_i and the pressure due to carcass stiffness p_c is 68.6 kPa (9.9 psi). Since $p_i + p_c < p_{cr}$, the tire behaves like an elastic wheel under the given operating conditions.

Following the procedure outlined in Section 2.4.2, the tire deflection δ_t is found by iteration to be 0.16 cm. Using Eqs. 2.65 and 2.66, the contact length l_t and sinkage z_0 of the elastic wheel are found to be 0.079 m (3 in.) and 0.026 m (1 in.), respectively. Since $l_t < b$, the contact length is indeed the smaller dimension of the loading area. With the values of l_t and z_0 known, the compaction resistance can be calculated using Eq. 2.70

$$R_c = \frac{0.47\left[(8.93/0.079) + 230.69\right]0.026^{1.44}}{1.44}$$

$$= 0.586 \text{ kN (132 lb)}$$

2.4.3 Motion Resistance of a Track

A rigid track, such as that used in agricultural tractors and their derivatives, may be considered similar to a plate. The normal pressure exerted on the track by the terrain can be considered equal to that beneath the plate at the same depth in a penetration test. If the normal load is uniformly distributed along the track, then the sinkage of the track can be predicted by one of the pressure-sinkage equations discussed previously. Using Bekker's equation, Eq. 2.36, the sinkage is

$$z_0 = \left(\frac{p}{k_c/b + k_\phi}\right)^{1/n}$$

$$= \left(\frac{W/bl}{k_c/b + k_\phi}\right)^{1/n} \tag{2.71}$$

The work done in compacting the soil and making a rut of length l, width b, and depth z_0 is given by

$$\text{Work} = bl\int_0^{z_0} p\,dz$$

Substituting for p from Eq. 2.36 yields

$$\text{Work} = bl\left(\frac{k_c}{b} + k_\phi\right)\left(\frac{z_0^{n+1}}{n+1}\right) \tag{2.72}$$

For a track with uniform pressure distribution, z_0 is given by Eq. 2.71, and

Eq. 2.72 can be rewritten as

$$\text{Work} = \frac{bl}{(n+1)(k_c/b + k_\phi)^{1/n}} \left(\frac{W}{bl}\right)^{(n+1)/n} \tag{2.73}$$

If the track is pulled a distance l in the horizontal direction, the work done by the towing force, which is equal to the magnitude of the motion resistance due to soil compaction R_c, should be balanced by the vertical work done in making a rut of length l as expressed by Eq. 2.73,

$$R_c l = \frac{bl}{(n+1)(k_c/b + k_\phi)^{1/n}} \left(\frac{W}{bl}\right)^{(n+1)/n}$$

and

$$R_c = \frac{b}{(n+1)(k_c/b + k_\phi)^{1/n}} \left(\frac{W}{bl}\right)^{(n+1)/n}$$

$$= \frac{1}{(n+1)b^{1/n}(k_c/b + k_\phi)^{1/n}} \left(\frac{W}{l}\right)^{(n+1)/n} \tag{2.74}$$

This is the equation for calculating the motion resistance due to soil compaction of a track with uniform pressure distribution, based on Bekker's pressure-sinkage relationship. Expressions for motion resistance based on other pressure-sinkage relationships may be derived in a similar way.

In soft ground with noticeable sinkage, bulldozing resistance acting at the front of the track is a significant component of the total motion resistance and should be taken into consideration. The bulldozing resistance of tracks can be predicted in the same way as that for wheels described previously.

It should be emphasized that Eq. 2.74 is applicable only where the normal load is uniformly distributed over the contact area. This kind of uniform pressure distribution may occur in tractors used in agriculture and construction industry with low ratio of road wheel spacing s_r to track pitch t_t (i.e., $s_r/t_t \leqslant 2$) and with proper location of the center of gravity. For flexible tracks, such as rubber belt tracks on pneumatic tired road wheels, or for tracks with high ratio of road wheel spacing to track pitch, the pressure distribution along the track will be nonuniform. Figure 2.37 shows the measured normal pressure distribution (at a depth of 0.23 m below soil surface) under various military tracked vehicles [2.26, 2.27]. For a very flexible track with relatively rigid road wheels, the normal pressure distribution under the track is similar to that under individual road wheels. Under these circumstances, the effect of the track may be neglected and

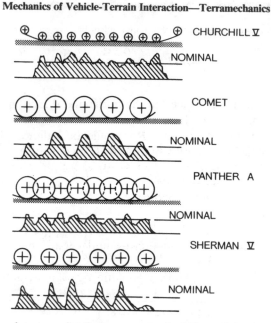

Fig. 2.37 Measured pressure distributions at a depth of 23 cm (9 in.) below the soil surface under various tracked vehicles. (Reproduced by permission from reference 2.26.)

the compaction resistance may be predicted by assuming that the vehicle is equivalent to a wheeled vehicle, and the consecutive road wheels are in multiple-pass operation, as suggested by Bekker [2.23]. Since under most conditions, the load distribution under the track is nonuniform, the use of the so-called nominal ground pressure, which is the weight of the vehicle divided by the projected track area, as a basis for predicting the performance of the track is not very meaningful. Rowland suggested that the mean maximum pressure, MMP, which is defined as the mean value of the maxima occurring under all the wheel stations, be used as a basic criterion for evaluating the mobility of tracked vehicles [2.26, 2.27].

Based on data obtained from testing off-road vehicles including tanks, reconnaissance vehicles, armoured personnel carriers, and military logistic vehicles, Rowland proposed the following empirical equations for predicting the mean maximum pressure for various track configurations [2.26, 2.27].

A Link and belt tracks on rigid road wheels

$$MMP = \frac{1.26W}{2n_r A_l b \sqrt{t_l D}} \, \text{kN/m}^2 \qquad (2.75)$$

B Belt tracks on pneumatic tired road wheels

$$MMP = \frac{0.5\,W}{2n_r b \sqrt{D\delta_t}}\,\mathrm{kN/m^2} \qquad (2.76)$$

where

W = vehicle weight, kN
n_r = number of wheel stations in one track
A_l = rigid area of link (or belt track cleat) as a proportion of track pitch
   multiplied by wheel width
b = track or pneumatic tire width, m
t_l = track pitch, m
D = outer diameter of road wheel or pneumatic tire, m
δ_t = radial deflection of pneumatic tire under load, m

The values of the mean maximum pressure of some vehicles are given in Table 2.2.

Table 2.2   Values of Mean Maximum Pressure of Tracked Vehicles

Vehicle	Track Configuration	Weight (kN)	Mean Max. Pressure (kN/m²)
Caterpillar D7 Tractor	Link Track	131	80
Vicker Vigor Tractor	Link Track	181	155
Armoured Personnel Carrier M.113	Link Track	108	119
Armoured Personnel Carrier M.114	Belt Track	68	137
Amphibious Carrier M.29C Weasel	Link Track	26.5	27
Volvo BV.202	Belt Track, Pneumatic Tires	42	33
Main Battle Tank M60	Link Track	510–545	221–236
Main Battle Tank Leopard II	Link Track	514	201
S-Tank	Link Track	370	267
Main Battle Tank Centurion X	Link Track	510	252

Source.   Reference 2.27.

Based on test results, Rowland has proposed a set of desirable values of mean maximum pressure for off-road vehicles under various terrain conditions. The suggested values are given in Table 2.3 [2.27].

Table 2.3   Desirable Values of Mean Maximum Pressure

| Terrain | Mean Maximum Pressure (kN/m^2) | | |
	Ideal (Multipass Operation)	Satisfactory	Maximum Acceptable (Mostly Trafficable at Single-Pass Level)
Wet fine grained soils			
Temperate	150	200	300
Tropical	90	140	240
Muskeg	30	50	60
Muskeg floating mat and European bogs	5	10	15
Snow	10	25–30	40

Source.   Reference 2.27.

2.4.4   Tractive Effort and Slip of a Track

The tractive effort of a track is produced by the shearing of the terrain as shown in Fig. 2.29. The maximum tractive effort F_{max} that can be developed by a track is determined by the shear strength of the terrain τ_{max} and the contact area A

$$F_{max} = A\tau_{max}$$

$$= A(c + \sigma \tan\phi)$$

$$= Ac + W\tan\phi \tag{2.77}$$

where W is the vertical load, and c and ϕ are apparent cohesion and angle of internal shearing resistance of the terrain, respectively. It can be seen that in frictional soil, such as dry sand, $c = 0$, the maximum tractive effort depends on the vehicle weight. The heavier the vehicle, the more tractive effort it can develop. The dimensions of the track do not affect the maximum tractive effort. For dry sand, the angle of internal shearing resistance is approximately equal to $35°$. The maximum tractive effort of a vehicle on dry sand is therefore approximately equal to 70% of vehicle weight. In cohesive soil, such as saturated clay, $\phi = 0$, the maximum tractive effort depends on the contact area of the track, and the weight has little effect. Thus, the dimensions of the track are crucial in this case; the larger the contact area, the higher the thrust the track can develop.

Equation 2.77 can only be used for predicting the maximum tractive effort of a tracked vehicle. In vehicle performance evaluation, it is, however, desirable to determine the variation of thrust with vehicle slip over the full operating range. To predict the relationship between thrust and slip, it is necessary to examine the development of shear displacement beneath a track, since shear stress is a function of shear displacement. The shear displacement at various points beneath a track is shown schematically in Fig. 2.38[2.1]. At point 1, the grouser is just coming into contact with the ground, it cannot develop the same shear displacement as the other grousers 2, 3, 4, and 5, since they have been shearing the ground for a certain period of time. The amount of horizontal shear displacement j accumulates consecutively along the contact length and reaches its maximum value at the rear of the contact area. To examine the development of shear displacement beneath a track quantitatively, the slip of a track i has to be defined first.

$$i = 1 - \frac{V}{r\omega} = 1 - \frac{V}{V_t} = \frac{V_t - V}{V_t} = \frac{V_j}{V_t} \qquad (2.78)$$

where V is the actual speed of the track, V_t is the theoretical speed which can be determined from the angular speed ω and radius of the pitch circle r of the sprocket, and V_j is the speed of slip of the track with reference to the ground. When the vehicle is slipping, V_j will be in the direction opposite to that of vehicle motion. On the other hand, when the vehicle is skidding, V_j will be in the same direction as that of vehicle motion. Since the track cannot stretch, the speed of slip V_j is the same for every point of the track in contact with the ground. The shear displacement j at a point located at

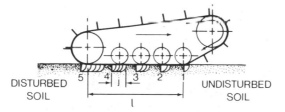

Fig. 2.38 Development of shear displacement under a track. (From *Theory of Land Locomotion* by M. G. Bekker, copyright © by the University of Michigan 1956, reproduced by permission of the University of Michigan Press.)

a distance x from the front of the contact area (Fig. 2.39) can be determined by

$$j = V_j t \qquad (2.79)$$

where t is the contact time of the point in question with the ground, and is equal to x/V_t. Rearranging Eq. 2.79, the expression for shear displacement j becomes

$$j = \frac{V_j x}{V_t} = ix \qquad (2.80)$$

This indicates that the shear displacement beneath a track increases linearly from the front to the rear of the contact area, as shown in Fig. 2.39. Since the development of shear stress is related to shear displacement as discussed previously, the shear stress distribution along the contact area can be found. For instance, to determine the shear stress developed at a point located at a distance x from the front of the contact area, the shear displacement at that point should first be calculated using Eq. 2.80. Making use of the shear stress-displacement relationship obtained from shear tests, as shown in Fig. 2.32, or from the semiempirical equation, such as Eq. 2.42 or Eq. 2.43, the shear stress at that point can then be determined. As an example, the shear stress distribution beneath a track on a particular type of terrain at a given slip is shown in Fig. 2.39. The total tractive effort developed by a track at a particular slip is represented by

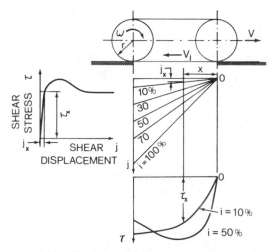

Fig. 2.39 Distribution of shear stress under a track.

the area beneath the shear stress curve in Fig. 2.39. Alternatively, if Eq. 2.43 is used to describe the shear stress-displacement relationship, the total tractive effort of a track can be calculated as follows:

$$F = b \int_0^l \tau \, dx$$

$$= b \int_0^l (c + \sigma \tan \phi)(1 - e^{-j/K}) \, dx \qquad (2.81)$$

The above equation indicates that the tractive effort of a track depends, among other factors, on the normal pressure distribution over the contact area. For a uniform normal pressure distribution σ is independent of x and equal to W/bl. In this case, the total tractive effort of a track is determined by

$$F = b \int_0^l \left(c + \frac{W}{bl} \tan \phi \right)(1 - e^{-ix/K}) \, dx$$

$$= (Ac + W \tan \phi) \left[1 - \frac{K}{il}(1 - e^{-il/K}) \right] \qquad (2.82)$$

Equation 2.82 expresses the functional relationship between tractive effort, vehicle design parameters, terrain values, and vehicle slip. If the slip is 100%, then Eqs. 2.82 and 2.77 are practically identical. Among the vehicle design parameters, the contact length of the track deserves special attention. Consider two tracked vehicles with identical ground contact area and vertical load (i.e., $A_1 = A_2$ and $W_1 = W_2$) that operate over the same terrain. However, the track length of one vehicle is twice that of the other (i.e., $l_1 = 2l_2$). To keep the total contact area the same, the width b_1 of the track with length l_1 is half that of the other (i.e., $b_1 = 0.5 b_2$). If these two tracked vehicles are to develop the same tractive effort, then from Eq. 2.82 the slip of the vehicle with contact length l_1 will be half that of the other with contact length l_2. It may be concluded, therefore, that in general, a short, stubby tracked vehicle will slip more than a long one, if they are to develop the same tractive effort.

The above analysis is applicable to predicting the tractive effort of a track with uniform normal pressure distribution. In practice, the normal pressure distribution is seldom uniform as mentioned previously. It is, therefore, of interest to assess the effect of normal pressure distribution on the tractive effort developed by a track. This problem has been investigated by Wills among others [2.18]. Consider the case of the multipeak

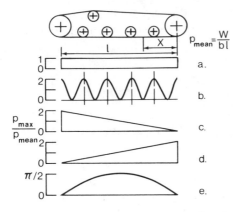

Fig. 2.40 Various types of idealized normal pressure distribution under a track. (Reproduced by permission of the *Journal of Agricultural Engineering Research* from reference 2.18.)

sinusoidal pressure distribution described by

$$\sigma = \frac{W}{bl}\left(1 + \cos\frac{2n\pi x}{l}\right) \tag{2.83}$$

where n is the number of periods, as shown in Fig. 2.40. In a frictional soil, the shear stress developed along the contact length can be expressed by

$$\tau = \frac{W}{bl}\tan\phi\left(1 + \cos\frac{2n\pi x}{l}\right)(1 - e^{-ix/K}) \tag{2.84}$$

and hence the tractive effort is given by

$$F = b\int_0^l \frac{W}{bl}\tan\phi\left(1 + \cos\frac{2n\pi x}{l}\right)(1 - e^{-ix/K})\,dx$$

$$= W\tan\phi\left[1 + \frac{K}{il}(e^{-il/K} - 1) + \frac{K(e^{-il/K} - 1)}{il(1 + 4n^2K^2\pi^2/i^2l^2)}\right] \tag{2.85}$$

The tractive effort of a track with other types of normal pressure distribution can be evaluated in a similar way. In the case of normal pressure increasing linearly from front to rear [i.e., $\sigma = 2(W/bl)(x/l)$] as shown in Fig. 2.40, the tractive effort of a track in frictional soil is given by

$$F = W\tan\phi\left[1 - 2\left(\frac{K}{il}\right)^2\left(1 - e^{-il/K} - \frac{il}{K}e^{-il/K}\right)\right] \tag{2.86}$$

In the case of normal pressure increasing linearly from rear to front, [i.e., $\sigma = 2(W/bl)(l-x)/l$], as shown in Fig. 2.40, the tractive effort in frictional soil is calculated by

$$F = 2W\tan\phi\left[1 - \frac{K}{il}(1 - e^{-il/K})\right]$$

$$- W\tan\phi\left[1 - 2\left(\frac{K}{il}\right)^2\left(1 - e^{-il/K} - \frac{il}{K}e^{-il/K}\right)\right] \qquad (2.87)$$

In the case of sinusoidal distribution with maximum pressure at the center and zero pressure at the front and rear end [*i.e.,* $\sigma = (W/bl)(\pi/2)\sin(\pi x/l)$] as shown in Fig. 2.40, the tractive effort is determined by

$$F = W\tan\phi\left[\frac{1 - (e^{-il/K} - 1)}{2(1 + i^2l^2/\pi^2K^2)}\right] \qquad (2.88)$$

Figure 2.41 shows the variation of the tractive effort with slip of a track with various types of normal pressure distribution discussed above. It can be seen that the normal pressure distribution does have some effect on the tractive effort.

Example 2.3   Two tracked vehicles with the same gross weight of 135 kN (30,350 lb) travel over a particular terrain, which is characterized by $n = 1.6$, $k_c = 4.37$ kN/m$^{2.6}$ (0.07 lb/in.$^{2.6}$), $k_\phi = 196.72$ kN/m$^{3.6}$ (0.08

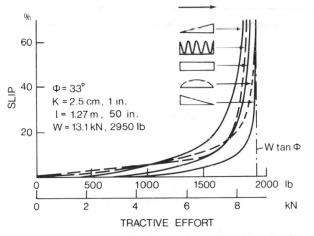

Fig. 2.41   Effect of normal pressure distribution on the tractive effort-slip characteristics of a track in sand. (Reproduced by permission of the *Journal of Agricultural Engineering Research* from reference 2.18.)

lb/in.$^{3.6}$), $K=5$ cm (2 in.), $c=1.0$ kPa (0.15 psi), $\phi=19.7°$, and $\gamma_s=2570$ N/m^3 (16 lb/ft^3). Both vehicles have the same ground contact area of 7.2 m^2 (77.46 ft^2). However, the width b and contact length l of the tracks of the two vehicles are not the same. For vehicle A, $b=1$ m (3.28 ft) and $l=3.6$ m (11.8 ft), and for vehicle B, $b=0.8$ m (2.62 ft) and $l=4.5$ m (14.76 ft). Estimate the motion resistance and thrust-slip characteristics of these two vehicles. In the calculations uniform ground contact pressure may be assumed.

Solution.

A   Motion resistance of vehicle A
Sinkage,

$$z_0=\left(\frac{P}{k_c/b+k_\phi}\right)^{1/n}=\left(\frac{135.0/7.2}{4.37/1+196.72}\right)^{0.625}$$

$$=0.227 \text{ m (9 in.)}$$

Compaction resistance,

$$R_c=2b\left(\frac{k_c}{b}+k_\phi\right)\frac{z_0^{n+1}}{n+1}$$

$$=2\times1\times201.09\times\frac{0.227^{2.6}}{2.6}$$

$$=3.28 \text{ kN (738 lb)}$$

Bulldozing resistance, from Eq. 2.60

$$R_b'=2b\left(0.67\,cz_0K_{pc}'+0.5z_0^2\gamma_s\,K_{p\gamma}'\right)$$

where

$$K_{pc}'=(N_c'-\tan\phi')\cos^2\phi'$$

and

$$K_{p\gamma}'=\left(\frac{2N_\gamma'}{\tan\phi'}+1\right)\cos^2\phi'$$

From Fig. 2.19, for $\phi = 19.7°$, $N_c' = 12$ and $N_\gamma' = 2$. Therefore,

$$K_{pc}' = 11.1 \text{ and } K_{p\gamma}' = 16.8$$

$$R_b' = 5.7 \text{ kN (1282 lb)}$$

Total external motion resistance for vehicle A

$$R_c + R_b' = 8.98 \text{ kN (2020 lb)}$$

B   Motion resistance of vehicle B
Sinkage,

$$z_0 = 0.226 \text{ m (9 in.)}$$

Compaction resistance,

$$R_c = 2.60 \text{ kN (585 lb)}$$

Bulldozing resistance,

$$R_b' = 4.56 \text{ kN (1024 lb)}$$

Total external motion resistance

$$R_c + R_b' = 7.16 \text{ kN (1609 lb)}$$

C   Thrust-slip characteristics of vehicle A

$$F = (2blc + W \tan\phi)\left[1 - \frac{K}{il}(1 - e^{-il/K})\right]$$

$$= F_{max}\left[1 - \frac{K}{il}(1 - e^{-il/K})\right]$$

$$F_{max} = 2 \times 1 \times 3.6 \times 1 + 135 \times 0.358$$

$$= 7.2 + 48.34 = 55.54 \text{ kN (12,486 lb)}$$

The thrust of vehicle A at various slips is given in Table 2.4

D   Thrust-slip characteristics of vehicle B
The maximum thrust of vehicle B will be the same as vehicle A, since the contact area and weight of the two vehicles are identical. The thrust-slip relationship will, however, be different, as the contact lengths

Table 2.4   Performance Characteristics of Vehicles *A* and *B*

Slip, i %			5	10	20	40	60	80
Vehicle A	Thrust	kN	40.54	47.82	51.68	53.62	54.25	54.57
		lb	9114	10,750	11,618	12,054	12,196	12,268
	Drawbar Pull[a]	kN	31.56	38.84	42.7	44.64	45.27	45.59
		lb	7094	8730	9598	10,034	10,176	10,248
Vehicle B	Thrust	kN	43.32	49.37	52.46	54.0	54.51	54.77
		lb	9739	11,099	11,794	12,140	12,254	12,313
	Drawbar Pull	kN	36.16	42.21	45.3	46.84	47.35	47.61
		lb	8130	9490	10,185	10,531	10,645	10,704

[a]Drawbar pull is equal to the thrust minus the total motion resistance.

of the two vehicles are not the same. The thrust of vehicle *B* at various slips is given in Table 2.4.

It can be seen that the performance of vehicle *B* is somewhat better than that of vehicle *A* in the terrain specified. For instance at 10% slip, the drawbar pull of vehicle *B* is approximately 9% higher than that of vehicle *A*.

2.4.5   Tractive Effort and Slip of a Wheel

To evaluate the relationship between tractive effort and slip of a rigid wheel, the development of shear displacement along the wheel-soil interface has to be determined first. The shear displacement developed along the contact area of a rigid wheel may be determined based on the analysis of the slip velocity V_j. For a rigid wheel, the slip velocity V_j of a point on the rim relative to the terrain is the tangential component of the absolute velocity at the same point, as illustrated in Fig. 2.42 [2.20]. The magnitude of the slip velocity V_j of a point on the rim defined by angle θ (Fig. 2.42) can, therefore, be expressed by [2.20].

$$V_j = r\omega\left[1 - (1 - i)\cos\theta\right] \tag{2.89}$$

It can be seen that the slip velocity for a rigid wheel varies with angle θ and slip.

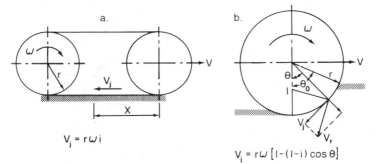

Fig. 2.42 Development of shear displacement under a wheel as compared with that under a track. (Reproduced by permission from reference 2.20.)

The shear displacement j along the wheel-soil interface is given by

$$j = \int_0^t V_j \, dt = \int_\theta^{\theta_0} r\omega \left[1 - (1-i)\cos\theta \right] \frac{d\theta}{\omega}$$

$$= r\left[(\theta_0 - \theta) - (1-i)(\sin\theta_0 - \sin\theta) \right] \qquad (2.90)$$

where θ_0 is the entry angle that defines the angle where a point on the rim comes into contact with the terrain (Fig. 2.42).

Based on the relationship between shear stress and shear displacement discussed previously, the shear stress distribution along the contact area of a rigid wheel can be determined. For instance, using Eq. 2.43, the shear stress distribution may be described by

$$\tau(\theta) = \left[c + \sigma(\theta)\tan\phi \right] (1 - e^{-j/K})$$

$$= \left[c + \sigma(\theta)\tan\phi \right] \left[1 - \exp\{ -(r/K)[\theta_0 - \theta - (1-i)(\sin\theta_0 - \sin\theta)] \} \right]$$

$$(2.91)$$

The normal pressure distribution along a rigid wheel $\sigma(\theta)$ may be estimated by Bekker's theory, which assumes that the normal pressure at the rim is equal to that beneath a horizontal plate at the same depth. The method for predicting normal pressure distribution proposed by Wong and Reece may also be used [2.20]. Figure 2.43 shows a comparison of the measured and predicted shear stress distribution on the rim of a rigid wheel with diameter 1.25 m (49 in.) and width 0.15 m (6 in.) on compact

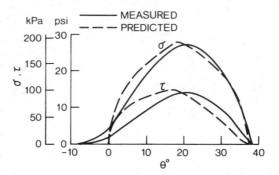

Fig. 2.43 Comparison of the measured and predicted normal and tangential stresses along the rim of a rigid wheel of 125×15 cm (49.4×6 in.) with load 88.96 kN (2000 lb) at 22.1% slip in compact sand. (Reproduced by permission from reference 2.20.)

sand [2.20]. It is seen that Eq. 2.91 can give fairly good prediction of tangential stresses around the rim of a rigid wheel.

Integrating the horizontal component of tangential stress over the entire contact area, the total tractive effort F can be determined.

$$F = \int_0^{\theta_0} \tau(\theta) \cos\theta \, d\theta \qquad (2.92)$$

It should be mentioned that the vertical component of shear stress at the contact area supports part of the vertical load on the wheel. This fact has been neglected in the simplified wheel-soil interaction model shown in Fig. 2.34. In a more complete analysis of wheel-soil interaction, the effect of shear stress should be taken into consideration, and the equations governing the performance characteristics of a rigid wheel are given by [2.20] for vertical load,

$$W = rb\left[\int_0^{\theta_0} \sigma(\theta) \cos\theta \, d\theta + \int_0^{\theta_0} \tau(\theta) \sin\theta \, d\theta \right] \qquad (2.93)$$

for drawbar pull,

$$F_d = rb\left[\int_0^{\theta_0} \tau(\theta) \cos\theta \, d\theta - \int_0^{\theta_0} \sigma(\theta) \sin\theta \, d\theta \right] \qquad (2.94)$$

and for wheel torque

$$M_w = r^2 b \int_0^{\theta_0} \tau(\theta) \, d\theta \qquad (2.95)$$

It should be pointed out that Eq. 2.91 is for the prediction of shear stress distribution along the contact area of a driven rigid wheel. For a towed

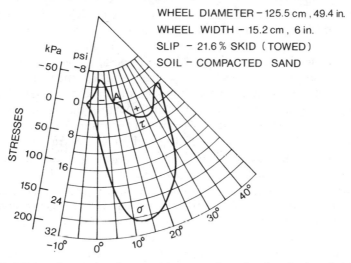

WHEEL DIAMETER – 125.5 cm , 49.4 in.

WHEEL WIDTH – 15.2 cm , 6 in.

SLIP – 21.6 % SKID (TOWED)

SOIL – COMPACTED SAND

Fig. 2.44 Measured normal and tangential stresses along the rim of a towed rigid wheel. (Reproduced by permission from reference 2.20.)

wheel, the shear stress changes its direction at a particular point on the wheel-soil interface, which may be called the transition point as shown in Fig. 2.44 [2.20]. It has been determined that this transition point corresponds to that where two flow zones in the soil beneath a towed wheel meet each other as shown in Fig. 2.21 [2.20]. Under the action of section AD of the rim, the soil in the region ABD moves upward while the rim rotates around the instantaneous center I. The soil therefore slides along AD in such a way as to produce shear stress in the direction opposite to that of wheel rotation. Between A and E the soil moves forward slowly while the wheel rim moves forward relatively fast. In this region, the shear stress therefore acts in the direction of wheel rotation. As a result, the resultant moment of the shear stresses about the wheel center will be zero.

The location of the transition point can be determined using the theory of plastic equilibrium described in Section 2.2. Since at the transition point, shear stress is zero, the normal stress (radial stress) at that point must be the major principal stress at the boundary of the soil mass. According to the theory of passive earth pressure, there must be two slip lines on either side of the axis of the major principal stress with an angle of $45° - \phi/2$, where ϕ is the angle of internal shearing resistance, as AF and AG shown in Fig. 2.45 [2.20]. It therefore follows that, if a point at the wheel-soil interface can be found where the slip lines have an angle of $45° - \phi/2$ with the radial, then this point must be the transition point. This indicates that, to locate the transition point, the slip line field at the boundary of the soil mass adjacent to the rim should be examined. It has been found that the tangent of the trajectory of soil particles at the junction of the two flow zones beneath a towed wheel coincides with the direction of the absolute velocity of the corresponding point on the rim. In solving problems of soil mechanics, it has been assumed often that the trajectories of soil particles in the flow zones represent one set of the slip lines. If this assumption is adopted, then it follows that at the transition point the direction of the absolute velocity of the rim coincides with one of the slip lines at the boundary of the soil mass. Based on the above consideration, it becomes evident that the problem of locating the transition point is now reduced to determining where the direction of the absolute velocity on the rim has an angle of $45° - \phi/2$ with the radial.

By referring to Fig. 2.45, it can be seen that the angle between the direction of the absolute velocity and the radius θ_r at different points of the rim can be determined from the kinematics of the wheel. For a towed wheel of radius r with skid i_s, the instantaneous center is at a distance of $\Delta r = i_s r/(1 - i_s)$ below the bottom-dead-center as shown in Fig. 2.45. The following relationship therefore can be established:

$$\frac{r}{r + \Delta r} = \frac{\sin\left[90° - (\theta + \theta_r)\right]}{\sin(90° + \theta_r)} = \frac{\cos(\theta + \theta_r)}{\cos\theta_r}$$

$$1 - i_s = \cos\theta - \sin\theta\,\tan\theta_r$$

$$\tan\theta_r = \frac{\cos\theta - (1 - i_s)}{\sin\theta} \tag{2.96}$$

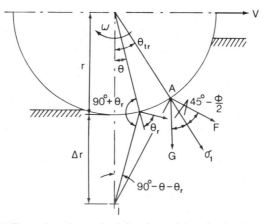

Fig. 2.45 Diagram illustrating the method for determining the location of the transition point of tangential stress for a towed rigid wheel. (Reproduced by permission from reference 2.20.)

Since at the transition point $\theta_r = 45° - \phi/2$, the angular position of the transition point θ_{tr} can be determined by solving

$$\tan(45° - \phi/2) = \frac{\cos\theta_{tr} - (1 - i_s)}{\sin\theta_{tr}} \tag{2.97}$$

It has been shown that the theory for locating the transition point described above works well [2.20]. Following this approach, Wong and Reece proposed a method for predicting the shear stress distribution along the wheel-soil interface and the performance of a towed wheel [2.20].

The method for predicting the tractive effort of a pneumatic tire depends on its mode of operation. If the sum of the inflation pressure p_i and the pressure produced by carcass stiffness p_c is greater than the critical pressure p_{cr} defined by Eq. 2.62, the tire behaves like a rigid wheel, and the shear stress distribution and tractive effort may be estimated by Eqs. 2.91 and 2.92, respectively. On the other hand, if the sum of p_i and p_c is less than p_{cr}, then a portion of the circumference of the tire will be flattened. The shear stress distribution on the flat portion and the tractive effort of the tire can be predicted in a similar way as that for a track discussed previously. In this case, the length of the flat portion of the tire has to be estimated first. It has been shown by Reece that this approach to the prediction of the tractive effort of an elastic tire yields satisfactory results [2.28].

REFERENCES

2.1 M. G. Bekker, *Theory of Land Locomotion*, University of Michigan Press, Ann Arbor, MI, 1956.

2.2 M. G. Bekker, *Off-the-Road Locomotion*, University of Michigan Press, Ann Arbor, MI, 1960.

2.3 M. G. Bekker, Introduction to Terrain-Vehicle Systems, University of Michigan Press, Ann Arbor, MI, 1969.

2.4 W. Söhne, Fundamentals of Pressure Distribution and Soil Compaction under Tractor Tires, *Agricultural Engineering*, May, 1958.

2.5 W. Söhne, Agricultural Engineering and Terramechanics, *Journal of Terramechanics*, Vol. 6, No. 4, 1969.

2.6 M. S. Osman, The Mechanics of Soil Cutting Blades, *Journal of Agricultural Engineering Research*, Vol. 9, No. 4, 1964.

2.7 K. Terzaghi, *Theoretical Soil Mechanics*, Wiley, New York, NY, 1966.

2.8 G. P. Tschebotarioff, Retaining Structures, in G. A. Leonards, Ed., *Foundation Engineering*, McGraw-Hill, New York, NY, 1962. Chap. 5.

2.9 A. Caquot and J. Kerisel, *Tables for the Calculation of Passive Pressure, Active Pressure and Bearing Capacity of Foundations* (revised translation by Ministry of Works, Chief Scientific Advisors' Division, London), Gauthier - Villars, Paris, 1948.

2.10   D. R. P. Hettiaratchi and A. R. Reece, The Calculation of Passive Soil Resistance, *Geotechnique*, Vol. 24, No. 3, 1974.

2.11   J. Y. Wong and A. R. Reece, Soil Failure Beneath Rigid Wheels, *Proceedings of the Second International Conference of the International Society for Terrain Vehicle Systems*, University of Toronto Press, Toronto, 1966.

2.12   J. Y. Wong, Behaviour of Soil Beneath Rigid Wheels, *Journal of Agricultural Engineering Research*, Vol. 12, No. 4, 1967.

2.13   L. L. Karafiath, Plasticity Theory and Stress Distribution Beneath Wheels, *Journal of Terramechanics*, Vol. 8, No. 2, 1971.

2.14   L. L. Karafiath and E. A. Nowatzki, *Soil Mechanics for Off-Road Vehicle Engineering*, Trans Tech Publications, Aedermannsdorf, Switzerland, 1978.

2.15   R. N. Yong and E. A. Fattah, Prediction of Wheel-Soil Interaction and Performance Using the Finite Element Method, *Journal of Terramechanics*, Vol. 13, No. 4, 1976.

2.16   W. L. Harrison, Vehicle Performance over Snow, U.S. Army Cold Regions Research and Engineering Laboratory, Technical Report 268, December 1975.

2.17   A. R. Reece, Principles of Soil-Vehicle Mechanics, *Proceedings of the Institution of Mechanical Engineers*, Vol. 180, Part 2A, 1965–1966.

2.18   B. M. D. Wills, The Measurement of Soil Shear Strength and Deformation Moduli and a Comparison of the Actual and Theoretical Performance of a Family of Rigid Tracks, *Journal of Agricultural Engineering Research*, Vol. 8, No. 2, 1963.

2.19   O. Onafeko and A. R. Reece, Soil Stresses and Deformations Beneath Rigid Wheels, *Journal of Terramechanics*, Vol. 4, No. 1, 1967.

2.20   J. Y. Wong and A. R. Reece, Prediction of Rigid Wheel Performance Based on the Analysis of Soil-Wheel Stresses, Part I and Part II, *Journal of Terramechanics*, Vol. 4, Nos. 1 and 2, 1967.

2.21   J. Y. Wong, Some Problems in the Mechanics of Soil-Wheel Interaction, *Proceedings of the Third International Conference of the International Society for Terrain Vehicle Systems*, Vol. 1, Essen, West Germany, 1969.

2.22   F. L. Uffelmann, The Performance of Rigid Cylindrical Wheels on Clay Soils, *Proceedings of the First International Conference on Soil Vehicle Mechanics*, Turin, Italy, 1961.

2.23   J. Y. Wong and M. G. Bekker, *Terrain Vehicle Systems Analysis*, Monograph, Department of Mechanical and Aeronautical Engineering, Carleton University, Ottawa, Canada, 1977.

2.24   J. Y. Wong, Performance of the Air Cushion-Surface Contacting Hybrid Vehicle for Overland Operation, *Proceedings of the Institution of Mechanical Engineers*, Vol. 186, 50/72, 1972.

2.25   M. G. Bekker and E. V. Semonin, Motion Resistance of Pneumatic Tires, *Journal of Automotive Engineering*, Vol. 6, No. 2, 1975.

2.26   D. Rowland, Tracked Vehicle Ground Pressure and Its Effect on Soft Ground Performance, *Proceedings of the Fourth International Conference of the International Society for Terrain Vehicle Systems*, Vol. 1, Stockholm, Sweden, 1972.

2.27   D. Rowland, A Review of Vehicle Design for Soft-Ground Operation, *Proceedings of the Fifth International Conference of the International Society for Terrain Vehicle Systems*, Vol. 1, Detroit, MI, 1975.

2.28   A. R. Reece, Theory and Practice of Off-the-Road Locomotion, *Proceedings of the Institution of Agricultural Engineers*, Vol. 20, No. 2, 1964.

PROBLEMS

2.1 The contact area of a tire on a fairly hard and dry soil may be approximated by an ellipse having a major axis of 30 cm (11.8 in.) and a minor axis of 20 cm (7.9 in.). The contact pressure is assumed to be a uniform 68.95 kPa (10 psi). For this type of soil, the concentration factor v is assumed to be 4. Calculate the resultant vertical stress σ_z in the soil at depths of 20 and 40 cm (7.9 and 15.8 in.) below the center of the contact area. At what depth below the center is the vertical stress one-tenth of the contact pressure?

2.2 A steel wheel with 18 lugs on a narrow rim is to be attached to an off-road wheeled vehicle to increase its traction over a wet soil. The outside diameter of the steel wheel across the tips of the lugs is 1.5 m (4.92 ft). The lugs are 25 cm (10 in.) wide and penetrate 12.5 cm (5 in) into the soil at the vertical position. Estimate the maximum tractive effort that the steel wheel can develop in a soil with $c = 13.79$ kPa (2 psi), $\phi = 5^0$, and $\gamma_s = 16$ kN/m^3 (102 lb/ft^3). Calculate also the driving torque required. The rim of the wheel is narrow, and its effect may be neglected. The surface of the lugs is assumed to be smooth.

2.3 A tracked vehicle with uniform contact pressure weighs 155.68 kN (35,000 lb). Each of its two tracks is 102 cm (40 in.) wide and 305 cm (120 in.) long. Estimate the motion resistance and thrust-slip relationship of the vehicle in a terrain with $n = 0.5$, $k_c = 0.77$ kN/m$^{(n+1)}$ (0.7 lb/in.$^{(n+1)}$), $k_\phi = 51.91$ kN/m$^{(n+2)}$ (1.2 lb/in.$^{(n+2)}$), $c = 5.17$ kPa (0.75 psi), $\phi = 11^\circ$, $K = 5$ cm (2 in.), and $\gamma_s = 16$ kN/m^3 (102 lb/ft^3). Estimate also the maximum drawbar pull the vehicle can develop. What will be the changes in its performance, if the width of the track is reduced by 20% and its length is increased by the same amount?

2.4 A four-wheel-drive tractor weighs 60.05 kN (12,000 lb), with equal weight distribution between the axles. Each of the four tires is 47 cm (18.5 in.) wide and 135 cm (53 in.) in diameter. The sum of the inflation pressure and the pressure due to carcass stiffness is 68.95 kPa (10 psi). Estimate the motion resistance and the maximum thrust of the vehicle in the terrain described in Problem 2.3. What improvement, if any, in the performance of the vehicle may be expected, if the inflation pressure is reduced by 13.79 kPa (2 psi)?

CHAPTER THREE
PERFORMANCE CHARACTERISTICS OF ROAD VEHICLES

Performance characteristics of a road vehicle are primarily concerned with its capability to accelerate, to decelerate, and to negotiate grades in straight-line motion. The tractive (or braking) effort and the resisting forces determine the performance potential of the vehicle and will be discussed in detail in this chapter. Procedures for predicting and evaluating the performance characteristics of road vehicles will also be presented.

3.1 EQUATION OF MOTION AND MAXIMUM TRACTIVE EFFORT

The major external forces acting on a two-axle vehicle are shown in Fig. 3.1. In the longitudinal direction, they include aerodynamic resistance R_a, rolling resistance of the front and rear tires R_{rf} and R_{rr}, drawbar load R_d, grade resistance R_g ($W \sin \theta_s$) and tractive effort of the front and rear tires F_f and F_r. For a rear-wheel-drive vehicle F_f is zero, whereas for a front-wheel-drive vehicle F_r is zero.

The equation of motion along the longitudinal axis of the vehicle is expressed by

$$m \frac{d^2x}{dt^2} = \frac{aW}{g} = F_f + F_r - R_a - R_{rf} - R_{rr} - R_d - R_g \qquad (3.1)$$

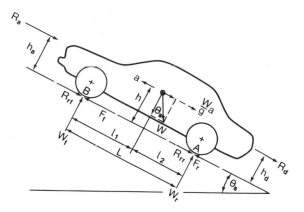

Fig. 3.1 Forces acting on a two-axle vehicle.

where d^2x/dt^2 or a is the linear acceleration of the vehicle, g is acceleration due to gravity, and m and W are vehicle mass and weight, respectively.

By introducing the concept of inertia force, the above equation may be rewritten as

$$F_f + F_r - \left(R_a + R_{rf} + R_{rr} + R_d + R_g + \frac{aW}{g} \right) = 0$$

or

$$F = R_a + R_r + R_d + R_g + \frac{aW}{g} \qquad (3.2)$$

where F is the total tractive effort and R_r is the total rolling resistance of the vehicle.

To evaluate the performance potential, the maximum tractive effort that the vehicle can develop has to be determined. There are two limiting factors to the maximum tractive effort of a road vehicle: one is determined by the coefficient of road adhesion and the normal load on the driven axle or axles; the other is determined by the characteristics of the power plant and the transmission. The smaller of these two determines the performance potential of the vehicle.

To predict the maximum tractive effort that the tire-ground contact can support, the normal loads on the axles have to be determined. They can be computed readily by summation of the moments about points A and B shown in Fig. 3.1. By summing moments about A, the normal load on the front axle W_f can be determined.

$$W_f = \frac{W l_2 \cos \theta_s - R_a h_a - h a W/g - R_d h_d \mp W h \sin \theta_s}{L} \qquad (3.3)$$

where l_2 is the distance between the rear axle and the center of gravity of the vehicle, h_a is the height of the point of application of the aerodynamic resistance, h is the height of the center of gravity, h_d is the height of drawbar, L is the wheelbase, and θ_s is the slope angle. When the vehicle is climbing a hill, the negative sign is used for the term $Wh\sin\theta_s$.

Similarly, the normal load on the rear axle can be determined by summing moments about B.

$$W_r = \frac{Wl_1\cos\theta_s + R_a h_a + haW/g + R_d h_d \pm Wh\sin\theta_s}{L} \qquad (3.4)$$

where l_1 is the distance between the front axle and the center of gravity of the vehicle. In the above expression, the positive sign is used for the term $Wh\sin\theta_s$ when the vehicle is climbing a hill.

For small angles of slope, $\cos\theta_s$ is approximately equal to 1. For passenger cars the height of the point of application of the aerodynamic resistance h_a and the height of the drawbar h_d may be assumed to be near the height of the center of gravity h. With these simplifications and assumptions, Eqs. 3.3 and 3.4 may be rewritten as

$$W_f = \frac{l_2}{L} W - \frac{h}{L}\left(R_a + \frac{aW}{g} + R_d \pm W\sin\theta_s\right) \qquad (3.5)$$

and

$$W_r = \frac{l_1}{L} W + \frac{h}{L}\left(R_a + \frac{aW}{g} + R_d \pm W\sin\theta_s\right) \qquad (3.6)$$

Substituting Eq. 3.2 into the above equations, one obtains

$$W_f = \frac{l_2}{L} W - \frac{h}{L}(F - R_r) \qquad (3.7)$$

and

$$W_r = \frac{l_1}{L} W + \frac{h}{L}(F - R_r) \qquad (3.8)$$

It should be noted that the first term on the right-hand side of each equation represents the static load on the axle when the vehicle is at rest on level ground. The second term on the right-hand side of each equation represents the dynamic component of the normal load.

The maximum tractive effort that the tire-ground contact can support can be determined in terms of the coefficient of road adhesion μ and vehicle parameters. For a rear-wheel-drive vehicle,

$$F_{max} = \mu W_r = \mu \left[\frac{l_1}{L} W + \frac{h}{L} (F_{max} - R_r) \right]$$

and

$$F_{max} = \frac{\mu W (l_1 - f_r h)/L}{1 - \mu h/L} \qquad (3.9)$$

where the total rolling resistance R_r is expressed as the product of the coefficient of rolling resistance f_r and the weight of the vehicle W. For a front-wheel-drive vehicle

$$F_{max} = \mu W_f = \mu \left[\frac{l_2}{L} W - \frac{h}{L} (F_{max} - R_r) \right]$$

and

$$F_{max} = \frac{\mu W (l_2 + f_r h)/L}{1 + \mu h/L} \qquad (3.10)$$

It should be noted that in deriving the above equations, transverse load transfer due to engine torque has been neglected, and that both the right- and left-hand side tires are assumed to have identical performance.

For a tractor-semitrailer vehicle, the calculation of the maximum tractive effort that the tire-ground contact can support is more involved than a two-axle vehicle. The major forces acting on a tractor-semitrailer are shown in Fig. 3.2. For most of the tractor-semitrailers, the tractor rear axle

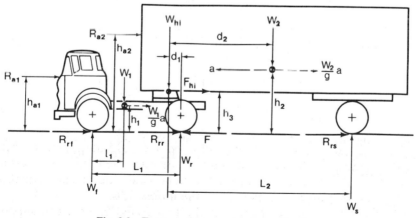

Fig. 3.2 Forces acting on a tractor-semitrailer.

is driven. To compute the maximum tractive effort as determined by the nature of tire-road adhesion, it is necessary to calculate the normal load on the tractor rear axle under operating conditions. This can be calculated by considering the tractor and the semitrailer as free bodies separately. By taking the semitrailer as a free body, the normal load on the semitrailer axle W_s, and the vertical and horizontal loads at the hitch point W_{hi} and F_{hi} can be determined.

The normal load on the semitrailer axle, for small angles of slope, is given by

$$W_s = \frac{W_2 d_2 + R_{a_2} h_{a_2} + h_2 a W_2/g \pm W_2 h_2 \sin\theta_s - F_{hi} h_3}{L_2} \tag{3.11}$$

where R_{a_2} is the aerodynamic resistance acting on the semitrailer, h_{a_2} is the height of the point of application of R_{a_2}, and W_2 is the weight of the semitrailer. Other parameters and dimensions are shown in Fig. 3.2. When the vehicle is climbing a hill, the positive sign for the term $W_2 h_2 \sin\theta_s$ in Eq. 3.11 should be used.

If $h_{a_2} \cong h_3 \cong h_2$, the expression for W_s may be simplified as

$$W_s = \frac{d_2}{L_2} W_2 + \frac{h_2}{L_2}\left(R_{a_2} + \frac{aW_2}{g} \pm W_2 \sin\theta_s - F_{hi}\right) \tag{3.12}$$

The longitudinal force at the hitch point is given by

$$F_{hi} = R_{a_2} + \frac{aW_2}{g} \pm W_2 \sin\theta_s + f_r W_s \tag{3.13}$$

Substituting Eq. 3.13 into Eq. 3.12, the expression for W_s becomes

$$W_s = \frac{W_2 d_2}{L_2 + f_r h_2}$$

and the load at the hitch point is given by

$$W_{hi} = W_2 - W_s = \left(1 - \frac{d_2}{L_2 + f_r h_2}\right) W_2 \tag{3.14}$$

$$= C_{hi} W_2$$

By taking the tractor as a free body and summing moments about the front tire-ground contact point, the normal load on the tractor rear axle W_r can be determined.

$$W_r = \frac{W_1 l_1 + R_{a_1} h_{a_1} + h_1 a W_1/g \pm W_1 h_1 \sin\theta_s + F_{hi} h_3 + (L_1 - d_1) W_{hi}}{L_1}$$

$$\tag{3.15}$$

where R_{a_1} is the aerodynamic resistance acting on the tractor, h_{a_1} is the height of the point of application of R_{a_1}, and W_1 is weight of the tractor. Other parameters and dimensions are shown in Fig. 3.2. When the vehicle is climbing a hill, the positive sign for the term $W_1 h_1 \sin\theta_s$ in Eq. 3.15 should be used.

If $h_{a_1} \cong h_3 \cong h_1$, the expression for W_r may be simplified as

$$W_r = \frac{W_1 l_1 + (R_{a_1} + aW_1/g \pm W_1 \sin\theta_s + F_{hi}) h_1 + (L_1 - d_1) W_{hi}}{L_1} \qquad (3.16)$$

By equating the forces acting on the tractor in the longitudinal direction, the following expression for the tractive effort F required can be obtained

$$F = R_{a_1} + \frac{aW_1}{g} \pm W_1 \sin\theta_s + f_r(W_1 + W_{hi}) + F_{hi} \qquad (3.17)$$

From Eqs. 3.16 and 3.17, the maximum tractive effort that the tire ground contact can support with tractor rear axle driven can be expressed by

$$F_{max} = \mu W_r = \frac{\mu[l_1 W_1 - h_1 f_r(W_1 + W_{hi}) + (L_1 - d_1) W_{hi}]/L_1}{1 - \mu h_1/L_1}$$

Substitution of Eq. 3.14 into the above equation yields

$$F_{max} = \frac{\mu[l_1 W_1 - h_1 f_r(W_1 + C_{hi} W_2) + (L_1 - d_1) C_{hi} W_2]/L_1}{1 - \mu h_1/L_1} \qquad (3.18)$$

The maximum tractive effort as determined by the nature of tire-road interaction imposes a fundamental limit on the vehicle performance characteristics including maximum speed, acceleration, gradability, and drawbar pull.

3.2 AERODYNAMIC FORCES AND MOMENTS

Aerodynamic resistance, aerodynamic lift, and aerodynamic pitching moment have significant effects on vehicle performance at moderate and higher speeds. The increasing emphasis on fuel economy and on energy conservation has stimulated new interest in improving the aerodynamic performance of road vehicles.

The aerodynamic resistance of the vehicle is derived from three sources:

1   Form drag, which is caused by the turbulence in the wake of the vehicle. It is a function of the shape of the vehicle body, particularly the shape of the rear part. This component is usually the most significant part of the aerodynamic resistance.
2   Skin friction, which is caused by the shear force exerted on the vehicle exterior surfaces by the air stream. For the normal surface finish of passenger cars, this component is approximately 10% of the total aerodynamic resistance.
3   Resistance due to air flow through the radiator system or the interior of the vehicle for purposes of cooling or ventilating. It is dependent on the design of flow passage; this component amounts to a few percent of the total drag.

The aerodynamic resistance is usually expressed in the following form

$$R_a = \frac{\rho}{2} C_D A_f V^2 \qquad (3.19)$$

where ρ is the air density, C_D is the coefficient of aerodynamic resistance that represents the combined effects of the three components described above, A_f is a characteristic area of the vehicle usually taken as the frontal area which is the projected area of the vehicle in the direction of travel, and V is the speed of the vehicle relative to the wind. It is interesting to note that aerodynamic resistance is proportional to the square of speed. Thus the horsepower required to overcome aerodynamic resistance increases with the cube of speed. If the speed of a vehicle is doubled, the power required for overcoming aerodynamic resistance increases eightfold. It should be mentioned that atmospheric conditions affect air density ρ. It is, therefore, necessary to establish a standard set of conditions to which all aerodynamic test data may be referred. The most widely used standard conditions are: temperature 288.5° Kelvin (15.5°C or 60°F) and barometric pressure 101.32 kPa (76 cm or 29.92 in. Hg). The coefficient of aerodynamic resistance can be obtained by wind-tunnel testing of a scale model or a full-scale vehicle. The deceleration method of road testing may also be used to determine the aerodynamic resistance [3.1]. Using this method, the vehicle is first run up to a certain speed, then the driveline is disconnected from the engine, and the vehicle decelerates. The deceleration of the vehicle due to the combined effects of the rolling resistance and the aerodynamic resistance is determined. By isolating the effect of the motion resistance from the test data, the aerodynamic resistance can be derived. It has been shown that this method can yield sufficiently accurate

Table 3.1 Coefficient of Aerodynamic Resistance

Vehicle Type	C_D (dimensionless)
Passenger car	0.3–0.6
Convertible	0.4–0.65
Racing car	0.25–0.3
Bus	0.6–0.7
Truck	0.8–1.0
Tractor-trailer	0.8–1.3
Motorcycle and rider	1.8

Source. Reference 3.2.

results. Representative values of the coefficient of aerodynamic resistance for various types of vehicle are given in Table 3.1 [3.2].

Figure 3.3 shows the values of the coefficient of aerodynamic resistance for passenger cars with various shapes [3.3]. In addition to the shape of the vehicle, the attitude of the vehicle defined by the angle of attack (i.e., the angle between the longitudinal axis of the vehicle and the horizontal ground plane), ground clearance, and other operational factors, such as radiator open or blanked, and window open or closed, also affect the coefficient of aerodynamic resistance. The variation of the angle of attack is normally due to changes in load or load distribution. Figure 3.4 shows the effect of the angle of attack on the values of C_D for three types of passenger car [3.4]. Figure 3.5 shows the effect of operational factors on the coefficient of aerodynamic resistance of a car [3.4].

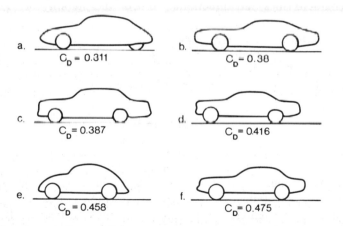

Fig. 3.3 Aerodynamic drag coefficients of passenger cars. (*a*) Citroen DS19; (*b*) Oldsmobile Toronado; (*c*) Mercedes 300SE; (*d*) Ford Falcon Futura; (*e*) VW 1200; (*f*) Ford Mustang. (Reproduced by permission of the Society of Automotive Engineers from reference 3.3.)

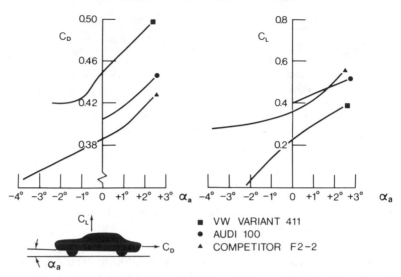

Fig. 3.4 Effect of the angle of attack on aerodynamic drag coefficient and aerodynamic lift coefficient of cars. (Reproduced by permission from The Effect of Various Parameters on the Aerodynamic Drag of Passenger Cars, by L. J. Janssen and W. H. Hucho, in *Advances in Road Vehicle Aerodynamics*, BHRA Fluid Engineering, Cranfield, England, 1973.)

Aerodynamic lift acting on a vehicle is caused by the pressure differential across the vehicle body from the bottom to the top. It may become significant at moderate speeds. The aerodynamic lift usually causes the reduction of the normal load on the tire-ground contact. Thus the performance characteristics and directional control and stability of the vehicle may be adversely affected. For racing cars, to improve its cornering and tractive capabilities, externally mounted aerodynamic surfaces that generate a downward aerodynamic force are widely used. This increases the normal load on the tire-ground contact.

The aerodynamic lift R_L acting on a vehicle may be expressed as

$$R_L = \frac{\rho}{2} C_L A_f V^2 \tag{3.20}$$

where C_L is the coefficient of aerodynamic lift usually obtained from wind-tunnel testing. Typical values of C_L for passenger cars vary in the range 0.2–0.5 using the frontal area of the vehicle as the characteristic area. As for the coefficient of aerodynamic resistance, it depends not only on the shape of the vehicle, but also on the attitude of the vehicle, ground clearance and other operational factors. Figure 3.4 shows the influence of the angle of attack on the coefficient of aerodynamic lift.

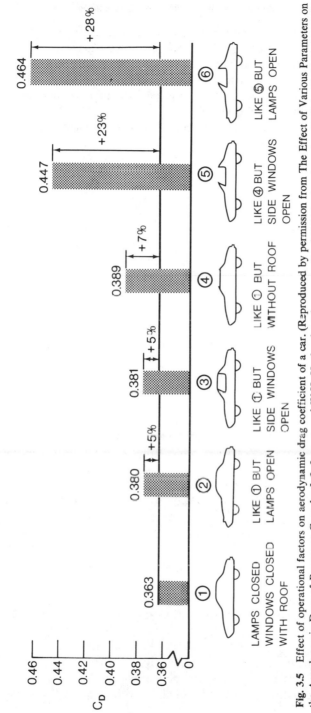

Fig. 3.5 Effect of operational factors on aerodynamic drag coefficient of a car. (Reproduced by permission from The Effect of Various Parameters on the Aerodynamic Drag of Passenger Cars, by L.J. Janssen and W.H. Hucho, in *Advances in Road Vehicle Aerodynamics*, BHRA Fluid Engineering, Cranfield, England, 1973.)

Aerodynamic pitching moment may also affect the behavior of a vehicle. This moment is the resultant of the moments of the aerodynamic resistance and aerodynamic lift about the center of gravity of the vehicle. It may cause significant load transfer from one axle to the other at moderate and higher speeds. Thus it would affect the performance as well as directional control and stability of the vehicle.

The aerodynamic pitching moment M_a is usually expressed by

$$M_a = \frac{\rho}{2} C_M A_f L_c V^2 \tag{3.21}$$

where C_M is the coefficient of aerodynamic pitching moment usually obtained from wind-tunnel testing and L_c is the characteristic length of the vehicle. The wheelbase or the overall length of the vehicle may be used as the characteristic length in Eq. 3.21. Most passenger cars have a value of C_M between 0.05 and 0.20 using the wheelbase as the characteristic length and the frontal area as the characteristic area.

3.3 VEHICLE POWER PLANT AND TRANSMISSION CHARACTERISTICS

As mentioned previously, there are two limiting factors to the performance of a road vehicle: one is the maximum tractive effort that the tire-ground contact can support; the other is the tractive effort that the engine torque with a given transmission can provide. The smaller of these two will determine the performance potential of the vehicle. At low gears with the engine throttle fully open, the tractive effort may be limited by the nature of tire-road adhesion. At higher gears, the tractive effort is usually determined by the engine and transmission characteristics. To predict the overall performance of a road vehicle, the engine and transmission characteristics must be taken into consideration. In this section, the general characteristics of vehicle power plants and transmissions will be presented.

3.3.1 Power Plant Characteristics

For vehicular applications, the ideal performance characteristics of a power plant are constant power output over the full speed range. Consequently, the engine output torque varies with speed hyperbolically as shown in Fig. 3.6. This will provide the vehicle with high tractive effort at low speeds where demands for acceleration, drawbar pull, or grade climbing capability are high. There are power plants that have power-torque-speed characteristics close to the ideal for vehicular applications, such as

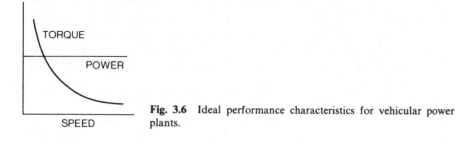

Fig. 3.6 Ideal performance characteristics for vehicular power plants.

series-wound electric motors and steam engines. Figure 3.7 shows the torque-speed characteristics of a series-wound d.c. motor. The internal combustion engine has less favorable performance characteristics and can be used only with a suitable transmission. Despite this short coming, it has found the widest application in automotive vehicles to date, because of its relatively high power to weight ratio, good fuel economy, low cost, and readiness for operation.

In addition to the continuous search for improving the efficiency, power-to-weight ratio, size, and economy of vehicular power plants, considerable emphasis has been placed on the control and reduction of undesirable exhaust emissions in recent years. Various technological options including further modification of the internal combustion engine are being investigated. In general, the two basic approaches to reducing undesirable emissions are to prevent them from forming and to remove them from the exhaust once formed. Improved combustion using fuel injection, stratified charge techniques and others can reduce undesirable emissions. Pollutants can also be removed after they have left the combustion chamber by injecting air into an exhaust manifold reactor for more complete oxidation, and by a catalytic converter in the direct-flame afterburner [3.5].

Alternatives to the internal combustion engine are also being studied [3.5]. They include gas turbine engines, Rankine-cycle external combustion

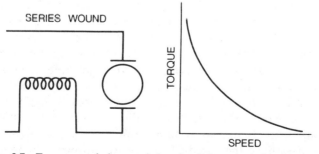

Fig. 3.7 Torque-speed characteristics of a series wound electric motor.

engines, noncondensing external combustion (Stirling-cycle) engines, electric propulsion systems, and hybrid power systems such as a combination of the internal combustion engine and electric propulsion. The gas turbine has several advantages as a vehicular power plant. It has a favorable power-to-weight ratio and can be used with a wide range of fuels. The carbon monoxide and hydrocarbon in the exhausts of a gas turbine are lower than those of an equivalent gasoline engine. There is evidence to suggest that nitrogen oxide emissions could also be reduced. The gas turbine is, however, not without drawbacks as an automotive power plant. The greatest disadvantage is its low efficiency and poor fuel economy under no load or partial load conditions that constitute a significant portion of the operation of automotive vehicles. The Rankine vapor-cycle external combustion engine has torque-speed characteristics close to the ideal. Coupling with its high overload capacity, the Rankine-cycle engine would eliminate the need for a transmission. It can use a wide range of hydrocarbon fuels and yet undesirable emissions including nitrogen oxides are very low. Among the disadvantages of this kind of power plant are the time required to put the engine into operation and relatively poor power-to-weight ratio. The Stirling-cycle engine utilizes alternate heating and cooling of the working medium, such as compressed helium and hydrogen gas, at constant volume to develop useful mechanical work. To date, it has rather poor power-to-weight ratio and is mechanically complex. The emission characteristics of the Stirling engine are, however, extremely good. It also has excellent performance characteristics at higher speeds, which suggest its potential value in a hybrid power system for automotive vehicles, where it could run continuously under optimum operating conditions [3.5].

Since the internal combustion engine is still the most commonly used power plant in automotive vehicles to date, it is appropriate to review the basic features of its characteristics that are essential to the prediction of vehicle performance. Representative characteristics of a gasoline engine and of a diesel engine are shown in Figs. 3.8 and 3.9, respectively. The internal combustion engine starts operating smoothly at a certain speed (the idle speed). Good combustion quality and maximum engine torque are reached at an intermediate engine speed. As speed increases further, the mean effective pressure decreases because of growing losses in the air-induction manifolds, and the engine torque declines. Power output, however, increases with the increase of speed up to the point of maximum power. Beyond this point, the engine torque decreases more rapidly with the increase of speed. This results in the decline of power output. In vehicular applications, the maximum permissible speed of the engine is usually set just above the speed of the maximum power output. Vehicles designed for traction, such as agricultural and industrial tractors, usually

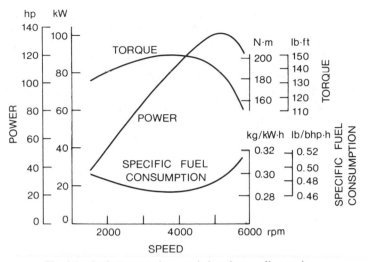

Fig. 3.8 Performance characteristics of a gasoline engine.

operate at much lower engine speeds, since the maximum torque and not power determines the limits to their tractive performance. To limit the maximum operating speed, engines for heavy-duty vehicles are often equipped with a governor.

It should be mentioned that engine-performance diagrams supplied by manufacturers usually represent the gross engine performance, which is the performance measured when all installations and accessories not essential

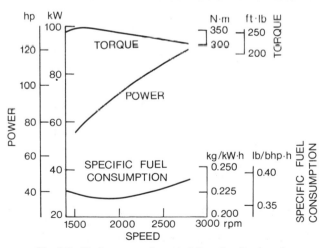

Fig. 3.9 Performance characteristics of a diesel engine.

to the operation are stripped off. The effective engine power available at the transmission input shaft is therefore reduced by the losses arising from accessories, such as the fan for the cooling system, the exhaust system, and the air cleaner. There are also auxiliaries such as electric generators that make a demand on engine power. In vehicle performance prediction, power consumption of all accessories over the full engine speed range should be evaluated and subtracted from the gross engine power to obtain the effective power available to the transmission input shaft.

Atmospheric conditions affect engine performance. To allow comparison of the performance of different engines on a common basis, standard atmospheric conditions are used. The most commonly used standard conditions are temperature $T_0 = 288.5°$ Kelvin (15.5°C or 60°F), barometric pressure $B_0 = 101.32$ kPa (76 cm or 29.92 in. Hg). For a gasoline engine, the relationship between engine power under standard atmospheric conditions P_0 and that under given atmospheric conditions P is given by [3.2]

$$P = \frac{P_0(B_a - B_v)}{B_0} \sqrt{\frac{T_0}{T}} \qquad (3.22)$$

where B_a and T are barometric pressure at the carburetor air inlet and ambient temperature (°K), respectively. B_v is vapor pressure, which represents the effect of air humidity. Usually it may be neglected except under

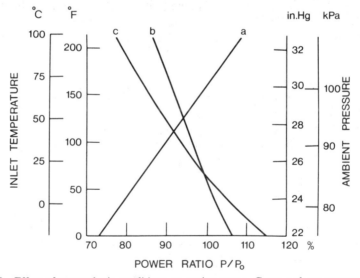

Fig. 3.10 Effect of atmospheric conditions on engine power. Curve *a* shows power ratio vs. ambient pressure; Curve *b* shows power ratio vs. intake temperature for gasoline engines; Curve *c* shows power ratio vs. intake temperature for diesel engines.

extreme conditions. For a diesel engine, the effects of atmospheric conditions on its performance characteristics are more complicated than those for a gasoline engine. As an approximation, the following relation may be used [3.2]

$$P = \frac{P_0(B_a - B_v)}{B_0} \frac{T_0}{T} \tag{3.23}$$

Atmospheric conditions can change engine performance considerably. The effects of engine inlet temperature and ambient pressure on engine performance are shown in Fig. 3.10 [3.2]. It can be seen that the higher the engine air inlet temperature and the lower the ambient pressure, the less the output power of the engine will be.

3.3.2   Transmission Characteristics

As mentioned previously, the power-torque-speed characteristics of the internal combustion engine are not suited for direct vehicle propulsion. A transmission, therefore, is required to provide the vehicle with the tractive effort-speed characteristics that will satisfy the load demands under various operating conditions. The term transmission includes all those systems employed for transmitting the engine power to the driven wheels or sprockets. There are three basic types of transmission for road vehicles: the manual gear transmission, the hydrodynamic (hydrokinetic) transmission, and the hydrostatic transmission.

Gear Transmissions

The manual gear transmission usually consists of a clutch, a gearbox, a propeller shaft, and a drive axle. As a general rule, the drive axle has a constant gear reduction ratio which is determined by the common practice requiring direct drive (nonreducing drive) in the gearbox in the highest gear. For vehicles requiring extremely high torque at low speeds, additional reduction gear (final drive) may be placed at the driven wheels. The gearbox provides a number of gear reduction ratios ranging from three to five for passenger cars and more for heavy commercial vehicles.

The gear ratio of the highest gear (i.e., the smallest ratio) is determined by the maximum vehicle speed required. The maximum tractive effort or the maximum gradability specified, on the other hand, determines the gear ratio of the lowest gear (i.e., the largest reduction ratio). Ratios between these two limits should be spaced in such a way that they will provide the tractive effort-speed characteristics as close to the ideal as possible, as shown in Fig. 3.11. In the first iteration, gear ratios between the highest

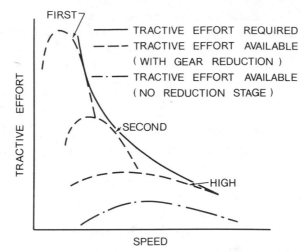

Fig. 3.11 Tractive effort-speed characteristics of a vehicle. (Reproduced by permission from reference 3.2.)

and the lowest gear may be selected using the geometric progression rule. The basis for this method for selecting gear ratios is to have the engine operating within the same speed range in each gear, as shown in Fig. 3.12. This would ensure that in each gear the fuel economy characteristics are similar.

For a four-speed gearbox, the following relationship can be established (see Fig. 3.12),

$$\frac{\xi_2}{\xi_1} = \frac{\xi_3}{\xi_2} = \frac{\xi_4}{\xi_3} = \frac{n_{e_2}}{n_{e_1}} = K_g$$

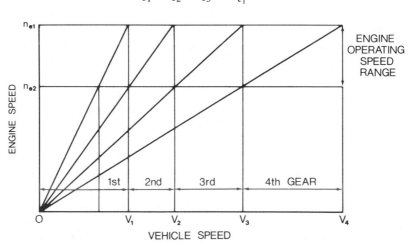

Fig. 3.12 Selection of gear ratios based on geometric progression rule.

and

$$K_g = \sqrt[3]{\frac{\xi_4}{\xi_1}} \qquad (3.24)$$

where ξ_1, ξ_2, ξ_3, and ξ_4 are the gear ratios of the first, second, third, and fourth gear, respectively. In a more general case, if the ratio of the highest gear ξ_n and that of the lowest gear ξ_1 have been determined, and the number of speeds of the gearbox n_g is known, the factor K_g can be determined by

$$K_g = \left(\frac{\xi_n}{\xi_1}\right)^{1/(n_g-1)} \qquad (3.25)$$

and

$$\xi_n = K_g \xi_{n-1}$$

For commercial vehicles, the gear ratios in the gearbox are often arranged in geometric progression. Table 3.2 gives the gear ratios used in an Allison gearbox designed for heavy-duty vehicles. It can be seen that the ratios of this gearbox are arranged in exact geometric progression.

Table 3.2

Allison Transmission Model HT70		Calculated Gear Ratios Based on the
Gear	Gear Ratios	Geometric Progression Rule[a]
1	3.0	3.0
2	2.28	2.28
3	1.73	1.73
4	1.31	1.31
5	1.00	1.00
6	0.76	0.76

[a]In the calculations, $\xi_1 = 3.0$, $\xi_6 = 0.76$, $n_g = 6$, and $K_g = \sqrt[5]{0.76/3.0} = 0.76$

For passenger cars, to suit the changing traffic conditions, the step between the ratios of the upper two gears is often closer than that based on geometric progression. This, in turn, affects the selection of the ratios of the lower gears.

In mechanical gear transmissions, there are losses due to friction between gear teeth and in the bearings, and oil churning. The following are representative values of the mechanical efficiency of various components:

clutch: 99%

each pair of gears: 95–97%

bearings and joints: 98–99%

Total mechanical efficiency of the transmission between the engine output shaft and driven wheels or sprockets is the product of the efficiencies of all the components in the driveline. As a first approximation, the following average values of overall mechanical efficiency of a manual gear-shift transmission may be used [3.2],

direct gear: 90%

other gears: 85%

transmission with very high reduction ratio: 75–80%.

For a vehicle with a gear transmission, the tractive effort of the vehicle is given by

$$F = \frac{M_e \xi_0 \eta_t}{r} \qquad (3.26)$$

Where M_e is the engine output torque, ξ_0 is overall reduction ratio of the transmission, η_t is overall transmission efficiency, and r is the radius of the tire (or sprocket). It is important to note that the maximum tractive effort that the tire-ground contact can support usually determines the traction capability of the vehicle at low gears.

The relationship between vehicle speed and engine speed is given by

$$V = \frac{n_e r}{\xi_0}(1 - i) \qquad (3.27)$$

where n_e is the engine speed and i is the slip of the vehicle running gear. For a road vehicle, the slip is usually assumed to be 2–5% under normal operating conditions. Figure 3.13 shows the variation of the tractive effort with speed for a passenger car equipped with a three-speed manual gear transmission [3.2].

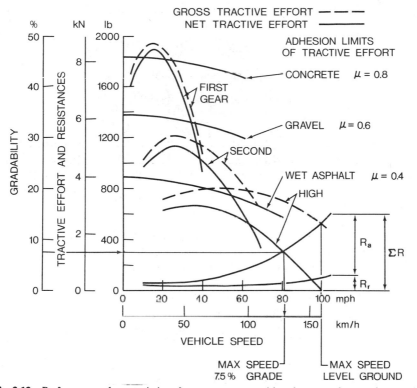

Fig. 3.13 Performance characteristics of a passenger car with a three-speed manual transmission. (Reproduced by permission from reference 3.2.)

Hydrodynamic Transmissions

Hydrodynamic transmissions are used widely in passenger cars in North America. They usually comprise a torque converter and an automatic gear box. The torque converter consists of at least three rotary elements known as the pump (impeller), the turbine, and the reactor, as shown in Fig. 3.14. The pump is connected with the engine shaft and the turbine connected with the output shaft of the converter, which in turn is coupled with the input shaft of a multispeed gearbox. The reactor is coupled to an external casing to provide a reaction on the fluid circulating in the converter. The function of the reactor is to enable the turbine to develop an output torque higher than the input torque of the converter, thus to obtain a torque multiplication. The reactor is usually mounted on a free wheel (one-way clutch) so that when the starting period has been completed and the turbine speed is approaching that of the pump, the reactor is in free

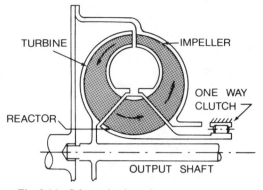

Fig. 3.14 Schematic view of a torque converter.

rotation. At this point, the converter operates as a fluid coupling with a ratio of output torque to input torque equal to 1.0 [3.6].

The major advantages of the hydrodynamic transmission may be summarized as follows:

1 When properly matched, it will not stall the engine.
2 It provides a flexible coupling between the engine and the driven wheels (or sprockets).
3 Together with a suitably selected multispeed gearbox, it provides torque-speed characteristics that approach the ideal.

The performance characteristics of a torque converter are usually described in terms of the following four parameters:

$$\text{Speed ratio } C_{sr} = \text{output speed/input speed}$$

$$\text{Torque ratio } C_{tr} = \text{output torque/input torque}$$

$$\text{Efficiency } \eta_c = \frac{\text{output speed} \times \text{output torque}}{\text{input speed} \times \text{input torque}}$$

$$= C_{sr} C_{tr}$$

$$\text{Capacity factor (size factor) } K_{tc} = \frac{\text{speed}}{\sqrt{\text{torque}}}$$

The capacity factor is an indication of the ability of the converter to absorb or to transmit torque, which is proportional to the square of rotating speed.

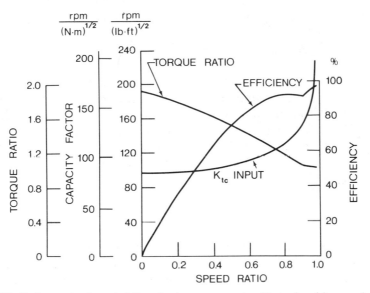

Fig. 3.15 Performance characteristics of a torque converter. (Reproduced by permission of the Society of Automotive Engineers from reference 3.7.)

Representative performance characteristics of the torque converter are shown in Fig. 3.15, in which torque ratio, efficiency, and input capacity factor, which is the ratio of input speed to the square root of input torque, are plotted against speed ratio [3.7]. Torque ratio of the converter reaches a maximum at stall condition where the speed ratio is zero. The torque ratio decreases as the speed ratio increases, and the converter eventually acts as a hydraulic coupling with torque ratio of 1.0. At this point, a small difference between the input and the output speed remains because of the slip between the pump (impeller) and the turbine. The efficiency of the converter is zero at stall condition and increases with the increase of the speed ratio. It reaches a maximum when the converter acts as a fluid coupling. The input capacity factor is an important parameter defining the operating conditions of the torque converter and governing the matching between the converter and the engine. The input capacity factor of the converter has a minimum value at stall condition and increases with the increase of the speed ratio.

Since the converter is driven by the engine, to determine the actual operating conditions of the converter, the engine operating point has to be specified. To characterize the engine operating conditions for purposes of determining the combined performance of the engine and the converter, an engine capacity factor K_e is introduced and is defined as

$$K_e = \frac{n_e}{\sqrt{M_e}}$$

where n_e and M_e are engine speed and torque, respectively. The variation of the capacity factor with speed for a particular engine is shown in Fig. 3.16 [3.7]. To achieve proper matching, the engine and the converter should have a similar range of capacity factor.

As mentioned above, the engine shaft is usually connected with the input shaft of the converter; therefore,

$$K_e = K_{tc}$$

The matching procedure begins with specifying the engine speed and engine torque. Knowing the engine operating point, one can determine the engine capacity factor K_e (Fig. 3.16). Since $K_e = K_{tc}$, the input capacity factor of the converter corresponding to the specific engine operating point is then known. For a particular value of the input capacity factor of the converter K_{tc}, the converter speed ratio and torque ratio can be determined from the converter performance characteristics, as shown in Fig. 3.15. The

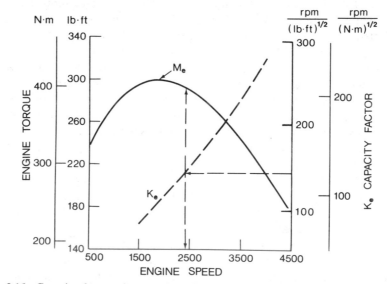

Fig. 3.16 Capacity factor of an engine. (Reproduced by permission of the Society of Automotive Engineers from reference 3.7.)

output torque and output speed of the converter are then given by

$$M_{tc} = M_e C_{tr} \tag{3.28}$$

and

$$n_{tc} = n_e C_{sr} \tag{3.29}$$

where M_{tc} and n_{tc} are output torque and output speed of the converter, respectively.

With the reduction ratios of the gearbox and the driven axle known, the tractive effort and speed of the vehicle can be calculated,

$$H = \frac{M_{tc}\xi_0\eta_t}{r} = \frac{M_e C_{tr}\xi_0\eta_t}{r} \tag{3.30}$$

and

$$V = \frac{n_{tc}r}{\xi_0}(1-i) = \frac{n_e C_{sr}r}{\xi_0}(1-i) \tag{3.31}$$

Figure 3.17 shows the variation of the tractive effort with speed for a passenger car equipped with a torque converter and a three-speed gearbox [3.7].

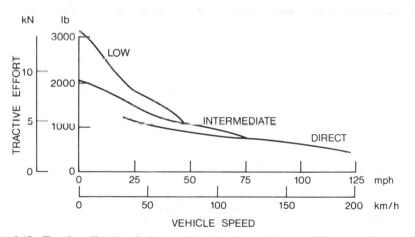

Fig. 3.17 Tractive effort-speed characteristics of a passenger car with automatic transmission. (Reproduced by permission of the Society of Automotive Engineers from reference 3.7.)

Example 3.1

An engine with torque-speed characteristics as shown in Fig. 3.16 is coupled with a torque converter with characteristics as shown in Fig. 3.15. Determine the output speed and output torque of the torque converter when the engine is operating at 2450 rpm with engine output torque of 393 N·m (290 lb·ft)

Solution. The engine capacity factor K_e

$$K_e = \frac{n_e}{\sqrt{M_e}} = \frac{2450}{\sqrt{393}} = 123 \text{ rpm}/(\text{N·m})^{\frac{1}{2}}$$

Since the capacity factor K_e is equal to that of the torque converter K_{tc}

$$K_{tc} = 123 \text{ rpm}/(\text{N·m})^{\frac{1}{2}}$$

From Fig. 3.15, when $K_{tc} = 123$, the speed ratio $C_{sr} = 0.9$ and the torque ratio $C_{tr} = 1.02$. Output speed of the torque converter n_{tc} is

$$n_{tc} = 0.9 \times 2450 = 2205 \text{ rpm}$$

Output torque of the torque converter M_{tc} is

$$M_{tc} = 393 \times 1.02 = 400 \text{ N·m (295 lb·ft)}$$

Efficiency of the torque converter under this operating condition is

$$\eta_c = 0.9 \times 1.02 = 91.8\%$$

Hydrostatic Transmissions

Hydrostatic transmissions are used in some road vehicles as well as off-road vehicles, particularly those of a specialized nature, and have enjoyed a certain degree of success [3.8]. Hydrostatic drives may be divided into three categories [3.9].

Constant Displacement Pump with Fixed Displacement Motor

This type of hydrostatic drive usually consists of a gear or vane pump driving a gear, vane, or piston motor through control valves. The maximum working pressure of the fluid in this type of system is usually about 20,685 kPa (3000 psi). This simple hydrostatic transmission has been quite

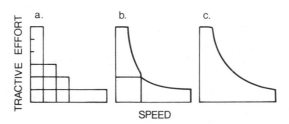

Fig. 3.18 Tractive effort-speed characteristics of a vehicle equipped with various types of hydrostatic transmission. (Reproduced by permission of the Council of the Institution of Mechanical Engineers from reference 3.9.)

widely used in construction machinery such as excavators to drive the tracks. Each gear pump drives its own hydraulic motor, which allows the tracks to be operated individually, thus providing a mechanism for forward and reverse motions as well as for steering. The tractive effort-speed characteristics of this system with a multispeed gearbox are illustrated in Fig. 3.18(a).

Variable Displacement Pump with Fixed Displacement Motor

This type of hydrostatic drive has certain advantages over the fixed displacement pump and motor system. Variable displacement pumps are piston pumps that permit higher pressure to be used. They also permit stepless speed control from zero to maximum. Closed loop fluid circuits can be employed to provide both forward and reverse motions and braking functions. To extend the tractive effort and vehicle speed range, a gear box is frequently employed. The performance characteristics of this type of system coupled with a two-speed gearbox are shown in Fig. 3.18(b).

Variable Displacement Pump and Motor

In this system the displacement of both the pump and the motor can be varied continuously. The performance characteristics of the vehicle are approaching the ideal ones as shown in Fig. 3.18(c). Although the performance and control of this type of transmission are beyond question, the problems of cost, reliability, maintenance, and service remain to be solved.

In comparison to hydrodynamic transmissions, hydrostatic drives can provide a more positive speed control and flexibility in vehicle layout. Figure 3.19 shows the efficiencies of a hydrostatic drive and a comparable hydrodynamic transmission (torque converter with a two-speed gear box) [3.8]. It appears that there is relatively little difference between the two

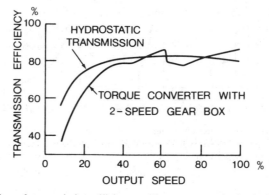

Fig. 3.19 Variation of transmission efficiency with output speed of a hydrodynamic transmission and a hydrostatic transmission. (Reproduced by permission of the Council of the Institution of Mechanical Engineers from reference 3.8.)

types of transmission from the point of view of efficiency over the operating range. However, for vehicles designed for traction spending much time operating with a high tractive effort at low speeds, the hydrostatic transmission seems to be more suitable. Figure 3.20 shows the fuel consumption and power output of a particular vehicle equipped with the two types of transmission [3.8]. It is apparent that the hydrostatic transmission permits full power to be developed by the engine once the output speed of the transmission is high enough. Thus a faster rate of work can be

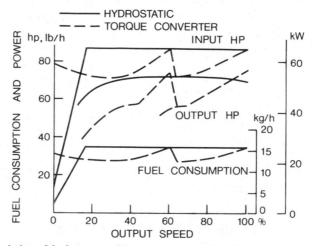

Fig. 3.20 Variation of fuel consumption and output power with output speed of a hydrodynamic transmission and a hydrostatic transmission. (Reproduced by permission of the Council of the Institution of Mechanical Engineers from reference 3.8.)

achieved with the hydrostatic drive. Tests of off-road vehicles equipped with hydrostatic transmission have shown improved productivity as compared with those equipped with mechanical gear transmission, even though the mechanical gear transmission has higher efficiency [3.8].

3.4 PREDICTION OF VEHICLE PERFORMANCE

The relationship between tractive effort and vehicle speed discussed in the previous section provides the basis for predicting the performance characteristics of a road vehicle. The passenger car with characteristics shown in Fig. 3.13 will be used as an example to illustrate the procedure for predicting acceleration characteristics and gradability.

To fully describe the performance of a vehicle, in addition to the relationship between tractive effort and vehicle speed, the resistance of the vehicle as a function of speed must also be determined. On level ground without drawbar load, the major resisting forces are rolling resistance R_r and aerodynamic resistance R_a, and they can be predicted using methods discussed previously. The variation of R_r and R_a with speed for the passenger car is shown in Fig. 3.13. The difference between the tractive effort and the resultant resisting force is the net thrust F_{net} available for accelerating the vehicle or for overcoming grade resistance. The intersection of the vehicle thrust and the resistance curves determines the maximum speed that the vehicle can achieve as shown in Fig. 3.13. It should be noted that the nature of tire-road adhesion imposes a fundamental limit on the maximum tractive effort. The maximum tractive efforts of the passenger car that the tire-ground contact can support on various surfaces including concrete, gravel, and wet asphalt are shown in the figure. They are determined using the method discussed in Section 3.1. It can be seen, for instance, that with the second gear engaged, the maximum tractive effort as determined by the engine torque and transmission characteristics is about 5.5 kN (1240 lb), whereas the maximum tractive effort on wet asphalt that the tire-road contact can support is only 4 kN (900 lb). This indicates that in fact the maximum tractive effort that the car can develop with the second gear engaged is 4 kN. Figure 3.13 also shows that with the second gear engaged, when the vehicle speed is below 112 km/h (70 mph), the tractive effort of the vehicle on wet asphalt is limited by the tire-road adhesion and not by the engine torque.

3.4.1 Acceleration Time and Distance

Having determined the net thrust of the vehicle as a function of speed, one can then compute the acceleration of the vehicle using Newton's second law. It should be noted, however, that the translational motion of the vehicle is coupled to the rotational motion of the components connected with the wheels including the engine and the driveline. Any change of translational speed of the vehicle will therefore be accompanied by the corresponding change of the rotational speed of the components coupled with the wheels. To take into account the effect of the inertia of the rotating parts on vehicle acceleration characteristics, a mass factor γ_m is introduced into the following equation for calculating vehicle acceleration a [3.2]

$$F - \Sigma R = F_{net} = \gamma_m ma \qquad (3.32)$$

where m is the vehicle mass.

γ_m can be determined from the moments of inertia of the rotating parts by

$$\gamma_m = 1 + \frac{\Sigma I_w}{mr^2} + \frac{\Sigma I \xi^2}{mr^2} \qquad (3.33)$$

where I_w is the mass moment of inertia of the wheels, I is the mass moment of inertia of the rotating components connected with the driveline having gear ratio ξ with respect to the driven wheel, and r is the rolling radius of the wheel. For passenger cars, the mass factor γ_m may be calculated using the following empirical relation [3.2]:

$$\gamma_m = 1.04 + 0.0025\xi_0^2 \qquad (3.34)$$

The first term on the right-hand side of the above equation represents the contribution of the rotating inertia of the wheels, while the second term represents the contribution of the inertia of the components rotating at the equivalent engine speed with overall gear reduction ratio ξ_0 with respect to the driven wheel.

In the evaluation of vehicle acceleration characteristics, time-speed and time-distance relationships are of prime interest. These relationships can be derived using the equation of motion of the vehicle in a differential form.

$$\gamma_m m \frac{dV}{dt} = F - \Sigma R = F_{net}$$

and

$$dt = \frac{\gamma_m m dV}{F_{net}} \qquad (3.35)$$

As can be seen from Fig. 3.13, the net tractive effort F_{net} available for accelerating the vehicle is a function of vehicle speed

$$F_{net} = f(V) \tag{3.36}$$

This makes the expression relating time and speed of the following form not easily integrable by analytic methods,

$$t = \gamma_m m \int_{V_1}^{V_2} \frac{dV}{f(V)} \tag{3.37}$$

To predict the time required to accelerate the vehicle from speed V_1 to V_2, the integration is best handled by numerical methods using a digital computer, although graphic methods of integration can also offer solutions of sufficient accuracy [3.2].

The distance S that the vehicle travels during an acceleration period from speed V_1 to V_2 can be calculated by integrating the following equation:

$$S = \int_{V_1}^{V_2} \frac{V \, dV}{F_{net}/\gamma_m m} = \gamma_m m \int_{V_1}^{V_2} \frac{V \, dV}{f(V)} \tag{3.38}$$

In the evaluation of the minimum acceleration time and distance, the engine is usually assumed to be operating at wide open throttle. It should be noted that a certain amount of time is required for gear changing during acceleration. For manual transmissions, gear changing causes a delay of 1–2s; for automatic transmissions, the delay is typically 0.5–1s. To obtain a more accurate estimate of acceleration time and distance, this delay should be taken into consideration.

Figure 3.21 shows the acceleration time-distance curve and the acceleration time-speed curve for a passenger car with a gross weight of 17.79 kN (4000 lb) and with thrust-speed characteristics as shown in Fig. 3.13 [3.2]. The kinks in the time-speed curve represent the delays caused by gear changing.

Example 3.2

A passenger car weighs 21.24 kN (4775 lb) including the four road wheels. Each of the wheels has a rolling radius of 33 cm (13 in.) and radius of gyration of 25.4 cm (10 in.), and weighs 244.6N (55 lb). The engine develops a torque of 325 N·m (240 lb·ft) at 3500 rpm. The equivalent mass of moment of inerita of the parts rotating at engine speed is 0.733 kg·m² (0.54 slug·ft²). The transmission efficiency is 85% and the total

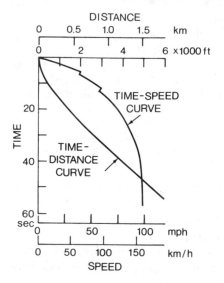

Fig. 3.21 Acceleration characteristics of a passenger car with a three-speed manual transmission. (Reproduced by permission from reference 3.2.)

reduction ratio of the driveline in the third gear is 4.28 to 1. The vehicle has a frontal area of 1.86 m² (20 ft²) and the aerodynamic drag coefficient is 0.38. The coefficient of rolling resistance is 0.02. Determine the acceleration of the vehicle on level road under these conditions.

Solution.

A　The mass factor γ_m for the vehicle in the third gear can be calculated using Eq. 3.33.

$$\gamma_m = 1 + \frac{\Sigma I_w + \Sigma I \xi^2}{mr^2}$$

$$= 1 + \frac{4 \times 1.61 + 0.733 \times 4.28^2}{2170 \times 0.33^2} = 1.084$$

B　The thrust of the vehicle F is determined using Eq. 3.26.

$$F = \frac{M_e \xi_0 \eta_t}{r} = 3585 \text{ N (806 lb)}$$

C　The vehicle speed V can be calculated using Eq. 3.27.

$$V = \frac{n_e r}{\xi_0}(1 - i)$$

Assume that $i = 3\%$, the vehicle speed V is

$$V = 98.7 \text{ km/h } (61.3 \text{ mph})$$

D The total resistance of the vehicle is the sum of the aerodynamic resistance R_a and rolling resistance R_r

$$\Sigma R = R_a + R_r = 755 \text{ N } (170 \text{ lb})$$

E The acceleration a of the vehicle can be determined using Eq. 3.32.

$$a = \frac{F - \Sigma R}{\gamma_m m} = 1.2 \text{ m/s}^2 \ (3.95 \text{ ft/s}^2)$$

3.4.2 Gradability

Gradability is usually defined as the maximum grade a vehicle can negotiate at a given speed (no acceleration). This parameter is primarily intended for the evaluation of the performance of heavy highway vehicles and off-road vehicles. On a slope at a constant speed, the tractive effort has to overcome grade resistance, rolling resistance and aerodynamic resistance

$$F = W \sin \theta_s + R_r + R_a$$

For relatively small value of θ_s, $\tan \theta_s \simeq \sin \theta_s$. Therefore the grade resistance may be approximated by $W \tan \theta_s$ or WG, where G is the grade in percent.

The maximum grade a vehicle can negotiate at a constant speed therefore is determined by the net tractive effort available at that speed

$$G = \frac{1}{W}(F - R_r - R_a) = \frac{F_{net}}{W} \tag{3.39}$$

Use can be made of the performance curves of a vehicle, such as those shown in Fig. 3.13, to determine the speed obtainable on each particular grade. For instance, the grade resistance of the passenger car with a weight of 17.79 kN (4000 lb) on a grade of 7.5% is 1.34 kN (300 lb). A horizontal line representing this grade resistance can be drawn on the diagram, which intersects the net tractive effort curve at a speed of 133 km/h (82 mph). This indicates that for the passenger car under consideration, the maximum speed obtainable at a grade of 7.5% is 133 km/h (82 mph). It should be noted that the limits of tractive effort set by the nature of tire-road adhesion usually determine the maximum gradability of the vehicle. For instance, it can be seen from Fig. 3.13 that the maximum grade the vehicle can negotiate on a gravel surface with $\mu = 0.6$ will be approximately 35%.

3.5   OPERATING FUEL ECONOMY

The operating fuel economy of a road vehicle depends on a number of factors including the fuel consumption characteristics of the engine, gear ratios of the transmission, and operating conditions of the vehicle. Typical fuel economy characteristics of a gasoline and a diesel engine are shown in Figs. 3.22 and 3.23, respectively [3.6]. They usually have reduced fuel economy at low throttle or low torque setting. Operation at low engine speed and high torque is always more economical than at higher speed and lower torque settings with the same power output. For instance, it can be seen from Fig. 3.22 that for the engine to develop 22 kW (30 hp) of power,

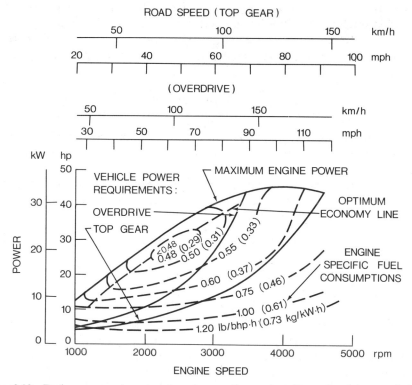

Fig. 3.22 Fuel economy characteristics of a gasoline engine. (Reproduced by permission from reference 3.6.)

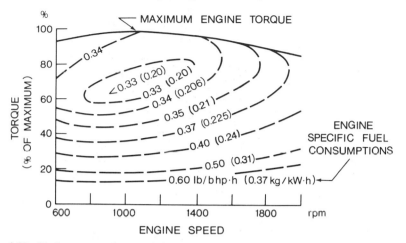

Fig. 3.23 Fuel economy characteristics of a diesel engine. (Reproduced by permission from reference 3.6.)

it can run at a speed of 2500 rpm or 4000 rpm. At 2500 rpm, the specific fuel consumption is below 0.29 kg/kW·h (0.48 lb/hp·h), whereas at 4000 rpm, it is 0.37 kg/kW·h (0.60 lb/hp·h). By connecting the engine operating points with the lowest specific fuel consumption for each power setting, an optimum fuel economy line (maximum efficiency line) of the engine can be drawn as shown in Fig. 3.22 [3.6].

For a given power requirement at a specific vehicle speed, the engine operating point is determined by the gear ratio of the transmission. Ideally, the gear ratio of the transmission can be continuously adjusted to any desired values so that the engine operating point will follow the optimum fuel economy line for all power settings. This requirement has stimulated the development of a variety of variable ratio drives including frictional drives, hydrodynamic drives, hydrostatic drives, and hydromechanical variable drives.

To further illustrate the effect of gear ratios of the transmission on the operating fuel economy of road vehicles, let us consider the overdrive gear of a passenger car as an example. As shown in Fig. 3.24, the gear ratio of the top gear in the transmission is usually selected in such a way that the curve representing the power available at the driven wheels meets the resultant resistance curve at a speed slightly higher than that of maximum power [3.6]. This typical choice of gear ratio provides the vehicle with sufficient reserve for acceleration and hill climbing. The vehicle power requirements at various vehicle speeds in top gear can be plotted in the engine performance diagram as shown in Fig. 3.22. It will be noted that a

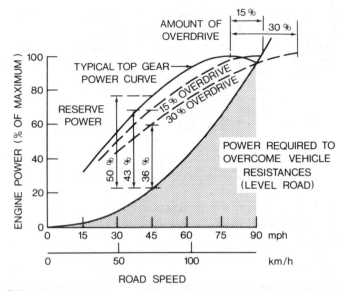

Fig. 3.24 Effect of overdrive gear on vehicle performance. (Reproduced by permission from reference 3.6.)

maximum vehicle speed of 145 km/h (90 mph) is equivalent to engine speed of 4500 rpm in top gear in the example shown, and that the power required to overcome the resultant resistance at that speed is about 32.8 kW (44 hp). When the engine is running at 4500 rpm and developing 32.8 kW (44 hp), the specific fuel consumption will be 0.40 kg/kW·h (0.65 lb/hp·h) as shown in Fig. 3.22. Thus in 1 hr at 145 km/h (90 mph) the vehicle will consume 13.1 kg (28.8 lb) of fuel in top gear.

If, however, an overdrive gear with gear ratio 30% less than that of the top gear is introduced into the transmission, the vehicle can still achieve a maximum speed of 145 km/h (90 mph) as shown in Fig. 3.24, but with reduced reserve for acceleration over the entire speed range. Owing to the lower gear ratio that an overdrive gear introduces, for the same vehicle speed the engine speed will be lower than that when using top gear as shown in Fig. 3.22. For instance, at a speed of 145 km/h (90 mph), with the overdrive gear the engine is running at 3400 rpm as compared with 4500 rpm when using top gear. Accordingly, using the overdrive gear the engine specific fuel consumption is reduced to 0.32 kg/kW·h (0.53 lb/hp·h) as compared with 0.40 kg/kW·h (0.65 lb/hp·h) when using top gear. Thus with the overdive gear, the vehicle will consume only 10.5 kg (23.1 lb) of fuel per hour at a speed of 145 km/h (90 mph). This represents a saving of fuel of approximately 20%. Although this example is for a particular engine and vehicle, most cars will show similar gains with an overdrive. In summary, the improvement in fuel economy obtained by an overdrive gear is an exploitation of the fact that for the same power output the internal combustion engine is always more economical to operate at low speed and high torque than at higher speed and lower torque settings.

3.6 BRAKING PERFORMANCE

Braking performance of motor vehicles is undoubtedly one of the most important characteristics that affect vehicle safety. With increasing emphasis on traffic safety in recent years, intensive efforts have been directed toward improving the braking performance. Safety standards that specify performance requirements of various types of brake system have been introduced in many countries.

In this section, the method of approach to the analysis of braking performance of motor vehicles will be presented. Criteria for the evaluation of braking capability and approaches to improving braking performance will be discussed.

3.6.1 Braking Characteristics of a Two-Axle Vehicle

The major external forces acting on a decelerating two-axle vehicle are shown in Fig. 3.25. The braking force F_b originating from the brake system and developed on the tire-road interface is the primary retarding force. When the braking force is below the limit of tire-road adhesion, the

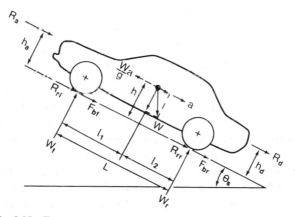

Fig. 3.25 Forces acting on a two-axle vehicle during braking.

braking force F_b is given by

$$F_b = \frac{M_b - \Sigma I \alpha_{an}}{r} \tag{3.40}$$

where M_b is the applied brake torque, I is the rotating inertia being decelerated, α_{an} is the corresponding angular deceleration, and r is the rolling radius of the tire.

In addition to the braking force, the rolling resistance of tires, aerodynamic resistance, transmission resistance, and grade resistance (when travelling on a slope) also affect vehicle motion during braking. Thus the resultant retarding force F_{res} can be expressed by

$$F_{res} = F_b + f_r W \cos\theta_s + R_a \pm W \sin\theta_s + R_t \tag{3.41}$$

where f_r is the rolling resistance coefficient, W is the vehicle weight, θ_s is the angle of the slope with the horizontal, R_a is the aerodynamic resistance, and R_t is the transmission resistance. When the vehicle is moving uphill, the positive sign for the term $W \sin\theta_s$ should be used. On a downhill grade, the negative sign should, however, be used. Normally, the magnitude of the transmission resistance is small and can be neglected in braking performance calculations.

During braking, there is load transfer from the rear axle to the front axle. By considering the equilibrium of moments about the front and rear tire-ground contact points, the normal loads on the front and rear axles, W_f and W_r, can be expressed as

$$W_f = \frac{1}{L}\left[Wl_2 + h\left(\frac{W}{g}a - R_a \pm W\sin\theta_s\right) \right] \tag{3.42}$$

and

$$W_r = \frac{1}{L}\left[Wl_1 - h\left(\frac{W}{g}a - R_a \pm W\sin\theta_s\right) \right] \tag{3.43}$$

where a is the deceleration. When the vehicle is moving uphill, the negative sign for the term $W\sin\theta_s$ should be used. In the above expression, it is assumed that the aerodynamic resistance is applied at the center of gravity of the vehicle and that there is no drawbar load.

By considering the force equilibrium in the longitudinal direction, the following relationship can be established

$$F_b + f_r W = F_{bf} + F_{br} + f_r W = \frac{W}{g}a - R_a \pm W\sin\theta_s \tag{3.44}$$

where F_{bf} and F_{br} are the braking forces of the front and rear axles, respectively.

Substituting Eq. 3.44 into Eqs. 3.42 and 3.43, the normal loads on the axles become

$$W_f = \frac{1}{L} \left[Wl_2 + h(F_b + f_r W) \right] \tag{3.45}$$

and

$$W_r = \frac{1}{L} \left[Wl_1 - h(F_b + f_r W) \right] \tag{3.46}$$

The maximum braking force that the tire-ground contact can support is determined by the normal load and the coefficient of road adhesion. With four-wheel brakes, the maximum braking forces on the front and rear axles are given by (assuming the maximum braking force of the vehicle $F_{bmax} = \mu W$),

$$F_{bf\,max} = \mu W_f = \frac{\mu W \left[l_2 + h(\mu + f_r) \right]}{L} \tag{3.47}$$

$$F_{br\,max} = \mu W_r = \frac{\mu W \left[l_1 - h(\mu + f_r) \right]}{L} \tag{3.48}$$

where μ is the coefficient of road adhesion. It should be noted that when the braking forces reach the values determined by Eqs. 3.47 and 3.48, tires are at the point of impending skid. Any variation would cause the tires to lock up.

It should be pointed out that the distribution of braking forces between the front and rear axles is a function of the design of brake system when no wheels are locked. For conventional brake systems, the distribution of braking forces is primarily dependent on the hydraulic (or pneumatic) pressures and brake cylinder (or chamber) areas in the front and rear brakes. From Eqs. 3.47 and 3.48 it can be seen that only when the distribution of braking forces between the front and rear axles is in exactly the same proportion as that of normal loads on the front and rear axles, will the maximum braking forces of the front and rear tires be developed at the same time.

$$\frac{K_{bf}}{K_{br}} = \frac{F_{bf\,max}}{F_{br\,max}} = \frac{l_2 + h(\mu + f_r)}{l_1 - h(\mu + f_r)} \tag{3.49}$$

where K_{bf} and K_{br} are the proportions of the total braking force on the front and rear axles, respectively, and are determined by the brake system design.

For instance, for a light truck with 68% of the static load on the rear axle ($l_2/L=0.32$, $l_1/L=0.68$), $h/L=0.18$, $\mu=0.85$ and $f_r=0.01$, the maximum braking forces of the front and rear tires that the tire-ground contact can support will be developed at the same time, only if the braking force distribution between the front and rear brakes satisfies the following requirement

$$\frac{K_{bf}}{K_{br}} = \frac{0.32+0.18(0.85+0.01)}{0.68-0.18(0.85+0.01)} = \frac{47}{53}$$

In other words, 47% of the total braking force must be placed on the front axle and 53% on the rear axle to achieve the optimum utilization of the potential braking capability of the vehicle. The braking force distribution that can ensure the maximum braking forces of the front and rear tires developed at the same time is referred to as the ideal braking force distribution. If the braking force distribution is not ideal, then either the front or the rear tires will lock up first.

When the rear wheels lock up first, the vehicle will lose directional stability [3.10]. This can be visualized with the aid of Fig. 3.26. The figure shows the top view of a two-axle vehicle acted upon by the braking force and the inertia force. When the rear tires lock, the capability of the rear tires to resist lateral force is reduced to zero. If some slight lateral movement of the rear tires is initiated by side wind, road camber, or centrigugal force, a yawing moment due to the inertia force about the yaw center of the front axle will be developed. As the yaw motion progresses, the moment arm of the inertia force increases, resulting in an increase in yaw acceleration. As the rear end of the vehicle swings around 90°, the

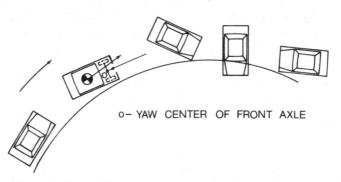

o— YAW CENTER OF FRONT AXLE

Fig. 3.26 Loss of directional stability due to lockup of rear tires.

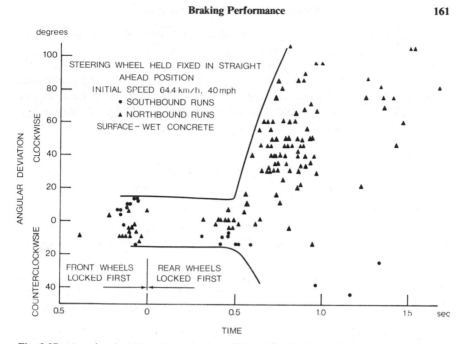

Fig. 3.27 Angular deviation of a car when all four wheels do not lock at the same instant. (Reproduced by permission of the Society of Automotive Engineers from reference 3.11.)

moment arm gradually decreases and eventually the vehicle rotates 180° with the rear end leading the front end. Figure 3.27 shows the measured angular deviation of a vehicle when the front and rear wheels do not lock at the same instant [3.11].

The lockup of front tires will cause a loss of directional control, and the driver will no longer be able to exercise effective steering. It should be pointed out, however, that front tires lockup does not cause directional instability. This is because whenever lateral movement of the front tires occurs, a self-correcting moment due to the inertia force of the vehicle about the yaw center of the rear axle will be developed. Consequently, it tends to bring the vehicle back to a straight line path.

Loss of steering control may be detected more readily by the driver and control may be regained by release or partial release of the brakes. Contrary to the case of front wheel lockup, when rear tires lock and the angular deviation of the vehicle exceeds a certain level, control cannot be regained even by complete release of the brakes and by the most skilful driving. This suggests that rear wheel lockup is a more critical situation, particularly on a road surface with low coefficient of adhesion. Since on slippery surfaces, the value of the braking force is low, the kinetic energy of the vehicle will dissipate at a slow rate and the vehicle will experience a serious loss of directional stability over a considerable distance. Because of the importance of the sequency of locking of the tires to vehicle behavior during braking, it is necessary to determine quantitatively the conditions under which the rear tires will lock first. To facilitate the understanding of the problem, only the braking force and rolling resistance will be considered in the following analysis. Thus

$$F_b + f_r W = F_{bf} + F_{br} + f_r W = \frac{W}{g} a \tag{3.50}$$

Substituting Eq. 3.50 into Eqs. 3.45 and 3.46 yields

$$W_f = \frac{W}{L} \left(l_2 + \frac{a}{g} h \right) \tag{3.51}$$

$$W_r = \frac{W}{L} \left(l_1 - \frac{a}{g} h \right) \tag{3.52}$$

The braking forces of the front and rear axles as determined by the brake system design are primarily related to the front and rear brake cylinder (or chamber) areas and are expressed by

$$F_{bf} = K_{bf} F_b = K_{bf} W \left(\frac{a}{g} - f_r \right) \tag{3.53}$$

and

$$F_{br} = K_{br} F_b = (1 - K_{bf}) F_b = (1 - K_{bf}) W \left(\frac{a}{g} - f_r \right) \tag{3.54}$$

The front tires approach impending lockup when

$$F_{bf} = \mu W_f \tag{3.55}$$

Substituting Eqs. 3.51 and 3.53 into Eq. 3.55 yields

$$K_{bf} W \left(\frac{a}{g} - f_r \right) = \mu W \left(\frac{l_2}{L} + \frac{a}{g} \frac{h}{L} \right) \tag{3.56}$$

From Eq. 3.56, the vehicle deceleration rate (in g units) associated with the impending lockup of the front wheels can be defined by

$$\left(\frac{a}{g} \right)_f = \frac{\mu l_2 / L + K_{bf} f_r}{K_{bf} - \mu h / L} \tag{3.57}$$

Similarly it can be shown that the rear tires approach impending lockup when the deceleration rate is

$$\left(\frac{a}{g}\right)_r = \frac{\mu l_1/L + (1-K_{bf})f_r}{1 - K_{bf} + \mu h/L} \tag{3.58}$$

For a given vehicle with a particular braking force distribution on a given road surface, the front tires will lock first, if

$$\left(\frac{a}{g}\right)_f < \left(\frac{a}{g}\right)_r \tag{3.59}$$

On the other hand, the rear wheels will lock first if

$$\left(\frac{a}{g}\right)_r < \left(\frac{a}{g}\right)_f \tag{3.60}$$

From the above analysis, it can readily be seen that for a given vehicle with a fixed braking force distribution, both front and rear tires will lock at the same deceleration rate only on a particular road surface. Under this condition, the maximum braking forces of the front and rear axles that the tire-ground contact can support are developed at the same time, which indicates an optimum utilization of the potential braking capability of the vehicle. Under all other conditions, either the front or the rear wheels will lock first, resulting in loss of either steering control or directional stability. This suggests that ideally the braking force distribution should be adjustable to ensure optimum braking performance under various operating conditions.

Based on the analysis described above, the interrelationships between the sequence of locking of wheels, the deceleration achievable prior to any wheel lockup, design parameters of the vehicle, and operating conditions can be quantitatively defined. As an illustrative example, Fig. 3.28 shows the braking characteristics of a light truck as a function of the braking effort distribution on the front axle under loaded and unloaded conditions [3.12]. For the loaded condition, the gross vehicle weight is 44.48 kN (10,000 lb) and for the unloaded case it is 26.69 kN (6000 lb). The ratio of the height of the center of gravity to the wheelbase is 0.18 for both loaded and unloaded conditions. The coefficient of road adhesion is 0.85.

In Fig. 3.28, the solid line and the dotted line represent the boundaries of the deceleration rate that the vehicle can achieve prior to the locking of any wheels under loaded and unloaded conditions, respectively. Lines OA and $O'A'$ represent the limiting values of deceleration rate the vehicle can achieve without locking the rear wheels, whereas lines AB and $A'B'$

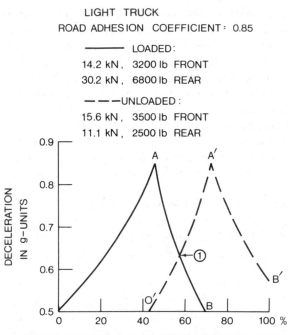

LIGHT TRUCK
ROAD ADHESION COEFFICIENT: 0.85

———— LOADED:
14.2 kN, 3200 lb FRONT
30.2 kN, 6800 lb REAR

— — —UNLOADED:
15.6 kN, 3500 lb FRONT
11.1 kN, 2500 lb REAR

FRONT BRAKING FORCE / TOTAL BRAKING FORCE

Fig. 3.28 Effect of braking effort distribution on the braking performance of a light truck. (Reproduced by permission of the Society of Automotive Engineers from reference 3.12.)

represent the limiting values of deceleration rate the vehicle can achieve without locking the front tires. Use can be made of Fig. 3.28 to determine the braking characteristics of the light truck under various operating conditions. For instance, if the brake system is designed to have 40% of the total braking force placed on the front axle, then for the loaded vehicle, the lockup of the rear tires will take place prior to the lockup of the front tires and the highest deceleration rate the vehicle can achieve just prior to rear tires lockup will be 0.75 g. Conversely, if 60% of the total braking force is placed on the front, then for the loaded case the lockup of the front tires will take place prior to that of the rear tires, and the highest deceleration rate the vehicle can achieve without locking of any wheels will be 0.6 g. It is interesting to note that to achieve the maximum deceleration rate of 0.85 g, which indicates the optimum utilization of the potential braking capability on a surface with a coefficient of road adhesion of 0.85, 47% of the total braking force on the front is required for the loaded case as compared to 72% for the unloaded case. Therefore, there is a difference of 25% in the optimum braking force distribution between the loaded and unloaded cases. A compromise in the selection of the braking force distribution has to be made. Usually the value of the braking force distribution on the front axle corresponding to the intersection of lines AB and $O'A'$, point 1, in Fig. 3.28 is selected. Under these circumstances, the maximum deceleration that the truck can achieve without locking any wheels under both loaded and unloaded conditions is 0.64 g on a surface with a coefficient of road adhesion of 0.85.

Figure 3.29 illustrates the braking characteristics of a passenger car [3.12]. Because the difference in vehicle weight between the loaded and unloaded cases for a passenger car is much smaller than that for a truck, the braking characteristics under these two conditions are very close, which can readily be seen from Fig. 3.29. To achieve the maximum deceleration rate of 0.85 g, 62% of the total braking force on the front is required for the loaded case as compared to 67% for the unloaded case, a difference of 5%. A braking force distribution with 64.5% of the total braking force on the front, corresponding to point 1 in Fig. 3.29, may be

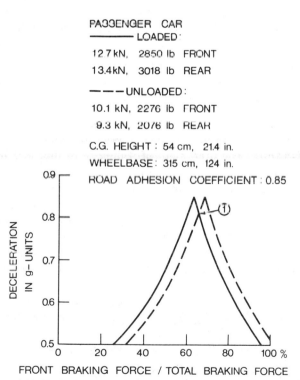

Fig. 3.29 Effect of braking effort distribution on the braking performance of a passenger car. (Reproduced by permission of the Society of Automotive Engineers from reference 3.12.)

selected as a compromise under these circumstances. The maximum deceleration that the vehicle can achieve prior to any wheel lockup under both loaded and unloaded conditions is therefore 0.82g.

The analysis and examples given above indicate the complex nature of the braking process. It is shown that the optimum braking force distribution, which ensures the maximum deceleration rate, varies with loading conditions of the vehicle, vehicle design parameters, and road surface conditions. In practice, the operating conditions vary in a wide range, thus for a given vehicle with a fixed braking force distribution, only under a specific set of loading and road conditions, will the maximum braking forces on the front and rear axles be developed at the same time and will the maximum deceleration rate be achieved. Under all other conditions, the achievable deceleration rate without causing loss of steering control or directional stability will be reduced. To improve the braking performance and to ensure steering control and directional stability under all possible operating conditions, antilock devices and the like have been introduced. The prime function of these devices is to prevent wheels from locking, thus the capability of the wheels to sustain side force can be maintained. The operating principles of the antilock system will be briefly described in Section 3.6.4.

Example 3.3

A passenger car weighs 21.24 kN (4775 lb) and has a wheelbase of 2.87 m (113 in.). The center of gravity is 1.27 m (50 in.) behind the front axle and 0.508 m (20 in.) above ground level. The braking effort distribution on the front wheels is 60%. The coefficient of rolling resistance is 0.02. Determine which set of the wheels will lock first on two road surfaces: one with a coefficient of adhesion $\mu = 0.8$ and the other with $\mu = 0.2$.

Solution.

A   On the road surface with $\mu = 0.8$, the vehicle deceleration associated with the impending lockup of the front wheels is determined by Eq. 3.57

$$\left(\frac{a}{g}\right)_f = \frac{\mu l_2 / L + K_{bf} f_r}{K_{bf} - \mu h / L} = \frac{0.8 \times 0.558 + 0.6 \times 0.02}{0.6 - 0.8 \times 0.177} = 1.0$$

The vehicle deceleration associated with the impending lockup of the rear wheels is determined by Eq. 3.58

$$\left(\frac{a}{g}\right)_r = \frac{\mu l_1 / L + (1 - K_{bf}) f_r}{1 - K_{bf} + \mu h / L} + \frac{0.8 \times 0.442 + 0.4 \times 0.02}{0.4 + 0.8 \times 0.177} = 0.67$$

Since $(a/g)_f > (a/g)_r$, the rear wheels will lock first on the road surface with $\mu = 0.8$.

B On the road surface with $\mu = 0.2$

$$\left(\frac{a}{g}\right)_f = \frac{0.2 \times 0.558 + 0.6 \times 0.02}{0.6 - 0.2 \times 0.177} = 0.219$$

$$\left(\frac{a}{g}\right)_r = \frac{0.2 \times 0.442 + 0.4 \times 0.02}{0.4 + 0.2 \times 0.177} = 0.221$$

Since $(a/g)_f < (a/g)_r$, the front wheels will lock first on the road surface with $\mu = 0.2$

3.6.2 Braking Efficiency and Stopping Distance

To characterize the braking performance of a road vehicle, braking efficiency may be used. Braking efficiency η_b is defined as the ratio of the maximum deceleration rate in g units (a/g) achievable prior to any wheel lockup to the coefficient of road adhesion μ, and is given by

$$\eta_b = \frac{a/g}{\mu} \tag{3.61}$$

The braking efficiency indicates the extent to which the vehicle utilizes the coefficient of road adhesion available during braking. Thus, when $a/g < \mu$, hence $\eta_b < 1.0$, the deceleration is less than the maximum achievable, resulting in unnecessarily long stopping distance. Referring to Fig. 3.28, if 57% of the total braking force is placed on the front, corresponding to point 1, the maximum deceleration achievable prior to any wheel lockup is 0.64 g. This indicates that on a surface with a coefficient of road adhesion of 0.85, the braking efficiency is 75.3%.

Stopping distance is another parameter widely used for evaluating the overall braking performance of a road vehicle. To predict the stopping distance, the basic principles in Dynamics are employed. The interrelationships between stopping distance, braking force, vehicle mass, and vehicle speed, in differential form, may be expressed as

$$ads = \left(\frac{F_b + \Sigma R}{\gamma_b W/g}\right) ds = V dV \tag{3.62}$$

where γ_b is an equivalent mass factor taking into account the mass moments of inertia of the rotating components involved during braking. Since during braking clutch is usually disengaged, the value of γ_b is not necessarily the same as that of γ_m used in the calculation of acceleration. For conventional automotive vehicles, γ_b may be taken as approximately 1.04.

Equation 3.62 may be integrated to determine the stopping distance S from an initial speed V_1 to a final speed V_2

$$S = \int_{V_2}^{V_1} \frac{\gamma_b W}{g} \frac{V dV}{F_b + \Sigma R} \tag{3.63}$$

Substituting Eq. 3.41 into the above equation and neglecting the transmission resistance R_t, Eq. 3.63 becomes

$$S = \frac{\gamma_b W}{g} \int_{V_2}^{V_1} \frac{V dV}{F_b + f_r W \cos\theta_s \pm W \sin\theta_s + R_a} \tag{3.64}$$

The aerodynamic resistance is proportional to the square of speed and it may be expressed as

$$R_a = \frac{\rho}{2} C_D A_f V^2 = C_{ae} V^2 \tag{3.65}$$

With substitution of $C_{ae} V^2$ for R_a and integration, stopping distance can be expressed by [3.2, 3.10]

$$S = \frac{\gamma_b W}{2g C_{ae}} \ln\left(\frac{F_b + f_r W \cos\theta_s \pm W \sin\theta_s + C_{ae} V_1^2}{F_b + f_r W \cos\theta_s \pm W \sin\theta_s + C_{ae} V_2^2} \right) \tag{3.66}$$

For final speed $V_2 = 0$, Eq. 3.66 reduces to the form

$$S = \frac{\gamma_b W}{2g C_{ae}} \ln\left(1 + \frac{C_{ae} V_1^2}{F_b + f_r W \cos\theta_s \pm W \sin\theta_s} \right) \tag{3.67}$$

For a given vehicle, if the braking force distribution and road conditions are such that the maximum braking forces of the front and rear wheels that the tire-ground contact can support are developed at the same time, that is braking efficiency $\eta_b = 100\%$, the minimum stopping distance will be achieved. In this case, the braking torque generated by the brakes have already overcome the inertia of the rotating parts connected with the wheels, the maximum braking forces developed at the tire-ground contact are retarding only the translational inertia. The mass factor γ_b is therefore one. The minimum stopping distance S_{min} can be expressed as,

$$S_{min} = \frac{W}{2g C_{ae}} \ln\left(1 + \frac{C_{ae} V_1^2}{\mu W + f_r W \cos\theta_s \pm W \sin\theta_s} \right) \tag{3.68}$$

If the braking efficiency η_b is less than 100% (i.e., the maximum deceleration rate in g units achievable prior to wheel lockup is less than the coefficient of road adhesion available), then the stopping distance will be longer than that determined using Eq. 3.68. In this case, the stopping distance may be calculated from

$$S = \frac{W}{2gC_{ae}} \ln\left(1 + \frac{C_{ae}V_1^2}{\eta_b\mu W + f_r W \cos\theta_s \pm W \sin\theta_s}\right) \tag{3.69}$$

It should be pointed out that in practice there is a time lag between the application of brakes and the full development of the braking force. This time lag depends on the response of the brake system. The actual stopping distance therefore will be longer than that calculated using the equations given above. In general, the distance the vehicle travels during the transient period between the application of brake and the attainment of steady-state braking has to be taken into consideration in determining the total stopping distance. In a first approximation, this additional stopping distance S_a may be calculated from

$$S_a - t_d V_1$$

where t_d is the response time of the brake system and V_1 the initial speed of the vehicle. For preliminary braking performance calculations, an average value of 0.3 s for t_d may be assumed [3.12]. The delay in applying brakes due to driver's reaction time further increases the actual stopping distance in practice. This reaction time usually varies from 0.5 to 2 s [3.2].

3.6.3 Braking Characteristics of a Tractor-Semitrailer

In comparison with a two-axle vehicle, the braking characteristics of a tractor-semitrailer are more complex. For a given two-axle vehicle, the load transfer is only a function of the deceleration rate, whereas for a tractor-semitrailer the load transfer during braking is dependent not only on the deceleration rate but also on the braking force of the trailer. Consequently, the optimum braking for a tractor-semitrailer is even more difficult to achieve than for a two-axle vehicle. A tractor-semitrailer during emergency braking could exhibit behavior of a more complex nature than that of a two-axle vehicle. In addition to the possibility of loss of directional control due to the lockup of tractor front wheels, directional instability of a tractor-semitrailer may be caused by the locking of either the tractor rear wheels or the semitrailer wheels. The locking of the tractor rear wheels first usually causes jack-knifing, which puts the vehicle completely out of control and often causes considerable damage both to the vehicle itself and to other road users. On the other hand, the lockup of the semitrailer wheels causes trailer swing. Although trailer swing has little effect on the stability of the tractor, it could be very dangerous to other road users, particularly to the oncoming traffic [3.13].

To reach a better understanding of the braking characteristics of a tractor-semitrailer, it is necessary to review its mechanics of braking. Figure 3.30 shows the major forces acting on a tractor-semitrailer during braking. To simplify the analysis, the aerodynamic drag and rolling resistance will be neglected.

The equilibrium equations are as follows:

A For the tractor

$$W_f + W_r = W_1 + W_{hi} \tag{3.70}$$

$$C_f W_f + C_r W_r = \frac{a}{g} W_1 + F_{hi} \tag{3.71}$$

$$\frac{a}{g} W_1 h_1 + F_{hi} h_3 + W_1 (L_1 - l_1 - d_1) + W_r d_1 = W_f (L_1 - d_1) \tag{3.72}$$

B For the semitrailer

$$W_{hi} + W_s = W_2 \tag{3.73}$$

$$F_{hi} + C_s W_s = \frac{a}{g} W_2 \tag{3.74}$$

$$W_2 d_2 + F_{hi} h_3 = \frac{a}{g} W_2 h_2 + W_s L_2 \tag{3.75}$$

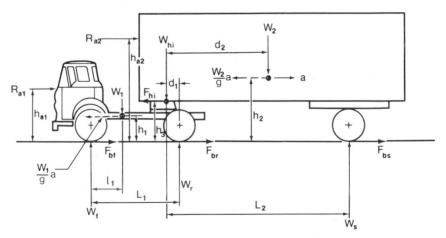

Fig. 3.30 Forces acting on a tractor-semitrailer during braking.

C For the tractor-semitrailer combination

$$W_f + W_r + W_s = W_1 + W_2 \tag{3.76}$$

$$C_f W_f + C_r W_r + C_s W_s = \frac{a}{g}(W_1 + W_2) \tag{3.77}$$

$$\frac{a}{g}W_1 h_1 + \frac{a}{g}W_2 h_2 + W_r L_1 + W_s[L_1 - d_1 + L_2]$$

$$= W_1 l_1 + W_2[L_1 - d_1 + d_2] \tag{3.78}$$

where W_{hi} is the vertical load on the fifth wheel, F_{hi} is the horizontal load on the fifth wheel, a is deceleration of the vehicle, C_f, C_r, and C_s are the ratios of the braking force to the normal load of the tractor front axle, rear axle, and semitrailer axle, respectively. Other parameters are shown in Fig. 3.30. It should be mentioned that the equations described above are applicable to tractors with single rear axle and semitrailers with single axle, or with tandem axle having equilization levers. For tractors and semitrailers having tandem axles without equalization, the equations have to be modified.

From the above equations, the normal loads on various axles can be expressed by the following:

A Tractor front axle

$$W_f = \frac{W_1[L_1 - l_1 + (a/g)h_1 + (C_r - a/g)h_3]}{L_1 + (C_r - C_f)h_3}$$

$$+ \frac{W_2[L_2 - d_2 + (C_s - a/g)h_3 + (a/g)h_2](d_1 + C_r h_3)}{(L_2 + C_s h_3)[L_1 + (C_r - C_f)h_3]} \tag{3.79}$$

B Tractor rear axle

$$W_r = \frac{W_1[l_1 - (a/g)h_1 + (a/g - C_f)h_3]}{L_1 + (C_r - C_f)h_3}$$

$$+ \frac{W_2[(L_2 - d_2) + (C_s - a/g)h_3 + (a/g)h_2][(L_1 - d_1) - C_f h_3]}{(L_2 + C_s h_3)[L_1 + (C_r - C_f)h_3]} \tag{3.80}$$

C   Semitrailer axle

$$W_s = \frac{W_2[d_2 + (h_3 - h_2)a/g]}{C_s h_3 + L_2} \tag{3.81}$$

It can be seen that to determine the normal loads on various axles of a given tractor-semitrailer, the deceleration rate and the braking force coefficient of the semitrailer axle C_s have to be specified. When the deceleration and the braking force of the semitrailer axle are known, the normal load on semitrailer axle can be determined from Eq. 3.81 and the vertical and horizontal loads on the fifth wheel, W_{hi} and F_{hi}, can be calculated from Eqs. 3.73 and 3.74. With the values of W_{hi} and F_{hi} known, from Eqs. 3.70 and 3.72, the normal loads on the front and rear axles of the tractor can be calculated.

For the optimum braking condition where the maximum braking forces of all axles that the tire-ground contact can support are developed at the same time, the brake force coefficients for all axles, and the deceleration rate in g units are equal to the coefficient of road adhesion, $C_f = C_r = C_s = a/g = \mu$. The expressions for normal axle loads given above can be simplified as follows:

A   Tractor front axle

$$W_f = \frac{W_1[L_1 - l_1 + \mu h_1]}{L_1} + \frac{W_2[L_2 - d_2 + \mu h_2](d_1 + \mu h_3)}{L_1(L_2 + \mu h_3)} \tag{3.82}$$

B   Tractor rear axle

$$W_r = \frac{W_1[l_1 - \mu h_1]}{L_1} + \frac{W_2[L_2 - d_2 + \mu h_2][L_1 - d_1 - \mu h_3]}{L_1(L_2 + \mu h_3)} \tag{3.83}$$

C   Semitrailer axle

$$W_s = \frac{W_2[d_2 + \mu(h_3 - h_2)]}{\mu h_3 + L_2} \tag{3.84}$$

Under the optimum braking condition, the braking forces on the axles are proportional to the corresponding normal loads. The required braking force distribution among the axles therefore can be determined from Eqs. 3.82–3.84. Figure 3.31 shows the variation of the optimum braking force distribution with the coefficient of road adhesion for a particular tractor-

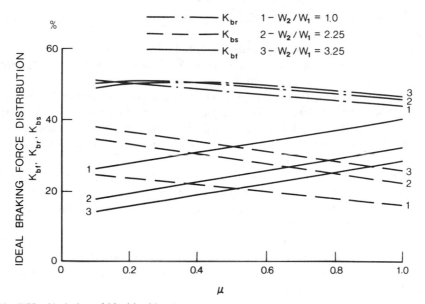

Fig. 3.31 Variation of ideal braking force distribution with coefficient of road adhesion of a tractor-semitrailer. (Reproduced by permission from reference [3.13].)

semitrailer under various loading conditions [3.13]. The parameters of the vehicle used in the analysis are as follows: $W_1 = 75.62$ kN (17,000 lb), $W_2 = 75.62$ kN (17,000 lb) (semitrailer empty), $W_2 = 170.14$ kN (38,250 lb) (semitrailer partially loaded), $W_2 = 245.75$ kN (55,250 lb) (semitrailer fully loaded), $L_1 = 5.0$ m (16.5 ft), $L_2 = 9.75$ m (32 ft), $l_1 = 2.75$ m (9 ft), $d_1 = 0.3$ m (1 ft), $d_2 = 4.88$ m (16 ft), $h_1 = 0.84$ m (2.75 ft), $h_2 = 2.44$ m (8 ft), and $h_3 = 0.98$ m (3.20 ft). It can be seen that the optimum value of the braking force distribution on the tractor rear axle K_{br} varies very little over a wide range of road and loading conditions. On the other hand, the optimum value of the braking force distribution on the tractor front axle K_{bf} and that on the semitrailer axle K_{bs} vary considerably with the coefficient of road adhesion and with the loading conditions of the semitrailer. This indicates that for a tractor-semitrailer combination with a fixed braking force distribution the optimum braking condition can be achieved only with a particular loading configuration over a specific road surface. Under all other conditions, one of the axles will lock first. As mentioned previously, the locking of tractor front wheels results in loss of steering control, the locking of tractor rear wheels first results in jack-knifing, and the locking of semitrailer wheels causes trailer swing. This indicates that the locking sequence of the wheels is of particular importance to the behavior of the tractor-semitrailer during braking. As jack-knifing is the most critical situation, the preferred locking sequence, therefore, appears to be tractor front wheels locking up first, then semitrailer wheels and then tractor rear wheels. A procedure for predicting the locking sequence of wheels of tractor-semitrailers has been developed by Wong and Guntur [3.13]. It has been shown that by careful selection of the braking force distribution among the axles coupled with the proper control of loading conditions, the preferred locking sequence may be achieved over a certain range of road conditions, thus minimizing the undesirable directional response. However, the loss of braking efficiency will result under certain operating conditions [3.13].

The dynamic behavior and directional response of tractor-semitrailers during braking is of practical importance to traffic safety. Extensive study has been made and the results have been reported in the literature including references 3.14–13.18.

To ensure steering control and directional stability and to improve braking performance of tractor-semitrailers under various operating conditions, antilock brake systems are used. Their operating principles will be discussed in the following section.

3.6.4 Antilock Brake Systems

As mentioned previously, when a tire is locked (i.e., 100% skid), the coefficient of road adhesion falls to its sliding value and its ability to sustain side force is reduced to almost null. As a result, the vehicle will lose directional control or stability, and the stopping distance will be longer than the minimum achievable. Figure 3.32 shows the general characteris-

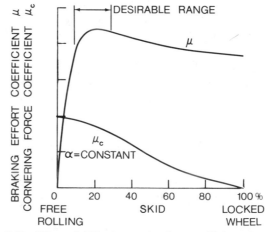

Fig. 3.32 Effect of skid on cornering force coefficient of a tire.

tics of the coefficient of braking effort μ and the coefficient of cornering force μ_c at a given slip angle, which is the ratio of cornering force to vertical load, as a function of skid for a pneumatic tire.

The prime function of an antilock system is to prevent the tire from locking and to keep the skid of the tire within a desired range such as that shown in Fig. 3.32. This will ensure that the tire can develop sufficiently high braking force for stopping the vehicle and at the same time can provide adequate cornering force for directional control and stability.

A modern antilock system usually consists of a sensor, a control unit, and a brake pressure modulator as shown in Fig. 3.33. In practice, the skid of a tire is difficult to measure directly, therefore, the control logic of the system is usually formulated based on some easily measurable parameters, such as the angular speed and/or the angular acceleration of the wheel.

The sensor is to monitor the parameters specified and to generate signals representative of those parameters. When the angular speed or angular acceleration of the wheel is used as the basic parameter, the sensor is mounted on the wheel. The signals generated by the sensor are transmitted to the control unit.

The control unit usually consists of four modules: a signal processing module, a module for predicting whether the wheel is at the point of locking, a module for determining whether the danger of locking the wheel is averted, and a module for generating a command signal for activating the pressure modulator.

In the control unit, after the signals generated by the sensor have been processed, the measured parameters and/or those derived from them are compared with the corresponding predetermined threshold values. When certain requirements that indicate the impending lockup of the wheel are met by the measured parameters and/or their derivatives, a command signal is sent to the modulator to release the brake. The methods for predicting the locking of the wheel used in some existing anitlock systems are described below [3.19, 3.20].

A   In some of the existing antilock devices, the locking of the wheel is predicted and a command signal is sent to the modulator to release the

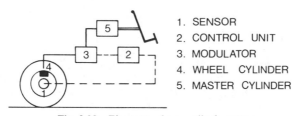

1. SENSOR
2. CONTROL UNIT
3. MODULATOR
4. WHEEL CYLINDER
5. MASTER CYLINDER

Fig. 3.33 Elements of an antilock system.

brake, whenever the product of the angular deceleration of the wheel and its rolling radius exceeds a predetermined value. In some systems, the threshold value used is in the range 1.5–2.5 g.

B In an antilock system designed for passenger cars, a signal proportional to the angular speed of the wheel is tracked by a track and hold circuit in the control unit, and when the equivalent linear deceleration of the center of the wheel is greater than 1.6 g, the tracked signal is held in a memory circuit for about 140 ms. During this period of time, if the actual angular speed of the wheel decreases by 5% of the already held value and at the same time if the deceleration of the vehicle measured is not higher than 0.5 g, it is predicted that the wheel is at the point of locking, and a command signal for releasing the brake is sent to the modulator. On the other hand, if the deceleration of the vehicle is higher than 0.5 g, locking of the wheel is predicted and the brake is released whenever the decrease in angular speed of the wheel is 15% of the already stored value.

During the braking process, the operating conditions of the wheel and of the vehicle are continuously monitored by the sensor and the control unit. After the danger of locking the wheel is predicted and the brake is released, another module in the control unit will determine at what point the brake should be reapplied. There are a variety of criteria employed in existing antilock systems; some of them are described below [3.19, 3.20].

A In some systems, a command signal will be sent to the modulator to reapply the brake, whenever the criteria for releasing the brake discussed previously are no longer satisfied.

B In certain devices, a fixed time delay is introduced to ensure that the brake is reapplied only when a fixed time has elapsed after the release of the brake.

C In some systems, the brake is reapplied as soon as the product of the angular acceleration of the wheel and the rolling radius exceeds a predetermined value, after the brake is released. Threshold values of linear acceleration in the range 3.0–6.0 g have been used.

The relative suitability of various types of control logic has been examined extensively in reference 3.19.

As an example, Fig. 3.34 shows the characteristics of an antilock system designed for heavy commercial vehicles. The variation of brake pressure, equivalent speed and acceleration of the wheel center (ωr and $\alpha_{an} r$), wheel skid, and vehicle speed with time during a braking maneuver is shown.

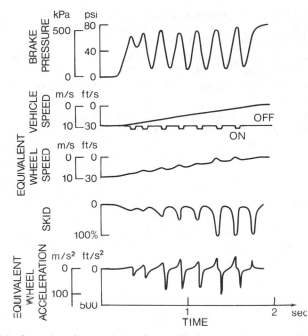

Fig. 3.34 Operating characteristics of an antilock system for commercial vehicles.

REFERENCES

3.1 G. Rousillon, J. Marzin, and J. Bourhis, Contribution to the Accurate Measurement of Aerodynamic Drag by the Deceleration Method, *Advances in Road Vehicle Aerodynamics 1973*, BHRA Fluid Engineering, Cranfield, England.

3.2 J. J. Taborek, Mechanics of Vehicles, *Machine Design*, 1957.

3.3 R. G. S. White, A Method of Estimating Automobile Drag Coefficient, *SAE Transactions*, Vol. 78, paper 690189, 1969.

3.4 L. J. Janssen and W. H. Hucho, The Effect of Various Parameters on the Aerodynamic Drag of Passenger Cars, *Advances in Road Vehicle Aerodynamics 1973*, BHRA Fluid Engineering, Cranfield, England.

3.5 R. V. Agres and R. P. McKenna, *Alternatives to the Internal Combustion Engine*, The Johns Hopkins University Press, Baltimore, MD, 1972.

3.6 J. G. Giles, *Gears and Transmissions*, Automotive Technology Series, Vol. 4, Butterworths, London, 1969.

3.7 H. I. Setz, Computer Predicts Car Acceleration, *SAE Transactions*, Vol. 69, 1961.

3.8 C. K. J. Price and S. A. Beasley, Aspects of Hydraulic Transmissions for Vehicles of Specialized Nature, *Proceedings of the Institution of Mechanical Engineers*, Vol. 178, Part 3C, 1963–1964.

3.9 R. Wardill, Why Has the British Manufacturer Been Hesitant to Adopt Hydrostatic Drives? Conference on Making Technology Profitable—Hydrostatic Drives, The Institution of Mechanical Engineers, London, 19–20 March, 1974.

3.10 D. E. Cole, *Elementary Vehicle Dynamics*, Department of Mechanical Engineering, University of Michigan, Ann Arbor, MI, 1971.

3.11 R. D. Lister, Retention of Directional Control When Braking, *SAE Transactions*, Vol. 74, paper 650092, 1965.

3.12 D. J. Bickerstaff and G. Hartley, Light Truck Tire Traction Properties and Their Effect on Braking Performance, *SAE Transactions*, Vol. 83, paper 741137, 1974.

3.13 J. Y. Wong and R. R. Guntur, Effects of Operational and Design Parameters on the Sequence of Locking of the Wheels of Tractor-Semitrailers, *Vehicle Systems Dynamics*, Vol. 7, No. 1, 1978.

3.14 J. R. Ellis, *Vehicle Dynamics*, Business Books, London, England, 1969.

3.15 E. C. Mikulcik, The Dynamics of Tractor-Semitrailer Vehicles: The Jackknifing Problem, *SAE Transactions*, Vol. 80, paper 710045, 1971.

3.16 R. W. Murphy, J. E. Bernard, and C. B. Winkler, A Computer Based Mathematical Method for Predicting the Braking Performance of Trucks and Tractor-Trailers, Report of the Highway Safety Research Institute, University of Michigan, September 1972.

3.17 C. B. Winkler, J. E. Bernard, P. S. Fancher, C. C. MacAdam, and T. M. Post, Predicting the Braking Performance of Trucks and Tractor-Trailers, Report of the Highway Safety Research Institute, University of Michigan, June, 1976.

3.18 R. R. Guntur and J. Y. Wong, Application of the Parameter Plane Method to the Analysis of Directional Stability of Tractor-Semitrailers. *Transactions of the ASME, Journal of Dynamic Systems, Measurement, and Control*, Vol. 100, No. 1, March, 1978.

3.19 R. R. Guntur and H. Ouwerkerk, Adaptive Brake Control System, *Proceedings of the Institution of Mechanical Engineers*, Vol. 186, 68/72, 1972.

3.20 J. Y. Wong, J. R. Ellis, and R. R. Guntur, *Braking and Handling of Heavy Commercial Vehicles*, Monograph, Department of Mechanical and Aeronautical Engineering, Carleton University, Ottawa, Canada, 1977.

PROBLEMS

3.1 A vehicle weighs 20.02 kN (4500 lb) and has a wheelbase of 279.4 cm (110 in.). The center of gravity is 127 cm (50 in.) behind the front axle and 50.8 cm (20 in.) above ground level. The frontal area of the vehicle is 2.32 m^2 (25 ft^2) and the aerodynamic drag coefficient is 0.45. The coefficient of rolling resistance is given by $f_r = 0.015 + 0.01 \ (V/100)^{2.5}$, where V is the speed of the vehicle in kilometers per hour. The rolling radius of the tires is 33 cm (13 in.). The coefficient of road adhesion is 0.8. Estimate the possible maximum speed of the vehicle on level ground and on a grade of 20% as determined by the maximum tractive effort that the tire-road contact can support, if the vehicle is (a) rear-wheel-drive, (b) front-wheel-drive, and (c) four-wheel drive. Plot the resultant resistance versus vehicle speed, and show the maximum thrust of the vehicle with the three types of drive.

3.2 The vehicle described in Problem 3.1 is equipped with an engine having torque-speed characteristics as shown in Fig. 3.16. The gear ratios of the gearbox are: first, 4.0; second, 2.4; third, 1.47; and fourth, 1.0. The gear ratio of the driven axle is 2.91. The transmission efficiency is 88%. Estimate the maximum speed of the vehicle on level ground and on a grade of 20% as determined by the tractive effort that the engine torque with the given transmission can provide, if the vehicle is rear-wheel-drive. Plot the vehicle thrust at various gears versus vehicle speed. What is the maximum thrust the vehicle can actually develop on a level road with a coefficient of adhesion of 0.8?

3.3 Estimate the possible minimum acceleration time and acceleration distance of the vehicle described in Problem 3.2 from stand still to a speed of 100 km/h (62 mph) on level road.

3.4 A vehicle is equipped with an automatic transmission consisting of a torque converter and a 3-speed gearbox. The torque converter and the engine characteristics are shown in Figs. 3.15 and 3.16, respectively. The total gear reduction ratio of the gearbox and the drive axle is 2.91 when the third gear is engaged. The combined efficiency of the gearbox and the drive axle is 0.90. The rolling radius of the tire is 33.5 cm (1.1 ft). Calculate the tractive effort and speed of the vehicle when the third gear is engaged and the engine is running at 2000 rpm with engine torque of 407 N·m (300 lb·ft). Determine also the overall efficiency of the transmission including the torque converter.

3.5 A passenger car weighs 12.45 kN (2800 lb) including the four road wheels. Each of the wheels has an effective diameter of 67 cm (2.2 ft) and radius of gyration of 27.9 cm (11 in.), and weighs 222.4 N (50 lb). The engine develops 44.8 kW (60 hp) at 4000 rpm and the equivalent weight of the rotating parts of the driveline at engine speed is 444.8 N (100 lb) with a radius of gyration of 10 cm (4 in.). The transmission efficiency is 88% and the total reduction ratio of the driveline in second gear is 6.98 to 1. The vehicle has a frontal area of 1.67 m² (18 ft²) and the aerodynamic drag coefficient is 0.45. The average coefficient of rolling resistance is 0.015. Calculate the acceleration of the vehicle on a level road under these conditions.

3.6 A passenger car weighs 20.02 kN (4500 lb) and has a wheelbase of 279.4 cm (110 in.). The center of gravity is 127 cm (50 in.) behind the front axle and 50.8 cm (20 in.) above ground level. In practice, the vehicle encounters a variety of surfaces with the coefficient of road adhesion ranging 0.2–0.8. With a view to avoiding the loss of directional stability on surfaces with a low coefficient of adhesion under emergency braking conditions, what would you recommend regarding the braking effort distribution between the front and rear axles?

3.7 For a particular tractor-semitrailer combination, the tractor weighs 66.72 kN (15,000 lb) and the semitrailer weighs 266.8 kN (60,000 lb). The wheelbase of the tractor is 381 cm (150 in.) and the trailer axle is 711 cm (280 in.) behind the rear axle of the tractor. The hitch point is 61 cm (24 in.) in front of the tractor rear axle and 101.6 cm (40 in.) above the ground level. The center of gravity of the tractor is 203.2 cm (80 in.) behind the tractor front axle and 96.5 cm (38 in.) above the ground. The center of gravity of the semitrailer is 330. 2 cm (130 in.) in front of the trailer axle and 177.8 cm (70 in.) above the ground. Calculate the normal loads on the axles and the forces acting at the hitch point, when the combination is being braked uniformly on all axles to produce a deceleration of 0.6 g. What is the required braking effort distribution between the axles under these circumstances?

CHAPTER FOUR

PERFORMANCE CHARACTERISTICS
OF OFF-ROAD VEHICLES

Depending on the functional requirements, different criteria are employed to evaluate the performance characteristics of various types of off-road vehicle. For tractors, their main function is to provide adequate draft to pull various types of implement and machinery, the drawbar performance is, therefore, of prime interest. It may be characterized by the ratio of drawbar pull to vehicle weight, drawbar horsepower, and drawbar efficiency. For cross-country transport vehicles, the transport productivity and efficiency are often used as basic criteria for evaluating their performance. For military vehicles, on the other hand, the maximum feasible operating speed between two specific points in a given area may be employed as a criterion for the evaluation of their agility.

Although differing criteria are used to assess the performance of different kinds of off-road vehicle, there is a basic requirement common to all cross-country vehicles, that is, the mobility over unprepared terrain. Mobility in the broad sense is concerned with the performance of the vehicle in relation to soft terrain, obstacle negotiation and avoidance, ride quality over rough terrain, and water crossing. The performance in soft terrain constitutes a basic problem in vehicle mobility, and a detailed analysis of the relationship between vehicle performance, vehicle design parameters, and the terrain is, therefore, of prime importance.

In this chapter methods for evaluating and predicting the tractive performance of cross-country vehicles will be discussed. Performance criteria for various types of off-road vehicle will also be examined in detail.

4.1 DRAWBAR PERFORMANCE

4.1.1 Drawbar Pull and Drawbar Power

For off-road vehicles designed for traction (i.e., tractors), the drawbar performance is of prime importance, as it represents the ability of the vehicle to pull or push various types of working machinery, including implements and construction and earthmoving equipment. Drawbar pull F_d is the force available at the drawbar and is equal to the difference between the tractive effort F and the resultant resisting force ΣR

$$F_d = F - \Sigma R \tag{4.1}$$

For a vehicle with known power plant and transmission characteristics, the tractive effort and vehicle speed can be determined using methods similar to those described in Chapter 3. It should be pointed out, however, that in cross-country operations the maximum tractive effort is often limited by the characteristics of vehicle-terrain interaction as described in Chapter 2. Furthermore, the development of thrust often results in considerable slip over unprepared terrain. Thus the drawbar pull and vehicle speed are functions of slip.

The resisting forces acting on an off-road vehicle include the internal resistance of the running gear, resistance due to vehicle-terrain interaction, obstacle resistance, grade resistance as well as aerodynamic drag.

Internal Resistance of the Running Gear

For wheeled vehicles the internal resistance of the running gear is mainly due to the hysteresis of tire materials, which has been discussed in Chapter 1. For tracked vehicles, the internal resistance of the track and the associated suspension system may be substantial. Frictional losses in track pins, driving sprocket, and sprocket hub and road wheel bearings constitute the major portion of the internal resistance of the track and the associated suspension system. Experimental results show that of the total power consumed in the track-suspension system, 63–75% is due to losses in the track itself for certain types of track. Among the operational parameters, track tension and vehicle speed have noticeable effects on the internal resistance as shown in Figs. 4.1 and 4.2, respectively [4.1, 4.2].

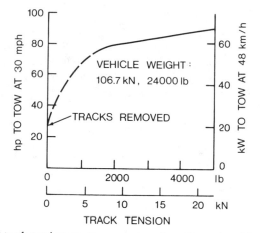

Fig. 4.1 Effect of track tension on power consumption. (Reproduced by permission of the Council of the Institution of Mechanical Engineers from reference 4.1.)

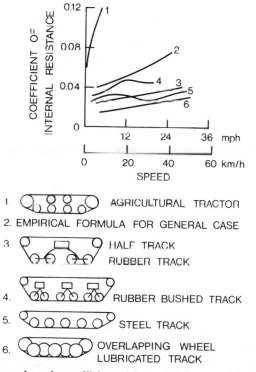

Fig. 4.2 Effect of speed on the coefficient of internal resistance of various types of track. (From *Introduction to Terrain-Vehicle Systems*, by M. G. Bekker, copyright © by the University of Michigan, 1969, reproduced by permission of the University of Michigan Press.)

183

Because of the complex nature of the internal resistance in the track and in the suspension system, it is difficult, if not impossible, to establish an analytic procedure to predict the internal resistance with sufficient accuracy. As a first approximation the following formula proposed by Bekker may be used for calculating the average value of the internal resistance R_{in} of a conventional tracked vehicle [4.2].

$$R_{in} = W(222 + 3V)$$ (4.2)

where R_{in} is in newtons, W is vehicle weight in tons, and V is vehicle speed in kilometers per hour.

For modern lightweight tracked vehicles, the internal resistance may be less and the empirical formula is [4.2]

$$R_{in} = W(133 + 2.5 V)$$ (4.3)

Resistance Due to Vehicle-Terrain Interaction

This type of resistance is the most significant one for off-road vehicles, and determines, to a great extent, the mobility of the vehicle over unprepared terrain. It includes the resistance due to compacting the terrain and bulldozing effect and may be predicted using the methods described in Chapter 2 or determined experimentally.

Ground Obstacle Resistance

In off-road operations, obstacles such as stumps and stones may be encountered. The obstacle resistance may be considered as a resisting force, usually variable in magnitude, acting parallel to the ground at a certain effective height. When the line of action of this resisting force does not pass through the center of gravity of the vehicle, it produces a moment that should be taken into consideration in formulating the equations of motion for the vehicle. In general, the value of the obstacle resistance is obtained from experiments.

Aerodynamic Resistance

Aerodynamic resistance is usually not a significant factor for off-road vehicles operating at speeds below 48 km/h (30 mph). For vehicles designed for higher speeds, such as military vehicles, aerodynamic resistance may have to be taken into consideration in performance calculations. The aerodynamic resistance can be predicted using the methods described in Chapter 3.

The aerodynamic drag coefficient mainly depends on the shape of the vehicle as mentioned previously. A value of 1.17 for the coefficient of aerodynamic resistance C_D has been reported for certain types of military off-road vehicle. For a tank weighing 50 tons and having a frontal area of 6.5 m² (70 ft²), the power required to overcome aerodynamic resistance at 48 km/h (30 mph) amounts to about 11.2 kW (15 hp). A light tracked vehicle weighing 10 tons and having a frontal area of 3.7 m² (40 ft²) may require 10.5 kW (14 hp) to overcome the aerodynamic resistance at a speed of 56 km/h (35 mph).

In addition to the resisting forces described above, the grade resistance must be taken into consideration, when the vehicle is climbing up a slope.

To characterize the drawbar performance, the slip of the running gear and the vehicle speed in each gear are usually plotted against tractive effort and drawbar pull, as shown in Figure 4.3. The product of drawbar pull and vehicle speed is usually referred to as the drawbar power that represents the potential productivity of the vehicle, that is, the rate at which productive work may be done. The drawbar power P_d is given by

$$P_d = F_d V = (F \quad \Sigma R) V_t (1 \quad i) \tag{4.4}$$

where V and V_t are the actual speed and the theoretical speed of the vehicle, respectively. Theoretical speed is the speed of the vehicle if there is no slip and is determined by the engine speed, reduction ratio of the transmission, and the radius of the tire (or sprocket). Usually, the variation of drawbar power with drawbar pull in each gear is also shown in the drawbar performance diagram. As an example, Fig. 4.4 shows the measured drawbar performance of a MF-165 tractor on tarmacadam [4.3]. The drawbar performance diagram provides a basis for comparing and evaluating the tractive performance of different tractors. It also provides

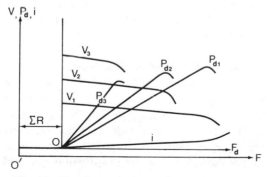

Fig. 4.3 Tractive performance diagram for tractors.

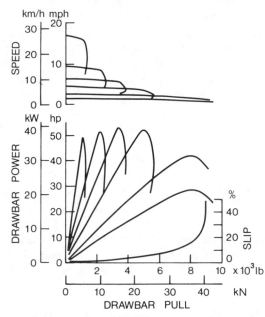

Fig. 4.4 Drawbar performance of an MF-165 tractor on tarmacadam. (Reproduced by permission of the *Journal of Agricultural Engineering Research* from reference 4.3.)

the operator with the required information to achieve proper matching of the tractor with the working machinery.

4.1.2   Tractive Efficiency

To characterize the efficiency of an off-road vehicle in transforming the engine power to the power available at the drawbar, the tractive efficiency is often used. It is defined as the ratio of drawbar power P_d to the corresponding power delivered by the engine P.

$$\eta_d = \frac{P_d}{P} = \frac{F_d V}{P} = \frac{(F - \Sigma R)V_t(1 - i)}{P} \qquad (4.5)$$

The power delivered by the engine may be expressed in terms of the power available at the driven wheels (or sprockets) and transmission efficiency η_t

$$P = \frac{FV_t}{\eta_t} \qquad (4.6)$$

Substituting Eq. 4.6 into Eq. 4.5, the expression for tractive efficiency becomes

$$\eta_d = \frac{(F - \Sigma R)}{F}(1-i)\eta_t = \frac{F_d}{F}(1-i)\eta_t$$

$$= \eta_m \eta_s \eta_t \tag{4.7}$$

where η_m is the efficiency of motion equal to F_d/F, and η_s is the efficiency of slip equal to $1-i$.

The efficiency of motion indicates the losses in transforming the tractive effort at the driven wheels to the pull at the drawbar. For motion resistance having a constant value, the efficiency of motion η_m increases with the increase of drawbar pull as shown in Fig. 4.5.

The efficiency of slip characterizes the power losses and also the reduction in speed of the vehicle due to slip of the running gear. Since slip increases with the increase of tractive effort and drawbar pull, the efficiency of slip decreases as the drawbar pull increases as shown in Fig. 4.5. Usually slip is a major source of power losses in the operation of off-road vehicles. Reduction of slip is, therefore, of practical significance in increasing the operational efficiency of off-road vehicles.

As can be seen from Eq. 4.7, the tractive efficiency is the product of the efficiency of transmission, efficiency of motion, and efficiency of slip. In general, it exhibits a peak at an intermediate value of drawbar pull, as shown in Fig. 4.5. To increase the tractive efficiency, optimization of the form and size of the vehicle running gear is of importance. In this respect, terramechanics described in Chapter 2 plays an important role.

Example 4.1 An off-road wheeled vehicle is equipped with an engine having torque-speed characteristics given in Table 4.1. The vehicle is to

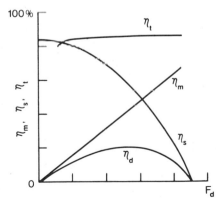

Fig. 4.5 Variation of tractive efficiency with drawbar pull.

Table 4.1   Engine Characteristics

Engine Speed n_e (rpm)	Engine Torque M_e	
	N·m	lb·ft
800	393	290
1200	650	479
1600	732	540
2000	746	550
2400	705	520
2800	610	450

operate on a soil with thrust-slip characteristics given in Table 4.2. The total motion resistance is 2.23 kN (500 lb). The transmission efficiency is 0.85, and the rolling radius of the tire is 0.76 m (2.5 ft). Determine the drawbar power and tractive efficiency of the vehicle when the 4th gear with a total reduction ratio $\xi = 20.5$ is engaged.

Table 4.2   Thrust-Slip Characteristics

Slip (%)	Thrust F	
	kN	lb
5	10.24	2303
10	16.0	3597
15	20.46	4600
20	24.0	5396
25	26.68	5998
30	28.46	6398
40	32.02	7199

Solution.   The thrust can be calculated using Eq. 3.26 in Chapter 3

$$F = \frac{M_e \xi_0 \eta_t}{r}$$

From Table 4.2, the slip at a particular thrust can be determined. The vehicle speed can be determined using Eq. 3.27 in Chapter 3.

$$V = \frac{n_e r}{\xi_0}(1 - i)$$

For a given engine operating point, vehicle speed and thrust are related. Therefore, the slip at a particular theoretical speed can be determined and the actual speed of the vehicle can be calculated. The results of the calculations for F and V are tabulated in Table 4.3. The drawbar pull is

Table 4.3 Drawbar Performance

Engine Speed n_e (rpm)	Thrust F		Slip (%)	Vehicle Speed V		Drawbar Pull F_d		Drawbar Power P_d		Transmission Efficiency η_t (%)	Efficiency of Slip η_s (%)	Tractive Efficiency η_d (%)
	kN	lb		km/h	mph	kN	lb	kW	hp			
800	9.01	2025	4.4	10.7	6.7	6.78	1525	20.1	27	85	95.6	61.1
1200	14.90	3350	9.0	15.3	9.5	12.67	2850	53.8	72.2	85	91.0	65.7
1600	16.78	3772	10.9	19.9	12.4	14.55	3272	80.4	107.8	85	89.1	65.6
2000	17.10	3844	11.23	24.9	15.5	14.87	3344	102.8	137.9	85	88.7	65.6
2400	16.16	3633	10.2	30.2	18.8	13.93	3133	116.8	156.7	85	89.8	65.8
2800	13.98	3143	8.3	36.0	22.4	11.74	2643	117.5	157.5	85	91.7	65.5

given by

$$F_d = F - \Sigma R$$

Since the total motion resistance is given, the drawbar pull can be calculated and the results are given in Table 4.3. The drawbar power can be determined using Eq. 4.4,

$$P_d = F_d V$$

and the tractive efficiency can be calculated by

$$\eta_d = \frac{F_d V}{P}$$

the results of the calculations for P_d and η_d are tabulated in Table 4.3.

It can be seen that the maximum drawbar efficiency of the vehicle under the operating conditions specified is approximately 66%, which indicates that 34% of the engine power is lost in the transmission, in overcoming the motion resistance, and in vehicle slip.

It should be mentioned that engines for off-road vehicles are often equipped with a governor to limit its maximum operating speed. When the engine characteristics over the operating range of the governor (i.e., between the full load and no load settings of the governor) are known, the drawbar performance of the vehicle in that range can be predicted in the same way as that described above.

In agriculture, earthmoving, logging, and cross-country transport, there is a growing demand for higher productivity. Consequently, there has been a steady increase in the installed power of new vehicles. For wheeled tractors to fully utilize the high engine power available and to maintain high tractive efficiency, four-wheel-drive has gained increasingly wide acceptance since the total weight of a four-wheel-drive tractor is utilized for the development of thrust, whereas only about 60–70% of the total weight is applied on the driven wheels of a two-wheel-drive vehicle. Consequently, over soft terrain, a four-wheel-drive tractor has the potential of developing higher thrust than an equivalent two-wheel-drive vehicle at the same slip. Furthermore, a four-wheel-drive vehicle may have a lower coefficient of rolling resistance than an equivalent two-wheel-drive vehicle [4.4]. However, for a four-wheel-drive tractor to achieve the optimum tractive efficiency, certain requirements have to be met. To define these requirements quantitatively, it is necessary to examine the tractive efficiency, particularly the efficiency of slip, of a four-wheel-drive off-road vehicle.

For a four-wheel-drive vehicle, the power losses due to slip occur at both the front and rear driven wheels. The slip efficiency η_{s_4} of a four-wheel-drive vehicle is determined by [4.5]

$$\eta_{s_4} = 1 - \frac{i_f V_{tf} F_f + i_r V_{tr} F_r}{V_{tf} F_f + V_{tr} F_r} \tag{4.8}$$

where V_{tf} and V_{tr} are the theoretical speed of the front and rear wheels, F_f and F_r are the tractive effort of the front and rear wheels, and i_f and i_r are the slip of the front and rear wheels, respectively.

There is a relationship between the speed of the front wheel and that of the rear wheel of a four-wheel-drive vehicle in straight line motion. The relationship can be expressed by

$$V_{tf}(1 - i_f) = V_{tr}(1 - i_r) = V \tag{4.9}$$

This is due to the fact that the front and rear wheels are connected with the same frame.

Therefore,

$$\eta_{s_4} = 1 - \frac{[(1 - i_r)/(1 - i_f)] i_f V_{tr} F_f + i_r V_{tr} F_r}{[(1 - i_r)/(1 - i_f)] V_{tr} F_f + V_{tr} F_r}$$

$$= 1 - \frac{i_f(1 - i_r) - (i_f - i_r) K_d}{(1 - i_r) - (i_f - i_r) K_d} \tag{4.10}$$

where K_d is the coefficient of thrust distribution and is equal to $F_r/(F_f + F_r)$. This shows that in general the efficiency of slip of a four-wheel-drive vehicle depends not only on the slips of the front and rear wheels, but also on the distribution of thrust between them.

From Eq. 4.10, it is clear that under a particular condition there must be an optimum thrust distribution that can make the efficiency of slip reach its peak. To find this optimum thrust distribution, the first partial derivative of η_{s_4} with respect to K_d is taken and set equal to zero.

$$\frac{\partial \eta_{s_4}}{\partial K_d} = \frac{(1 - i_f)(1 - i_r)(i_f - i_r)}{[(1 - i_r) - (i_f - i_r) K_d]^2} = 0 \tag{4.11}$$

This condition can only be satisfied if the slip of the front wheels or that of the rear wheels is 100%, or the slip of the front wheels is equal to that of the rear wheels. When the slip of either the front or the rear wheels is 100%, the vehicle cannot move forward at all, and the tractive efficiency is equal to zero. Therefore, under normal operating conditions, only when the slip of the front wheels equals that of the rear wheels, will the first partial derivative be zero. This is the necessary condition for achieving the maximum efficiency of slip.

The above analysis leads to an interesting result. It shows that for the most efficient operation of a four-wheel-drive vehicle, the slip of the front wheels must be the same as that of the rear wheels. In other words, the optimum thrust distribution will make the slips of the front and rear wheels equal. Only in this case can the efficiency of slip reach its peak. It is interesting to point out that when the slips of the front and rear wheels are equal, $i_f = i_r$, the efficiency of slip, η_{s_4}, is simply equal to $1 - i_f$ or $1 - i_r$, and the coefficient of thrust distribution no longer has any effect on the efficiency of slip (see Eq. 4.10). As an example, Fig. 4.6 shows the variation of the efficiency of slip with the coefficient of thrust distribution of a four-wheel-drive vehicle on farm soil [4.5].

Since the thrust distribution affects the tractive efficiency of a four-wheel-drive vehicle considerably, it is of importance to analyze the factors that in practice affect the thrust distribution. Generally speaking, there are two basic factors: first, the type of coupling between the front and rear axles, which may be rigid coupling, interaxle differential, over-running clutch, etc; second, the difference in theoretical speed (wheel speed when no slip or skid occurs) between the front and rear wheels.

A difference in theoretical speed often exists under operating conditions, and is usually caused by the variation of the radii of the front or rear tires,

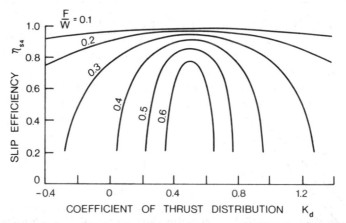

Fig. 4.6 Effect of thrust distribution between the driven axles on the slip efficiency of a four-wheel-drive tractor. (Reproduced by permission from reference 4.5.)

owing to unequal tire pressure, uneven wear of tires, or load transfer. When the size of the front tire is smaller than that of the rear one, sometimes it is difficult to provide exactly the right gear ratio for them, and this also causes the difference in theoretical speed between them.

The most common configuration of four-wheel-drive off-road vehicles has rigid coupling between the front and rear driven axles. For this type of vehicle, the ratio of the angular speed of the front wheel to that of the rear wheel is fixed. The relationship between the slip of the front wheel and that of the rear wheel is therefore a function of the ratio of the theoretical speed of the front wheel to that of the rear wheel, K_v

$$i_r = 1 - \frac{V_{tf}}{V_{tr}}(1 - i_f) = 1 - K_v(1 - i_f) \qquad (4.12)$$

The variation of i_r with i_f and K_v is shown in Fig. 4.7. When the theoretical speed ratio K_v is equal to 0.85 (i.e., the theoretical speed of the front wheel is 85% of that of the rear wheel) and i_r is less than 15%, the front wheel skids and develops negative thrust (braking force). On the other hand when K_v is equal to 1.15 (i.e., the theoretical speed of the front wheel is 15% higher than that of the rear wheel) and i_f is less than 13%, the rear wheel skids and also develops negative thrust. In both cases, the maximum forward thrust of the vehicle is reduced and torsional wind-up in the transmission inevitably occurs. This results in the increase of stress in the components of the driveline and the reduction of transmission efficiency.

Since wheel slip is related to thrust as described in Chapter 2, the thrust distribution between the front and rear driven axles depends on the theoretical speed ratio. Figure 4.8 shows the relationship between the coefficient of thrust distribution K_d and the theoretical speed ratio K_v of a four-wheel-drive vehicle having equal weight distribution between the axles

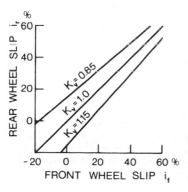

Fig. 4.7 Effect of theoretical speed ratio on the slips of the front and rear tires of a four-wheel-drive tractor with rigid interaxial coupling. (Reproduced by permission from reference 4.5)

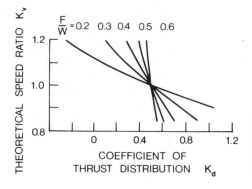

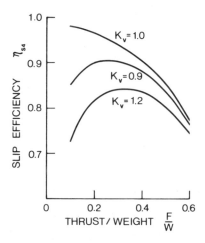

Fig. 4.8 Variation of coefficient of thrust distribution with theoretical speed ratio of a four-wheel-drive tractor with rigid interaxial coupling. (Reproduced by permission from reference 4.5.)

at various values of thrust/weight ratio, F/W, on a farm soil [4.5]. It is shown that when the value of thrust/weight ratio is high (i.e., the vehicle is pulling a heavy load), the difference in theoretical speed has less effect on the thrust distribution. It is interesting to note that when the thrust/weight ratio is 0.2 and the theoretical speed ratio K_v is 0.9, the coefficient of thrust distribution K_d is equal to 1.0. This indicates that the vehicle is essentially a rear-wheel-drive vehicle, and that the potential advantage of four-wheel-drive has not been realized.

Since the theoretical speed ratio K_v affects the relationship between the slip of the front wheel and that of the rear wheel, and hence the thrust distribution between the driven axles, the slip efficiency η_{s_4} is a function of the theoretical speed ratio. Figure 4.9 shows the variation of the slip efficiency with the thrust/weight ratio for a four-wheel-drive vehicle at various theoretical speed ratios. It can be seen that when the theoretical

Fig. 4.9 Variation of slip efficiency with thrust/weight ratio at various theoretical speed ratios of a four-wheel-drive tractor with rigid interaxial coupling. (Reproduced by permission from reference 4.5.)

speed ratio K_v is equal to 1.0, the slip of the front wheel equals that of the rear wheel and the slip efficiency is an optimum.

The results of the above analysis indicates that care must be taken in the design and operation of four-wheel-drive off-road vehicles to achieve the optimum efficiency. For a four-wheel-vehicle with rigid coupling between the driven axles to achieve high efficiency of operation, the theoretical speed of the front wheel and that of the rear wheel must be equal, so that the slip of the front wheel and that of the rear wheel are equal under operating conditions. This requires that the rolling radii of the tires be equal (when the front and rear tires are of the same size) under working conditions, an important matter that the vehicle operator must control.

4.1.3 Coefficient of Traction

In the evaluation of the drawbar performance of off-road vehicles, the ratio of the drawbar pull to the proportion of the vehicle weight applied to the driven wheels W_d, which is usually referred to as the coefficient of traction μ_{tr}, is a widely used parameter. It is expressed by

$$\mu_{tr} = \frac{F_d}{W_d} = \frac{F \ \Sigma R}{W_d} \tag{4.13}$$

It should be pointed out that since drawbar pull is a function of slip, the coefficient of traction of different vehicles should be compared at the same slip. Figure 4.10 shows a comparison of the coefficient of traction of a two-wheel-drive with a comparable four-wheel-drive tractor on farm soil [4.4].

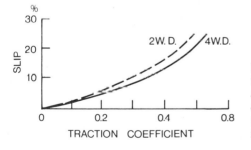

Fig. 4.10 Variation of coefficient of traction with slip for a two-wheel-drive and a four-wheel-drive tractor. (Reproduced by permission of the Council of the Institution of Mechanical Engineers from reference 4.4.)

4.1.4 Weight to Power Ratio for Off-Road Vehicles

For off-road vehicles designed for traction, the desirable weight-to-engine-power ratio is determined by the necessity for the optimum utilization of the engine power to produce the required drawbar pull. It is, therefore, a function of the operating speed. From Eq. 4.6, the relationship between the vehicle-weight-to-engine-power ratio and operating speed can be expressed by [4.6]

$$P = \frac{FV_t}{\eta_t} = \frac{(F_d + \Sigma R)V_t}{\eta_t}$$

$$= \frac{(W_d \mu_{tr} + Wf_r)V}{(1-i)\eta_t} \tag{4.14}$$

and

$$\frac{W}{P} = \frac{(1-i)\eta_t}{(\mu_{tr} W_d / W + f_r)V} = \frac{(1-i)\eta_t}{(\mu_{tr} K_w + f_r)V} \tag{4.15}$$

where W is the total vehicle weight, f_r is the coefficient of motion resistance, and K_w is called the weight utilization factor and is the ratio of W_d to W. The weight utilization factor K_w is less than unity for a two-wheel-drive tractor and is equal to unity for a four-wheel-drive or a tracked vehicle. If there is load transfer from the implement to the vehicle, the value of K_w may be greater than unity.

Equation 4.15 indicates that for a vehicle designed for a given range of operating speed, the weight-to-engine-power ratio should be within a particular range, so that a specific level of tractive efficiency can be maintained. Figure 4.11 shows the variation of the desirable weight-to-

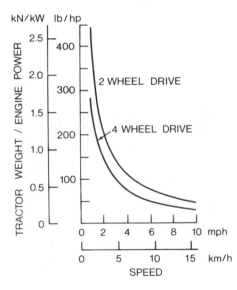

Fig. 4.11 Variation of the optimum weight to power ratio with operating speed for a two-wheel-drive and a four-wheel-drive tractor. (Reproduced by permission of the Council of the Institution of Mechanical Engineers from reference 4.6.)

engine-power ratio with operating speed of a two-wheel-drive and a four-wheel-drive tractor under a particular operating environment [4.6].

In agriculture attempts are being made to achieve higher productivity in the field by increasing the operating speed of the tractor-implement system. This would require the development of appropriate implements as well as tractors, so that the full advantage of high-speed operation can be realized. Equation 4.15 provides guiding principles for the selection of the design and performance parameters of tractors designed for operation at increased speeds. It shows that to achieve the optimum utilization of engine power and to maintain high tractive efficiency, the increase of the operating speed must be accompanied by the corresponding reduction of the tractor weight-to-engine-power ratio.

4.2 FUEL ECONOMY OF CROSS-COUNTRY OPERATIONS

The fuel economy of off-road vehicles depends not only on the fuel consumption characteristics of the engine, but also on the transmission characteristics, internal resistance of the running gear, external resisting forces, drawbar pull, and operating speed. When the resultant resisting force, drawbar pull, and operating speed are known, the required engine output power P is determined by

$$P = \frac{(\Sigma R + F_d)V}{(1-i)\eta_t} \qquad (4.16)$$

The fuel consumed per hour of operation u_h can then be calculated by

$$u_h = Pu_s \qquad (4.17)$$

where u_s is the specific fuel consumption of the engine in kg/kW·h (or lb/hp·h). For changing operating conditions, the basic equations given above can still be used to compute step by step the changing power requirements and fuel consumption.

The motion resistance and slip of an off-road vehicle over a given terrain affect the power requirements and are dependent, to a great extent, on the design of the running gear and vehicle configuration as discussed in Chapter 2. Consequently, the tractive performance of the vehicle has considerable effects on the fuel economy of cross-country operations. This may be illustrated by the following example.

Example 4.2 Referring to Example 2.3 in Chapter 2, if vehicles A and B are to pull a load with resistance of 40.03 kN (9000 lb), estimate the difference in fuel consumption of the two vehicles when traveling at a speed of 10 km/h (6.2 mph). In the calculations an average specific fuel consumption of 0.30 kg/kW·h (0.49 lb/hp·h) may be assumed.

Solution.   Referring to Example 2.3, the motion resistance of vehicle A is 8.98 kN (2020 lb) and that of vehicle B is 7.16 kN (1609 lb). Both vehicles have a weight of 135 kN (30,350 lb). The internal resistance of the two vehicles traveling at 10 km/h may be estimated using Eq. 4.2.

$$R_{in} = W(222 + 3V) = 3.47 \text{ kN } (780 \text{ lb}).$$

A   To pull the load with a resistance of 40.03 kN (9000 lb), vehicle A should develop a thrust, F, equal to the sum of the resultant motion resistance and drawbar pull.

$$F = \Sigma R + F_d = 8.98 + 3.47 + 40.03 = 52.48 \text{ kN } (11{,}800 \text{ lb})$$

From Table 2.4, to develop this thrust, the slip of vehicle A is 28.3%. Assume that the transmission efficiency η_t is 0.85. The engine power required for vehicle A traveling at 10 km/h (6.2 mph) can be calculated using Eq. 4.16.

$$P = \frac{(\Sigma R + F_d)V}{(1-i)\eta_t} = 239 \text{ kW } (320 \text{ hp})$$

The fuel consumption per hour of operation is

$$u_h = Pu_s = 71.6 \text{ kg/h } (157 \text{ lb/h})$$

B   To pull the load specified, the thrust that vehicle B should develop is

$$F = 7.16 + 3.47 + 40.03 = 50.66 \text{ kN } (11{,}389 \text{ lb})$$

From Table 2.4, to develop this thrust, the slip of vehicle B is 14.2%. The required engine power for vehicle B traveling at 10 km/h (6.2 mph) is

$$P = 193 \text{ kW } (258 \text{ hp})$$

The fuel consumption per hour of operation

$$u_h = 57.7 \text{ kg/h } (127 \text{ lb/h})$$

The results indicate that vehicle A consumes about 24% more fuel than vehicle B, because vehicle A has higher motion resistance and slip than vehicle B under the circumstances. The difference in tractive performance between the two vehicles is due to the difference in the dimensions of the tracks. This illustrates the importance of the design of the running gear of off-road vehicles to the fuel economy of cross-country operations.

The operational fuel economy of various types of cross-country vehicle may also be evaluated using parameters reflecting the productive work performed by the vehicle. For instance, for an agricultural tractor, the operational fuel economy may be expressed in terms of fuel consumed for work performed in unit area, u_a

$$u_a = \frac{Pu_s}{B_m V_m} \tag{4.18}$$

where B_m is the working width of the implement or machinery which the tractor pulls and V_m is the average operating speed.

To evaluate the fuel economy of a tractor in developing drawbar power, the fuel consumption per unit drawbar power per hour u_d may be used as a criterion.

$$u_d = \frac{u_h}{P_d} = \frac{Pu_s}{P\eta_m \eta_s \eta_t} = \frac{u_s}{\eta_m \eta_s \eta_t} \tag{4.19}$$

Where u_h is the fuel consumed per hour of operation, P is the engine power, P_d is the drawbar power, u_s is the specific fuel consumption of the engine, η_m is the efficiency of motion, η_s is the efficiency of slip, and η_t is the transmission efficiency.

In the University of Nebraska's test programs, the energy obtained at the drawbar E_d per unit volume of fuel consumed, u_e, is used as an index for evaluating fuel economy [4.2]

$$u_e = \frac{E_d}{u_t} = \frac{F_d V t}{u_t} = \frac{P_d t}{u_t} \tag{4.20}$$

where u_t is the fuel consumed during time t.

For cross-country transporters, the fuel consumption per unit payload transported over a unit distance, u_{tr}, may be used as a criterion for evaluating fuel economy

$$u_{tr} = \frac{Pu_s}{W_p V_m} \tag{4.21}$$

where W_p is the payload. u_{tr} may be expressed in liters per ton·kilometer or gallons per ton·mile.

When operating in areas where fuel is not readily available, special fuel carriers have to be used to supply the payload carriers with the required fuel. Thus, the total fuel consumption per unit payload transported should include the consumption of the fuel carriers [4.2].

4.3   TRANSPORT PRODUCTIVITY AND TRANSPORT EFFICIENCY

The absolute criterion for comparing one commercial off-road transporter with another is the relative cost of transporting a unit payload on a particular route. This involves not only the performance and fuel consumption characteristics of the vehicle, but also factors not known before a vehicle has been operated, such as load factor and customer's preference. However, there exist certain basic performance criteria that enable some assessment and comparison to be made in the preliminary stage of development. Some of these are discussed below.

Transport productivity, which is defined as the product of payload and the average cross-country speed through a specific region, may be used as a criterion for evaluating the performance of off-road transporters. For an existing vehicle, the average speed may be measured experimentally. However, for a vehicle under development, the prediction of its average operating speed through a particular region may be quite complex, as the terrain conditions may vary considerably.

In addition to vehicle tractive performance, a number of other factors, such as its ability in obstacle negotiation, its mobility in riverine environment, and the driver-vehicle response to ground roughness, also affect the cross-country speed of the vehicle.

To characterize the efficiency of a transport system, transport efficiency η_{tr}, which is defined as the ratio of the transport productivity to the corresponding power input to the system, may also be used.

$$\eta_{tr} = \frac{W_p V}{P} \tag{4.22}$$

where W_p is payload and P is the power input to the system. The transport efficiency as defined has three basic components, namely the lift/drag ratio C_{ld} (the ratio of the vehicle total weight to the resultant motion resistance), structural efficiency η_{st} (the ratio of the payload to the vehicle total weight), and propulsive efficiency η_p

$$\eta_{tr} = \frac{W_p V}{P} = \frac{W_p V}{(\Sigma R)V/\eta_p} = \frac{W}{\Sigma R}\frac{W_p}{W}\eta_p$$

$$= C_{ld}\eta_{st}\eta_p \qquad (4.23)$$

The propulsive efficiency includes the transmission efficiency and slip efficiency of the vehicle.

The reciprocal of transport efficiency expressed in terms of power consumption per unit transport productivity may also be used to characterize the performance of a transport system. Figure 4.12 shows a comparison of the power consumption per unit transport productivity, expressed in terms of kW/ton·km/h (or hp/ton·mile/h), of a tracked vehicle, an air cushion trailer, and an air cushion vehicle under various terrain conditions [4.7]. The terrain conditions are characterized by constants k_c, k_ϕ, and n, which are defined in Chapter 2.

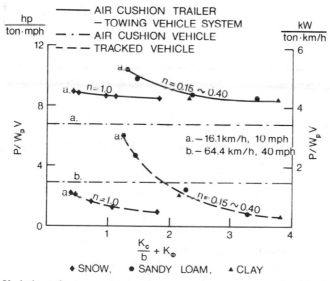

Fig. 4.12 Variation of power consumption per unit transport productivity with terrain conditions for various types of off-road transport vehicle. (Reproduced by permission from reference 4.7.)

4.4 MOBILITY MAP AND MOBILITY PROFILE

To characterize the mobility of military vehicles, the maximum feasible speed between two points in a given region may be used as a basic criterion [4.8]. The maximum feasible speed is a highly aggregated parameter representing the net results of numerous interactions between the vehicle and the operational environment. This criterion has found increasingly wide acceptance, particularly among military startegic planners and military vehicle operators.

To predict the maximum feasible speed, various computer models, such as AMC-71 and AMM-75, have been developed [4.8, 4.9]. In view of the variation of environmental conditions in the field, in these computer models, the area of interest is first divided into patches, within each of which the terrain is considered sufficiently uniform to permit the use of the maximum speed of the vehicle in straight line motion to define its mobility.

For these computer models, the characteristics of the terrain, the vehicle, and the driver are required as inputs. Terrain surface composition, surface geometry, vegetation, and linear geometry, such as stream cross section, and water speed and depth, have to be specified. Vehicle geometric characteristics, inertia characteristics and mechanical characteristics together with the driver's reaction time, recognition distance, and ride comfort limits also have to be defined.

For the computer models, the terrain is classified into three categories: areal patch, linear feature segment, such as a stream, ditch, or embankment, and road or trail segment.

When a vehicle is crossing an areal terrain unit, the maximum speed may be limited by one or a combination of the following factors:

1 The tractive effort available for overcoming the resisting forces due to sinkage, slope, obstacles, vegetation, etc.

2 The driver's tolerance to ride discomfort when traversing rough terrain and to obstacle impacts

3 The driver's reluctance to proceed faster than the speed at which the vehicle would be able to decelerate to a stop, within the limited visibility distance prevaling in that patch

4 Vehicle maneuverability to avoid obstacles

5 The acceleration and deceleration between obstacles, and speed reduction due to maneuvering to avoid obstacles.

The speed limited by each of the above factors is calculated and compared, and the maximum attainable speed within a particular terrain patch is determined.

When the vehicle is traversing a linear feature segment, such as a stream, man-made ditch, canal, escarpment, railroad and highway embankment, appropriate models are used to determine the maximum attainable speed. In the models, the time required to enter and cross the segment and that required to egress from it are taken into consideration. Both include allowance for engineering effort, such as winching and excavating, whenever required.

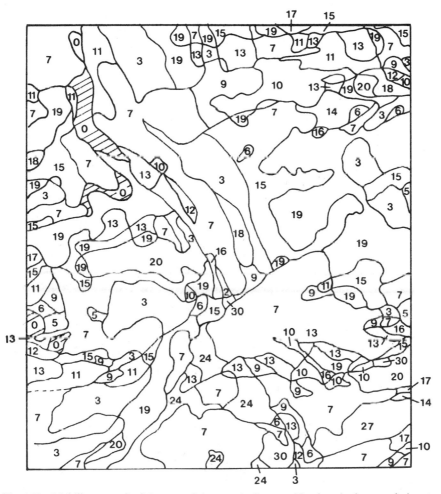

Fig. 4.13 Mobility map of a 2.5 ton truck in a particular area. Numbers in the map designate maximum achievable speed in miles per hour; cross-hatched areas indicate where the vehicle is immobile. (Reproduced by permission of the Society of Automotive Engineers from reference 4.8.)

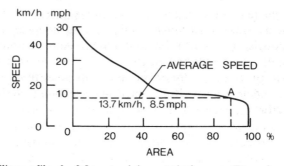

Fig. 4.14 Mobility profile of a 2.5 ton truck in a particular area. (Reproduced by permission of the Society of Automotive Engineers from reference 4.8.)

To predict the maximum attainable speed of a vehicle on roads or trails, in addition to the speed limited by the motion resistance, the speeds limited by ride discomfort, visibility, tire characteristics, and road curvature have to be taken into consideration. The least of these speeds is taken as the maximum feasible speed for the road or trail segment.

The results obtained from the analysis may be conveniently shown in a mobility map as that illustrated in Fig. 4.13 [4.8]. The numbers in the map indicate the speed of which a particular vehicle is capable in each patch throughout the region under consideration. This provides the basis for selecting the optimum route for the vehicle to maximize the average speed through a given area. The information contained in the mobility map may be generalized in a mobility profile shown in Fig. 4.14 [4.8], which conveys a complete statistical description of vehicle mobility in a particular area. It indicates the speed at which the vehicle can sustain as a function of the percentage of the total area under consideration. For instance, the intercept of 90% point (point A) in Fig. 4.14 indicates that the vehicle can achieve an average speed of 13.7 km/h (8.5 mph) over 90% of the area. The mobility map and mobility profile are suitable formats for characterizing vehicle mobility for many purposes, such as operational planning and effectiveness analysis.

4.5 SELECTION OF VEHICLE CONFIGURATIONS FOR OFF-ROAD OPERATIONS

Vehicle configuration can generally be defined in terms of form, size, weight, and power [4.2]. Selection of vehicle configuration is primarily based on mission and operational requirements and on the environment in which the vehicle is expected to operate. In addition, fuel economy, safety, cost, impact on the environment, reliability, maintainability, and other factors have to be taken into consideration. To define an optimum vehicle configuration for a given mission and environment, a system analysis approach should therefore be adopted.

The analysis of terrain-vehicle systems usually begins with defining mission requirements, such as the type of work to be performed, the kind of payload to be transported, and the operational characteristics of the vehicle system, including output rates, cost, and economy. The physical and geometric properties of the terrain over which the vehicle is expected to operate are collected as inputs. Competitive vehicle concepts with probability of accomplishing the specified mission requirements are chosen, based on past experience and future development trends. The operational characteristics and performance of the vehicle candidates are then analyzed and compared. In the evaluations, the methods and techniques discussed in Chapter 2 and in the preceding sections of this chapter may be employed. As a result of the system analysis, an order of merit for the vehicle candidates is established, from which an optimum vehicle configuration is selected [4.2].

Thus, selection of vehicle configuration for a given mission and environment is a complex process, and it is not possible to define the optimum configuration without detailed analysis. However, based on the current state of the art of off-road transport technology, some generalization of the merits and limitations of existing vehicle configurations may be made. Broadly speaking, there are currently four basic types of ground vehicle capable of operating over a specific range of unprepared terrain: wheeled vehicles, tracked vehicles, air cushion vehicles, and hybrid vehicles.

Wheeled Vehicles

Referring to the analysis of the tractive performance of off-road vehicles given in Chapter 2 and in the preceding sections of this chapter, the maximum drawbar pull to weight ratio of a vehicle may be expressed by

$$\frac{F_d}{W} = \frac{F - \Sigma R}{W} = \frac{cA + W\tan\phi - f_r W}{W}$$

$$= \frac{c}{p} + \tan\phi - f_r \qquad (4.24)$$

This equation indicates that for a given terrain with specific values of cohesion and angle of internal shearing resistance, c and ϕ, the maximum drawbar pull to weight ratio is a function of the contact pressure p and the coefficient of motion resistance f_r. The lower the contact pressure and the coefficient of motion resistance, the higher the maximum drawbar pull to weight ratio will be. Since the contact pressure and the motion resistance are dependent on the design of the vehicle, the proper selection of vehicle configuration is of utmost importance.

For given overall dimensions and gross weight, a tracked vehicle will have larger contact area than a wheeled vehicle. Consequently, the ground contact pressure, and hence the sinkage and external motion resistance of the tracked vehicle, would generally be lower than that of an equivalent wheeled vehicle. Furthermore, a tracked vehicle has longer contact length than a wheeled vehicle of the same overall dimensions. Thus, the slip of a tracked vehicle is usually lower than that of an equivalent wheeled vehicle for the same thrust. As a result, the mobility of the tracked vehicle is generally superior to that of the wheeled vehicle in difficult terrain.

The wheeled vehicle is, however, a more suitable choice than the tracked one, when frequent on-road travel and high road speeds are required.

Tracked Vehicles

Although the tracked vehicle has the capability of operating over a wide range of unprepared terrain, to fully realize its potential, careful attention must be given to the design of the track system. The nominal ground pressure of the tracked vehicle (i.e., the ratio of the vehicle gross weight to the nominal ground contact area) has been quite widely used as a design parameter of relevance to soft ground performance. However, the shortcomings in its general use are now evident both in its neglect of the actual pressure variation under the track and in its inability to distinguish between track designs giving different soft ground mobility. It has been shown that the vehicle sinkage and hence motion resistance depend on the maximum pressure exerted by the vehicle on the ground and not the nominal pressure. Therefore, it is of prime importance that the design of the track system should give as uniform contact pressure on the ground as possible under normal operating conditions. For low-speed tracked vehicles, fairly uniform ground contact pressure could be achieved by using a relatively rigid track with a long track pitch and a large number of small diameter road wheels. For high-speed tracked vehicles, to minimize the vibration of the vehicle and of the track, relatively large road wheels with considerable suspension travel and short track pitch are required. This would result in a rather nonuniform pressure distribution under the track. The overlapping road wheel arrangement shown in Fig. 2.37 provides a possible compromise in meeting the conflicting requirements for soft ground mobility and for high speed. Pneumatic tracks and pneumatic cushion devices have also been proposed to provide a uniform pressure distribution on the ground.

Experience and analysis have shown that the method of steering is also of importance to the mobility of tracked vehicles in difficult terrain. Articulated steering provides the vehicle with better mobility and maneuverability than skid-steering over soft terrain. In addition, the characteristic tail-down attitude of the conventional tracked vehicles due to slip-sinkage is alleviated, to a certain extent, by using articulation. Articulated steering also makes it possible for the vehicle to achieve a more rational form, since a long, narrow vehicle encounters less external resistance over soft ground than does a short, wide vehicle with the same contact area. It has also been shown that the ride of an articulated vehicle is significantly better than that of a comparable vehicle with skid-steering. The greater contact length is the prime reason, since it minimizes the amplitude of pitch oscillation. From an environmental point of view, articulated steering causes less damage to the terrain during maneuvering than skid-steering. A detailed analysis of the characteristics of various steering methods for tracked vehicles will be given in Chapter 6.

The characteristics of the transmission also play a significant role in vehicle mobility over soft ground. Generally speaking, automatic transmission is preferred as it allows gear changing without interruption of power flow to the running gear.

Air-Cushion Vehicles

A vehicle wholly supported by an air cushion and propelled by a propeller or fan air can operate over level terrain of low bearing capacity at relatively high speeds. It has, however, very limited capabilities in slope climbing, slope traversing, and obstacle crossing. Its maneuverability in confined space is generally poor without a ground contact device. Existing air thrust devices are relatively inefficient and could not generate sufficient thrust at low speeds. Over rugged terrain, skirt damage could pose a serious problem, while over snow or sandy terrain, visibility could be considerably reduced by a cloud of small particles formed around the vehicle. With the current state of the art, the potential of the air cushion vehicle with air propulsion can only be fully exploited over relatively flat and smooth terrain at high speeds. A detailed analysis of the performance of air-cushion vehicles will be given in Chapter 8.

Hybrid Vehicles

Hybrid vehicles are those that employ two or more forms of running gear, such as the half-tracked vehicle with front wheel steering, the air-cushion assist wheeled vehicle and the air-cushion assist tracked vehicle. The performance and characteristics of the air-cushion assist wheeled vehicle will be analyzed in detail in Chapter 8. It can be said, however, that the use of the wheel as a directional control device for the air-cushion vehicle is quite effective. However, the use of the wheel as a traction device over difficult terrain has severe limitations as mentioned previously.

Over exceedingly soft and cohesive terrain, such as deep mud or semi-liquid swamp, the air-cushion assist tracked vehicle may have some merits from the mobility viewpoint. This is because over this type of terrain, the air cushion can be used to carry a high proportion of the vehicle weight, thus minimizing the sinkage and motion resistance of the vehicle. The track could then be used solely as a propulsive device. Since in cohesive type of terrain, the thrust is mainly a function of track contact area and the cohesion of the terrain, and is more or less independent of the normal load, a track with suitable dimensions may provide the vehicle with the necessary thrust and mobility. However, the added weight, size, and expense of the air-cushion assist device must be carefully weighed against the benefits obtainable.

REFERENCES

4.1 G. V. Cleare, Factors Affecting the Performance of High-Speed Track Layers, *Proceedings of the Institution of Mechanical Engineers*, Vol. 178, Part 2A, No. 2, 1963–1964.

4.2 M. G. Bekker, *Introduction to Terrain-Vehicle Systems*, University of Michigan Press, Ann Arbor, MI 1969.

4.3 Z. Kolozsi and T. T. McCarthy, The Prediction of Tractor Field Performance, *Journal of Agricultural Engineering Research*, Vol. 19, pp. 167–172, 1974.

4.4 L. E. Osborne, Ground-Drive Systems for High-Powered Tractors, *Proceedings of the Institution of Mechanical Engineers*, Vol. 184, Part 3Q, 1969–1970.

4.5 J. Y. Wong, Optimization of the Tractive Performance of Four-Wheel-Drive Off-Road Vehicles, *SAE Transactions*, Vol. 79, paper 700723, 1970.

4.6 A. R. Reece, The Shape of the Farm Tractor, *Proceedings of the Institution of Mechanical Engineers*, Vol. 184, Part 3Q, 1969–1970.

4.7 J. Y. Wong, On the Application of Air Cushion Technology to Overland Transport, *High Speed Ground Transportation Journal*, Vol. 6, No. 3, 1972.

4.8 C. J. Nuttall, Jr., A. A. Rula, and H. J. Dugoff, Computer Model for Comprehensive Evaluation of Cross-Country Vehicle Mobility, *SAE Transactions*, paper 740426, 1974.

4.9 M. P. Jurkat, C. J. Nuttall, and P. W. Haley, The U.S. Army Mobility Model (AMM-75), *Proceedings of the Fifth International Conference of the International Society for Terrain-Vehicle Systems*, Vol. IV, Detroit, MI, 1975.

PROBLEMS

4.1 Calculate the drawbar power and tractive efficiency of the off-road vehicle described in Example 4.1 at various operating speeds when the third gear with a total reduction ratio of 33.8 is engaged.

4.2 An off-road vehicle pulls an implement that has a resistance of 17.79 kN (4000 lb). The motion resistance of the vehicle is 6.672 kN (1500 lb). Under these circumstances, the slip of the running gear is 35%. The transmission efficiency is 0.80. What percentage of the power is lost in converting engine power into drawbar power?

4.3 A four-wheel-drive off-road vehicle has a rigid coupling between the front and rear driven axles. The thrust-slip characteristics of the front and rear axles are identical and are the same as those given in Table 4.2. Owing to unequal tire pressure and uneven wear of tires, the theoretical speed of the front tires is 6% higher than that of the rear tires. The motion resistance of the vehicle is 2.23 kN (500 lb). The vehicle is to pull an implement that has a resistance of 20.02 kN (4500 lb). Determine whether or not torsional wind-up in the transmission will occur. Determine also the thrust distribution between the front and rear axles and the slip efficiency of the vehicle.

4.4 If the four-wheel-drive off-road vehicle described in Problem 4.3 is equipped with an overrunning clutch between the front and rear driven axles, so that the front axle will not be driven until the slip of the rear tires is up to 10%, determine the thrust distribution between the driven axles and the slip efficiency of the vehicle, when it pulls an implement that has a resistance of 20.02 kN (4500 lb). The motion resistance of the vehicle is 2.23 kN (500 lb).

4.5 A two-wheel-drive tractor with a weight utilization factor of 75% is to be designed mainly for operation in the speed range 10–15 km/h (6.2–9.3 mph). Both the transmission efficiency and slip efficiency are in the range 80–90%. The average value of the coefficient of motion resistance is 0.1, and that of the traction coefficient is 0.4. Determine the appropriate range of the power-to-weight ratio for the tractor.

4.6 An off-road transporter with a gross weight of 44.48 kN (10,000 lb) carries a payload of 17.79 kN (4000 lb). The coefficient of motion resistance of the vehicle is 0.15. Both the transmission efficiency and slip efficiency are 0.80. If the transporter travels at a speed of 15 km/h (9.3 mph) and the average specific fuel consumption of the engine is 0.32 kg/kW·h (0.52 lb/hp·h), determine the fuel consumed in transporting 1 ton of payload for 1 km (or 1 ton of payload for 1 mile). Calculate also the transport productivity, the power consumption per unit productivity, and the transport efficiency of the vehicle system.

CHAPTER FIVE

HANDLING CHARACTERISTICS
OF ROAD VEHICLES

Handling characteristics of a road vehicle are concerned with its response to steering commands and to environmental inputs affecting the direction of motion of the vehicle, such as wind and road disturbances. There are two basic problems in vehicle handling: one is the control of the vehicle to a desired path; the other is the stabilization of the direction of motion against external disturbances.

The vehicle as a rigid body has six degrees of freedom as shown in Fig. 5.1. The motions associated with sideslip (motion along the y axis), yaw (rotation about the z axis), and roll (rotation about the roll axis) are usually referred to as lateral motions of the vehicle. The behavior of the vehicle in these modes determines, to a great extent, its handling characteristics.

This chapter is intended to serve as an introduction to the study of vehicle handling. A simplified linear vehicle model in which the suspension is neglected will be examined. This model demonstrates the effects of tire properties, location of the center of gravity, and forward speed of the vehicle on the handling behavior, and leads to conclusions of practical importance about directional stability and control. The response of the vehicle to a steering wheel displacement and the stability characteristics associated with a fixed steering wheel, which are usually referred to as fixed-control characteristics, will be analyzed.

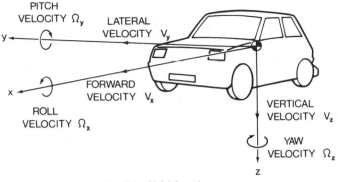

Fig. 5.1 Vehicle axis system.

5.1 STEERING GEOMETRY

In examining the handling characteristics of a road vehicle, it is convenient to begin with the discussion of the cornering behavior of the vehicle at low speeds with the effect of the centrifugal force being neglected. For road vehicles, steering is normally effected by changing the heading of the front wheels through the steering system. At low speeds, there is a simple relation between the direction of motion of the vehicle and the steering wheel angle, and the turning behavior mainly depends on the geometry of the steering linkage. The prime consideration in the design of the steering system geometry is minimum tire scrub during cornering. This requires that during the turn all tires should be in pure rolling without lateral sliding. To satisfy this requirement, the wheels should follow curved paths with radii originating from a common center as shown in Fig. 5.2. This

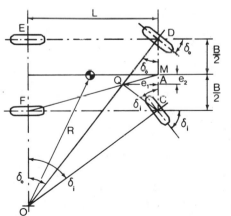

Fig. 5.2 Basic steering geometry.

establishes the proper realtionship between the steer angle of the inside front wheel δ_i and that of the outside front wheel δ_o. From Fig. 5.2, it can be readily seen that the steer angles δ_i and δ_o should satisfy the following relationship

$$\cot\delta_o - \cot\delta_i = \frac{B}{L} \qquad (5.1)$$

where B and L are the track (or tread) and wheelbase of the vehicle, respectively.

The steering geometry that satisfies Eq. 5.1 is usually referred to as the Ackerman steering geometry.

The relationship between δ_i and δ_o that satisfies Eq. 5.1 can be illustrated graphically. Referring to Fig. 5.2, first connect the midpoint of the front axle M with the center of the inside rear wheel F. Then lay out the steer angle of the outside front wheel δ_o from the front axle. Line DO intersects line MF at Q. Connect point Q with the center of the inside front wheel C, then angle $\angle QCM$ is the steer angle of the inside front wheel δ_i that satisfies Eq. 5.1. This can be proved from the geometric relations shown in Fig. 5.2,

$$\cot\delta_o = \frac{B/2 + e_2}{e_1}$$

$$\cot\delta_i = \frac{B/2 - e_2}{e_1}$$

and

$$\cot\delta_o - \cot\delta_i = \frac{2e_2}{e_1} \qquad (5.2)$$

Since triangle $\triangle MAQ$ is similar to triangle $\triangle MCF$,

$$\frac{e_2}{e_1} = \frac{B/2}{L}$$

Eq. 5.2 can then be rewritten as

$$\cot\delta_o - \cot\delta_i = \frac{B}{L}$$

The results of the above analysis indicates that if the steer angles of the front wheels δ_i and δ_o satisfy Eq. 5.1, then by laying out the steer angles δ_i

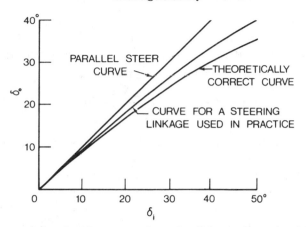

Fig. 5.3 Characteristics of various types of steering linkages. (Reproduced by permission from reference 5.1.)

and δ_o from the front axle, the intersection of the noncommon sides of δ_i and δ_o (i.e., point Q in Fig. 5.2) will lie on the straight line connecting the midpoint of the front axle and the center of the inside rear wheel (i.e., line MF in Fig. 5.2).

Figure 5.3 shows the relationship between δ_o and δ_i that satisfies Eq. 5.1 for a vehicle with $B/L = 0.56$, as compared to a parallel steer curve ($\delta_i = \delta_o$) and that for a typical steering geometry used in practice [5.1].

To evaluate the characteristics of a particular steering linkage with respect to the Ackerman steering geometry, a graphic method may be employed. First, the steer angles of the inside front wheel δ_i with suitable increment are laid out from the initial position of the steer arm CH as shown in Fig. 5.4. Then, from the pivot of the inside steer arm H, an arc is struck with a radius equal to the length of the tie rod HI. This intersects the arc generated by the steer arm of the outside front wheel DI. The intersection then defines the corresponding steer angle of the outside front wheel δ_o. By laying out the steer angles of the inside front wheel δ_i and the corresponding steer angles of the outside front wheel δ_o from the front axle, the noncommon sides of δ_i and δ_o will intersect at points 0_1, 0_2, and 0_3, as shown in Fig. 5.4. If the steering geometry satisfies Eq. 5.1, the intersections of the noncommon sides of δ_i and δ_o will lie on the straight line MF as mentioned previously. The deviation of the curve connecting 0_1, 0_2, and 0_3 from line MF is therefore an indication of the error of the steering geometry with respect to the Ackerman criterion. Steering geometry with an error curve that deviates excessively from line MF shown in Fig. 5.4 will exhibit considerable tire scrub during cornering. This results in excessive tire wear and increased steering effort.

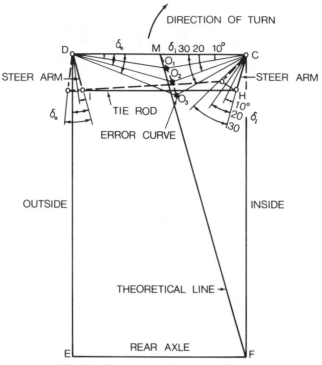

Fig. 5.4   Error curve of a steering linkage.

It should be mentioned that the graphic method described above is only applicable to the type of coplaner steering linkage shown in Fig. 5.4, which is commonly used in vehicles with front beam axles. For vehicles with front independent suspensions, the steering linkage will be more complex. Dependent on the type of independent suspension used, the front wheels may be steered via a three-piece tie rod or by a rack and pinion with outer tie rods. The approach for constructing steering error curves for these linkages is similar to that described above. The procedure, however, is more involved.

5.2   STEADY-STATE HANDLING CHARACTERISTICS

Steady-state handling performance is concerned with the directional behavior of a vehicle during a turn under non-time-varying conditions. An example of a steady-state turn is a vehicle negotiating a curve with constant radius at constant forward speed. In the analysis of steady-state handling behavior, the inertia properties of the vehicle are not involved.

When a vehicle is negotiating a turn at moderate or higher speeds, the effect of the centrifugal force acting at the center of gravity can no longer be neglected. To balance the centrifugal force, the tires must develop appropriate cornering forces. As discussed in Chapter 1, a side force acting on a tire produces a side slip angle. Thus, when a vehicle is negotiating a turn at moderate or higher speeds, the four tires will develop appropriate slip angles. To simplify the analysis, the pair of tires on an axle are represented by a single tire with double the cornering stiffness as shown in Fig. 5.5. The handling characteristics of the vehicle depend, to a great extent, on the relationship between the slip angles of the front and rear tires, α_f and α_r.

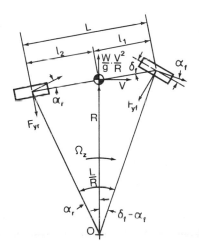

Fig. 5.5 Simplified steady-state handling model.

The steady-state handling response of a vehicle at moderate and higher speeds will have a more complex relation with the steering input than that at low speeds. From the geometry shown in Fig. 5.5, the relationship between the steer angle of the front tire δ_f, turning radius R, wheel base L, and the slip angles of the front and rear tires α_f and α_r is given by [5.2, 5.3]

$$\delta_f - \alpha_f + \alpha_r = \frac{L}{R}$$

or

$$\delta_f = \frac{L}{R} + \alpha_f - \alpha_r \qquad (5.3)$$

This indicates that the steer angle δ_f required to negotiate a given curve is a function of not only the turning radius R but also the front and rear slip angles α_f and α_r. The slip angles α_f and α_r are dependent on the side forces acting on the tires and their cornering stiffness. The cornering forces on the front and rear tires F_{yf} and F_{yr} can be determined from the equilibrium of the vehicle in the lateral direction. For small steer angles, the cornering forces acting at the front and rear tires are approximately given by

$$F_{yf} = \frac{W}{g} \frac{V^2}{R} \frac{l_2}{L} \tag{5.4}$$

$$F_{yr} = \frac{W}{g} \frac{V^2}{R} \frac{l_1}{L} \tag{5.5}$$

where W is the total weight of vehicle, g is the acceleration due to gravity, V is vehicle forward speed, and other parameters are shown in Fig. 5.5.

The normal load on each of the front wheels W_f and that on each of the rear wheels W_r under static conditions are expressed by

$$W_f = \frac{Wl_2}{2L}$$

$$W_r = \frac{Wl_1}{2L}$$

Equations 5.4 and 5.5 can be rewritten as

$$F_{yf} = 2W_f \frac{V^2}{gR} \tag{5.6}$$

$$F_{yr} = 2W_r \frac{V^2}{gR} \tag{5.7}$$

The slip angles α_f and α_r therefore are given by

$$\alpha_f = \frac{F_{yf}}{2C_{\alpha f}} = \frac{W_f}{C_{\alpha f}} \frac{V^2}{gR} \tag{5.8}$$

$$\alpha_r = \frac{F_{yr}}{2C_{\alpha r}} = \frac{W_r}{C_{\alpha r}} \frac{V^2}{gR} \tag{5.9}$$

where $C_{\alpha f}$ and $C_{\alpha r}$ are the cornering stiffness of each of the front and rear tires, respectively. As described in Chapter 1, the cornering stiffness of a given tire varies with a number of operational parameters including inflation pressure, normal load, tractive (or braking) effort, and lateral force. It may be regarded as a constant only within a limited range of operating conditions.

Substituting Eqs. 5.8 and 5.9 into Eq. 5.3, the expression for the steer angle δ_f required to negotiate a given curve becomes [5.2, 5.3]

$$\delta_f = \frac{L}{R} + \left(\frac{W_f}{C_{\alpha f}} - \frac{W_r}{C_{\alpha r}} \right) \frac{V^2}{gR}$$

$$= \frac{L}{R} + K_{us} \frac{V^2}{gR} \tag{5.10}$$

where K_{us} is usually referred to as the understeer coefficient, and is expressed in radians. Equation 5.10 is the fundamental equation governing the steady-state handling behavior of a road vehicle. It indicates that the steer angle required to negotiate a given curve depends on the wheelbase, weight distribution, forward speed, and tire cornering stiffness.

Dependent on the values of the understeer coefficient K_{us} or the relationship between the slip angles of the front and rear tires, the steady-state handling characteristics may be classified into three categories: neutral steer, understeer, and oversteer [5.2].

5.2.1   Neutral Steer

When the understeer coefficient $K_{us} = 0$, which is equivalent to the slip angles of the front and rear tires being equal (i.e., $\alpha_f = \alpha_r$, and $W_f/C_{\alpha f} = W_r/C_{\alpha r}$), the steer angle δ_f required to negotiate a given curve is independent of forward speed and is given by

$$\delta_f = \frac{L}{R} \tag{5.11}$$

A vehicle having this handling property is said to be neutral steer. Its characteristics for a constant radius turn are represented by a horizontal line in the steer angle-speed diagram shown in Fig. 5.6.

For a nuetral steer vehicle, when it is accelerated in a constant radius turn, the driver should maintain the same steering wheel position. In other words, when it is accelerated with the steering wheel fixed, the turning radius remains the same, as illustrated in Fig. 5.7. When a neutral steer vehicle moving on a straight course is subjected to a side force acting at the center of gravity, equal slip angles will be developed at the front and rear tires (i.e., $\alpha_f = \alpha_r$). As a result, the vehicle follows a straight line path at an angle to the original as shown in Fig. 5.8.

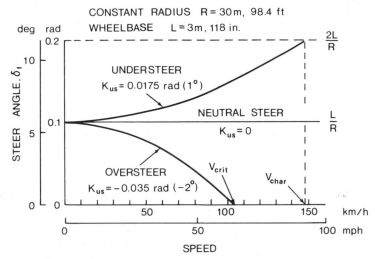

Fig. 5.6 Relationships between steer angle and speed of neutral steer, understeer, and oversteer vehicles.

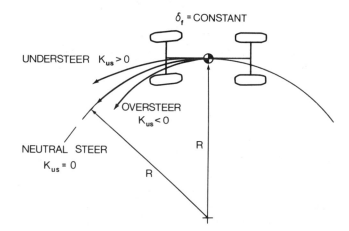

Fig. 5.7 Curvature responses of neutral steer, understeer, and oversteer vehicles at a fixed steer angle.

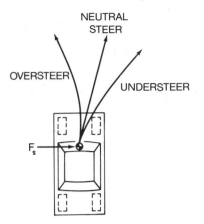

Fig. 5.8 Directional responses of neutral steer, understeer, and oversteer vehicles subjected to a side force at the center of gravity.

5.2.2 Understeer

When the understeer coefficient $K_{us} > 0$, which is equivalent to the slip angle of the front tire α_f being greater than that of the rear tire α_r (i.e., $\alpha_f > \alpha_r$ and $W_f / C_{\alpha f} > W_r / C_{\alpha r}$), the steer angle δ_f required to negotiate a given curve increases with the square of vehicle forward speed. A vehicle with this handling property is said to be understeer. Its characteristics for a constant radius turn are represented by a parabola in the steer angle-speed diagram shown in Fig. 5.6.

For an understeer vehicle, when it is accelerated in a constant radius turn, the driver must increase the steer angle. In other words, when it is accelerated with the steering wheel fixed, the turning radius increases, as illustrated in Fig. 5.7. When a side force acts at the center of gravity of an understeer vehicle, the front tires will develop a slip angle greater than that of the rear tires (i.e., $\alpha_f > \alpha_r$). As a result, a yaw motion is initiated and the vehicle turns away from the side force as shown in Fig. 5.8.

For an understeer vehicle, a characteristic speed V_{char} may be identified. It is the speed at which the steer angle required to negotiate a turn is equal to $2L/R$, as shown in Fig. 5.6. From Eq. 5.10,

$$V_{char} = \sqrt{\frac{gL}{K_{us}}} \tag{5.12}$$

5.2.3 Oversteer

When the understeer coefficient $K_{us} < 0$, which is equivalent to the slip angle of the front tire α_f being less than that of the rear tire α_r (i.e., $\alpha_f < \alpha_r$

and $W_f/C_{\alpha f} < W_r/C_{\alpha r}$), the steer angle δ_f required to negotiate a given curve decreases with the increase of vehicle forward speed. A vehicle with this handling property is said to be oversteer. The relationship between the required steer angle and forward speed for this kind of vehicle at a constant radius turn is illustrated in Fig. 5.6.

For an oversteer vehicle, when it is accelerated in a constant radius turn, the driver must decrease the steer angle. In other words, when it is accelerated with the steering wheel fixed, the turning radius decreases, as illustrated in Fig. 5.7. When a side force acts at the center of gravity of an oversteer vehicle originally proceeding in a straight line, the front tires will develop a slip angle less than that of the rear tires (i.e., $\alpha_f < \alpha_r$). As a result, a yaw motion is initiated, and the vehicle turns into the side force as illustrated in Fig. 5.8.

For an oversteer vehicle, a critical speed V_{crit} can be identified. It is the speed at which the steer angle required to negotiate any turn is zero as shown in Fig. 5.6. From Eq. 5.10,

$$V_{crit} = \sqrt{\frac{gL}{-K_{us}}} \qquad (5.13)$$

It should be noted that for an oversteer vehicle the understeer coefficient K_{us} in the above equation has a negative sign. It will be shown later that the critical speed also represents the speed above which an oversteer vehicle exhibits directional instability.

The prime factors controlling the steady-state handling characteristics of a vehicle are the weight distribution of the vehicle and the cornering stiffness of the tires. A front-engined, front-wheel-drive vehicle with large proportion of the vehicle weight on the front tires may tend to exhibit understeer behavior. A rear-engined, rear-wheel-drive car with large proportion of the vehicle weight on the rear tires, on the other hand, may tend to have oversteer characteristics [5.1]. Changes of weight distribution will alter the handling behavior of a vehicle.

A number of design and operational parameters affect the cornering stiffness of tires, thus the handling performance of the vehicle. Mixing of radial-ply with bias-ply tires in a vehicle may have serious consequences in its handling characteristics. Installing laterally stiff radial-ply tires on the front and relatively flexible bias-ply tires on the rear may change an otherwise understeer vehicle to an oversteer one. Lowering the inflation pressure in the rear tires can have similar effects, as the cornering stiffness of a tire usually decreases with the decrease of inflation pressure. The lateral load transfer from the inside tire to the outside tire on an axle during cornering will increase the slip angle required to generate a specific cornering force as discussed in Chapter 1. Thus lateral load transfer will affect the handling behavior of the vehicle. The application of driving or braking torque to the tire during a turn will also affect the cornering behavior of the vehicle, as driving or braking torque modifies the cornering properties of the tire as mentioned in Chapter 1. For a rear-wheel-drive vehicle, the application of tractive effort during a turn reduces the cornering stiffness of the rear tires, producing an oversteering effect. On the other hand, for a front-wheel-drive car, the application of tractive effort during a turn reduces the cornering stiffness of the front tires, thus introducing an understeering effect.

It should also be mentioned that the effects of roll steer (the steering motion of the front or rear wheels due to the rolling motion of the sprung mass relative to the unsprung mass), roll camber (the change in camber of the wheels due to the motion of the sprung mass relative to the unsprung mass), and compliance steer (the steering motion of the wheels with respect to the sprung mass resulting from compliance in, and forces on, the suspension and steering linkages) would be significant under certain circumstances, and that they should be taken into account in a more comprehensive analysis of vehicle handling. The effect of these factors can, however, be included in a modified form of the understeer coefficient K_{us}, and Eq. 5.10, which describes the steady-state handling performance, still holds.

In summary, there are a number of design and operational factors that would affect the understeer coefficient of a vehicle and hence its handling characteristics. For a practical vehicle, the understeer coefficient would vary with operating conditions. Figure 5.9 shows the changes in the understeer coefficient, expressed in degrees, with lateral acceleration for four different types of car [5.4]. Curve 1 represents the characteristics of a

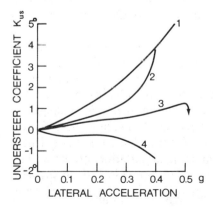

Fig. 5.9 Variation of understeer coefficient with lateral acceleration of various types of car. 1—a conventional front engine/rear-wheel-drive car; 2—a European front engine/front-wheel-drive car; 3—a European rear engine/rear-wheel-drive car; 4—an American rear engine/rear-wheel-drive car. (Reproduced by permission from reference 5.4.)

conventional front-engine/rear-wheel-drive car. It shows that the understeer coefficient increases sharply with the increase of lateral acceleration. Curve 2 represents the behavior of a European front-engine/front-wheel-drive car. It exhibits similar characteristics. The characteristics of a European rear-engine/rear-wheel-drive car are represented by curve 3. It indicates that the vehicle exhibits understeer behavior up to lateral acceleration of approximately 0.5 g, above which it tends to become oversteer. The behavior of an American rear-engine/rear-wheel-drive compact car is represented by curve 4. It shows that the vehicle exhibits oversteer characteristics in the full operating range.

Among the three types of steady-state handling behavior, oversteer is not desirable from directional stability point of view, which will be discussed later in this chapter. It is considered desirable for a road vehicle to have a small degree of understeer up to a certain level of lateral acceleration, such as 0.4 g, with increasing understeer beyond this point [5.4] This would have the advantages of sensitive response associated with a small degree of understeer during the majority of cornering conditions. The increased understeer at higher lateral accelerations, on the other hand, would provide the required stability during tight turns.

Example 5.1 A passenger car has a weight of 20.105 kN (4520 lb) and a wheel base of 3.2 m (10.5 ft). The weight distribution on the front axle is 53.5% and that on the rear axle is 46.5% under static conditions.

A   If the cornering stiffness of each of the front tires is 38.92 kN/rad (8750 lb/rad) and that of the rear tires is 38.25 kN/rad (8600 lb/rad), determine the steady-state handling behavior of the vehicle.

B   If the front tires are replaced by a pair of radial tires, each of which has a cornering stiffness of 47.82 kN/rad (10,750 lb/rad), and the rear tires remain unchanged, determine the steady-state handling behavior of the vehicle under these circumstances.

Solution.

A   The understeer coefficient of the vehicle is

$$K_{us} = \frac{W_f}{C_{\alpha f}} - \frac{W_r}{C_{\alpha r}} = \frac{20,105 \times 0.535}{2 \times 38,920} - \frac{20,105 \times 0.465}{2 \times 38,250}$$

$$= 0.016 \text{ rad } (0.92°)$$

The vehicle is understeer and the characteristic speed is

$$V_{char} = \sqrt{\frac{gL}{K_{us}}} = 44.3 \text{ m/s} = 159 \text{ km/h } (99 \text{ mph})$$

B When a pair of radial tires with higher cornering stiffness are installed in the front axle, the understeer coefficient of the vehicle is

$$K_{us} = \frac{20,105 \times 0.535}{2 \times 47,820} - \frac{20,105 \times 0.465}{2 \times 38,250} = -0.0097 \text{ rad } (-0.56°)$$

The vehicle is oversteer and the critical speed is

$$V_{crit} = \sqrt{\frac{gL}{-K_{us}}} = 56.8 \text{ m/s} = 204 \text{ km/h (127 mph)}$$

5.3   STEADY-STATE RESPONSE TO STEERING INPUT

A vehicle may be regarded as a control system upon which various inputs are imposed. During a turning maneuver the steer angle induced by the driver can be considered as input to the system and the motion variables of the vehicle, such as yaw velocity, lateral acceleration, and curvature may be regarded as outputs. The ratio of the yaw velocity, lateral acceleration or curvature to the steering input can then be used for comparing the response characteristics of different vehicles [5.2, 5.3].

5.3.1   Yaw Velocity Response

Yaw velocity gain is an often used parameter for comparing the steering response of road vehicles. It is defined as the ratio of the steady state yaw velocity to the steer angle. Yaw velocity Ω_z of the vehicle under steady-state conditions is the ratio of the forward speed V to the turning radius R. From Eq. 5.10, the yaw velocity gain G_{yaw} is given by

$$G_{yaw} = \frac{\Omega_z}{\delta_f} = \frac{V}{L + K_{us} V^2 / g} \tag{5.14}$$

Eq. 5.14 gives the yaw velocity gain with respect to the steer angle of the front wheel. If the yaw velocity gain with respect to the steering wheel displacement is desired, the value obtained from Eq. 5.14 should be divided by the steering gear ratio.

For a neutral steer vehicle, the understeer coefficient K_{us} is zero, the yaw velocity gain increases linearly with the increase of forward speed as shown in Fig. 5.10. For an understeer vehicle, the understeer coefficient K_{us} is positive. The yaw velocity gain first increases with the increase of forward speed and reaches a maximum at a particular speed as shown in Fig. 5.10. It can be proved that the maximum yaw velocity gain occurs at the characteristic speed V_{char} mentioned previously.

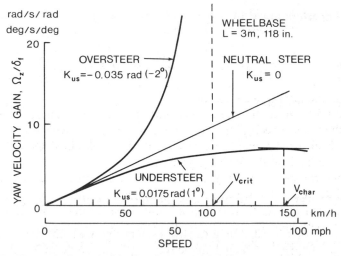

Fig. 5.10 Yaw velocity gain characteristics of neutral steer, understeer, and oversteer vehicles.

For an oversteer vehicle, the understeer coefficient K_{us} is negative, the yaw velocity gain increases with the forward speed at an increasing rate as shown in Fig. 5.10. Since K_{us} is negative, at a particular speed the denominator of Eq. 5.14 is zero, and the yaw velocity gain approaches infinity. This speed is the critical speed V_{crit} of an oversteer vehicle discussed previously.

The results of the above analysis indicate that from the point of view of handling response to steering input, an oversteer vehicle is more sensitive than a neutral steer one, and in turn a vehicle with neutral steer characteristics is more responsive than an understeer one. Since yaw velocity of a vehicle is an easily measured parameter, the yaw velocity gain-speed characteristics can be obtained from tests. The handling behavior of a vehicle can then be evaluated from the yaw velocity gain characteristics. For instance, if the yaw velocity gain of a vehicle is found to be greater than the forward speed divided by the wheel base (i.e., neutral steer response) the vehicle is oversteer, and if it is less, it is understeer.

5.3.2 Lateral Acceleration Response

Lateral acceleration gain that is defined as the ratio of the steady-state lateral acceleration to the steer angle is another commonly used parameter for evaluating the steering response of a vehicle. By rearranging Eq. 5.10, the lateral acceleration gain G_{acc} is given by

$$G_{acc} = \frac{V^2/gR}{\delta_f} = \frac{a_y/g}{\delta_f} = \frac{V^2}{gL + K_{us}V^2} \qquad (5.15)$$

where a_y is the lateral acceleration.

Equation 5.15 gives the lateral acceleration gain with respect to the steer angle of the front wheel. If the lateral acceleration gain with respect to the steering wheel displacement is desired, the value obtained from Eq. 5.15 should be divided by the steering gear ratio.

For a neutral steer vehicle, the value of the understeer coefficient K_{us} is zero, the lateral acceleration gain is proportional to the square of forward speed as shown in Fig. 5.11(a). For an understeer vehicle, the value of the understeer coefficient K_{us} is positive, the lateral acceleration gain increases with speed and approaches a finite value asymptotically as shown in Fig. 5.11(a). At very high speed, the first term in the denominator of Eq. 5.15 is much smaller than the second term, and the lateral acceleration gain approaches a value of $1/K_{us}$.

For an oversteer vehicle, the value of the understeer coefficient K_{us} is negative. The lateral acceleration gain increases with the increase of forward speed at an increasing rate, as the denominator of Eq. 5.15 decreases with the increase of speed. At a particular speed, the denominator of Eq. 5.15 becomes zero, and the lateral acceleration gain approaches infinity. It can be shown that this speed is the critical speed of an oversteer vehicle.

5.3.3 Curvature Response

The ratio of the steady-state curvature $1/R$ to the steer angle δ_f is another parameter commonly used for evaluating the response characteristics of a vehicle. From Eq. 5.10, this parameter is expressed by

$$\frac{1/R}{\delta_f} = \frac{1}{L + K_{us}V^2/g} \qquad (5.16)$$

Equation 5.16 gives the curvature response with respect to the steer angle of the front wheel. If the curvature response with respect to the steering wheel displacement is desired, the value obtained from Eq. 5.16 should be divided by the steering gear ratio.

For a neutral steer vehicle, the understeer coefficient K_{us} is zero, the curvature response is independent of forward speed as shown in Fig. 5.11(b). For an understeer vehicle, the understeer coefficient K_{us} is positive,

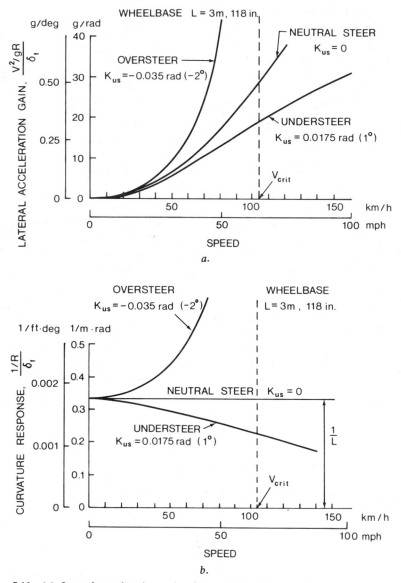

Fig. 5.11 (*a*) Lateral acceleration gain characteristics of neutral steer, understeer, and oversteer vehicles. (*b*) Curvature response of neutral steer, understeer and oversteer vehicles.

the curvature response decreases as the forward speed increases as shown in Fig. 5.11(b).

For an oversteer vehicle, the understeer coefficient K_{us} is negative, the curvature response increases with the forward speed. At a particular speed, the curvature response approaches infinity as shown in Fig. 5.11(b). This means that the turning radius approaches zero, and the vehicle spins and loses control. This speed is in fact the critical speed V_{crit} of an oversteer vehicle discussed previously.

The results of the above analysis illustrate that from the steering response point of view, the oversteer vehicle has the most sensitive handling characteristics, while the understeer vehicle is least responsive.

Example 5.2 A passenger car has a weight of 20.105 kN (4520 lb) and a wheelbase of 3.2 m (10.5 ft). The ratio of the distance between the center of gravity of the vehicle and the front axle to the wheelbase is 0.465. The cornering stiffness of each of the front tires is 38.92 kN/rad (8750 lb/rad) and that of the rear tires is 38.25 kN/rad (8600 lb/rad). The steering gear ratio is 25. Determine the yaw velocity gain and the lateral acceleration gain of the vehicle with respect to the steering wheel displacement.

Solution. The understeer coefficient of the vehicle is

$$K_{us} = \frac{W_f}{C_{\alpha f}} - \frac{W_r}{C_{\alpha r}} = \frac{20,105 \times 0.535}{2 \times 38,920} - \frac{20,105 \times 0.465}{2 \times 38,250} = 0.016 \text{ rad } (0.92°)$$

From Eq. 5.14, the yaw velocity gain with respect to the steering wheel displacement is

$$G_{yaw} = \frac{\Omega_r}{\delta_f \xi_s} = \frac{V}{(L + K_{us} V^2/g)\xi_s}$$

where ξ_s is the steering gear ratio. The yaw velocity gain of the vehicle as a function of forward speed is shown in Fig. 5.12. From Eq 5.15, the lateral acceleration gain with respect to steering wheel angle is

$$G_{acc} = \frac{a_y/g}{\delta_f \xi_s} = \frac{V^2}{(gL + K_{us} V^2)\xi_s}$$

The lateral acceleration gain of the vehicle as a function of forward speed is also shown in Fig. 5.12.

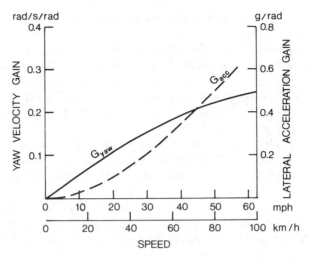

Fig. 5.12   Yaw velocity gain and lateral acceleration gain characteristics of a passenger car.

5.4   TESTING OF HANDLING CHARACTERISTICS

To determine the actual handling behavior of a road vehicle under steady-state conditions, various types of test can be conducted on a skid pad which in essence is a large, flat paved area. Three types of test can be distinguished: the constant radius test, the constant forward speed test, and the constant steer angle test. During the tests, the steer angle, forward speed, and yaw velocity (or lateral acceleration) of the vehicle are usually measured. Yaw velocity can be measured by a rate-gyro or determined by the lateral acceleration divided by vehicle forward speed. Lateral acceleration can be measured by an accelerometer or determined by the product of yaw velocity and vehicle forward speed. Based on the relationship between the steer angle and lateral acceleration or yaw vevelocity obtained from tests, the handling characteristics of the vehicle can be evaluated.

5.4.1   Constant Radius Test

In this test, the vehicle is driven along a curve with a constant radius at various speeds. The steer angle δ_f or the angle of the steering wheel required to maintain the vehicle on course at various forward speeds together with the corresponding lateral acceleration are measured. The steady-state lateral acceleration can also be deduced from vehicle forward speed and the given turning radius. The results can be plotted as shown in Fig. 5.13 [5.5]. The handling behavior of the vehicle can then be de-

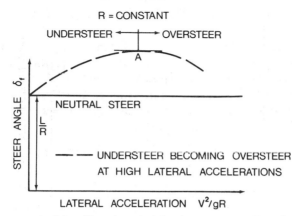

Fig. 5.13 Assessment of handling characteristics by constant radius of turn tests (From *Vehicle Dynamics*, by J. R. Ellis, Business Books, 1969, reproduced by permission of the author.)

termined from the slope of the steer angle-lateral acceleration curve. From Eq. 5.10, for a constant turning radius, the slope of curve is given by

$$\frac{d\delta_f}{d(a_y/g)} = K_{us} \tag{5.17}$$

This indicates that the slope of the curve represents the value of the understeer coefficient.

If the steer angle required to maintain the vehicle on a constant radius turn is the same for all forward speeds (i.e., the slope of the steer angle-lateral acceleration curve is zero), as shown in Fig. 5.13, the vehicle is neutral steer. The vehicle is considered to be understeer, when the slope of the steer angle-lateral acceleration curve is positive, which indicates the value of the understeer coefficient K_{us} being greater than zero, as shown in Fig. 5.13. The vehicle is considered to be oversteer, when the slope of the curve is negative, which indicates the value of the understeer coefficient K_{us} being less than zero, as illustrated in Fig. 5.13.

For a practical vehicle, owing to the nonlinear behavior of tires and suspensions, load transfer, and the effects of tractive (or braking) effort, the value of the understeer coefficient K_{us} varies with operating conditions. A curve rather than a straight line to represent the steer angle-lateral acceleration relationship is to be expected. It is possible for a vehicle to have understeer characteristics at low lateral accelerations and oversteer characteristics at high lateral accelerations as shown in Fig. 5.13.

5.4.2   Constant Speed Test

In this test, the vehicle is driven at constant forward speed at various turning radii. The steer angle and the lateral acceleration are measured. The results can be plotted as shown in Fig 5.14 [5.5]. The handling behavior of the vehicle can then be determined from the slope of the steer angle-lateral acceleration curve. From Eq. 5.10, for a constant speed turn, the slope of the curve is given by

$$\frac{d\delta_f}{d(a_y/g)} = \frac{gL}{V^2} + K_{us} \qquad (5.18)$$

If the vehicle is neutral steer, the value of the understeer coefficient K_{us} will be zero and the slope of the steer angle-lateral acceleration line will be a constant of gL/V^2, as shown in Fig. 5.14 [5.5].

The vehicle is considered to be understeer, when the slope of the steer angle-lateral acceleration curve is greater than the neutral steer response for a given forward speed (i.e., gL/V^2), which indicates that the value of the understeer coefficient K_{us} is positive as shown in Fig. 5.14. The vehicle is considered to be oversteer, when the slope of the curve is less than the neutral steer response for a given forward speed (i.e., gL/V^2), which indicates that the value of the understeer coefficient K_{us} is negative, as shown in Fig. 5.14.

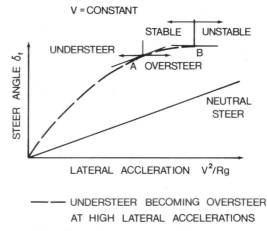

Fig. 5.14 Assessment of handling characteristics by constant speed tests (From *Vehicle Dynamics*, by J. R. Ellis, Business Books, 1969, reproduced by permission of the author.)

When the slope of the curve is zero

$$\frac{gL}{V^2} + K_{us} = 0$$

and

$$V^2 = \frac{gL}{(-K_{us})} = V_{crit}^2$$

This indicates that the oversteer vehicle is operating at the critical speed, and that the vehicle is directionally unstable.

If, during the tests, steer angle and yaw velocity are measured, then the slope of the steer angle-yaw velocity curve can also be used to evaluate the steady state handling behavior of the vehicle in a similar way.

5.4.3 Constant Steer Angle Test

In this test, the vehicle is driven with fixed steer angle at various forward speeds. The lateral accelerations at various speeds are measured. From the test results, the curvature $1/R$, which can be calculated from the measured lateral acceleration and forward speed by $1/R = a_y/V^2$, is plotted against lateral acceleration as shown in Fig. 5.15. The handling behavior can then be determined by the slope of the curvature-lateral acceleration curve. From Eq. 5.10, for a constant steer angle, the slope of the curve is given by

$$\frac{d(1/R)}{d(a_y/g)} = -\frac{K_{us}}{L} \tag{5.19}$$

If the vehicle is neutral steer, the value of the understeer coefficient K_{us} will be zero and the slope of the curvature-lateral acceleration line is zero.

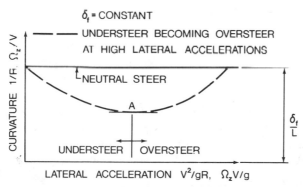

Fig. 5.15 Assessment of handling characteristics by fixed steer angle tests.

The characteristics of a neutral steer vehicle are therefore represented by a horizontal line as shown in Fig. 5.15.

The vehicle is considered to be understeer, when the slope of the curvature-lateral aceleration curve is negative, which indicates that the value of the understeer coefficient K_{us} is positive, as shown in Fig. 5.15. The vehicle is considered to be oversteer, when the slope of the curvature-lateral acceleration curve is positive, which indicates the value of the understeer coefficient K_{us} is negative.

In general, the constant radius test is the simplest and requires little instrumentation. The steer angle and forward speed are the only essential parameters that require to be measured during the test, as the steady-state lateral acceleration can be deduced from the vehicle forward speed and the given turning radius. The constant speed test is more representative of the actual road behavior of a vehicle than the constant radius test, as the driver usually maintains a more or less constant speed in a turn and turns the steering wheel by the required amount to negotiate the curve. The constant steer angle test, on the other hand, is easy to execute. Both the constant speed and constant steer angle tests would require, however, the measurement of the lateral acceleration or yaw velocity.

5.5 TRANSIENT RESPONSE CHARACTERISTICS

Between the application of steering input and the attainment of steady-state motion, the vehicle is in a transient state. The behavior of the vehicle in this period is usually referred to as transient response characteristics. The overall handling qualities of a vehicle depend, to a great extent, on its transient behavior. The optimum transient response of a vehicle is that which has the fastest response with a minimum of oscillation in the process of approaching the steady-state motion.

In analyzing the transient response, the inertia properties of the vehicle must be taken into consideration. During a turning maneuver, the vehicle is in translation as well as in rotation. To describe its motion, it is convenient to use a set of axes fixed to and moving with the vehicle body, because with respect to these axes the mass moments of inertia of the vehicle are constant, whereas with respect to axes fixed in space the mass moments of inertia vary as the vehicle changes its orientation.

To formulate the equations of transient motion for a vehicle during a turning maneuver, it is necessary to express the absolute acceleration of the center of gravity of the vehicle (i.e., the acceleration with respect to axes fixed in space) using the reference frame attached to the vehicle body [5.6].

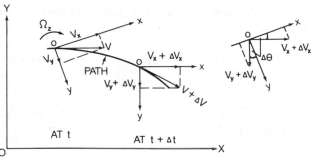

Fig. 5.16 Analysis of the motions of a vehicle using axes fixed to the vehicle body.

Let ox and oy be the longitudinal and lateral axes fixed to the vehicle body with origin at the center of gravity, and let V_x and V_y be the components of the velocity V of the center of gravity along the axes ox and oy, respectively, at time t as shown in Fig. 5.16. As the vehicle is in both translation and rotation during a turn, at time $t + \Delta t$, the direction and magnitude of the velocity of the center of gravity as well as the orientation of the longitudinal and lateral axes of the vehicle change, as shown in Fig. 5.16. The change of the velocity component parallel to ox axis is

$$(V_x + \Delta V_x)\cos\Delta\theta - V_x - (V_y + \Delta V_y)\sin\Delta\theta$$

$$= V_x \cos\Delta\theta + \Delta V_x \cos\Delta\theta - V_x - V_y \sin\Delta\theta - \Delta V_y \sin\Delta\theta$$

$$(5.20)$$

Consider that $\Delta\theta$ is small and neglect second-order terms, the above expression becomes

$$\Delta V_x - V_y \Delta\theta \tag{5.21}$$

The component along the longitudinal axis of the absolute acceleration of the center of gravity of the vehicle can be obtained by dividing the above expression by Δt. In the limit, this gives

$$a_x = \frac{dV_x}{dt} - V_y \frac{d\theta}{dt} = \dot{V}_x - V_y \Omega_z \tag{5.22}$$

The component dV_x/dt (or $\dot{V}_x$) is due to the changing magnitude of the velocity component V_x and is directed along the ox axis, and the component $V_y \, d\theta/dt$ (or $V_y \Omega_z$) is due to the rotation of the velocity component

V_y. Following a similar approach, the component of the absolute acceleration of the center of gravity of the vehicle along the lateral axis is

$$a_y = \frac{dV_y}{dt} + V_x \frac{d\theta}{dt} = \dot{V}_y + V_x \Omega_z \qquad (5.23)$$

Referring to Fig. 5.17, for a vehicle having plane motion, the equations
of motion using axes fixed to the vehicle body are given by

$$m(\dot{V}_x - V_y \Omega_z) = F_{xf} \cos \delta_f + F_{xr} - F_{yf} \sin \delta_f \qquad (5.24)$$

$$m(\dot{V}_y + V_x \Omega_z) = F_{yr} + F_{yf} \cos \delta_f + F_{xf} \sin \delta_f \qquad (5.25)$$

$$I_z \dot{\Omega}_z = l_1 F_{yf} \cos \delta_f - l_2 F_{yr} + l_1 F_{xf} \sin \delta_f \qquad (5.26)$$

where I_z is the mass moment of inertia of the vehicle about the z axis (see
Fig. 5.1).

In deriving the above equations, it is assumed that the vehicle body is
symmetric about the longitudinal plane (i.e., xoz plane in Fig. 5.1) and that
roll motion of the vehicle body is neglected.

If the vehicle is neither accelerating nor decelerating in the longitudinal
direction, Eq. 5.24 may be omitted and the lateral motions of the vehicle
are governed by Eqs. 5.25 and 5.26.

The slip angles α_f and α_r can be defined in terms of vehicle motion
variables Ω_z and V_y. Referring to Fig. 5.17 and using the usual small angle

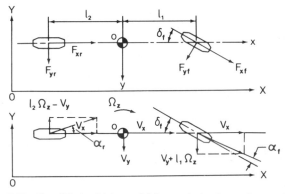

Fig. 5.17 Simplified vehicle model for analysis of transient motions.

assumptions,

$$\alpha_f = \delta_f - \frac{l_1 \Omega_z + V_y}{V_x} \tag{5.27}$$

$$\alpha_r = \frac{l_2 \Omega_z - V_y}{V_x} \tag{5.28}$$

The lateral forces acting on the front and rear tires are a function of the corresponding slip angle and cornering stiffness and are expressed by

$$F_{yf} = 2C_{\alpha f}\alpha_f \tag{5.29}$$

$$F_{yr} = 2C_{\alpha r}\alpha_r \tag{5.30}$$

Combining Eqs. 5.25–5.30, and assuming that the steer angle is small and F_{xf} is zero, the equations of lateral motions of a vehicle with steer angle as the only input variable become

$$m\dot{V}_y + \left[mV_x + \frac{2l_1 C_{\alpha f} - 2l_2 C_{\alpha r}}{V_x} \right] \Omega_z + \left[\frac{2C_{\alpha f} + 2C_{\alpha r}}{V_x} \right] V_y = 2C_{\alpha f}\ \delta_f(t) \tag{5.31}$$

$$I_z \dot{\Omega}_z + \left[\frac{2l_1^2 C_{\alpha f} + 2l_2^2 C_{\alpha r}}{V_x} \right] \Omega_z + \left[\frac{2l_1 C_{\alpha f} - 2l_2 C_{\alpha r}}{V_x} \right] V_y = 2l_1 C_{\alpha f}\ \delta_f(t) \tag{5.32}$$

In the above equations, $\delta_f(t)$ represents the steer angle of the front wheel as a function of time. If, in addition to the steer angle, external forces or moments, such as aerodynamic forces and moments, are acting on the vehicle, they should be added to the right-hand side of Eqs. 5.31 and 5.32 as input variables.

When the input variables, such as the steer angle and external disturbing forces, and the initial conditions are known, the response of the vehicle, expressed in terms of yaw velocity Ω_z and lateral velocity V_y as functions of time, can be determined by solving the differential equations. As an example, Fig. 5.18 shows the yaw velocity responses to a step input of steering angle of 0.01 rad (0.57°) for a station wagon with different types of tire traveling at 96 km/h (60 mph) [5.7]. Figure 5.19 shows the yaw velocity responses to a step input of aerodynamic side force of 890 N (200 lb) for the same vehicle [5.7].

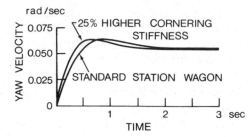

Fig. 5.18   Yaw velocity response of a station wagon to a step input of steer angle of 0.01 rad at 96 km/h (60 mph). (Reproduced by permission of the Society of Automotive Engineers from reference 5.7.)

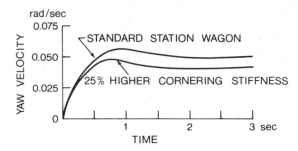

Fig. 5.19   Yaw velocity response of a station wagon to a step input of lateral force of 890 N (200 lb) at 96 km/h (60 mph). (Reproduced by permission of the Society of Automotive Engineers from reference 5.7.)

5.6   DIRECTIONAL STABILITY

Directional stability of a vehicle is concerned with its ability to stabilize its direction of motion against disturbances. A vehicle is considered to be directionally stable if it returns to a steady-state regime within a finite time after the disturbance is removed. A directionally unstable vehicle diverges more and more from the original path even after the disturbance is removed. The disturbance may arise from crosswind, momentary forces acting on the tires from the road, slight movements of the steering wheel, and a variety of other causes.

In many cases, a vehicle may be simplified to a linear dynamic system. The equations of lateral motions are a set of linear differential equations with constant coefficients as shown in Eqs. 5.31 and 5.32. When the vehicle is initially subject to a disturbance, after the disturbance is removed, the yaw and lateral velocities, Ω_z and V_y, will vary with time exponentially $e^{\Psi t}$, and the stability of the vehicle is determined by the value of Ψ. If Ψ is real and positive, the values of yaw and lateral velocities will increase exponentially with time and the vehicle will be directionally unstable. A real and negative value of Ψ indicates that motions of the vehicle converge to a steady state in a finite time and that the vehicle is directionally stable. If Ψ is complex with positive real part, the motions will be oscillatory with increasing amplitudes and thus the system will be directionally unstable. A complex value of Ψ with negative real part indicates that the motions are oscillatory with decreasing amplitudes and thus the vehicle is directionally stable.

To evaluate the directional stability of a vehicle, it is, therefore, necessary to determine the values of Ψ. Since only the motion of the vehicle after disturbance is of interest in the evaluation of stability, steering input and the like are taken to be zero. This is equivalent to the examination of the free vibration of the vehicle in the lateral direction after the initial disturbance is removed. To obtain the values of Ψ, the following solutions to the differential equations for lateral motions (i.e., Eq. 5.31 and 5.32) are assumed

$$V_y = A_1 e^{\Psi t} \tag{5.33}$$

$$\Omega_z = A_2 e^{\Psi t} \tag{5.34}$$

Then

$$\dot{V}_y = A_1 \Psi e^{\Psi t} \tag{5.35}$$

$$\dot{\Omega}_z = A_2 \Psi e^{\Psi t} \tag{5.36}$$

On substituting these values into Eqs. 5.31 and 5.32, and setting the right-hand sides of the equations to zero, the equations become

$$mA_1\Psi + \left[\frac{2C_{\alpha f} + 2C_{\alpha r}}{V_x}\right]A_1 + \left[\frac{mV_x^2 + 2l_1 C_{\alpha f} - 2l_2 C_{\alpha r}}{V_x}\right]A_2 = 0 \tag{5.37}$$

$$I_z A_2\Psi + \left[\frac{2l_1 C_{\alpha f} - 2l_2 C_{\alpha r}}{V_x}\right]A_1 + \left[\frac{2l_1^2 C_{\alpha f} + 2l_2^2 C_{\alpha r}}{V_x}\right]A_2 = 0 \tag{5.38}$$

The above equations can be rewritten as

$$mA_1\Psi + a_1 A_1 + a_2 A_2 = 0 \tag{5.39}$$

$$I_z A_2\Psi + a_3 A_1 + a_4 A_2 = 0 \tag{5.40}$$

where

$$a_1 = \frac{2C_{\alpha f} + 2C_{\alpha r}}{V_x}$$

$$a_2 = \frac{mV_x^2 + 2l_1 C_{\alpha f} - 2l_2 C_{\alpha r}}{V_x}$$

$$a_3 = \frac{2l_1 C_{\alpha f} - 2l_2 C_{\alpha r}}{V_x}$$

$$a_4 = \frac{2l_1^2 C_{\alpha f} + 2l_2^2 C_{\alpha r}}{V_x}$$

Equations 5.39 and 5.40 are known as the amplitude equations, which are linear homogeneous algebraic equations. It can be shown that to obtain a nontrivial solution for Ψ, the determinant of the amplitudes must be equal to zero. Thus

$$\begin{vmatrix} m\Psi + a_1 & a_2 \\ a_3 & I_z\Psi + a_4 \end{vmatrix} = 0 \tag{5.41}$$

Expanding the determinant yields the characteristic equation

$$mI_z\Psi^2 + (I_z a_1 + ma_4)\Psi + (a_1 a_4 - a_2 a_3) = 0 \tag{5.42}$$

It can be shown that if $(I_z a_1 + ma_4)$ and $(a_1 a_4 - a_2 a_3)$ are both positive, then Ψ must be either a negative real number or a complex number having negative real part. The terms $I_z a_1$ and ma_4 are clearly always positive, hence it follows that the vehicle is directionally stable if $a_1 a_4 - a_2 a_3$ is positive. It can be shown that the condition for $a_1 a_4 - a_2 a_3 > 0$ is

$$L + \frac{V_x^2}{g}\left(\frac{W_f}{C_{\alpha f}} - \frac{W_r}{C_{\alpha r}} \right) > 0$$

or

$$L + \frac{V_x^2}{g} K_{us} > 0 \tag{5.43}$$

where K_{us} is the understeer coefficient defined previously. This indicates that the examination of the directional stability of a vehicle is now reduced to determining the conditions under which Eq. 5.43 is satisfied. When the understeer coefficient K_{us} is positive, Eq. 5.43 is always satisfied. This implies that when a vehicle is understeer, it is always directionally stable. When the understeer coefficient K_{us} is negative, which indicates that the vehicle is oversteer, the vehicle is directionally stable only if the speed of the vehicle is below a specific value

$$V_x < \sqrt{\frac{gL}{-K_{us}}} \qquad (5.44)$$

This specific speed is in fact the critical speed V_{crit} of an oversteer vehicle discussed previously. This indicates that an oversteer vehicle will be directionally stable only if it operates at a speed lower than the critical speed.

The analysis of vehicle handling presented in this chapter is based on a simplified vehicle model. For a practical vehicle, the lateral motions are coupled with the longitudinal motions, that is, motions in fore and aft (motion along the x axis shown in Fig. 5.1), pitch (rotation about the y axis), and bounce (motion along the z axis). The coupling is through mechanisms such as changes in cornering properties of tires with the application of tractive or braking effort, fore and aft load transfer, and changes of the steering characteristics of the vehicle due to motions of the vehicle body relative to the unsprung parts. More complete evaluations of the handling behavior of road vehicles, in which the interactions of longitudinal motions with lateral motions are taken into consideration, have been made [5.5, 5.8–5.10].

It should also be pointed out that in practice the handling of a vehicle involves the continuous interaction of the driver with the vehicle. To perform a comprehensive examination of vehicle handling qualities, the characteristics of the human driver therefore should be included. This topic is, however, beyond the scope of the present text.

REFERENCES

5.1 J. G. Giles, Ed., *Steering, Suspension and Tyres*, Automotive Technology Series Vol. 1, Butterworths, London, England, 1968.

5.2 R. T. Bundorf, The Influence of Vehicle Design Parameters on Characteristic Speed and Understeer, *SAE Transactions*, Vol. 76, 1968.

5.3 D. E. Cole, *Elementary Vehicle Dynamics*, Department of Mechanical Engineering, University of Michigan, Ann Arbor, MI., 1971.

5.4   J. Fenton, Ed., *Handbook of Automotive Design Analysis*, Butterworths, London, England.

5.5   J. R. Ellis, *Vehicle Dynamics*, Business Books, London, England, 1969.

5.6   W. Steeds, *Mechanics of Road Vehicles*, Iliffe & Sons, London, England, 1960.

5.7   R. T. Bundorf, D. E. Pollock, and M. C. Hardin, Vehicle Handling Response to Aerodynamic Inputs, Society of Automotive Engineers, paper 716B, June, 1963.

5.8   L. Segel, Theoretical Prediction and Experimental Substantiation of the Response of the Automobile to Steering Control, *Proceedings of the Institution of Mechanical Engineers*, Automobile Division, 1956–1957.

5.9   D. W. Whitcomb and W. F. Milliken, Jr., Design Implications of a General Theory of Automobile Stability and Control, *Proceedings of the Institution of Mechanical Engineers*, Automobile Division, 1956–1957.

5.10   H. S. Radt and H. B. Pacejka, Analysis of the Steady State Turning Behavior of an Automobile, *Proceedings of the Institution of Mechanical Engineers, Symposium on the Control of Vehicles during Braking and Cornering*, June, 1963.

PROBLEMS

5.1   Design a suitable coplaner steering linkage for a truck with front beam axle. The ratio of tread (track) to wheelbase of the truck is 0.40. The characteristics of the linkage should be as close as possible to those of the Ackerman steering geometry.

5.2   A passenger car weighs 20.02 kN (4500 lb) and has a wheelbase of 279.4 cm (110 in.). The center of gravity is 127 cm (50 in.) behind the front axle. If a pair of radial-ply tires, each of which has a cornering stiffness of 45.88 kN/rad (180 lb/degree), are installed in the front, and a pair of bias-ply tires, each of which has a cornering stiffness of 33.13 kN/rad (130 lb/degree), are installed in the rear, determine whether the vehicle is understeer or oversteer. Calculate also the characteristic or critical speed of the vehicle.

5.3   A sports car weighs 9.919 kN (2230 lb) and has a wheelbase of 2.26 m (7.4 ft). The center of gravity is 1.22 m (4 ft) behind the front axle. The cornering stiffness of each front tire is 58.62 kN/rad (230 lb/degree) and that of each rear tire is 71.36 kN/rad (280 lb/degree). The steering gear ratio is 20:1. Determine the steady-state yaw velocity gain and lateral acceleration gain of the vehicle in the forward speed range of 10 to 160 km/h (6.2 to 99.4 mph).

5.4   The sports car described in Problem 5.3 has a mass moment of inertia about a vertical axis passing through its center of gravity of 1031 kg·m^2 (760 slug·ft^2). If the car is given a step input of steering wheel angle of 60° at a speed of 80.5 km/h (50 mph), determine its transient yaw velocity response.

CHAPTER SIX
STEERING OF TRACKED VEHICLES

The handling characteristics of tracked vehicles have certain unique features and are quite different from those of wheeled vehicles. A separate treatment of the steering of tracked vehicles is therefore required. There are a number of possible methods that can accomplish the steering of a tracked vehicle. These include skid-steering, steering by articulation, and curved track steering.

In skid-steering, the thrust of one track is increased and that of the other is reduced, so as to create a turning moment to overcome the moment of turning resistance due to the skidding of the tracks on the ground and the rotational inertia of the vehicle, as shown in Fig. 6.1. Since the moment of turning resistance is usually considerable, significantly more power may be required during a turn than in straight line motion. Furthermore, braking of the inside track is often required in making a turn. This results in a reduction of the maximum resultant forward thrust that the vehicle can develop. Over weak terrain, this often leads to immobilization.

For tracked vehicles consisting of two or more units, steering may be accomplished by rotating one unit against the other using a steering joint to make the vehicle follow a prescribed, curved path, as shown in Fig. 6.2 [6.1]. In articulated steering, turning is initiated by the steering joint between the two units and no adjustment of the thrusts of the tracks is required. Thus, the resultant forward thrust of the vehicle can be maintained during a turn. Articulated steering can therefore provide tracked

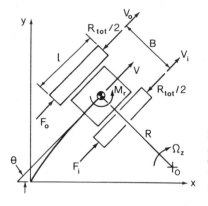

vehicles with better mobility during turning maneuver than skid-steering.

Another method for directional control of tracked vehicles is that of curved track steering. To initiate a turn, the laterally flexible track is laid down on the ground in a curve as shown in Fig. 6.3 [6.2]. This can be achieved using various kinds of mechanical arrangement, one of which is illustrated in Fig. 6.3. In this particular arrangement, each of the road wheels of the track is mounted on an axis inclined at a suitable angle from the vertical in a longitudinal plane, so that movement around these axes displaces the lower part of the wheels to form a curved track. Steering

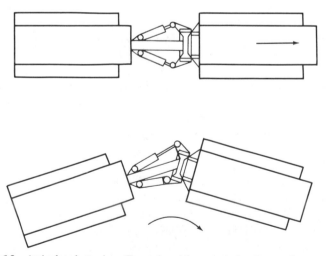

Fig. 6.2 Articulated steering. (Reproduced by permission from reference 6.1.)

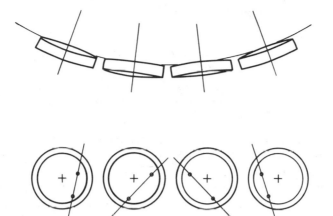

Fig. 6.3 Curved track steering. (Reproduced by permission from reference 6.2.)

movement of the road wheels may be activated by a conventional steering wheel through racks and pinions and individual push rods [6.2]. The main advantage of this steering method is that less power is required in making a turn as compared with skid-steering. However, owing to the limitations of the lateral flexibility of the track, the minimum turning radius of the vehicle is quite large. To achieve smaller turning radius, a supplementary steering mechanism, such as skid-steering, has to be added. Thus not only does the complexity of design of the vehicle increase, but also the potential advantages of curved track steering in power saving may not be realized.

Among the various steering methods available for tracked vehicles, the skid-steering and articulated steering are commonly used. The principles of these two steering methods will therefore be discussed in detail in this chapter.

6.1 KINETICS OF SKID-STEERING

The turning behavior of a tracked vehicle using skid steering depends on the thrusts of the outside and inside tracks, F_o and F_i, resultant resisting force R_{tot}, moment of turning resistance M_r exerted on the track by the ground, and vehicle parameters as shown in Fig. 6.1. The simple case of steering at low speeds on a level ground will be examined first. The problem of steering of tracked vehicles at high speeds will be discussed later. At low speeds, the centrifugal force may be neglected, and the behavior of the vehicle can be described by the following two equations of motion

$$m\frac{d^2s}{dt^2} = F_o + F_i - R_{tot} \tag{6.1}$$

$$I_z\frac{d^2\theta}{dt^2} = \frac{B}{2}(F_o - F_i) - M_r \tag{6.2}$$

where s is the displacement of the center of gravity of the vehicle, θ is angular displacement of the vehicle, B is the tread of the vehicle (i.e., the spacing between the center lines of the tracks), I_z and m are the mass moment of inertia of the vehicle about the vertical axis passing through its center of gravity and the mass of the vehicle, respectively. With known initial conditions, the above two differential equations can be integrated and the trajectory of the center of gravity and the orientation of the vehicle can be determined as discussed by Bekker [6.3].

Under steady-state conditions, there are no linear and angular accelerations

$$F_o + F_i - R_{tot} = 0 \tag{6.3}$$

$$\frac{B}{2}(F_o - F_i) - M_r = 0 \tag{6.4}$$

The thrusts of the outside and inside tracks required to achieve a steady-state turn are therefore expressed by

$$F_o = \frac{R_{tot}}{2} + \frac{M_r}{B} = \frac{f_r W}{2} + \frac{M_r}{B} \tag{6.5}$$

$$F_i = \frac{R_{tot}}{2} - \frac{M_r}{B} = \frac{f_r W}{2} - \frac{M_r}{B} \tag{6.6}$$

where f_r is the coefficient of motion resistance of the vehicle and W is vehicle weight.

To determine the values of the thrusts F_o and F_i, the moment of turning resistance M_r must be known. This can be determined experimentally or analytically. If the normal pressure is uniformly distributed along the track, the lateral resistance per unit length of the track R_l can be expressed by

$$R_l = \frac{\mu_t W}{2l} \tag{6.7}$$

where μ_t is the coefficient of lateral resistance and l is the contact length of

Table 6.1 Values of Lateral Resistance of Tracks Over Various Surfaces

Track Material	Coefficient of Lateral Resistance μ_t		
	Concrete	Hard Ground (not paved)	Grass
Steel	0.50–0.51	0.55–0.58	0.87–1.11
Rubber	0.90–0.91	0.65–0.66	0.67–1.14

Source. Reference 6.4.

the track. The value of μ_t depends not only on the terrain but also on the design of the track. Over soft terrain, the vehicle sinks into the ground and the tracks together with the grousers will be sliding on the surface as well as displacing the soil laterally during steering. The lateral forces acting on the tracks and the grousers due to displacing the soil laterally form part of the lateral resistance. Table 6.1 shows the values of μ_t for steel and rubber tracks over various types of ground [6.4].

By referring to Fig. 6.4, we can see that the resultant moment of the lateral resistance about the centers of the two tracks M_r (i.e., moment of

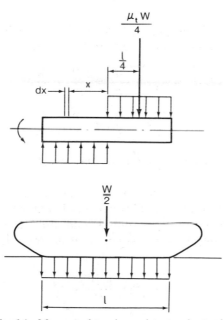

Fig. 6.4 Moment of turning resistance of a track.

turning resistance) can be determined by

$$M_r = 4 \frac{W\mu_t}{2l} \int_0^{l/2} x\,dx = \frac{\mu_t Wl}{4} \tag{6.8}$$

Accordingly, Eqs. 6.5 and 6.6 can be rewritten in the following form

$$F_o = \frac{f_r W}{2} + \frac{\mu_t Wl}{4B} \tag{6.9}$$

$$F_i = \frac{f_r W}{2} - \frac{\mu_t Wl}{4B} \tag{6.10}$$

It should be emphasized that the value of M_r as calculated by Eq. 6.8 is for a vehicle with a uniform normal pressure distribution turning at low speeds on level ground. Under other operating conditions, the expression for M_r will be different [6.3].

Equations 6.9 and 6.10 are of fundamental importance and lead to conclusions of practical significance regarding the steerability of a tracked vehicle. As discussed in Chapter 2, the maximum thrust of a track is limited by terrain properties and vehicle parameters. For the outside track

$$F_o \leqslant cbl + \frac{W\tan\phi}{2} \tag{6.11}$$

Where b is track width and c and ϕ are the cohesion and the angle of internal shearing resistance of the terrain, respectively.

Substituting Eq. 6.9 into Eq. 6.11

$$\frac{f_r W}{2} + \frac{\mu_t Wl}{4B} \leqslant cbl + \frac{W\tan\phi}{2}$$

and

$$\frac{l}{B} \leqslant \frac{1}{\mu_t}\left(\frac{4cA}{W} + 2\tan\phi - 2f_r\right)$$

where A is the contact area of one track. This indicates that to enable a tracked vehicle to steer without spinning the outside track, the ratio of track length to tread of the vehicle, l/B, must satisfy the following condition:

$$\frac{l}{B} \leqslant \frac{2}{\mu_t}\left(\frac{c}{p} + \tan\phi - f_r\right) \tag{6.12}$$

where p is the normal pressure which is equal to $W/2A$.

On a sandy terrain with $c=0$, $\phi=30°$, $\mu_t=0.5$, and $f_r=0.1$, the value of l/B should be less than 1.9. In other words, if the ratio of contact length to tread of a tracked vehicle is greater than 1.9, the vehicle will not be able to steer on the terrain specified. On a clay-type terrain, with $c=3.45$ kPa (0.5 psi), $\phi=10°$, $p=6.9$ kpa (1 psi), $\mu_t=0.4$, and $f_r=0.1$, the value of l/B must be less than 2.88. These examples show the importance of the ratio of contact length to tread of a tracked vehicle to its steerability.

From Eq. 6.10, it can also be seen that if $\mu_t l/2B > f_r$, the thrust of the inside track F_i will be negative. This implies that to achieve a steady-state turn, braking of the inside track is required. For instance, with $\mu_t=0.5$, $f_r=0.1$, and $l/B=1.5$, the value of $\mu_t l/2B$ will be greater than that of f_r, which indicates that braking force has to be applied to the inside track. Since the forward thrust of the outside track of a given vehicle is limited by terrain properties as shown by Eq. 6.11, the application of braking force to the inside track during a turn reduces the maximum resultant forward thrust of the vehicle, and thus the mobility of the vehicle over weak terrain will be adversely affected. Figure 6.5 shows the ratio of the maximum resultant forward thrust as limited by the track-terrain interaction during a turn to that when in straight line motion as a function of the coefficient of lateral friction μ_t, for a tracked vehicle with $l/B=1.5$ operating over a terrain with $c=0$, $\phi=30°$, and $f_r=0.1$. It can be seen that as the value of μ_t increases from 0.2 to 0.5, the maximum resultant forward thrust available during a steady-state turn decreases from 74 to 35% of that when moving in a straight line.

On hard grounds, the resultant of the longitudinal and lateral forces acting on a track during a turn may be assumed to obey the law of Coulomb friction. The resultant force is limited by the coefficient of friction and the normal load on the track, and acts in the direction

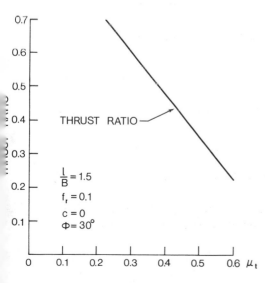

Fig. 6.5 Effect of the value of coefficient of lateral resistance on the maximum thrust available during a turn.

opposite to the relative motion of the track with respect to the ground. Based on these assumptions, the steering characteristics of tracked vehicles have been analyzed in detail by Steeds [6.5].

Example 6.1 A tracked vehicle weighs 155.68 kN (35,000 lb) and has a tread of 203.2 cm (80 in.). Each of the two tracks has a contact length of 304.8 cm (120 in.) and a width of 76.2 cm (30 in.). The contact pressure is assumed to be uniform. The vehicle travels over a terrain with cohesion $c = 3.45$ kPa (0.5 psi) and the angle of internal shearing resistance $\phi = 25°$. Over this terrain, the coefficient of motion resistance f_r is 0.15 and the coefficient of lateral resistance μ_t is 0.5.

A Determine the steerability of the vehicle over the terrain specified, if the skid steering method is employed.

B Determine the required thrusts of the outside and inside tracks during a steady-state turn.

Solution.

A From Eq. 6.12, the limiting value for the ratio of track length to tread is

$$\frac{l}{B} = \frac{2}{\mu_t}\left(\frac{c}{p} + \tan\phi - f_r\right) = 1.67$$

Since the ratio of track length to tread of the vehicle, l/B, is 1.5, which is less than the limiting value of 1.67, the vehicle is steerable over the terrain specified.

B The thrusts of the outside and inside tracks required during a steady-state turn can be determined using Eqs. 6.9 and 6.10.

$$F_o = \frac{f_r W}{2} + \frac{\mu_t W l}{4B} = 40.87 \text{ kN (9188 lb)}$$

$$F_i = \frac{f_r W}{2} - \frac{\mu_t W l}{4B} = -17.52 \text{ kN } (-3938 \text{ lb})$$

The results indicate that brakes have to be applied to the inside track during the turn.

6.2 KINEMATICS OF SKID-STEERING

In Fig. 6.1 a tracked vehicle is turning about the center 0. When the sprocket of the outside track is rotating at an angular speed of ω_o and that of the inside track is rotating at an angular speed of ω_i, and the tracks do not slip, the turning radius R and the yaw velocity of the vehicle Ω_z can be expressed by

$$R = \frac{B}{2} \frac{(r\omega_0 + r\omega_1)}{(r\omega_0 - r\omega_1)} = \frac{B(K_s + 1)}{2(K_s - 1)} \tag{6.13}$$

$$\Omega_z = \frac{r\omega_0 + r\omega_i}{2R} = \frac{r\omega_i(K_s - 1)}{B} \tag{6.14}$$

where r is the radius of the sprocket and K_s is the angular speed ratio ω_o/ω_i.

It should be pointed out, however, that during a turning maneuver appropriate thrust or braking force must be applied to the tracks as described previously. As a consequence, the tracks will slip or skid, depending on whether a forward thrust or a braking force is applied. The outside track always develops a forward thrust and therefore it slips. On the other hand, the inside track may develop a forward thrust or a braking force depending on the magnitude of the turning resistance moment M_r and other factors as defined by Eq. 6.6. When the slip (or skid) of the tracks is taken into consideration, the turning radius R' and yaw velocity Ω_z' are given by

$$R' = \frac{B[r\omega_o(1 - i_o) + r\omega_i(1 - i_i)]}{2[r\omega_o(1 - i_o) - r\omega_i(1 - i_i)]}$$

$$= \frac{B[K_s(1 - i_o) + (1 - i_i)]}{2[K_s(1 - i_o) - (1 - i_i)]} \tag{6.15}$$

$$\Omega_z' = \frac{r\omega_o(1 - i_o) + r\omega_i(1 - i_i)}{2R'}$$

$$= \frac{r\omega_i[K_s(1 - i_o) - (1 - i_i)]}{B} \tag{6.16}$$

where i_o and i_i are the slip of the outside track and that of the inside track, respectively. For a given vehicle over a particular terrain, the values of i_o and i_i depend on the thrusts F_o and F_i. The relationship between thrust and slip can be determined using the methods described in Chapter 2. When braking force is applied to the inside track, the track skids. Equations 6.15 and 6.16 still hold; however, i_i will have a negative value.

To illustrate the effect of track slip on the steering characteristics of a tracked vehicle, the ratio of the turning radius with track slipping R' to that without slipping R is plotted against the speed ratio $K_s = \omega_o/\omega_i$ in Fig.

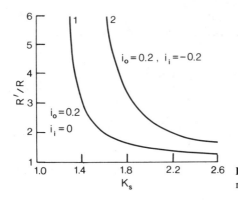

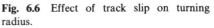

Fig. 6.6 Effect of track slip on turning radius.

6.6. Curve 1 shows the relationship between R'/R and K_s when the outside track slips at 20% and the inside track is disconnected from the transmission by declutching. Curve 2 shows the variation of the value of R'/R with K_s when the outside track slips and the inside track skids. This occurs when the outside track develops a forward thrust and a braking force is applied to the inside track.

It is shown that the value of R'/R is always greater than unity. Thus the effect of track slip is to increase the turning radius for a given speed ratio K_s.

6.3   SKID-STEERING AT HIGH SPEEDS

In the above analysis of the mechanics of skid-steering, low-speed operation is assumed and the effect of the centrifugal force is neglected. When a tracked vehicle is turning at moderate and higher speeds, or with a relatively small turning radius, the centrifugal force may be significant and its effect should be taken into consideration.

Consider that a tracked vehicle is in a steady-state turn on level ground. To achieve equilibrium in the lateral direction, the resultant lateral force exerted on the track by the ground must be equal to the centrifugal force as shown in Fig. 6.7. Assume that the normal pressure distribution along the track is uniform, then to satisfy the equilibrium condition in the lateral direction, the center of turn must lie at a distance s_0 in front of the transverse center line of the track-ground contact area, AC, as shown in Fig. 6.7. The distance s_0 can be determined by the following equation [6.3]:

$$\left(\frac{l}{2} + s_0\right)\frac{\mu_t W}{l} - \left(\frac{l}{2} - s_0\right)\frac{\mu_t W}{l} = \frac{WV^2}{gR'}\cos\beta$$

$$s_0 = \frac{lV^2}{2\mu_t gR'}\cos\beta = \frac{la_y}{2\mu_t g}\cos\beta \qquad (6.17)$$

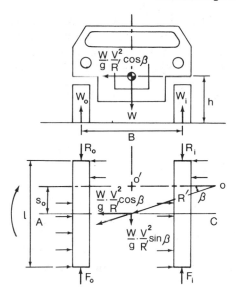

Fig. 6.7 Forces acting on a tracked vehicle during a turn at moderate or higher speeds. (From *Theory of Land Locomotion*, by M. G. Bekker, copyright © by the University of Michigan, 1956, reproduced by permission of the University of Michigan Press.)

where a_y is the lateral acceleration of the center of gravity of the vehicle.

Since the turning radius R' is usually large compared with the contact length of the track l, β would be small and accordingly $\cos\beta$ may be assumed to be equal to 1. Equation 6.17 can be rewritten as follows:

$$s_0 = \frac{la_y}{2\mu_t g} \tag{6.18}$$

As a consequence of the shifting of the center of turn, the equivalent moment of turning resistance M_r will have two components: one is the moment of the lateral resistance exerted on the tracks by the ground about $0'$ and the other is the moment of the centrifugal force about $0'$

$$M_r = \frac{\mu_t W}{l}\left[\int_0^{l/2+s_0} x\,dx + \int_0^{-(l/2-s_0)} x\,dx\right] - \frac{WV^2 s_0}{gR'}$$

$$= \frac{\mu_t W}{2l}\left(\frac{l^2}{2}+2s_0^2\right) - \frac{WV^2 s_0}{gR'} \tag{6.19}$$

Substituting Eq. 6.18 into Eq. 6.19, the equivalent moment of turning resistance M_r becomes

$$M_r = \frac{\mu_t Wl}{4}\left(1 - \frac{V^4}{g^2 R^2 \mu_t^2}\right)$$

$$= \frac{\mu_t Wl}{4}\left(1 - \frac{a_y^2}{g^2 \mu_t^2}\right) \tag{6.20}$$

The above equation indicates that when the centrifugal force is taken into consideration, the equivalent moment of turning resistance is reduced.

The centrifugal force also causes lateral load transfer. Thus the longitudinal motion resistance of the outside and inside track, R_o and R_i, will not be identical

$$R_o = \left(\frac{W}{2} + \frac{hWV^2}{BgR'} \right) f_r \tag{6.21}$$

$$R_i = \left(\frac{W}{2} - \frac{hWV^2}{BgR'} \right) f_r \tag{6.22}$$

where h is the height of the center of gravity of the vehicle.

Furthermore, the centrifugal force has a component along the longitudinal axis of the vehicle, $WV^2 s_0/gR'^2$. This component has to be balanced by the thrusts developed by the tracks. Therefore, when the centrifugal force is taken into account, the thrusts required to maintain the vehicle in a steady-state turn are expressed by [6.3]

$$F_o = \left(\frac{W}{2} + \frac{hWV^2}{BgR'} \right) f_r + \frac{WV^2 s_0}{2gR'^2} + \frac{\mu_t Wl}{4B} \left[1 - \left(\frac{V^2}{gR'\mu_t} \right)^2 \right]$$

$$= \left(\frac{W}{2} + \frac{hWa_y}{Bg} \right) f_r + \frac{Wa_y s_0}{2gR'} + \frac{\mu_t Wl}{4B} \left[1 - \left(\frac{a_y}{g\mu_t} \right)^2 \right] \tag{6.23}$$

$$F_i = \left(\frac{W}{2} - \frac{hWV^2}{BgR'} \right) f_r + \frac{WV^2 s_0}{2gR'^2} - \frac{\mu_t Wl}{4B} \left[1 - \left(\frac{V^2}{gR'\mu_t} \right)^2 \right]$$

$$= \left(\frac{W}{2} - \frac{hWa_y}{Bg} \right) f_r + \frac{Wa_y s_0}{2gR'} - \frac{\mu_t Wl}{4B} \left[1 - \left(\frac{a_y}{g\mu_t} \right)^2 \right] \tag{6.24}$$

Figure 6.8 illustrates the required ratios of the thrust to vehicle weight for the outside and inside tracks, F_o/W and F_i/W, as a function of lateral acceleration in g-units, a_y/g, for a given vehicle on a particular terrain. It can be seen that as the lateral acceleration increases, the ratio of the thrust to vehicle weight for the outside track F_o/W decreases. This is mainly due to the fact that the moment of the centrifugal force about the center of turn increases with the increase of lateral acceleration. As a consequence, the equivalent moment of turning resistance decreases with the increase of lateral acceleration. It can also be noted that the ratio of the thrust to vehicle weight for the inside track F_i/W is usually negative, which implies that braking of the inside track is required to maintain a steady-state turn.

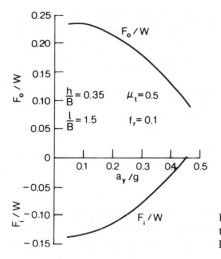

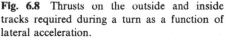

Fig. 6.8 Thrusts on the outside and inside tracks required during a turn as a function of lateral acceleration.

The magnitude of the braking force of the inside track decreases, however, as the lateral acceleration increases. This is again mainly due to the decrease of the equivalent moment of turning resistance with the increase of lateral acceleration.

Equations 6.23 and 6.24 specify the thrusts of the outside and inside tracks required under a steady-state turn for a given vehicle speed and turning radius. However, to achieve a specific turning radius and vehicle speed, certain kinematic relationships have to be satisfied. These include the relationship between turning radius, vehicle speed, track slips, and sprocket speeds. To determine the required sprocket speeds for a specific turning radius and vehicle speed, the slips of the outside and inside tracks, i_o and i_i, should be determined. To do this, the required thrusts F_o and F_i should first be calculated using Eqs. 6.23 and 6.24. Then from the relationship between thrust and slip discussed in Chapter 2, the values of i_o and i_i can be obtained. The required angular speed ratio K_s for a given turning radius R' can be determined from Eq. 6.15

$$K_s = \frac{(2R' + B)(1 - i_i)}{(2R' - B)(1 - i_o)} \tag{6.25}$$

The angular speeds of the sprockets, ω_o and ω_i, required to achieve a specific vehicle forward speed V can then be obtained from Eq. 6.16

$$\omega_i = \frac{2V}{r[K_s(1 - i_o) + (1 - i_i)]} \quad \text{and} \quad \omega_o = K_s \omega_i \tag{6.26}$$

It can be seen that when the effect of the centrifugal force is taken into consideration, the analysis of the turning maneuver becomes more involved.

6.4 POWER CONSUMPTION OF SKID-STEERING

When a tracked vehicle is traveling in a straight line, the power consumption P_{st} due to the motion resistance R_{tot} is

$$P_{st} = R_{tot} V_{st} = f_r W V_{st} \tag{6.27}$$

where V_{st} is vehicle speed in straight line motion.

It should be mentioned that power loss due to slip of the vehicle running gear may also be significant over unprepared terrain. In the following analysis of power consumption during a turning maneuver, the power loss due to slip is, however, neglected in order to simplify the analysis.

When a tracked vehicle is making a steady-state turn, power is consumed by the motion resistance, the moment of turning resistance, and the braking torque in the steering system. The power required during a turn P_t can be expressed by [6.6]

$$P_t = R_{tot} V + M_r \Omega_z + M_b \omega_b \tag{6.28}$$

where V is the speed of the center of gravity of the vehicle during a turn, M_b is the frictional torque of the brake (or clutch) in the steering system, and ω_b is the relative angular velocity of the frictional elements in the brake (or clutch). When the brake is fully applied and there is no relative motion between the frictional elements, the power loss in the brake will be zero.

The ratio of the power consumption during a steady-state turn to that in straight line motion can be expressed by

$$\frac{P_t}{P_{st}} = \frac{V}{V_{st}} + \frac{M_r \Omega_z}{f_r W V_{st}} + \frac{M_b \omega_b}{f_r W V_{st}}$$

$$= \frac{V}{V_{st}} \left(1 + \frac{M_r}{f_r W R} + \frac{M_b \omega_b}{f_r W V} \right) \tag{6.29}$$

For a given tracked vehicle on a particular terrain, the power ratio P_t / P_{st} depends on the ratios of V / V_{st}, $M_r / f_r W R$ and $M_b \omega_b / f_r W V$, which in turn are dependent, to a great extent, on the characteristics of the steering system used. The characteristics and the corresponding power ratio P_t/P_{st} of some typical steering systems for tracked vehicles will be discussed in the next section.

6.5 STEERING MECHANISMS FOR TRACKED VEHICLES

There are various types of steering mechanism available for tracked vehicles using the principles of skid-steering.

6.5.1 Clutch/Brake Steering System

This system is shown schematically in Fig. 6.9. To initiate a turn the inside track is disconnected from the driveline by declutching and the brake is usually applied. The outside track is driven by the engine and generates a forward thrust. The thrust on the outside track and the braking force on the inside track form a turning moment that steers the vehicle. This steering system is very simple but the steering brake usually absorbs considerable power during a turn. The clutch/brake steering system is therefore mainly used in low-speed tracked vehicles such as farm tractors and construction vehicles.

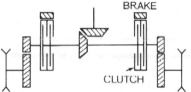

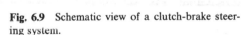

Fig. 6.9 Schematic view of a clutch-brake steering system.

Consider a turning maneuver in which the inside track of the vehicle is disconnected from the driveline by declutching and the brake is fully applied. The inside track thus has zero forward speed. The vehicle will be turning about the center of the inside track and the minimum turning radius R_{min} will be equal to $B/2$. Assume that during the turn, the engine is running at the same speed as that prior to turning. It is obvious that with the clutch/brake steering system, the forward speed of the center of gravity of the vehicle at the minimum turning radius will be half of that prior to turning, and $V/V_{st}=0.5$. Since the brake of the inside track is fully applied, there will be no power loss in the brake. The power ratio P_t/P_{st} for a tracked vehicle with a clutch/brake steering system at the minimum turning radius is therefore given by

$$\frac{P_t}{P_{st}} = 0.5\left(1 + \frac{M_r}{f_r WB/2}\right) \tag{6.30}$$

Assume that the normal pressure under the track is uniformly distributed and the vehicle is turning at low speeds. The moment of turning resistance M_r is given by Eq. 6.8, and Eq. 6.30 can be rewritten as follows:

$$\frac{P_t}{P_{st}} = 0.5\left(1 + \frac{\mu_t l}{2f_r B}\right) \tag{6.31}$$

For a tracked vehicle with a clutch/brake steering system, having $l/B = 1.5$ and operating over a terrain with coefficient of lateral resistance $\mu_t = 0.5$ and coefficient of motion resistance $f_r = 0.1$, the power consumption during a steady-state turn at the minimum turning radius will be 2.375 times that when the vehicle is traveling in a straight line. This indicates that considerably more power is required during a turning meneuver as compared to straight-line motion. If the power loss due to track slip is included, the total power consumption during a turn will be even higher.

6.5.2   Controlled Differential Steering System

This type of steering system is shown schematically in Fig. 6.10. Gear A is driven through a gearbox by the engine. In straight-line motion, brakes B_1 and B_2 are not applied and gears C_1, C_2, D_1, and D_2 form an ordinary differential. For steering, the brake of the inside track, such as B_2, is applied. This results in a reduction of the speed of the inside track and a corresponding increase of the speed of the outside track. Thus the forward speed of the center of gravity of the vehicle during a turn will be the same

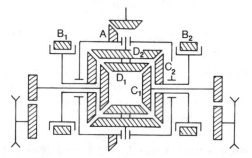

Fig. 6.10   Schematic view of a controlled differential steering system.

as that in straight-line motion for a given engine speed. A kinematic analysis of the controlled differential will show that the relationship between the angular speed of the sprocket of the outside track ω_o to that of the inside track ω_i can be expressed by

$$K_s = \frac{\omega_o}{\omega_i} = \frac{K_{di} + 1 - K_{di}\omega_{B2}}{K_{di} - 1 + K_{di}\omega_{B2}} \qquad (6.32)$$

where K_{di} is the gear ratio of the differential and is equal to $N_{D2}N_{C1}/N_{D1}N_{C2}$, where N_{C1}, N_{C2}, N_{D1}, and N_{D2} are the number of teeth of the gears C_1, C_2, D_1, and D_2 in the differential, respectively, and ω_{B2} is the angular speed of the brake drum B_2. If brake B_2 is fully applied and the drum does not slip, Eq. 6.32 can be rewritten as follows:

$$K_s = \frac{K_{di} + 1}{K_{di} - 1} \qquad (6.33)$$

It should be noted that when brake B_2 is fully applied, the minimum turning radius is achieved. From Eq. 6.13, the minimum turning radius of a tracked vehicle with a controlled differential steering system is therefore expressed by

$$R_{min} = \frac{B}{2}\left(\frac{K_s + 1}{K_s - 1}\right) = \frac{BK_{di}}{2} \qquad (6.34)$$

The power ratio P_t/P_{st} for a tracked vehicle with a controlled differential steering system at the minimum turning radius is given by

$$\frac{P_t}{P_{st}} = \frac{V}{V_{st}}\left(1 + \frac{M_r}{f_r W R_{min}}\right)$$

$$= 1 + \frac{M_r}{f_r W B K_{di}/2} \qquad (6.35)$$

where $V/V_{st} = 1$ as mentioned previously.

When the normal pressure under the track is uniformly distributed and the vehicle is turning at low speeds, Eq. 6.35 can be rewritten as

$$\frac{P_t}{P_{st}} = 1 + \frac{\mu_t l}{2 f_r B K_{di}} \qquad (6.36)$$

For a vehicle with $l/B = 1.5$ and $K_{di} = 2.0$, and operating over a terrain with $\mu_t/f_r = 5$, the power consumption during a steady-state turn at the minimum turning radius will be 2.875 times that when the vehicle is traveling in a straight line.

6.5.3 Planetary Gear Steering System

One of the simplest forms of planetary gear steering system for tracked vehicles is shown schematically in Fig. 6.11. The input from the engine is through bevel gearing to shaft A, which is connected, through the planetary gear train, with the sprockets of the tracks.

In the system shown, the input to the gear train is through sun gear B and the output is through arm C, which is connected to the sprocket. In straight-line motion, both clutches are engaged and brakes are released. For steering, the clutch on the inside track is disengaged and the brake is applied to ring gear D. If the brake is fully applied to hold the ring gear fixed, the angular speed of the sprocket of the inside track is determined by

$$\omega_i = \omega_a \left(\frac{N_B}{N_B + N_D} \right) \tag{6.37}$$

where ω_a is the angular speed of shaft A, and N_B and N_D are the number of teeth of the sun gear and the ring gear, respectively. Since the angular speed of the sprocket of the outside track ω_o is the same as ω_a, the speed ratio K_s can be expressed by

$$K_s = \frac{\omega_o}{\omega_i} = \frac{N_B + N_D}{N_B} \tag{6.38}$$

It should be noted that if the engine speed is kept constant, then the forward speed of the center of gravity of the vehicle will be less during a turn than in straight-line motion. The forward speed of the vehicle V

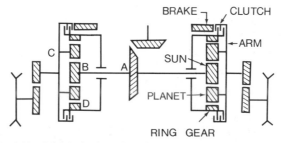

Fig. 6.11 Schematic view of a planetary gear steering system.

during a turn is determined by

$$V = \frac{(\omega_o + \omega_i)r}{2} = \frac{\omega_i r(K_s + 1)}{2} \tag{6.39}$$

It should also be mentioned that when the brake is fully applied on one side, the minimum turning radius is achieved. The minimum turning radius R_{min} is expressed by

$$R_{min} = \frac{B}{2}\left(\frac{K_s + 1}{K_s - 1}\right) = \frac{B}{2}\left(\frac{2N_B + N_D}{N_D}\right) \tag{6.40}$$

When a tracked vehicle with a planetary gear steering system is turning at the minimum turning radius, the power ratio P_t/P_{st} is expressed by

$$\frac{P_t}{P_{st}} = \frac{V}{V_{st}}\left(1 + \frac{M_r}{f_r W R_{min}}\right)$$

$$= \frac{(K_s + 1)}{2K_s}\left(1 + \frac{M_r}{f_r W B(K_s + 1)/2(K_s - 1)}\right) \tag{6.41}$$

For a vehicle with uniform normal pressure distribution and turning at low speeds, Eq. 6.41 can be rewritten as

$$\frac{P_t}{P_{st}} = \frac{1}{2K_s}\left[(K_s + 1) + \frac{\mu_t l(K_s - 1)}{2f_r B}\right] \tag{6.42}$$

For $K_s = 2$, $l/B = 1.5$, and $\mu_t/f_r = 5$, the power consumption during a steady-state turn at the minimum turning radius will be 1.68 times that when the vehicle is in straight line motion.

The results of the analysis of the characteristics of various steering systems described above indicate that considerably more power is required during a turn than in straight-line motion. To reduce the power requirements during a turn using the skid-steering principle, a number of regenerative steering systems have been developed for high-speed tracked vehicles [6.7].

6.6 ARTICULATED STEERING

For vehicles consisting of two or more units, steering can be effected by rotating one unit against the other to make the vehicle follow a prescribed curved path. This kind of steering method is referred to as steering by

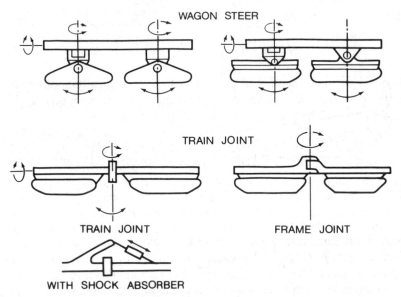

Fig. 6.12 Various configurations of articulated steering. (Reproduced by permission from reference 6.1.)

articulation or articulated steering. There are two principal configurations of articulated steering. One is usually called wagon steer as shown in Fig. 6.12. This configuration is for vehicles having a common frame but with two separate chassis. Steering is effected by rotating both or one of the two tracked chassis about a vertical axis. Normally the tracked chassis have freedom in pitch to allow good ground contact over rough surfaces. The wagon steer configuration has been adopted in some heavy tracked transporters as shown in Fig. 6.13. Another articulated steering configuration uses a train joint to connect separate vehicle units as shown in Fig. 6.12.

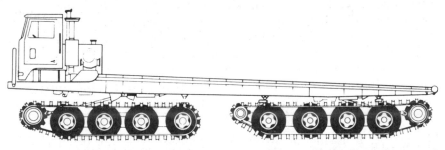

Fig. 6.13 An off-road transporter with wagon steer, Foremost Husky Eight (Courtesy of Canadian Foremost Ltd.)

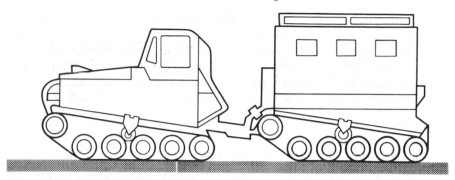

Fig. 6.14   An articulated vehicle with train joint, Volvo BV 202 (Courtesy of Volvo BM AB.)

Steering is achieved by rotating one unit against the other. Usually the design of the joint allows the two units to have freedom in pitch and roll within a certain range. Articulated steering with train joint has been adopted in vehicles for use over marginal terrain as shown in Fig. 6.14.

In comparison with the skid-steering method, articulated steering requires much less power to execute a turn. Furthermore, using articulated steering the resultant forward thrust of the vehicle can be maintained during a turn, whereas a net reduction in the maximum resultant forward thrust is accompanied by skid-steering. Thus over marginal terrain, articulated steering can provide the vehicle with better mobility than skid-steering. In addition, to satisfy the steerability criterion, the ratio of contact length to tread of a vehicle must be in a certain range when using skid-steering. For a heavy tracked transporter to meet the required ratio of contact length to tread, the vehicle will be too wide to be practical. This is the basic reason why articulated steering is widely used in heavy tracked transporters. Articulated steering also makes it possible for heavy tracked vehicles to achieve a more rational form, since a long, narrow vehicle encounters less obstacle resistance and motion resistance over unprepared terrain than a short, wide vehicle with the same track contact area.

Moreover, the ride quality of articulated tracked vehicles is better than that of comparable vehicles with skid-steering. The greater contact length of the articulated vehicle is the principal reason, as it reduces the amplitude of pitch oscillation over given surface irregularities. The characteristic tail-down attitude of conventional tracked vehicles due to slip-sinkage is alleviated by using articulation, since the interacting forces between the two units through the articulation joint tend to keep the whole vehicle in a level attitude. Field experience has also shown that the handling quality of articulated vehicles is satisfactory even at speeds up to 72 km/h (45 mph) in some cases [6.1].

It should be mentioned, however, that the minimum turning radius of an articulated tracked vehicle is larger than that of an equivalent vehicle with skid-steering. The first cost of the articulated vehicle is usually higher than that of a similar vehicle with skid-steering, particularly for smaller size vehicles, since the articulated vehicle has at least two separate units or chassis which necessitate the replication of suspension and track systems [6.1].

REFERENCES

6.1   C. J. Nuttall, Some Notes on the Steering of Tracked Vehicles by Articulation, *Journal of Terramechanics*, Vol. 1, No. 1, 1964.

6.2   L. F. Little, The Alecto Tracklayer, *Journal of Terramechanics*, Vol. 1, No. 2, 1964.

6.3   M. G. Bekker, *Theory of Land Locomotion*, University of Michigan Press, Ann Arbor, MI, 1956.

6.4   I. Hayashi, Practical Analysis of Tracked Vehicle Steering Depending on Longitudinal Track Slippage, *Proceedings of the 5th International Conference of the International Society for Terrain-Vehicle Systems*, Vol. II, Detroit-Houghton, MI, 1975.

6.5   W. Steeds, Tracked Vehicles, *Automobile Engineer*, April, 1950.

6.6   I. D. Lvov, *Theory of Tractors* (in Russian), National Scientific and Technical Publishers, Moscow, 1960.

6.7   W. Steeds, *Mechanics of Road Vehicles*, Iliffe and Sons, London, England, 1960.

PROBLEMS

6.1   A tracked vehicle with skid steering is to be designed for operation over various types of terrain ranging from desert sand with $c=0$ and $\phi=35°$ to heavy clay with $c=20.685$ kPa (3 psi) and $\phi=6°$. The average value of coefficient of motion resistance is 0.15 and that of the coefficient of lateral resistance is 0.5. The vehicle has a uniform contact pressure of 13.79 kPa (2 psi). Select a suitable value for the ratio of contact length to tread for the vehicle.

6.2   A tracked vehicle weighs 155.68 kN (35,000 lb) and has a contact length of 304.8 cm (120 in.) and a tread of 203.2 cm (80 in.). The vehicle has a uniform contact pressure and is equipped with a clutch/brake steering system. On a sandy terrain, the value of the coefficient of motion resistance is 0.15 and that of the coefficient of lateral resistance is 0.5. The angle of internal shearing resistance of the terrain ϕ is 30° and the shear modulus K is 5 cm (2 in.).

A   Determine the thrusts of the outside and inside tracks required to execute a steady-state turn.

B If during the turn, the sprocket of the outside track, with radius of 0.305 m (1 ft), is rotating at 10 rad/s, and the inside track is disconnected from the driveline by declutching and the brake is applied, determine the turning radius and yaw velocity of the vehicle during the turn. The slip of the running gear during the turn should be taken into account in the calculations.

6.3 Referring to Problem 6.2, estimate the maximum drawbar pull that the tracked vehicle could develop during a steady-state turn. Calculate also the ratio of the maximum drawbar pull available during a steady-state turn to that in straight-line motion under the conditions specified.

6.4 A tracked vehicle is equipped with a controlled differential steering system having a gear ratio of 3:1. The vehicle weighs 155.68 kN (35,000 lb), and has a tread of 203.2 cm (80 in.) and a contact length of 304.8 cm (120 in.). The contact pressure of the track is assumed to be uniform. On a particular terrain, the value of the coefficient of motion resistance is 0.15 and that of the coefficient of lateral resistance is 0.5. Determine the minimum turning radius of the vehicle. Calculate also the power required to maintain a steady-state turn at the minimum turning radius, when the speed of the center of gravity of the vehicle is 10 km/h (6.2 mph).

CHAPTER SEVEN

VEHICLE RIDE CHARACTERISTICS

Ride quality is concerned with the sensation or feel of the passenger in the environment of a vehicle. Ride comfort problems mainly arise from vibrations of the vehicle, which may be induced by a variety of sources including surface irregularities, aerodynamic forces, and vibrations of the engine and transmission. Usually the surface irregularity acts as a major source that excites the vibration of the vehicle.

The objective of the study of vehicle ride is to provide guiding principles for the control of the vibration of the vehicle so that the passenger's sensation of discomfort does not exceed a certain level. To achieve this objective, it is essential to have a basic understanding of human response to vibration, the vibrational behavior of the vehicle and the characteristics of surface irregularities.

7.1 HUMAN RESPONSE TO VIBRATION

In general, passenger ride comfort (or discomfort) boundaries are difficult to determine. Considerable research has, however, been conducted by a number of investigators to define ride comfort limits. Various methods for assessing human response to vibration have been developed [7.1]. They include subjective ride assessment, shake table tests, ride simulator experiments and ride measurements in vehicles [7.1]. In general these methods attempt to correlate the response of test subjects in qualitative terms, such as "uncomfortable" and "extremely uncomfortable," with vibrational parameters such as displacement, velocity, acceleration, and jerk over the frequency range of interest.

The assessment of human response to vibration is complex in that the results are influenced by the variations in individual sensitivity, and the diversity of test method and sensation level used by different investigators. Over the years, numerous ride comfort criteria have been proposed. Figure 7.1 shows one of such criteria for vertical vibration suggested in the *Ride and Vibration Data Manual J6a* of the Society of Automotive Engineers [7.2]. The recommended limits shown in the figure are also referred to as Janeway's comfort criterion. It defines the acceptable amplitude of vibration as a function of frequency. It can be seen that as the frequency increases the allowable amplitude decreases considerably. The Janeway comfort criterion consists of three simple relationships, each of which covers a certain frequency range, as shown in Fig. 7.1. In the frequency range $1-6$ Hz, the peak value of jerk, which is the product of the amplitude and the cube of the circular frequency, should not exceed 12.6 m/s^3 (496 in./s^3). For instance, at 1 Hz (2π rad/s), the recommended limit for amplitude is 12.6 $m \cdot s^{-3}/(2\pi \ s^{-1})^3 = 0.0508$ m (2 in.). In the frequency range $6-20$ Hz, the peak value of acceleration, which is the product of the amplitude and the square of the circular frequency, should be less than 0.33 m/s^2 (13 in./s^2), whereas in the range $20-60$ Hz, the peak value of velocity, which is the product of the amplitude and the circular frequency, should not exceed 2.7 mm/s (0.105 in./s).

Recently, a general guide for defining the human tolerance to whole body vibration has been developed and agreed upon as the International Standard ISO 2631, 1974 [7.3, 7.4]. This guide is recommended for the evaluation of vibrational environments in transport vehicles as well as in industry, and defines three distinct limits for whole body vibration in the frequency range $1-80$ Hz:

A Exposure limits, which are related to the preservation of safety (or health) and should not be exceeded without special justification.

B Fatigue or decreased proficiency boundaries, which are related to the preservation of working efficiency, and apply to such tasks as driving a road vehicle or a tractor.

C Reduced comfort boundaries, which are concerned with the preservation of comfort, and in transport vehicles they are related to such functions as reading, writing, and eating in a vehicle.

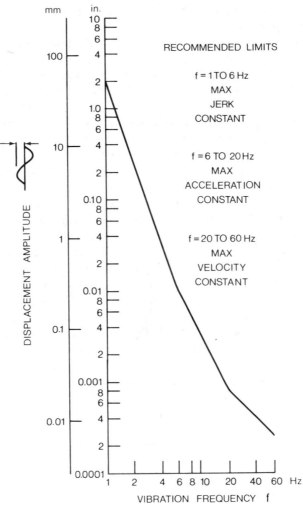

Fig. 7.1 Limits of vertical vibration recommended by Janeway. (Reproduced by permission of the Society of Automotive Engineers from reference 7.2.)

Figure 7.2(a) shows the fatigue or decreased proficiency boundaries for vertical vibration (head-to-foot or along the z axis in Fig. 7.3), which are defined in terms of root mean square values (rms) of acceleration as a function of frequency for various exposure times. It can be seen that as the average daily exposure time increases, the boundary lowers. The fatigue or decreased proficiency boundaries for lateral vibration (side-to-side or along the y axis, and chest-to-back or along the x axis in Fig. 7.3) are

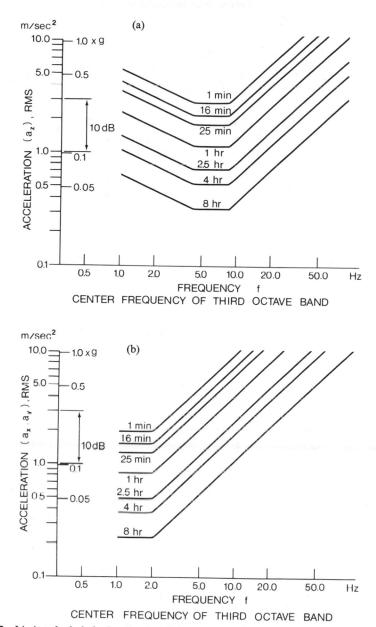

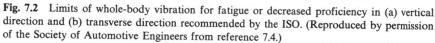

Fig. 7.2 Limits of whole-body vibration for fatigue or decreased proficiency in (a) vertical direction and (b) transverse direction recommended by the ISO. (Reproduced by permission of the Society of Automotive Engineers from reference 7.4.)

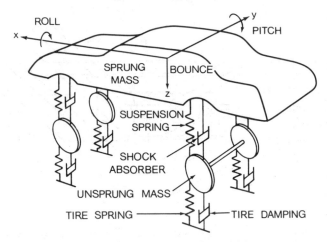

Fig. 7.3 A seven-degrees-of-freedom ride model for passenger cars.

shown in Fig. 7.2(b). When vibration takes place in more than one direction simultaneously, corresponding boundaries apply to each vectorial component in the three axes [7.3]. The exposure limits for safety (or health) reasons are obtained by raising the fatigue or decreased proficiency boundaries shown in Fig. 7.2(a) and (b) by a factor of two (6 dB higher), whereas the reduced comfort boundaries are obtained by lowering the boundaries shown in Fig. 7.2(a) and (b) by a factor of 3.15 (10 dB lower).

It should be pointed out that most of the data used in establishing ride comfort criteria were obtained using sinusoidal inputs, whereas actual vehicle vibration is usually of a random nature. Hence, the ride comfort criteria thus far proposed may require revision as new data are available.

Having defined a specific ride comfort criterion, the designer should then select an appropriate suspension system to ensure that the level of vehicle vibration is below the specified limits when operating over a particular range of environments.

7.2   VEHICLE RIDE MODELS

To study the ride quality of ground vehicles, various ride models have been developed. For a passenger car with independent front suspension, a seven-degrees-of-freedom model as shown in Fig. 7.3 may be used. In this model, the pitch, bounce, and roll of the vehicle body, as well as the bounce of the two front wheels, and the bounce and roll (tramp) of the

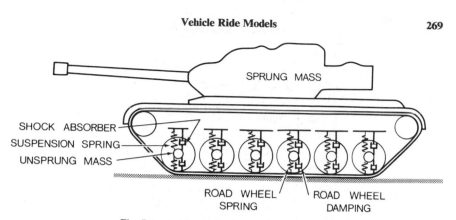

Fig. 7.4 A ride model for a military vehicle.

solid rear axle are taken into consideration. The mass of the vehicle body is usually referred to as the sprung mass, whereas the mass of the running gear together with the associated components is referred to as the unsprung mass. For a cross-country military vehicle shown in Fig. 7.4, a fifteen-degrees-of-freedom model may be used, which includes the pitch, bounce, and roll of the vehicle body and the bounce of each road wheel.

To study the vibrational characteristics of the vehicle, equations of motion based on Newton's second law for each mass have to be formulated. Natural frequencies and amplitude ratios can be determined by considering the principal modes (normal modes) of vibration of the system. When the excitation of the system is known, the response can, in principle, be determined by solving the equations of motion. However, as the degrees of freedom of the system increase, the analysis becomes increasingly complex. Digital or analog computer simulations are usually employed.

A vehicle represents a complex vibration system with many degrees of freedom. It is possible, however, to simplify the system by considering only

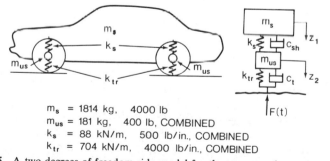

$$m_s = 1814 \text{ kg}, \quad 4000 \text{ lb}$$
$$m_{us} = 181 \text{ kg}, \quad 400 \text{ lb, COMBINED}$$
$$k_s = 88 \text{ kN/m}, \quad 500 \text{ lb/in., COMBINED}$$
$$k_{tr} = 704 \text{ kN/m}, \quad 4000 \text{ lb/in., COMBINED}$$

Fig. 7.5 A two-degrees-of-freedom ride model for the sprung and unsprung mass.

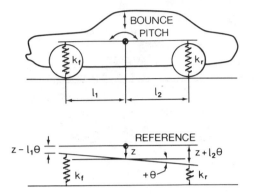

Fig. 7.6 A two-degrees-of-freedom ride model for pitch and bounce of the sprung mass.

some of the major motions of the vehicle. For instance, to obtain a qualitative insight into the functions of the suspension, particularly the effects of the sprung and unsprung mass on vehicle vibration, a linear model with two degrees of freedom as shown in Fig. 7.5 may be used. On the other hand, to reach a better understanding of the pitch and bounce vibration of the vehicle body, a two-degrees-of-freedom model as shown in Fig. 7.6 may be employed.

7.2.1 Two-Degrees-of-Freedom Vehicle Model for Sprung and Unsprung Mass

The two-degrees-of-freedom model shown in Fig. 7.5 includes an unsprung mass representing the wheels and associated components and a sprung mass representing the vehicle body. Their motions in the vertical direction can be described by two coordinates z_1 and z_2 with origins at the static equilibrium positions of the sprung and unsprung mass, respectively. By applying Newton's second law to the sprung and unsprung mass separately, the equations of motion of the system can be obtained.

For the sprung mass

$$m_s \ddot{z}_1 + c_{sh}(\dot{z}_1 - \dot{z}_2) + k_s(z_1 - z_2) = 0 \tag{7.1}$$

and for the unsprung mass

$$m_{us} \ddot{z}_2 + c_{sh}(\dot{z}_2 - \dot{z}_1) + k_s(z_2 - z_1) + c_t \dot{z}_2 + k_{tr} z_2 = F(t) \tag{7.2}$$

where m_s is the sprung mass, m_{us} is the unsprung mass, c_{sh} is the damping coefficient of the shock absorber, c_t is the damping coefficient of the tire, k_s is the stiffness of the suspension spring, k_{tr} is the equivalent spring stiffness of the tire, and $F(t)$ is the excitation that is usually acting on the wheels and is induced by surface irregularities. If the excitation of the system is known, then in principle the resulting vibrations of the sprung and unsprung mass can be determined by solving Eqs. 7.1 and 7.2.

To obtain a qualitative insight into the ride characteristics of the vehicle, an approximate method of analysis may be employed. For a typical North American passenger car, the values of the basic parameters of the system may be close to those shown in Fig. 7.5. It can be seen that the sprung mass is of an order of magnitude higher than the unsprung mass, and so is the tire stiffness in relation to the spring stiffness of the suspension. In a first approximation, the natural frequencies of the sprung and unsprung mass, f_{n-s} and f_{n-us}, can therefore be estimated by the following equations

$$f_{n-s} = \frac{1}{2\pi} \sqrt{\frac{k_s k_{tr}/(k_s + k_{tr})}{m_s}} \tag{7.3}$$

and

$$f_{n-us} = \frac{1}{2\pi} \sqrt{\frac{k_s + k_{tr}}{m_{us}}} \tag{7.4}$$

With the values shown in Fig. 7.5, it can be found that the natural frequency of the sprung mass is approximately equal to 1 Hz and that the natural frequency of the unsprung mass is approximately 10 Hz. The natural frequency of the sprung mass is thus widely separated from that of the unsprung mass.

If the wheel hits a bump, the impulse will set the wheel into oscillation. When the vehicle is over the bump, the unsprung mass will be in free oscillation at its own natural frequency f_{n-us}. For the sprung mass, however, the excitation will be the vibration of the unsprung mass. The ratio of the frequency of excitation to the natural frequency of the sprung mass is therefore equal to f_{n-us}/f_{n-s}. Since the value of f_{n-us} is an order of magnitude higher than that of f_{n-s}, the amplitude of oscillation transmitted to the sprung mass will be very small. As can be seen from Fig. 7.7, when the ratio of the frequency of excitation to the natural frequency of the system is high, the transmissibility ratio which is the ratio of output to input of a vibrating system is very low. Thus, excellent vibration isolation for the sprung mass (i.e., vehicle body) is achieved in this case.

When the vehicle travels over an undulating surface, the excitation will normally consist of a wide range of frequencies. As can be seen from Fig. 7.7, high-frequency inputs can be effectively isolated through the action of the suspension because of the low natural frequency of the sprung mass. Low frequency excitation can, however, be transmitted to the vehicle body,

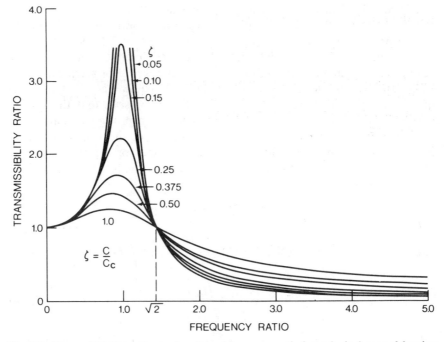

Fig. 7.7 Transmissibility ratio as a function of frequency ratio for a single-degree-of-freedom system.

as the transmissibility ratio is high when the frequency of excitation is close to the natural frequency of the system.

7.2.2 Two-Degrees-of-Freedom Vehicle Model for Pitch and Bounce

Because of the wide separation of the natural frequencies of the sprung and unsprung mass, the up and down linear motion (bounce) and the angular motion (pitch) of the vehicle body and the motion of the wheels may be considered to exist almost independently. The bounce and pitch of the vehicle body can therefore be studied using the model shown in Fig. 7.6. In this model damping is neglected.

By applying Newton's second law and using the static equilibrium position as the origin for both the linear displacement of the center of gravity z and angular displacement of the vehicle body θ, the equations of motion for the system can be formulated.

For free vibrations, the equation of motion for bounce is

$$m_s \ddot{z} = - k_f(z - l_1\theta) - k_r(z + l_2\theta) \tag{7.5}$$

and the equation of motion for pitch is

$$I_y \ddot{\theta} = m_s r_y^2 \ddot{\theta} = k_f l_1 (z - l_1 \theta) - k_r l_2 (z + l_2 \theta) \tag{7.6}$$

where k_f is the front spring stiffness, k_r is the rear spring stiffness, I_y and r_y are the mass moment of inertia and radius of gyration of the vehicle body about the y axis (Fig. 7.3), respectively.

By letting

$$D_1 = \frac{1}{m_s} (k_f + k_r)$$

$$D_2 = \frac{1}{m_s} (k_r l_2 - k_f l_1)$$

$$D_3 = \frac{1}{I_y} (k_f l_1^2 + k_r l_2^2) = \frac{1}{m_s r_y^2} (k_f l_1^2 + k_r l_2^2)$$

Equations 7.5 and 7.6 can be rewritten as

$$\ddot{z} + D_1 z + D_2 \theta = 0 \tag{7.7}$$

$$\ddot{\theta} + D_3 \theta + \frac{D_2}{r_y^2} z = 0 \tag{7.8}$$

It is evident that D_2 is the coupling coefficient for the bounce and pitch motions, and these motions uncouple when $k_f l_1 = k_r l_2$. With $k_f l_1 = k_r l_2$, a force applied to the center of gravity induces only bounce motion, while a moment applied to the body produces only pitch motion. In this case, the natural frequencies for the uncoupled bounce and pitch motions are

$$\omega_{nz} = \sqrt{D_1} \tag{7.9}$$

$$\omega_{n\theta} = \sqrt{D_3} \tag{7.10}$$

It is found that this would result in poor ride.

In general, the pitch and bounce motions are coupled and an impulse at the front or rear wheels excites both motions. To obtain the natural frequencies for the coupled bounce and pitch motions, the principal modes of vibration are considered. The solutions to the equations of motion (i.e., Eqs. 7.5 and 7.6) can be expressed in the form of

$$z = Z \cos \omega_n t \tag{7.11}$$

$$\theta = \Theta \cos \omega_n t \tag{7.12}$$

where ω_n is the natural frequency and Z and Θ are the amplitudes of bounce and pitch, respectively.

Substituting the above equations into Eqs. 7.7 and 7.8, one obtains

$$(D_1 - \omega_n^2)Z + D_2\Theta = 0 \tag{7.13}$$

$$\left(\frac{D_2}{r_y^2}\right)Z + (D_3 - \omega_n^2)\Theta = 0 \tag{7.14}$$

Solving the above equations, one obtains the frequency equation for the principal modes:

$$\omega_n^4 - (D_1 + D_3)\omega_n^2 + \left(D_1 D_3 - \frac{D_2^2}{r_y^2}\right) = 0 \tag{7.15}$$

From Eq. 7.15, two natural frequencies ω_{n_1} and ω_{n_2} can be obtained

$$\omega_{n_1}^2 = \frac{1}{2}(D_1 + D_3) - \sqrt{\frac{1}{4}(D_1 - D_3)^2 + \frac{D_2^2}{r_y^2}} \tag{7.16}$$

$$\omega_{n_2}^2 = \frac{1}{2}(D_1 + D_3) + \sqrt{\frac{1}{4}(D_1 - D_3)^2 + \frac{D_2^2}{r_y^2}} \tag{7.17}$$

These frequencies for coupled motions ω_{n_1} and ω_{n_2} always lie outside of the frequencies for uncoupled motions ω_{nz} and $\omega_{n\theta}$.

From Eqs. 7.13 or 7.14, the amplitude ratios of the bounce and pitch oscillations for the two natural frequencies ω_{n_1} and ω_{n_2} can be determined. For ω_{n_1}

$$\left.\frac{Z}{\Theta}\right|_{\omega_{n_1}} = \frac{D_2}{\omega_{n_1}^2 - D_1} \tag{7.18}$$

and for ω_{n_2}

$$\left.\frac{Z}{\Theta}\right|_{\omega_{n_2}} = \frac{D_2}{\omega_{n_2}^2 - D_1} \tag{7.19}$$

It can be shown that the two amplitude ratios will have opposite signs.

To further illustrate the characteristics of bounce and pitch modes of oscillation, the concept of oscillation center is introduced. The location of the oscillation center is denoted by l_0 measured from the center of gravity and can be determined from the amplitude ratios. Thus, one center is associated with ω_{n_1}, and the other with ω_{n_2}.

For ω_{n_1}

$$l_{01} = \frac{D_2}{\omega_{n_1}^2 - D_1} \qquad (7.20)$$

and for ω_{n_2}

$$l_{02} = \frac{D_2}{\omega_{n_2}^2 - D_1} \qquad (7.21)$$

When the value of the amplitude ratio is negative, the oscillation center will be located to the right of the center of gravity of the vehicle body, in accordance with the sign conventions for z and θ, as shown in Fig. 7.8. On the other hand, when the value of the amplitude ratio is positive, the oscillation center will be located to the left of the center of gravity. In general, a road input at the front or rear wheel will cause a moment about each oscillation center and therefore will excite both bounce and pitch oscillations. In other words, the body motion will be the sum of the oscillations about the two centers.

Usually, the oscillation center that lies outside of the wheelbase is called the bounce center, and the associated natural frequency is called the bounce frequency. On the other hand, the oscillation center that lies inside

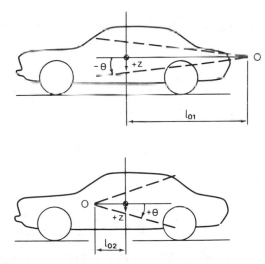

Fig. 7.8 Oscillation centers for pitch and bounce of the sprung mass.

of the wheelbase is called the pitch center, and the associated natural
frequency is called the pitch frequency.

Example 7.1   Determine the pitch and bounce frequencies and the location of oscillation centers of an automobile with the following data:

    sprung mass $m_s = 1500$ kg (weight 3300 lb)
    radius of gyration $r_y = 1.2$ m (3.94 ft)
    distance between front axle and center of gravity $l_1 = 1.4$ m (4.59 ft)
    distance between rear axle and center of gravity $l_2 = 1.7$ m (5.57 ft)
    front spring stiffness $k_f = 35$ kN/m (2398 lb/ft)
    rear spring stiffness $k_r = 38$ kN/m (2604 lb/ft)

Solution.   The constants D_1, D_2, and D_3 are first calculated as follows:

$$D_1 = \frac{k_f + k_r}{m_s} = \frac{35000 + 38000}{1500} = 48.7 \text{ s}^{-2}$$

$$D_2 = \frac{k_r l_2 - k_f l_1}{m_s} = \frac{38000 \times 1.7 - 35000 \times 1.4}{1500} = 10.4 \text{ m} \cdot \text{s}^{-2}$$

$$D_3 = \frac{k_f l_1^2 + k_r l_2^2}{m_s r_y^2} = \frac{35000 \times 1.4^2 + 38000 \times 1.7^2}{1500 \times 1.2^2} = 82.6 \text{ s}^{-2}$$

$$\left(\frac{D_2}{r_y}\right)^2 = 75.1 \text{ s}^{-4}$$

$$D_3 + D_1 = 131.3 \text{ s}^{-2}$$

$$D_3 - D_1 = 33.9 \text{ s}^{-2}$$

The natural frequencies can be obtained as

$$\omega_{n_1}^2 = \frac{1}{2}(D_1 + D_3) - \sqrt{\frac{1}{4}(D_1 - D_3)^2 + \left(\frac{D_2}{r_y}\right)^2}$$

$$= 65.65 - \sqrt{287.3 + 75.1} = 46.6 \text{ s}^{-2}$$

$$\omega_{n_1} = 6.83 \text{ s}^{-1} \text{ or } f_{n_1} = 1.09 \text{ Hz}$$

$$\omega_{n_2}^2 = \frac{1}{2}(D_1 + D_3) + \sqrt{\frac{1}{4}(D_1 - D_3)^2 + \left(\frac{D_2}{r_y}\right)^2}$$

$$= 65.65 + \sqrt{287.3 + 75.1} = 84.7 \text{ s}^{-2}$$

$$\omega_{n_2} = 9.2 \text{ s}^{-1} \text{ or } f_{n_2} = 1.46 \text{ Hz}$$

The location of oscillation centers can be determined using Eqs. 7.20 and 7.21.

For ω_{n_1}

$$l_{01} = \left.\frac{Z}{\Theta}\right|_{\omega_{n_1}} = \frac{D_2}{\omega_{n_1}^2 - D_1} = \frac{10.4}{46.6 - 48.7} = -4.95 \text{ m (195 in.)}$$

and for ω_{n_2}

$$l_{02} = \left.\frac{Z}{\Theta}\right|_{\omega_{n_2}} = \frac{D_2}{\omega_{n_2}^2 - D_1} = \frac{10.4}{84.7 - 48.7} = +0.29 \text{ m (11.5 in.)}$$

This indicates that one oscillation center is situated at a distance of 4.95 m (195 in.) to the right of the center of gravity and the other is located at a distance of 0.29 m (11.5 in.) to the left of the center of gravity, as shown in Fig. 7.8.

For most cars, the natural frequency for bounce is in the range of 1.0–1.2 Hz, and the natural frequency for pitch is slightly higher than that for bounce. For cars with coupled front-rear suspension systems, the natural frequency for pitch may be lower than that for bounce. In roll, the natural frequency is usually higher than those for bounce and pitch, because of the limits imposed on roll angles and the effect of antiroll bars. The natural frequency for roll usually varies in the range 1.5–2.0 Hz for cars.

The location of the oscillation centers has practical significance to ride behavior. One case of interest is that when the motions of bounce and pitch are uncoupled (i.e., $k_f l_1 = k_r l_2$). In this case, one oscillation center will be at the center of gravity and the other will be at an infinite distance from the center of gravity. The other case of interest is that when $r_y^2 = l_1 l_2$. In this case, one oscillation center will be located at the point of attachment of the front spring and the vehicle body (or its equivalent), and the other at the point of attachment of the rear spring and the body. This can be verified by setting $l_{01} = l_2$ and $l_{02} = l_1$ in Eqs. 7.20 and 7.21, respectively. It should also be noted that under these circumstances, the two-degrees-of-freedom model for pitch and bounce shown in Fig. 7.6 can be represented by a dynamically equivalent system with two concentrated masses at the front and rear attachment points (or their equivalents) as shown in Fig. 7.9. The equivalent concentrated mass at the front will be $m_s l_2/(l_1 + l_2)$ and that at the rear will be $m_s l_1/(l_1 + l_2)$. The equivalent system is in fact two single-degree-of-freedom systems with natural frequency $\omega_{nf} = \sqrt{k_f(l_1 + l_2)/m_s l_2}$ for the front, and natural frequency $\omega_{nr} = \sqrt{k_r(l_1 + l_2)/m_s l_1}$ for the rear. Thus, there is no interaction between the front and rear suspensions, and input at one end (front or rear) causes no motion of the other. This is a

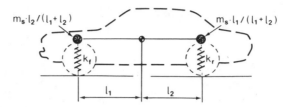

Fig. 7.9 Equivalent vibrating system having two concentrated masses for the vehicle body.

desirable condition for good ride. For practical vehicles, however, this condition often cannot be satisfied. Currently, the ratios of $r_y^2/l_1 l_2$ vary from approximately 0.8 for sports cars through 0.9–1.0 for conventional passenger cars to 1.2 and above for some front-wheel-drive cars.

In considering the natural frequencies for the front and rear ends, it should be noted that excitation from the road to a moving vehicle will affect the front wheels first and the rear wheels later. Consequently, there is a time lag between the excitation at the front and that at the rear. This results in a pitching motion of the vehicle body. To minimize this pitching motion, the equivalent spring rate and the natural frequency of the front end should be slightly less than those of the rear end. This ensures that both ends of the vehicle will move in phase (i.e., the vehicle body is merely bouncing) within a short time after the front end is excited. From the point of view of passenger ride comfort, pitching is more annoying than bouncing. The desirable ratio of the natural frequency of the front end to that of the rear end depends on the wheelbase of the vehicle, the average driving speed, and road conditions.

7.3 INTRODUCTION TO RANDOM VIBRATION

7.3.1 Surface Profile as a Random Function

In early attempts to investigate vehicle ride characteristics, excitation from the ground of the form of sine waves, step functions, or triangular waves was used. While these inputs could provide a basis for comparative evaluation of various designs, they could not serve as a valid basis for studying the actual ride behavior of the vehicle, since surface profiles are rarely of simple forms. Later, it is found that ground profiles should be more realistically described as a random function as shown in Fig. 7.10. The characteristic of a random function is that its instantaneous value cannot be predicted in a deterministic manner. For instance, the height of the surface profile z above a reference plane at any particular point, such as A, is not predictable as a function of the distance x between the point in

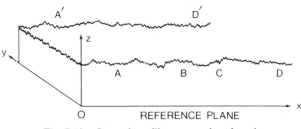

Fig. 7.10 Ground profile as a random function.

question and the origin shown in Fig. 7.10, if the surface profile is truly random in the popular sense of the term. However, certain properties of random functions can be described statistically. For instance, the mean or the mean square value of a random function can be determined by averaging, and the frequency content of the function can be established by methods based on Fourier analysis.

There are certain concepts of random functions that are of practical importance. Referring to the surface profile shown in Fig. 7.10, if the statistical properties of the portion of the road between A and B are the same as those of any other portion such as CD, then in practical terms the random function representing the surface profile is said to be stationary. This means that under these circumstances the statistical properties of the surface profile derived from a portion of the road can be used to define the properties of the entire section of the road surface. If the statistical properties of the surface profile on one plane such as AD are the same as that on any parallel plane such as $A'D'$, then in practical terms the random function representing the surface profile is said to be ergodic. Thus, if the random function is stationary or ergodic, the analysis will be simplified to a great extent.

The frequency composition of a random function is of importance. It may be established by methods based on Fourier analysis. For instance, after obtaining the surface profile shown in Fig. 7.10, one can perform a frequency analysis to make an estimate of the amplitudes for various wavelengths present [7.5]. The amplitude can then be plotted against the wavelength as shown in Fig. 7.11. In many cases, there are seldom any distinct wavelengths; therefore, an average value for the amplitude over a certain waveband is determined. Under certain circumstances, the relationship between amplitude and wavelength may be smoothed, and the amplitude may be expressed as a continuous function of wavelength as shown by the dotted line in Fig. 7.11.

In random vibrations, the mean square value of amplitude, and not the value of amplitude, is of prime interest, since it is associated with the average energy. For a harmonic component $z_n(x)$ with amplitude Z_n and

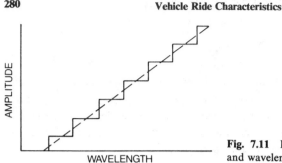

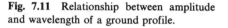

AMPLITUDE

WAVELENGTH

Fig. 7.11 Relationship between amplitude and wavelength of a ground profile.

wavelength l_{wn}, it can be expressed as

$$z_n(x) = Z_n \sin\left(\frac{2\pi x}{l_{wn}}\right) = Z_n \sin \Omega_n x$$

where $\Omega_n = 2\pi/l_{wn}$ is the circular spatial frequency of the harmonic component expressed in rad/m (rad/ft).

The mean square value of the component $\bar{z}_n^2$ is

$$\bar{z}_n^2 = \frac{1}{l_{wn}} \int_0^{l_{wn}} \left[Z_n \sin\left(\frac{2\pi x}{l_{wn}}\right) \right]^2 dx$$

$$= \frac{Z_n^2}{2} \tag{7.22}$$

For a function containing a number of discrete frequencies, its frequency content can be expressed in terms of the mean square values of the components, and the result is a discrete spectrum shown in Fig. 7.12. In general, the mean-square contribution in each frequency interval $\Delta\Omega$ is of interest. By letting $S(n\Omega_0)$ be the density of the mean square value in the interval $\Delta\Omega$ at frequency $n\Omega_0$, the following relation can be obtained

$$S(n\Omega_0)\Delta\Omega = \frac{Z_n^2}{2} = \bar{z}_n^2 \tag{7.23}$$

$\bar{z}_n^2$

$\Delta\Omega$

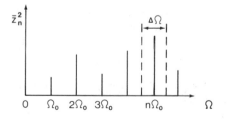

0   Ω_0 $2\Omega_0$ $3\Omega_0$ $n\Omega_0$ Ω

Fig. 7.12 Discrete frequency spectrum of a periodic function.

and the discrete spectral density becomes

$$S(n\Omega_0) = \frac{Z_n^2}{2\Delta\Omega} = \frac{\bar{z}_n^2}{\Delta\Omega} \tag{7.24}$$

If the function contains a large number of frequencies, the discrete spectral density function $S(n\Omega_0)$ becomes more or less a continuous spectral density function $S(\Omega)$, such as that shown in Fig. 7.13. The mean square value of the function $z(x)$ is then given by

$$\bar{z}^2 = \int_0^\infty S(\Omega)\,d\Omega \tag{7.25}$$

It should be noted that the mean square value of the function in any frequency band of interest, such as Ω_1 to Ω_2 shown in Fig. 7.13, can be calculated as follows:

$$\bar{z}_{\Omega_1 \to \Omega_2}^2 = \int_{\Omega_1}^{\Omega_2} S(\Omega)\,d\Omega \tag{7.26}$$

It may be mentioned that the determination of spectral densities from random data has been greatly facilitated by the availability of analog and digital spectral density analyzers [7.6]. The analyzer performs the filtering operation by heterodyning the random data signal past a highly selective narrow band-pass filter with a given center frequency. The instantaneous value of the filtered signal is squared, and the squared instantaneous value over the sampling time is then averaged to obtain the mean square value. Division of the mean square value by the bandwidth, the average spectral density at the given center frequency is obtained. As the center frequency of the narrow band-pass filter is varied, the spectral densities at a series of selected center frequencies can be determined and a plot of the spectral density versus frequency is obtained. Alternatively, an analyzer can be constructed with a collection of contiguous narrow band-pass filters that together cover the frequency range of interest. For this kind of multiple filter analyzer, no frequency scan is needed for obtaining a spectrum. Multiple filter analyzers are widely used in practice.

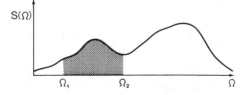

Fig. 7.13 Continuous spectral density curve.

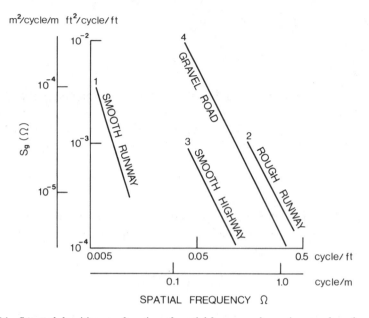

Fig. 7.14 Spectral densities as a function of spatial frequency for various roads and runways. (Reproduced by permission of the Society of Automotive Engineers from reference 7.7.)

When the surface profile is regarded as a random function, it can be characterized by a spectral density function. Figure 7.14 shows the spectral densities for profile amplitude as a function of spatial frequency for some runways and highways, and Fig. 7.15 shows the spectral density functions of various types of unprepared terrain [7.7, 7.8]. The spatial frequency Ω is the inverse of wavelength l_w (i.e., $\Omega = 1/l_w$) and is expressed in cycles per meter (or cycles per foot). The spectral density for profile amplitude is expressed in m²/cycle/m (or ft²/cycle/ft).

It has been found that the relationships between the spectral density and spatial frequency for the ground profiles shown in Figs. 7.14 and 7.15 can be approximated by

$$S_g(\Omega) = C_{sp}\Omega^{-N} \qquad (7.27)$$

where $S_g(\Omega)$ is the spectral density function of the surface profile, and C_{sp} and N are constants. Fitting this expression to the curves shown in Figs. 7.14 and 7.15 yields the values of C_{sp} and N as given in Table 7.1. N is a dimensionless constant, while the dimensions of C_{sp} vary with the value of N.

For vehicle vibration analysis, it is more convenient to express the spectral density of surface profiles in terms of temporal frequency in hertz

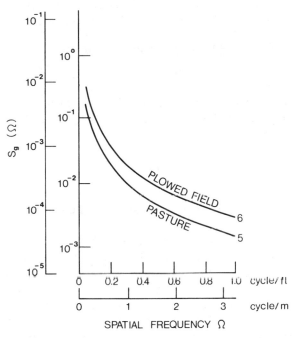

Fig. 7.15 Spectral densities as a function of spatial frequency for two types of unprepared terrain. (Reproduced by permission from reference 7.8.)

Table 7.1 Values of C_{sp} and N for Spectral Density Functions for Various Surfaces

No.	Description	N	C_{sp}	C'_{sp}
1	Smooth runway	3.8	4.3×10^{-11}	1.6×10^{-11}
2	Rough runway	2.1	8.1×10^{-6}	2.3×10^{-5}
3	Smooth highway	2.1	4.8×10^{-7}	1.2×10^{-6}
4	Highway with gravel	2.1	4.4×10^{-6}	1.1×10^{-5}
5	Pasture	1.6	3.0×10^{-4}	1.6×10^{-3}
6	Plowed field	1.6	6.5×10^{-4}	3.4×10^{-3}

Source. References 7.7 and 7.8.
Note:

C_{sp} is the value used for computing $S_g(\Omega)$ in $m^2/cycle/m$
C'_{sp} is the value used for computing $S_g(\Omega)$ in $ft^2/cycle/ft$
The numbers in the Table refer to the curves shown in Figs. 7.14 and 7.15.

than in terms of spatial frequency, since vehicle vibration is a function of time. The transformation of spatial frequency Ω in cycles/m (or cycles/ft) to temporal frequency f in hertz is that of the speed of the vehicle

$$f \text{ Hz} = \Omega(\text{cycle/m}) \, V \, (\text{m/sec})$$

$$= \Omega(\text{cycle/ft}) \, V \, (\text{ft/sec}) \tag{7.28}$$

The transformation of spectral density of surface profile expressed in terms of spatial frequency $S_g(\Omega)$ to that in terms of temporal frequency $S_g(f)$ is that of the speed of the vehicle

$$S_g(f) = \frac{S_g(\Omega)}{V} \tag{7.29}$$

7.3.2   Frequency Response Function

For a linear system, a direct linear relationship between input and output exists. This relationship, which also holds for random functions, is shown in the block diagram of Fig. 7.16 for a vehicle system. The vehicle system, characterized by its transfer function, modifies the input representing surface irregularities to the output representing the vibration of the vehicle. The transfer function or frequency response function is defined as the ratio of the output to input under steady-state conditions. For instance, if the vehicle is simplified to a single-degree-of-freedom system, and both the input due to surface irregularities and the output representing the vibration of the sprung mass are expressed in the same unit (i.e., displacement, velocity, or acceleration), the modulus of the transfer function $H(f)$ is expressed by

$$|H(f)| = \left| \sqrt{\frac{1 + (2\zeta f/f_n)^2}{\left[1 - (f/f_n)^2\right]^2 + \left[2\zeta f/f_n\right]^2}} \right| \tag{7.30}$$

where f is the frequency of excitation, f_n is the natural frequency of the system and ζ is the damping ratio. It is noted that in this case the transfer function $H(f)$ is simply the transmissibility ratio shown in Fig. 7.7.

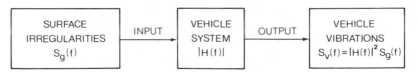

Fig. 7.16   Input and output of a linear vehicle system.

If, however, the surface irregularity as input is defined in terms of displacement and the vibration of the sprung mass as output is measured in acceleration, then the modulus of the transfer function $H(f)$ will take the following form

$$|H(f)| = \left| (2\pi f)^2 \sqrt{\frac{1 + (2\zeta f/f_n)^2}{\left[1 - (f/f_n)^2\right]^2 + \left[2\zeta f/f_n\right]^2}} \right| \tag{7.31}$$

The squared values of the moduli of two transfer functions representing two simplified, single-degree-of-freedom vehicle models, one with a bounce natural frequency of 3.5 Hz and a damping ratio of 0.1 and the other with a bounce natural frequency of 1.0 Hz and a damping ratio of 0.5, are shown in Fig. 7.17 [7.8]. The transfer functions shown are for predicting vehicle response having displacement as input and acceleration as output.

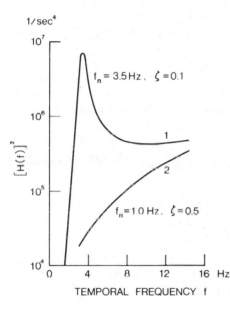

Fig. 7.17 The square of the moduli of the transfer functions of two simplified vehicle models with different natural frequencies and damping ratios. (Reproduced by permission from reference 7.8.)

If the transfer function of a system is known or given, then in general the relationship between the input of a system $z_g(t)$ and its output $z_v(t)$, both of which are functions of time, can be expressed as

$$z_v(t) = |H(f)| z_g(t) \tag{7.32}$$

Accordingly, the mean square values of the input $\bar{z}_g^2$ and output $\bar{z}_v^2$ can be related by

$$\bar{z}_v^2 = |H(f)|^2 \bar{z}_g^2 \tag{7.33}$$

Based on the definition of spectral density given by Eq. 7.24, and from the above equation, the relationship between the spectral density of the input $S_g(f)$ and the spectral density of the output $S_v(f)$ of the system is given by

$$S_v(f) = |H(f)|^2 S_g(f) \tag{7.34}$$

This indicates that the spectral density of the output $S_v(f)$ is related to the spectral density of the input $S_g(f)$ through the square of the modulus of the transfer function for a linear system.

Equation 7.34 holds regardless of the measure in which the input and output spectral densities are defined. For instance, if $S_g(f)$ is the spectral density for the amplitude of the terrain profile, $S_v(f)$ can be the spectral density for the acceleration of the sprung mass of the vehicle, provided that an appropriate transfer function is used. In the evaluation of vehicle ride quality, the spectral density for the acceleration of the sprung mass as a function of frequency is of prime interest.

7.3.3 Evaluation of Vehicle Vibration in Relation to Ride Comfort Criterion

After the spectral density function for acceleration of the vehicle has been obtained, further analysis is required to relate it to any ride comfort criterion that may be selected. For instance, if the fatigue or decreased proficiency boundaries for vertical vibration suggested by the International Standard ISO 2631 shown in Fig. 7.2 are adopted, then the transformation of the spectral density function into root mean square values of acceleration as a function of frequency is necessary. As mentioned previously, the mean square value of acceleration within a certain frequency band can be determined by integrating the corresponding spectral density function over the same frequency range. In practice, a series of discrete center frequencies within the range of interest is first selected. To determine the mean square value of acceleration at a given center frequency f_c, the spectral density function is integrated over a one-third-octave band of which the upper cut-off frequency is $\sqrt[3]{2}$ times the lower. In other words, by integrating the spectral density function over a frequency band of 0.89 to 1.12 f_c, the mean square value of acceleration at a given center frequency f_c can be obtained. The root mean square (rms) value of acceleration at each center frequency f_c can then be calculated by

$$\text{rms acceleration} = \left[\int_{0.89 f_c}^{1.12 f_c} S_v(f) \, df \right]^{1/2} \tag{7.35}$$

where $S_v(f)$ is the spectral density function for the acceleration of the vehicle. After obtaining the root mean square values of acceleration of the vehicle at a series of center frequencies within the range of interest, one can then evaluate the vibration of the vehicle against the limits specified.

Figure 7.18 shows the measured root mean square values of vertical and lateral accelerations at the driver's seat of a North American passenger car traveling at a speed of 80 km/h (50 mph) over smooth highway as compared with the reduced comfort boundaries recommended by the International Standard ISO 2631 [7.9].

It should be pointed out that the procedure described above is for a simplified vehicle model with a single degree of freedom. A practical vehicle has many degrees of freedom, and between the driver and the vehicle there is a seat suspension. In addition, more than one random input is imposed on the vehicle. In the case of a passenger car, there are four inputs, one to each wheel. The interaction of the random inputs with each other becomes important in determining the output. The consideration of cross-spectral densities is essential, and the time-lag of the input at the rear wheel with respect to the front wheel should also be taken into account. All these would make the analysis much more complex than that described above. However, analytical techniques based on random vibration theory

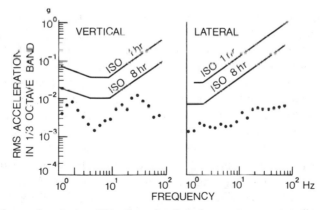

Fig. 7.18 Measured vertical and lateral acceleration of a passenger car traveling at 80 km/h (50 mph) over a smooth road. (Reproduced by permission of the American Society of Mechanical Engineers from reference 7.9.)

are being developed into a practical tool to evaluate vehicle ride quality under various operating conditions [7.7].

REFERENCES

7.1 B. D. Van Deusen, Human Response to Vehicle Vibration, *SAE Transactions*, Vol. 77, paper 680090, 1969.

7.2 Ride and Vibration Data Manual, Society of Automotive Engineers, SAE J6a, 1965.

7.3 C. M. Harris and C. E. Crede, *Shock and Vibration Handbook*, 2nd edition, McGraw-Hill, New York, NY, 1976.

7.4 L. F. Stikeleather, G. O. Hall, and A. O. Radke, A Study of Vehicle Vibration Spectra as Related to Seating Dynamics, *SAE Transactions*, Vol. 81, paper 720001, 1973.

7.5 M. A. Macaulay, Measurement of Road Surfaces, in G. H. Tidbury, Ed., *Advances in Automobile Engineering, Part I*, Pergamon Press, Oxford, England, 1963.

7.6 J. S. Bendat and A. G. Piersol, *Random Data: Analysis and Measurement Procedures*, Wiley-Interscience, New York, NY, 1971.

7.7 B. D. Van Deusen, Analytical Techniques for Designing Riding Quality into Automotive Vehicles, *SAE Transactions*, Vol. 76, paper 670021, 1968.

7.8 J. Y. Wong, Effect of Vibration on the Performance of Off-Road Vehicles, *Journal of Terramechanics*, Vol. 8, No. 4, 1972.

7.9 A. J. Healy, Digital Processing of Measured Random Vibration Data for Automobile Ride Evaluation, *ASME Publication*, AMD-Vol. 24, 1977.

7.10 D. E. Cole, *Elementary Vehicle Dynamics*, Department of Mechanical Engineering, University of Michigan, Ann Arbor, MI, 1971.

PROBLEMS

7.1 The sprung parts of a passenger car weigh 11.12 kN (2500 lb) and the unsprung parts weigh 890 N (200 lb). The combined stiffness of the suspension springs is 45.53 kN/m (260 lb/in.) and that of the tires is 525.35 kN/m (3000 lb/in.). Determine the two natural frequencies of bounce motions of the sprung and unsprung mass. Calculate the amplitudes of the sprung and unsprung parts, if the car travels at a speed of 48 km/h (30 mph) over a road of sine wave form with wavelength of 9.15 m (30 ft) and amplitude of 5 cm (2 in.). Determine also the speed at which the tires will cease to remain continuously in contact with the road surface.

7.2 Owing to the wide separation of the natural frequency of the sprung parts from that of the unsprung parts, the bounce and pitch motions of the vehicle body and the wheel motions exist almost independently. The sprung parts of a vehicle weigh 9.786 kN (2200 lb), its center of gravity is 106.7 cm (42 in.) behind the front axle and the wheelbase is 228.6 cm (90 in.). The combined stiffness of the springs of the front suspension is 24.52

kN/m (140 lb/in.) and that of the rear suspension is 26.27 kN/m (150 lb/in.). The radius of gyration of the sprung parts about a horizontal transverse axis through the center of gravity is 0.915 m (3.0 ft). Calculate the natural frequencies of pitch and bounce motions of the vehicle body. Determine also the location of the oscillation centers.

7.3 If the vehicle described in Problem 7.2 travels over a concrete highway with expansion joints 15.24 m (50 ft) apart, calculate the speeds at which bounce motion and pitch motion of the vehicle body are most apt to arise.

7.4 If the radius of gyration of the sprung parts of the vehicle described in Problem 7.2 can be varied, determine the conditions under which the oscillation centers of the vehicle body will be located at the points of attachment of the front and rear springs. Calculate also the natural frequencies of the sprung parts.

7.5 A tractor with bounce natural frequency of 3.5 Hz and damping ratio of 0.1 travels at a speed of 5 km/h (3.1 mph) over a plowed field of which the surface roughness characteristics are described in Table 7.1. Determine the root mean square values of vertical acceleration of the tractor over the frequency range 1–40 Hz. Evaluate whether the vibration of the vehicle is acceptable for an 8-hr duration based on the International Standard ISO 2631.

CHAPTER EIGHT

INTRODUCTION TO AIR-CUSHION VEHICLES

An air-cushion vehicle may be defined as a surface vehicle that is supported by a cushion of pressurized air. The cushion performs two basic functions: to separate the vehicle from the surface, thus reducing or eliminating surface contact and the associated resistance, and to provide the vehicle with a suspension system.

Since practical air-cushion concepts emerged in the 1950s, they have found applications in overwater as well as overland transport. In this chapter, the performance of the principal types of air-cushion system will be discussed. The characteristics unique to air-cushion vehicles will also be examined.

8.1 AIR-CUSHION SYSTEMS AND THEIR PERFORMANCE

There are two principal types of air cushion system: plenum chamber and peripheral jet.

8.1.1 Plenum Chamber

Figure 8.1 shows the basic features of a simple plenum chamber [8.1]. The majority of current air-cushion vehicles employ essentially plenum cham-

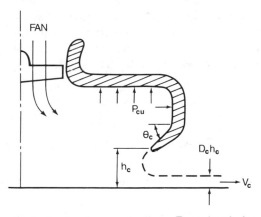

Fig. 8.1 Geometry of a simple plenum chamber. (Reproduced, by permission, from *Hovercraft Design and Construction*, by G. H. Elsley and A. J. Devereux, copyright © by Elsley and Devereux, 1968.)

ber configuration Pressurized air is pumped into the chamber by a fan or a compressor to form an air cushion that supports the vehicle. Under steady-state conditions, the air being pumped into the chamber is just sufficient to replace the air leaking under the peripheral gap, and the weight of the vehicle W is equal to the lift F_{cu} generated by the cushion pressure p_{cu}.

$$F_{cu} = W = p_{cu}A_c \tag{8.1}$$

where A_c is the effective cushion area.

For most current designs, the cushion pressure varies in the range 1.2–3.3 kPa (25–70 lb/ft²) for overwater and overland vehicles. For high-speed guided ground transport vehicles, cushion pressure of 4.2 kPa (87 lb/ft²) has been used.

Assume that the air inside the chamber is essentially at rest. From Bernoulli's theorem, the velocity of air escaping under the peripheral gap V_c is given by

$$V_c = \sqrt{\frac{2p_{cu}}{\rho}} \tag{8.2}$$

where ρ is the density of air. The total volume flow of air from the cushion Q is given by

$$Q = V_c h_c l_{cu} D_c = h_c l_{cu} D_c \sqrt{\frac{2p_{cu}}{\rho}} \tag{8.3}$$

where h_c is the clearance height, l_{cu} is the cushion perimeter, and D_c is the discharge coefficient. The discharge coefficient is primarily a function of wall angle θ_c shown in Fig. 8.1 and the length of the wall. For a long wall and nonviscous fluid, the values of D_c are as follows:

θ_c	0	45°	90°	135°	180°
D_c	0.50	0.537	0.611	0.746	1.000

In practice, because of the viscosity of the air, the values of D_c tend to be slightly less than those given above.

The power required to sustain the air cushion at the peripheral gap P_a is given by

$$P_a = p_{cu} Q$$

$$= h_c l_{cu} D_c p_{cu}^{3/2} \left(\frac{2}{\rho} \right)^{1/2} \tag{8.4}$$

Substituting Eq. 8.1 into the above equation, one obtains

$$P_a = h_c l_{cu} D_c \left(\frac{W}{A_c} \right)^{3/2} \left(\frac{2}{\rho} \right)^{1/2} \tag{8.5}$$

This equation shows that the power required to sustain the cushion in the plenum chamber varies with the clearance height and the perimeter, and that for a given vehicle it is proportional to the weight of the vehicle raised to the power of $3/2$. It should be noted that in determining the power required to drive the fan, intake losses, ducting losses, diffusion losses, and fan efficiency should be taken into consideration.

Consider that an air jet with the same amount of volume flow Q and having the same air velocity V_c as those of the air cushion is directly used to generate a lift force. The lift force F_l generated by the change of momentum of the air jet is given by

$$F_l = \rho Q V_c \tag{8.6}$$

An augmentation factor K_a which is a measure of the effectiveness of an air-cushion system as a lift generating device can be defined as

$$K_a = \frac{F_{cu}}{F_l} = \frac{p_{cu} A_c}{\rho Q V_c} = \frac{A_c}{2 h_c l_{cu} D_c} \tag{8.7}$$

Introducing the concept of hydraulic diameter D_h

$$D_h = \frac{4 A_c}{l_{cu}} \tag{8.8}$$

Equation 8.7 becomes

$$K_a = \frac{D_h}{8 h_c D_c} \tag{8.9}$$

This expression shows that the higher the ratio of the hydraulic diameter D_h to the clearance height h_c, the more effective the air-cushion system will be. Useful guidelines for the selection of the configuration and dimensions of air-cushion vehicles can be drawn from this simple equation.

Currently there are two principal forms of plenum chamber in use, one with a flexible skirt and the other with a combination of flexible skirt and sidewall, as shown in Fig. 8.2. The prime reason for using the flexible skirt is to allow the vehicle to have relatively large clearance between the hard structure and the supporting surface, while at the same time keeping the clearance height under the skirt sufficiently small to enable the power required for lift to remain within reasonable limits. A combination of flexible skirt and sidewall is used in marine air-cushion vehicles in which the air can only leak through the gaps in the front and rear of the vehicle. The air in the cushion is prevented from leaking along the sides by rigid sidewalls immersed in the water. Thus the power required to sustain the cushion is reduced. The sidewalls can also contribute to the directional stability of the vehicle.

There are many variants of the plenum chamber configuration with a flexible skirt. Figure 8.3 shows the multiple-cone skirt system used in Bertin Terraplane BC7 [8.2]. The conical form ensures that the shape of the skirt under pressure is stable. The system can provide the vehicle with sufficient roll and pitch stability. When the vehicle rolls, the air gap of the

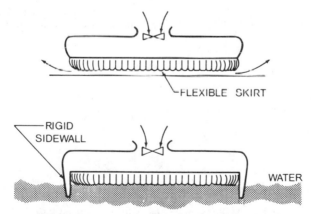

FLEXIBLE SKIRT

RIGID SIDEWALL

WATER

Fig. 8.2 Flexible skirted plenum chamber and rigid sidewall plenum chamber.

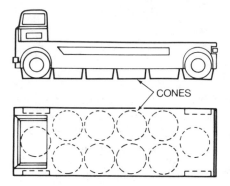

Fig. 8.3 Multiple-cone skirt system used in Bertin Terraplane BC7. (Reproduced from reference 8.2.)

cone on the downgoing side is reduced. Consequently, the air flow from that side decreases and the cushion pressure increases. This together with the decrease of cushion pressure in the cone on the upgoing side provides a restoring moment that tends to bring the vehicle back to its original position. This system is also less sensitive to loss of lift over ditches than the single-plenum-chamber configuration. The multiple-cone system shown in Fig. 8.3 requires, however, more power to sustain the cushion than an equivalent single plenum chamber, because the ratio of the periphery of the leakage gap to the cushion area is higher than that of a single plenum chamber. In other words, the equivalent hydraulic diameter of the multiple-cone skirt system is lower than that of an equivalent single plenum chamber. To reduce the volume flow, a peripheral skirt around the multiple cones may be added as shown in Fig. 8.4. This also increases the effective cushion area, although the cushion pressure between the cones is lower than that inside the cones.

The performance of the multiple-cone system with a peripheral skirt may be evaluated analytically as shown by Wong [8.3]. Consider that the cushion pressure inside the cones is p_{cu} and that between the peripheral

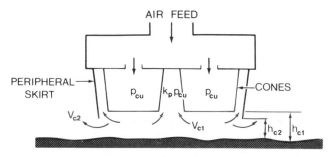

Fig. 8.4 Multiple-cone system with a peripheral skirt.

skirt and the cones is $k_p p_{cu}$, and assume that the air inside the cushion is substantially at rest, then from Bernoulli's theorem, the velocity of the air escaping under the peripheral skirt V_{c_2} is given by

$$V_{c_2} = \left(\frac{2 k_p p_{cu}}{\rho} \right)^{1/2} \tag{8.10}$$

and the total volume flow from the peripheral skirt Q_2 is given by

$$Q_2 = h_{c_2} l_{c_2} D_{c_2} \left(\frac{2 k_p p_{cu}}{\rho} \right)^{1/2} \tag{8.11}$$

where h_{c_2}, l_{c_2}, and D_{c_2} are the clearance height, perimeter, and discharge coefficient of the peripherial skirt, respectively.

Under steady-state conditions, the total lift force generated by the system is given by

$$F_{cu} = W = p_{cu} A_{c_1} + k_p p_{cu} A_{c_2}$$

where A_{c_1} is total cushion area of the cones and A_{c_2} is the cushion area between the peripheral skirt and the cones. The cushion pressure p_{cu} required to support the vehicle weight is expressed by

$$p_{cu} = \frac{W}{A_{c_1} + k_p A_{c_2}} \tag{8.12}$$

Based on the assumptions of inviscid, incompressible flow, the total volume of air escaping under the cones Q_1 is equal to that escaping under the peripheral skirt Q_2

$$Q_1 = n_c h_{c_1} l_{c_1} D_{c_1} \left[\frac{2(1 - k_p) p_{cu}}{\rho} \right]^{1/2} = Q_2 \tag{8.13}$$

where n_c is the number of cones, and h_{c_1}, l_{c_1}, and D_{c_1} are the clearance height, perimeter, and discharge coefficient of the cone, respectively.

The power required to sustain the air cushion is given by

$$P_a = p_{cu} Q_1 = p_{cu} Q_2$$

$$= h_{c_2} l_{c_2} D_{c_2} \left[\frac{W}{(A_{c_1} + k_p A_{c_2})} \right]^{3/2} \left(\frac{2 k_p}{\rho} \right)^{1/2} \tag{8.14}$$

Based on Eqs. 8.11 and 8.13, an expression for the pressure ratio k_p can be derived, and

$$k_p = \frac{n_c^2 h_{c_1}^2 l_{c_1}^2 D_{c_1}^2}{n_c^2 h_{c_1}^2 l_{c_1}^2 D_{c_1}^2 + h_{c_2}^2 l_{c_2}^2 D_{c_2}^2} \tag{8.15}$$

It is found that the value of k_p calculated from the above equation is very close to that quoted in the literature. It is interesting to note that the difference between the clearance heights h_{c_1} and h_{c_2} affects the pressure ratio k_p, hence the characteristics of the cushion system.

The augmentation factor K_a of a multiple-cone system with a peripheral skirt is given by

$$K_a = \frac{A_{c_1} + k_p A_{c_2}}{2 k_p h_{c_2} l_{c_2} D_{c_2}} \tag{8.16}$$

It can be shown that, other conditions being equal, the augmentation factor of the multiple-cone system with a peripheral skirt would be much higher than that of an equivalent system without a peripheral skirt.

Another flexible skirt system of plenum chamber type is the segmented skirt developed by the Hovercraft Development Ltd. (HDL) as shown in Fig. 8.5(a) [8.4, 8.5]. The unique feature of this type of skirt system is that the segments are unattached to one another. Consequently, when moving over a rough surface, only the segments in contact with the obstacles will deflect. When a segment is damaged or even removed, adjacent segments expand under cushion pressure and tend to fill the gap. Furthermore, the drag of the segmented skirt is found to be less than that of a continuous skirt because of its higher flexibility. The performance of the segmented skirt system may be predicted using the theory for a simple plenum chamber described previously.

Figure 8.5(b) shows the bag and finger skirt developed by the British Hovercraft Corporation (BHC) [8.4]. The fingers in this skirt system have the same characteristics as those of the segments in the segmented skirt. The cushion air is fed from the bag through holes into the fingers. A diaphragm is installed in the bag to help prevent the vertical oscillation of the skirt system.

Example 8.1 A multiple cone cushion system with a peripheral skirt similar to that shown in Fig. 8.4 has the following parameters:

gross vehicle weight, W	48.93 kN (11,000 lb)
number of cones, n_c	8
perimeter of each cone, l_{c_1}	3.6 m (11.8 ft)

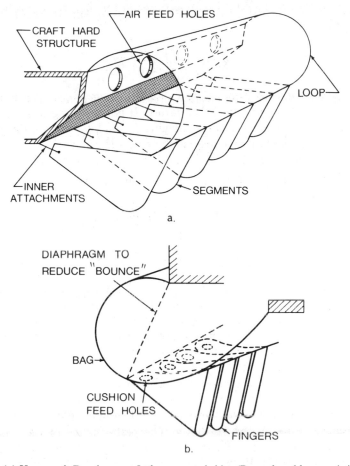

Fig. 8.5 (*a*) Hovercraft Development Ltd. segmented skirt. (Reproduced by permission of R. L. Trillo from reference 8.5.) (*b*) British Hovercraft Corporation bag and finger skirt. (Reproduced by permission of the Society of Automotive Engineers from reference 8.4.)

perimeter of the peripheral skirt, l_{c_2}	17.5 m (57.5 ft)
total cushion area of the cones, A_{c_1}	8.2 m² (88.3 ft²)
cushion area between the cones and the peripheral skirt, A_{c_2}	9.6 m² (103.3 ft²)
clearance heights, h_{c_1} and h_{c_2}	2.5 cm (1 in.)
discharge coefficients, D_{c_1} and D_{c_2}	0.60

Determine the power required to generate the lift and the augmentation factor.

Solution. From Eq. 8.15, for $D_{c_1} = D_{c_2}$ and $h_{c_1} = h_{c_2}$, the pressure ratio k_p is obtained by

$$k_p = \frac{n_c^2 l_{c_1}^2}{n_c^2 l_{c_1}^2 + l_{c_2}^2} = 0.73$$

From Eq. 8.12, the required cushion pressure p_{cu} is determined by

$$p_{cu} = \frac{W}{(A_{c_1} + k_p A_{c_2})} = 3.22 \text{ kPa } (67 \text{ lb/ft}^2)$$

From Eq. 8.14, the power required to sustain the cushion is obtained by

$$P_a = \left[\frac{W}{(A_{c_1} + k_p A_{c_2})} \right]^{3/2} \left(\frac{2k_p}{\rho} \right)^{1/2} h_{c_2} l_{c_2} D_{c_2}$$

$$= 53.4 \text{ kW } (71.6 \text{ hp})$$

From Eq. 8.16, the augmentation factor K_a is determined by

$$K_a = \frac{A_{c_1} + k_p A_{c_2}}{2 k_p h_{c_2} l_{c_2} D_{c_2}} = 39$$

8.1.2   Peripheral Jet

In the early days of development of air-cushion technology, the peripheral jet system was used. This system is schematically shown in Fig. 8.6. In this system, a curtain of air is produced around the periphery by ejecting air downward and inward from a nozzle. This curtain of air helps contain the cushion under the vehicle and reduces air leakage. Thus it could offer higher operational efficiency than the simple plenum chamber.

In addition to the lift force generated by the cushion pressure, the air jet also provides a small amount of vertical lift. Under steady-state conditions, the weight of the vehicle W is balanced by the lifting force F_{cu}

$$F_{cu} = W = p_{cu} A_c + J_j l_j \sin \theta_j$$

where J_j is the momentum flux of the air jet per unit length of nozzle, which is the product of jet velocity and mass flow per unit nozzle length, l_j is the nozzle perimeter, and θ_j is the angle of the nozzle from the horizontal.

There are a number of theories for predicting the performance of peripheral jet systems. Among them, the so-called "exponential theory" is

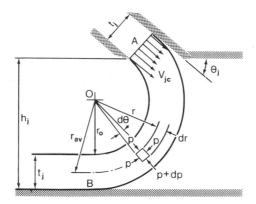

Fig. 8.6 Geometry of a peripheral jet system.

one of the most commonly used. In this theory, it is assumed that from the outlet of the nozzle (point A) to the point of ground contact (point B) the jet maintains its thickness as well as its circular path, and that the air is inviscid and incompressible. The total pressure p_j is assumed to be constant across the jet with a static pressure gradient within it. The distribution of static pressure p across the jet must satisfy the boundary conditions, that is, $p = 0$ at the outside and $p = p_{cu}$ at the cushion side.

Consider a small element of the jet at a distance r from the center of curvature 0. The pressure difference across the element is balanced by the centrifugal force, and the equation of equilibrium for the element is given by

$$(p + dp)(r + dr)\,d\theta - pr\,d\theta - p\,dr\,d\theta = \frac{\rho V_{jc}^2}{r} r\,dr\,d\theta$$

where V_{jc} is the velocity of the element. Neglecting second-order terms, one can rewrite the above equation as

$$\frac{dp}{dr} = \frac{\rho V_{jc}^2}{r} \tag{8.17}$$

Since the total pressure p_j is assumed to be constant across the jet, from Bernoulli's theorem the following relation is obtained

$$p_j = p + \frac{\rho V_{jc}^2}{2} \tag{8.18}$$

Substituting Eq. 8.17 into Eq. 8.18, one obtains

$$\frac{dp}{p_j - p} = \frac{2dr}{r} \tag{8.19}$$

Since the variation of r is limited, the value of r in the above equation may be considered to be constant and equal to the average radius of curvature of the path r_{av}. Integrating Eq. 8.19 and substituting the limits: $r = r_o, p = 0;\ r = r_o + t_j, p = p_{cu}$, one obtains the following expression relating cushion pressure p_{cu} and the total pressure of the jet p_j

$$\frac{p_{cu}}{p_j} = 1 - e^{-2t_j/r_{av}} \tag{8.20}$$

where t_j is the thickness of the jet or nozzle width. Noting that $r_{av} \approx h_j/(1 + \cos\theta_j)$, one obtains

$$\frac{p_{cu}}{p_j} = 1 - e^{-2t_j(1 + \cos\theta_j)/h_j} \tag{8.21}$$

where h_j is the clearance height.

The total volume flow Q_j is given by

$$Q_j = \int_{r_o}^{r_o + t_j} l_j V_{jc}\, dr$$

$$= \frac{l_j h_j}{1 + \cos\theta_j}\sqrt{\frac{2p_j}{\rho}}\left[1 - \sqrt{1 - p_{cu}/p_j}\,\right] \tag{8.22}$$

and the power required is

$$P_{aj} = p_j Q_j = \frac{l_j h_j (1 - e^{-x})p_{cu}^{3/2}(2/\rho)^{1/2}}{(1 + \cos\theta_j)(1 - e^{-2x})^{3/2}} \tag{8.23}$$

where $x = t_j(1 + \cos\theta_j)/h_j$.

For given values of h_j, l_j, p_{cu}, and θ_j, the power requirement is a minimum for

$$\frac{\partial P_{aj}}{\partial x} = 0$$

which gives $x = 0.693$. The minimum power $P_{aj\,min}$ is expressed by

$$P_{aj\,min} = \frac{4l_j h_j p_{cu}^{3/2}(2/\rho)^{1/2}}{3\sqrt{3}\,(1 + \cos\theta_j)} \tag{8.24}$$

Comparing the power requirement of a simple plenum chamber with that of a peripheral jet having the same cushion pressure and similar dimensions ($l_j = l_c$ and $h_j = h_c$), one may obtain the following power ratio

$$\frac{P_a}{P_{aj\,min}} = \frac{3\sqrt{3}\;D_c(1+\cos\theta_j)}{4} \tag{8.25}$$

Assume that $\theta_j = 45°$ and $D_c = 0.6$, the power requirement of a simple plenum chamber will be 33% higher than that of an equivalent peripheral jet system. The augmentation factor K_{aj} for a peripheral jet system is expressed by

$$K_{aj} = \frac{p_{cu}A_c + J_j l_j \sin\theta_j}{J_j l_j}$$

$$= \frac{p_{cu}A_c}{J_j l_j} + \sin\theta_j$$

$$= \frac{p_{cu}D_h}{4J_j} + \sin\theta_j \tag{8.26}$$

The momentum flux per unit nozzle length J_j can be determined by

$$J_j = \int_{r_o}^{r_o+l_j} \rho V_{jc}^2\,dr$$

$$= \int_{r_o}^{r_o+l_j} 2(p_j - p)\,dr$$

$$= \int_0^{p_{cu}} r\,dp = r_{av}p_{cu} \tag{8.27}$$

Substituting Eq. 8.27 into Eq. 8.26, one obtains

$$K_{aj} = \frac{D_h}{4r_{av}} + \sin\theta_j$$

$$= \frac{D_h}{4h_j}(1+\cos\theta_j) + \sin\theta_j \tag{8.28}$$

Comparing the augmentation factor of a simple plenum chamber with that of a peripheral jet system having the same hydraulic diameter and clearance height, one can obtain the following ratio:

$$\frac{K_{aj}}{K_a} = 2D_c\left(1+\cos\theta_j + 4\sin\theta_j\,\frac{h_j}{D_h}\right) \tag{8.29}$$

Assume that $D_c = 0.6$, $\theta_j = 45°$, and $h_j/D_h = 0.001$, the augmentation factor of a peripheral jet system is approximately twice that of an equivalent simple plenum chamber.

Although in theory the peripheral jet system appears to be superior to the plenum chamber, in practice it is not necessarily so. It has been found that using flexible nozzles for the peripheral jet system, difficulties arise in maintaining the jet width and angle, and in excessive nozzle wear. Using relatively hard nozzles, on the other hand, would induce high surface drag. Moreover, the advent of flexible skirt enables the clearance height and hence power requirements for lift to be reduced considerably, while maintaining sufficient clearance between the hard structure and the supporting surface. On some current vehicles, the designed clearance height is only a few millimeters. This renders the power saving aspect of the peripheral jet system rather insignificant. All of these have led to the use of essentially plenum chamber configuration in almost all of current air-cushion vehicles.

8.2 RESISTANCE OF AIR-CUSHION VEHICLES

There are drag components unique to air-cushion vehicles, which require special attention. For overland operations, in addition to aerodynamic resistance, there are momentum drag, trim drag, and skirt contact drag. For overwater operations, additional wave-making drag, wetting drag, and drag due to waves have to be taken into account.

As mentioned previously, the introduction of flexible skirts permits considerable reduction of clearance height and hence power for lift. It should be pointed out, however, that the reduction of clearance height would likely increase the skirt contact drag thus increasing the power for propulsion. Apparently, a proper balance between the reduction of lift power and the associated increase in propulsion power has to be struck to achieve a minimum total power requirement.

The aerodynamic resistance of an air cushion vehicle can be evaluated using the methods discussed in Chapter 3. Typical values for the coefficient of aerodynamic resistance C_D obtained from wind-tunnel tests range from 0.25 for SR.N2 to 0.38 for SR.N5 based on frontal area [8.1]. For a surface effect ship, a value of 0.5 for C_D has been reported [8.5].

Momentum Drag

To sustain the cushion, air is continuously drawn into the cushion system. When the vehicle is moving, the air is effectively accelerated to the speed of the vehicle. This generates a resisting force in the direction of the air relative to the vehicle, which is usually referred to as momentum drag R_m. The momentum drag can be expressed by

$$R_m = \rho Q V_a \tag{8.30}$$

where V_a is the speed of air relative to the vehicle, and Q is the volume flow of the cushion system. This momentum drag is unique to air-cushion vehicles.

It should be noted that part of the power to overcome momentum drag may be recovered from utilizing the dynamic pressure of the airstream at the inlet of the fan to generate the cushion pressure. The dynamic pressure of the airstream at the intake of the fan p_d is given by

$$p_d = \frac{\rho V_a^2}{2} \tag{8.31}$$

Assume that the efficiency of the cushion system including the fan and ducting is η_{cu}, then the power that can be recovered from generating the cushion pressure is given by

$$P_r = \frac{\eta_{cu} \rho Q V_a^2}{2} \tag{8.32}$$

Since the power required to overcome momentum drag P_m is equal to $\rho Q V_a^2$, the ratio of P_r to P_m is

$$\frac{P_r}{P_m} = \frac{\eta_{cu} \rho Q V_a^2}{2 \rho Q V_a^2} = \frac{\eta_{cu}}{2} \tag{8.33}$$

This indicates that if the efficiency of the cushion system η_{cu} is 100%, half of the power expended in overcoming the momentum drag can be recovered.

Trim Drag

If the cushion base of the vehicle is not horizontal, the lift force that is perpendicular to the cushion base will have a horizontal component. This horizontal component is given by

$$R_{tr} = p_{cu} A_c \sin \theta_t \tag{8.34}$$

where θ_t is the trim angle (i.e., the angle between the cushion base and the horizontal). R_{tr} may be a drag or a thrust component dependent upon whether the vehicle is trimmed nose up or down.

Skirt Contact Drag

For overland operations, contact between the skirt and the ground may be inevitable, particularly at low clearance heights. This gives rise to a drag component commonly known as skirt contact drag R_{sk}. The physical origin of this drag component appears to be derived from the following major sources: friction between the skirt and the ground, and the deformation of the skirt and of the terrain including vegetation due to skirt-ground interaction [8.6]. A reliable method for predicting skirt contact drag is lacking, although from experience it is known that cushion pressure, clearance height, skirt material, and the strength and geometry of the terrain surface have significant influence on the skirt contact drag. The value of skirt contact drag is usually obtained from experiments. Table 8.1 gives the values of the coefficient of towing resistance of two air-cushion trailers and a self-propelled air-cushion vehicle over various types of terrain [8.7, 8.8]. One of the air-cushion trailers is equipped with a Bertin-type multiple-cone system with a peripheral skirt and built by HoverJak, the other is equipped with the Hovercraft Development Ltd. segmented skirt and built by Terracross [8.7]. The self-propelled air-cushion vehicle is a Bell SK-5 equipped with the type of fingered skirt developed by British Hovercraft Corporation [8.8]. The coefficient of towing resistance is defined as the ratio of the towing resistance to the total vehicle weight.

It should be mentioned that for the air-cushion trailer built by Hover-Jak, 2% of the total vehicle weight is carried by the guided wheels, whereas for the one built by Terracross, 7% of the vehicle weight is carried by the guided wheels. The values given in Table 8.1 for the air-cushion trailers include, therefore, both the skirt contact drag and the rolling resistance of the guided wheels. The values given in Table 8.1 for the Bell SK-5 may be considered to be those of the coefficient of skirt contact drag, since no guided wheels were used.

Knowing the value of the coefficient of skirt contact drag C_{sk}, one can calculate the skirt contact drag R_{sk} from the following equation

$$R_{sk} = C_{sk} W \tag{8.35}$$

where W is the total vehicle weight.

In logged-over areas with stumps, average values of coefficient of towing resistance range 0.06–0.24 for an air-cushion trailer equipped with Bertin-type multiple-cone system having a peripheral skirt [8.9].

Table 8.1   Coefficient of Towing Resistance

Type of Vehicle	Type of Air-Cushion System	Terrain	Coefficient of Towing Resistance	Total Vehicle Weight (kN)
Air-cushion trailer by HoverJak	multiple-cone system with peripheral skirt	concrete, dry flat rock, dry	0.002–0.005 0.014–0.018	148.3 (34,000 lb)
		dry mud sandy road	0.011–0.016 0.023	130.8 (30,000 lb)
Air-cushion trailer by Terracross	H.D.L. type skirt	wet flat rock	0.018	143.5 (30,000 lb)
		water or mud wet mud dry mud churned marsh	0.015 0.019 0.022–0.037 0.035	206.9 (50,000 lb)
Self-propelled air-cushion vehicle Bell SK-5	B.H.C. type fingered skirt	rough hummocky snow, hard glazed surface	0.002	58.1 (13,060 lb)
		rock strewn creek bed, left rough	0.012–0.022	
		rock strewn creek bed, graded level	0.020–0.030	
		swamp grass, tufts in water	0.006–0.034	
		light brush on rough ground	0.075–0.25	

Source.   References 8.7 and 8.8.

Total Overland Drag

For a vehicle wholly supported by an air cushion operating overland, the total drag consists of aerodynamic resistance, momentum drag, trim drag, and skirt contact drag. It should be pointed out that although wholly air-cushion-supported vehicles can function overland, they are relatively difficult to maneuver and control in constricted space and in the traverse of a slope. The longitudinal slope that this type of vehicle can negotiate is also limited. To solve these problems, surface contacting devices such as wheels, tracks and the like may be used. In this type of arrangement, the air cushion is used to carry a proportion of the vehicle weight, while leaving sufficient surface contact for directional control, positioning, and possibly for traction and braking. A vehicle that uses air cushion together with surface contacting devices for support is usually referred to as a hybrid vehicle.

For the hybrid vehicle, the resistance of the surface-contacting device must be taken into consideration in computing the total overland drag. The resistance of wheels and tracks over unprepared terrain can be predicted using the methods described in Chapter 2. It is found that among the design parameters, the load distribution between the air cushion and the surface-contacting device has considerable effect on the total power consumption of the hybrid vehicle [8.3]. Figure 8.7 shows the variation of power consumption with the ratio of the load supported by the air cushion W_a to the total vehicle weight W for a particular hybrid vehicle equipped with tires over clay [8.3]. It is shown that for a given hybrid vehicle over a particular type of terrain, there is an optimum load distribution that could minimize the power consumption. Figure 8.8 shows the variation of the optimum load distribution with terrain conditions for a particular hybrid vehicle equipped with tires [8.3].

Another type of overland vehicle system employing air-cushion technology is the air-cushion trailer-towing vehicle system [8.10]. It consists of two separate units: an air-cushion trailer and a towing vehicle. Figure 8.9

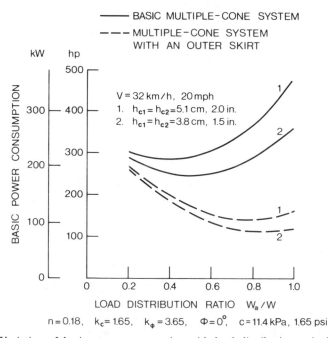

Fig. 8.7 Variation of basic power consumption with load distribution ratio for a hybrid vehicle in clay; the values of k_c and k_ϕ are in U.S. customary units. (Reproduced by permission from reference 8.3.)

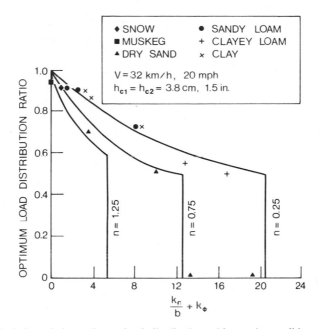

Fig. 8.8 Variation of the optimum load distribution with terrain conditions for a hybrid vehicle equipped with a multiple-cone system having a peripheral skirt; the values of k_c and k_ϕ are in U.S. customary units. (Reproduced by permission from reference 8.3.)

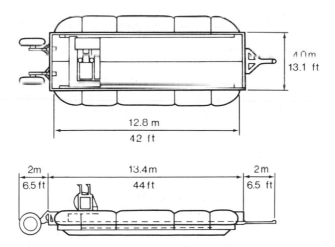

Fig. 8.9 An air-cushion trailer with segmented skirt built by Terracross. (Reproduced by permission from reference 8.7.)

shows schematically an air-cushion trailer built by Terracross [8.7]. The towing vehicle is usually a conventional tracked or wheeled vehicle. The system offers the convenience of an ordinary tractor-trailer unit. It should be mentioned, however, that since the air-cushion trailer is not self-propelled, the mobility of the system depends on the towing vehicle. This restricts the use of this system to areas where the conventional towing vehicle can operate effectively. The towing vehicle has to develop sufficient drawbar pull to overcome the total drag acting on the air-cushion trailer, which includes the skirt contact drag, resistance of guided wheels, and trim drag. This type of system normally operates at low speeds; aerodynamic resistance and momentum drag acting on the air cushion trailer would be insignificant and may be neglected.

As mentioned previously, one of the basic functions of the air-cushion system is to support the vehicle weight. As a consequence, power is required to generate the cushion lift. To compare the relative merits of an air cushion vehicle with a conventional ground vehicle on a rational basis, the power required to generate the lift by the cushion should be considered equivalent to part of the power required to overcome the motion resistance of a conventional vehicle. The concept of the equivalent coefficient of motion resistance f_{eq} for a vehicle wholly supported by an air cushion is proposed. It is defined as

$$f_{eq} = \frac{P_a}{WV} + \frac{R_m + R_a + R_{sk}}{W} \qquad (8.36)$$

where P_a is the power required to sustain the air cushion, W is the total weight of the vehicle, and V is the vehicle speed. It is noted that the equivalent coefficient of motion resistance of an air-cushion vehicle depends on operating speeds.

For a hybrid vehicle partly supported by air cushion and partly supported by surface contacting devices such as tracks or wheels, the equivalent coefficient of motion resistance is defined as

$$f_{eq} = \frac{P_a}{WV} + \frac{R_m + R_a + R_{sk} + R_r}{W} \qquad (8.37)$$

where R_r is the motion resistance of the surface contacting device. Figure 8.10 shows the variation of the equivalent coefficient of motion resistance with operating speed for a particular hybrid vehicle equipped with tires over clay, loose sand, and snow [8.10].

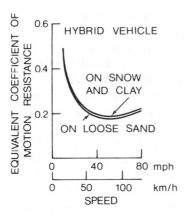

0   40   80 mph
0   50   100   km/h
SPEED

Fig. 8.10 Variation of the equivalent coefficient of motion resistance with speed of a hybrid vehicle. (Reproduced by permission from reference 8.10.)

Wave-Making Drag

When an air-cushion vehicle travels over water, waves will be generated as shown in Fig. 8.11. The vehicle tends to align itself with the wave and the cushion base will be inclined. Thus the lift force produces a rearward component that is commonly known as the wave making drag.

To reach a better understanding of the mechanism that generates the wave making drag, it is instructive to consider the nature of the interaction

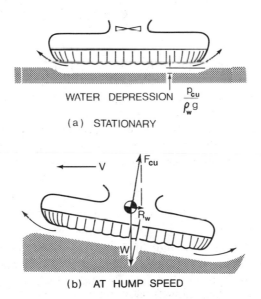

WATER DEPRESSION $\dfrac{p_{cu}}{\rho_w g}$

(a) STATIONARY

(b) AT HUMP SPEED

Fig. 8.11 Formation of wave-making drag.

between the air cushion and the water. When the vehicle is on cushion over water at zero forward speed, the water will be depressed by an amount equal to $p_{cu}/\rho_w g$, where g is the acceleration due to gravity and ρ_w is the density of the water, as shown in Fig. 8.11(a). When the vehicle travels forward, the water under the front part of the vehicle is just coming under the action of the cushion pressure, whereas under the rear part of the vehicle the water surface has been subjected to cushion pressure for a certain period of time. As a consequence, the water surface will be inclined downward toward the rear. As the vehicle tends to align itself with the water surface, the cushion base will take a nose up attitude, as shown in Fig. 8.11(b). The rearward component of the lift force perpendicular to the cushion base gives rise to the wave-making drag. The magnitude of this drag component increases with speed and reaches a maximum at a particular speed that is usually referred to as the hump speed. As vehicle speed further increases, the time during which the cushion interacts with the water surface becomes shorter. Consequently, the depression of the water becomes less, and the water surface under the vehicle begins to approach level again. The wave-making drag, therefore, decreases accordingly.

The wave-making drag may be predicted with sufficient accuracy by various methods. For a relatively long and narrow air-cushion vehicle, a two-dimensional theory for predicting the wave-making drag R_w based on Lamb's work has been proposed by Crewe and Egginton [8.1, 8.11]

$$R_w = \frac{2p_{cu}^2 A_c}{l\rho_w g}\left(1 - \cos\frac{gl}{V^2}\right)$$

or

$$\frac{R_w l}{p_{cu}^2 A_c} = \frac{2}{\rho_w g}\left(1 - \cos\frac{gl}{V^2}\right) \tag{8.38}$$

where l is the length of the cushion, p_{cu} is cushion pressure, A_c is cushion area, V is vehicle forward speed, and $V/\sqrt{gl}$ is the Froude number. The variation of $R_w l/p_{cu}^2 A_c$ with the Froude number is shown in Fig. 8.12 [8.1]. It is shown that the wave-making drag is a maximum when the Froude number is 0.56 and $\cos(gl/V^2)$ is equal to -1. This condition is commonly known as the hump and the associated drag is called hump drag. It is interesting to note that the wave-making drag is proportional to the square of cushion pressure.

A more accurate method for predicting wave-making drag that takes the shape of the planform of the vehicle into account has been developed by Newman and Poole [8.12]. It should be mentioned that water depth also

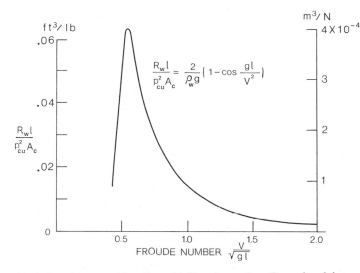

Fig. 8.12 Variation of wave-making drag with Froude number. (Reproduced, by permission, from *Hovercraft Design and Construction*, by G. H. Elsley and A. J. Devereux, copyright © by Elsley and Devereux, 1968.)

affects the wave-making drag. Over shallow water the wave-making drag is higher than that over deep water [8.12].

Wetting Drag

Wetting drag is a drag component due to spray striking the skirt and skirt-water contact. Although it is known that clearance height, cushion pressure, vehicle size and shape, and vehicle speed have influence over the magnitude of the wetting drag, no satisfactory method exists for the prediction of this drag component. A common practice to determine the wetting drag is to measure the total drag over calm water by model or full-scale tests, and then subtract those drag components that are known or calculable. Thus, wetting drag R_{wet} is given by [8.1, 8.5].

$$R_{wet} = R_{tot}(\text{calm water}) - R_a - R_m - R_w - R_{tr}(\text{if any}) \qquad (8.39)$$

where R_{tot} (calm water) is the total drag measured over calm water.

Drag Due to Waves

So far no theoretical method is available for the prediction of the drag due to waves. Its value is obtained from model or full-scale tests [8.1, 8.5].

Taking the difference between the total drag over waves, R_{tot} (over waves), and that over calm water, R_{tot} (calm water), at the same speed, one can obtain the drag due to waves R_{wave}.

$$R_{wave} = R_{tot}(\text{over waves}) - R_{tot}(\text{calm water}) \qquad (8.40)$$

It has been shown that wave height, cushion pressure, skirt depth, and vehicle speed have significant effects on the drag due to waves.

Total Overwater Drag

For overwater operations, the total drag of an air-cushion vehicle consists of aerodynamic resistance, momentum drag, wave-making drag, wetting drag, and drag due to waves. Figure 8.13 shows the relative order of magnitude of various drag components as a function of vehicle speed for overwater operations [8.5]. For vehicles with sidewalls, additional sidewall drag, mainly due to skin friction over the immersed surface, should also be taken into account.

It should be noted that the power consumption of an air-cushion vehicle consists of two major parts: power for lift and power for propulsion. In designing an air-cushion vehicle, power for lift and power for propulsion should, therefore, not be considered in isolation. For instance, increasing the clearance height or volume flow would reduce the skirt contact drag and hence power for propulsion. However, as discussed previously, power for lift is proportional to clearance height. Thus a compromise has to be made in selecting the clearance height so that total power requirement would be a minimum and it should also be compatible with other criteria such as skirt wear and ride comfort.

Example 8.2   The air-cushion vehicle described in Example 8.1 is to be used in overland transport. The frontal area of the vehicle is 6.5 m² (70 ft²) and the aerodynamic drag coefficient is 0.35. The coefficient of skirt contact drag is estimated to be 0.04. Determine the total drag of the vehicle over level ground at a speed of 20 km/h (12.4 mph).

Solution.   The total overland drag includes momentum drag, aerodynamic drag, and skirt contact drag.

A   The momentum drag R_m is given by Eq. 8.30.

$$R_m = \rho Q V_a = \rho \left[h_{c2} l_{c2} D_{c2} \left(\frac{2k_p P_{cu}}{\rho} \right)^{1/2} \right] V_a$$

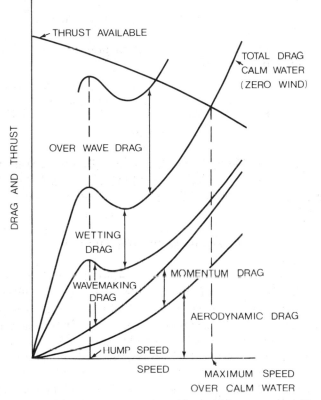

Fig. 8.13 Characteristics of drags of an air-cushion vehicle over water. (Reproduced by permission of R. L. Trillo from reference 8.5.)

Substituting the appropriate values given into the above equation, one obtains

$$R_m = 117.6 \text{ N } (26.4 \text{ lb})$$

B The aerodynamic drag R_a can be determined using Eq. 3.19.

$$R_a = \frac{\rho}{2} C_D A_f V^2 = 44.8 \text{ N } (10 \text{ lb})$$

C The skirt contact drag R_{sk} can be estimated using Eq. 8.35.

$$R_{sk} = C_{sk} W = 1957 \text{ N } (440 \text{ lb})$$

Total overland drag is the sum of the above three drag components.

$$R_{\text{tot}} = R_m + R_a + R_{sk} = 2.119 \text{ kN (476.4 lb)}$$

The results indicate that the momentum drag and aerodynamic drag are insignificant at low speeds.

8.3 SUSPENSION CHARACTERISTICS OF AIR-CUSHION SYSTEMS

One of the major functions of an air cushion is to act as a suspension system for the vehicle. To define its characteristics as a suspension, the stiffness and damping in bounce (or heave), roll, and pitch must be determined.

8.3.1 Heave (or Bounce) Stiffness

The heave (or bounce) stiffness can be derived from the relationship between the lift force and vertical displacement. For a simple plenum chamber, this relationship depends, to a great extent, on the fan character-istics. For a practical plenum chamber system, the ducting between the fan and the cushion and the feeding arrangements for the cushion also have significant influence on its stiffness and damping characteristics. Consider that a simple plenum chamber is in equilibrium at an initial clearance height h_{co} with initial cushion pressure p_{co} and volume flow Q_o. Neglecting ducting losses, the fan will operate at point A as shown in Fig. 8.14. Consider that the cushion system is disturbed from its equilibrium position and the clearance height decreases by an amount of Δh_c. Accordingly, the volume flow will decrease by an amount of ΔQ_o and the pressure will increase from p_{co} to $p_{co} + \Delta p_c$. The operating point of the fan shifts from A to A'. Thus, a restoring force which tends to bring the cushion system back to its original equilibrium position is created and the system is stable in heave.

If the parameters of the cushion system and the fan characteristics are known, the heave stiffness about an equilibrium position can be predicted [8.13]. An approximate method for predicting the stiffness of a simple plenum chamber is described below to illustrate the procedures involved.

The general relationship between pressure and volume flow of a fan commonly used in air-cushion vehicles is expressed by

$$p = f(Q)$$

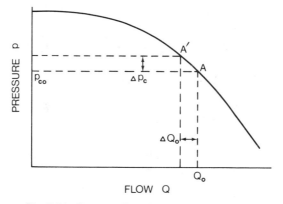

Fig. 8.14   Pressure-flow characteristics of a fan.

and

$$\frac{dp}{dQ} = f'(Q) \qquad f'(Q) < 0 \tag{8.41}$$

where $f'(Q)$ is the slope of the pressure-flow characteristic curve of the fan.

The volume flow from the cushion for a simple plenum chamber is governed by Eq. 8.3 and the relationship between cushion pressure and air escaping velocity is given by Eq. 8.2. By differentiating Eqs. 8.2 and 8.3, the following relationships can be obtained.

From Eq. 8.2

$$dV_c = \frac{dp_{cu}}{\rho V_c} \tag{8.42}$$

and from Eq. 8.3

$$dQ_c = h_c l_{cu} D_c dV_c + V_c l_{cu} D_c dh_c \tag{8.43}$$

Substituting Eq. 8.42 into Eq. 8.43, one obtains

$$dQ_c = h_c l_{cu} D_c \frac{dp_{cu}}{\rho V_c} + V_c l_{cu} D_c dh_c \tag{8.44}$$

Neglecting pressure and flow losses between the fan and the cushion (i.e., $p = p_{cu}$ and $Q = Q_c$), and combining Eqs. 8.41 and 8.44, one can obtain

$$dp_{cu} \left[\frac{1}{f'(Q_c)} - \frac{h_c l_{cu} D_c}{\rho V_c} \right] = V_c l_{cu} D_c dh_c$$

or

$$\frac{dp_{cu}}{\rho V_c^2/2}\left[\frac{\rho V_c}{h_c l_{cu} D_c f'(Q_c)}-1\right]=\frac{2l_{cu}D_c dh_c}{h_c l_{cu}D_c}\qquad(8.45)$$

Since $p_{cu}=\rho V_c^2/2$, the above equation can be written as

$$\frac{dp_{cu}}{p_{cu}}=\left[\frac{2}{\rho V_c/h_c l_{cu}D_c f'(Q_c)-1}\right]\frac{dh_c}{h_c}\qquad(8.46)$$

The lift force generated by the cushion F_{cu} is equal to $p_{cu}A_c$; the above equation, therefore, can be rewritten as

$$\frac{dF_{cu}}{dh_c}=\left[\frac{2}{\rho V_c/h_c l_{cu}D_c f'(Q_c)-1}\right]\frac{F_{cu}}{h_c}$$

$$=K_h\frac{F_{cu}}{h_c}\qquad(8.47)$$

Equation 8.47 gives the equivalent heave stiffness of a simple plenum chamber about the equilibrium position. It can be seen that the heave stiffness is strongly dependent on the slope of the pressure-flow characteristic curve of the fan $f'(Q)$. Since the value of $f'(Q)$ varies with the operating point of the fan, bounce stiffness is a function of operating conditions. The general characteristics of lift-displacement relationship of a simple plenum chamber under steady-state conditions are shown in Fig. 8.15 [8.5]. It can be seen that the air cushion is essentially a nonlinear system. However, for motions with small amplitudes about an equilibrium position, the system may be linearized.

The damping characteristics of an air-cushion system may be de-

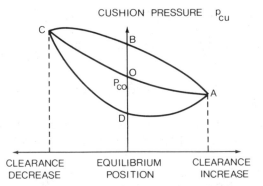

Fig. 8.15 Variation of lift force with clearance height of a simple plenum chamber. (Reproduced by permission of R. L. Trillo from reference 8.5.)

termined experimentally, for instance, using a dynamic heave table [8.5]. The cushion system being tested is mounted above the heave table, which can move up and down relative to the cushion with various amplitudes and frequencies. At a particular amplitude and frequency, the variation of lift force with displacement in a complete cycle is measured. If the system possesses damping, the variation of lift force with displacement will follow different paths during the upward and downward strokes of the table as shown in Fig. 8.15. The area enclosed by curve $ABCDA$ represents the degree of damping the cushion system possesses. The damping of an air cushion is usually not of simple viscous type. It is asymmetric and dependent upon the frequency of motion. However, to simplify the analysis, an equivalent viscous damping coefficient c_{eq} for the air cushion may be derived on the basis of equal energy dissipation

$$c_{eq} = \frac{U}{\pi \omega Z^2} \qquad (8.48)$$

where U is the actual energy dissipated in the air cushion during a cycle that is represented by the area enclosed by curve $ABCDA$ in Fig. 8.15, and ω and Z are the circular frequency and amplitude of the heave table, respectively.

Figure 8.16 shows schematically an air-cushion system designed for high-speed guided vehicles [8.14]. One of its unique features is the inclusion of a damper to provide the vehicle with sufficient damping to achieve the required ride quality.

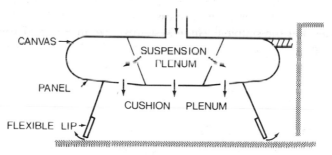

Fig. 8.16 An air-cushion system designed for high-speed guided vehicles. (Reproduced by permission from reference 8.14.)

8.3.2 Roll Stiffness

Stability in roll and pitch of air-cushion vehicles may be achieved by two methods: differential pressure and differential area. The multiple-cone system developed by Bertin obtains stability in roll and pitch from the

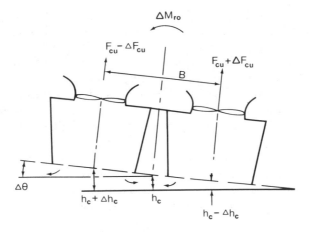

Fig. 8.17 Roll stability by differential pressure.

pressure differential between the downgoing side and the upgoing side of the skirt system as shown in Fig. 8.17. When the vehicle rolls, the clearance height on the downgoing side decreases. From previous analysis, it is known that the volume flow will decrease and the cushion pressure will increase. On the upgoing side, however, the cushion pressure will decrease, because of the increase of clearance height and volume flow. The increase of lift force on the downgoing side and the decrease of lift force on the upgoing side form a restoring moment that tends to bring the cushion system back to its equilibrium position.

Consider that the simple cushion system shown in Fig. 8.17 rolls a small angle $\Delta\theta$ with respect to the equilibrium position. The clearance height on the downgoing side will decrease by an average amount of Δh_c

$$\Delta h_c = (B/2)\Delta\theta \tag{8.49}$$

where B is the beam of the cushion.

On the upgoing side, the clearance height will increase by the same amount. From Eq. 8.47, the restoring moment ΔM_{ro} corresponding to the angular displacement $\Delta\theta$ is expressed by

$$\Delta M_{ro} = B\Delta F_{cu} = \frac{BF_{cu}K_h}{h_c}\Delta h_c$$

$$= \frac{B^2 F_{cu}K_h}{2h_c}\Delta\theta \tag{8.50}$$

In the limit the roll stiffness of the system K_r is given by

$$K_r = \frac{dM_{ro}}{d\theta} = \frac{B^2 F_{cu} K_h}{2h_c} \qquad (8.51)$$

Figure 8.18 shows the variation of the restoring moment coefficient C_{ro}, which is equal to $2M_{ro}/WB'$, with roll angle, for a 1/5 scale model of the Bertin BC 8 air cushion vehicle [8.15]. In Fig. 8.18, the effects of the difference in clearance height between the cones and the peripheral skirt on the roll characteristics are illustrated. When the roll angle exceeds a certain range and the downgoing side of the skirt comes into contact with the ground, the roll characteristics of the multiple-cone system may change significantly and considerable hysteresis has been observed [8.16].

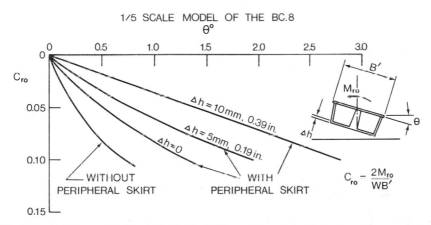

Fig. 8.18 Roll characteristics of the Bertin BC.8 cushion system. (Reproduced by permission from French Air Cushion Vehicle Developments, by J. Bertin, *Canadian Aeronautics and Space Journal*, January, 1968.)

Roll and pitch stability can also be achieved by using inflated bags (or keels) to divide the cushion into compartments. This method has been used by British Hovercraft Corporation in their skirt systems as shown in Fig. 8.19(a) [8.4]. The air pressure in the fan plenum is common to all compartments. However, when the vehicle rolls, on the upgoing side the flow increases, and consequently the cushion pressure decreases because of increased pressure losses through the cushion feed holes shown in Fig. 8.5(b). On the downgoing side, the flow decreases and the cushion pressure increases accordingly. As a result, a restoring moment is generated, which tends to return the system to its original equilibrium position. This method

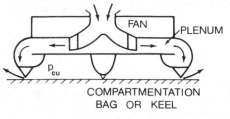

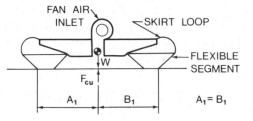

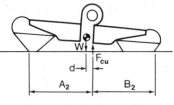

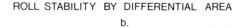

$A_1 + B_1 < A_2 + B_2$

ROLL STABILITY BY DIFFERENTIAL AREA

b.

Fig. 8.19 (*a*) Roll stability by compartmentation. (Reproduced by permission of the Society of Automotive Engineers from reference 8.4.) (*b*) Roll stability by differential area. (Reproduced by permission from reference 8.7.)

of achieving roll and pitch stability is essentially based on the principle of differential pressure.

The method for obtaining stability in roll and pitch by differential area has been employed by Hovercraft Development Ltd. in the design of their skirt systems. Stability is achieved by the outward movement of the downgoing side of the skirt, thus increasing the cushion area of the downgoing side as shown in Fig. 8.19(b) [8.7]. Consequently, the lift force on the downgoing side increases and a restoring moment is generated.

8.4 DIRECTIONAL CONTROL OF AIR-CUSHION VEHICLES

For vehicles wholly supported on an air cushion, their relative freedom from the surface presents unique problems in directional control. The methods for directional control may be divided into four main categories: aerodynamic control surfaces, differential thrust, thrust vectoring, and control ports. These methods are illustrated in Fig. 8.20 [8.2].

Using aerodynamic control surfaces such as rudders in the slipstream of the air propeller could provide an effective means for directional control of vehicles wholly supported on an air cushion. However, their effectiveness reduces with the decrease of slipstream velocity at low thrust. The control surfaces may also induce adverse rolling moment if the center of pressure of these surfaces is high relative to the center of gravity of the vehicle.

An adequate degree of directional control may be achieved by differential thrust produced by twin propellers fixed side by side as shown in Fig. 8.20. The differential thrust may be obtained by controlling propeller pitch and/or rotating speed. It should be noted, however, that decreasing the thrust on one of the propellers reduces the total forward thrust available and hence vehicle speed. In this fixed side-by-side propeller configuration,

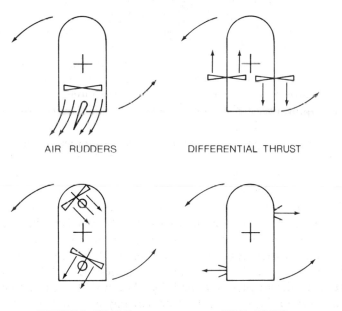

AIR RUDDERS   DIFFERENTIAL THRUST

ROTATING PYLONS   PUFF-PORTS

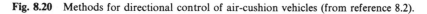

Fig. 8.20 Methods for directional control of air-cushion vehicles (from reference 8.2).

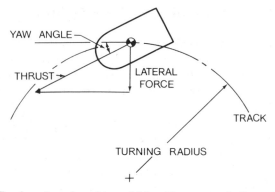

Fig. 8.21 Turning of an air-cushion vehicle with a yaw angle (from reference 8.2).

the thrust is parallel to the longitudinal axis of the vehicle. To provide a lateral force to balance the centrifugal force during a turning maneuver, the vehicle has to operate with a certain yaw angle as shown in Fig. 8.21 [8.2].

Using fore and aft swivelling pylon-mounted propellers, yawing moment and side force required for direction control can be generated. For some current designs, the swivel angle is confined to 30° on either side of the longitudinal axis to limit the magnitude of the adverse roll moment. Compared with the fixed side-by-side propeller arrangement, swivelling pylon-mounted propellers can generate higher yawing moment since the propellers can be mounted further from the center of gravity of the vehicle and less forward thrust is lost for a given yawing moment.

By discharging pressurized air from the so-called puff-ports located at each corner of the vehicle, yawing moment and side force can be provided. They are usually used as an auxiliary device to supplement other control devices.

To further improve the directional control of air-cushion vehicles, surface contacting devices, such as wheels for overland operations and retractable water rods for overwater operations, have been used. For overland operations, the wheels carry a proportion of the vehicle weight to provide the vehicle with the required cornering force for directional control. The load carried by the wheels ranges 2–30% of the total vehicle weight in existing designs, depending on whether the wheels are also used as a propulsive device or not. It has been found that using the wheel as a directional control device is quite effective [8.3].

The cornering force that a wheel can develop for control purposes consists of two major components: the lateral shearing force on the contact area; the lateral force resulting from the normal pressure exerted on the

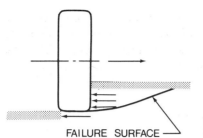

Fig. 8.22 Development of cornering force of a wheel on deformable surfaces.

FAILURE SURFACE

sidewall of the wheel, which is similar in nature to that acting on a bulldozer blade or a retaining wall as illustrated in Fig. 8.22. The magnitude of this force depends on the sinkage of the wheel and terrain properties and may be predicted by the earth pressure theory of soil mechanics discussed in Chapter 2.

As an example, Fig. 8.23 shows the variation of the maximum lateral acceleration a_y that can be sustained under a steady-state turn with load distribution for a particular hybrid vehicle with tires over clay [8.3]. The lateral acceleration shown is calculated from the maximum cornering force that can be developed by the tires of the vehicle. The possible minimum turning radius of the vehicle at a forward speed of 16 km/h (10 mph) is also plotted as a function of load distribution in Fig. 8.23 [8.3].

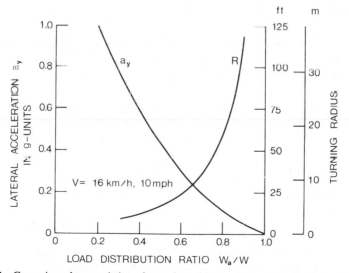

Fig. 8.23 Cornering characteristics of an air-cushion vehicle with wheels for directional control in clay. (Reproduced by permission from reference 8.3.)

For overwater air-cushion vehicles, methods similar to those for controlling the direction of ships may be employed. For instance, rudders immersed in the water have been used in air-cushion vehicles with rigid sidewalls for purposes of directional control.

REFERENCES

8.1   G. H. Elsley and A. J. Devereux, *Hovercraft Design and Construction*, Cornell Maritime Press Inc., 1968.

8.2   National Research Council of Canada, Air Cushion Vehicles—Their Potential for Canada, December 1969.

8.3   J. Y. Wong, Performance of the Air-Cushion-Surface-Contacting Hybrid Vehicle for Overland Operation, *Proceedings of the Institution of Mechanical Engineers*, Vol. 186, 50/72, 1972.

8.4   P. A. Sullivan, A Review of the Status of the Technology of the Air Cushion Vehicle, *SAE Transactions*, Vol. 80, paper 710183, 1971.

8.5   R. L. Trillo, *Marine Hovercraft Technology*, Leonard Hill, London, England, 1971.

8.6   H. S. Fowler, The Air Cushion Vehicle as a Load Spreading Transport Device, *Journal of Terramechanics*, Vol. 12, No. 2, 1975.

8.7   P. L. Eggleton and J. Laframboise, Field Evaluation of Towed Air Cushion Rafts, Report of Transportation Development Agency, TDA-500-166, Ministry of Transport, Ottawa, Canada, 1974.

8.8   R. A. Liston, Operational Evaluation of the SK-5 Air Cushion Vehicle in Alaska, U.S. Army Cold Regions Research and Engineering Laboratory Report TR 413, 1973.

8.9   C. R. Silversides, T. B. Tsay, and H. M. Mucha, Effect of Obstacles and Ground Clearance Upon the Movement of an ACV Platform. Forest Management Institute, Information Report FMR-X-62, Department of the Environment, Ottawa, Canada, 1974.

8.10   J. Y. Wong, On the Applications of Air Cushion Technology to Overland Transport, *High Speed Ground Transportation Journal*, Vol. 6, No. 3, 1972.

8.11   P. R. Crewe and W. J. Egginton, The Hovercraft—a New Concept in Maritime Transport, *Quarterly Transactions of Royal Institute of Naval Architects*, No. 3, July, 1960.

8.12   J. N. Newman and F. A. P. Poole, The Wave Resistance of a Moving Pressure Distribution in a Canal, *Schifftechnik*, Vol. 9, No. 45, 1962.

8.13   P. Guienne, Stability of the Terraplane on the Ground, *Hovering Craft and Hydrofoil*, July, 1964.

8.14   J. P. Morel and C. Bonnat, Air Cushion Suspension for Aerotrain: Theoretical Schemes for Static and Dynamic Operation, in H. B. Pacejka, Ed., *Proceedings of the IUTAM Symposium on the Dynamics of Vehicles on Roads and Railway Tracks*, Swets and Zeitlinger B. V., Amsterdam, 1975.

8.15   J. Bertin, French Air Cushion Vehicle Developments, *Canadian Aeronautics and Space Journal*, Vol. 14, No. 1, January 1968.

8.16   P. A. Sullivan, M. J. Hinchey, and R. G. Delaney, An Investigation of the Roll Stiffness Characteristics of Three Flexible Skirted Cushion Systems, Institute for Aerospace Studies, University of Toronto, Report No. 213, 1977.

8.17   J. Y. Wong, On the Application of Air Cushion Technology to Off-Road Transport, *Canadian Aeronautics and Space Journal*, Vol. 19, No. 1, January 1973.

PROBLEMS

8.1 An air-cushion vehicle has a gross weight of 80.06 kN (18,000 lb). Its planform is essentially of rectangular shape, 6.09 m (20 ft) wide and 12.19 m (40 ft) long. The cushion system is of plenum chamber type. It operates at an average daylight clearance of 2.54 cm (1 in.). Determine the power required to sustain the air cushion. Calculate also the augmentation factor.

8.2 An air-cushion vehicle has the same weight and planform as those of the vehicle described in Problem 8.1 but is equipped with a multiple-cone system with a peripheral skirt. It has eight cones with diameter of 2.44 m (8 ft). The average daylight clearance of the cones is 2.54 cm (1 in.) and that of the peripheral skirt is 1.9 cm (0.75 in.). Determine the power required to generate cushion lift using a suitable peripheral skirt.

8.3 The air-cushion vehicle described in Problem 8.2 is employed for overland transport. The frontal area of the vehicle is 16.26 m^2 (175 ft^2) and the aerodynamic drag coefficient is 0.38. The value of the coefficient of skirt contact drag over a particular terrain is 0.03. Determine the total overland drag of the vehicle in the speed range 5–30 km/h (3.1–18.6 mph). Calculate also the total power requirements, including both for lift and for propulsion, over the speed range.

8.4 Determine the equivalent coefficient of motion resistance of the air-cushion vehicle described in Problem 8.3 over the speed range 5–30 km/h (3.1–18.6 mph).

8.5 The air-cushion vehicle described in Problem 8.1 is employed for overwater transport. The frontal area of the vehicle is 16.26 m^2 (175 ft^2) and the aerodynamic drag coefficient is 0.38. Neglecting the wetting drag, determine the total overwater drag of the vehicle in the speed range 10–60 km/h (6.2 to 37.3 mph) over calm, deep water. Calculate also the total power requirements of the vehicle over the speed range.

8.6 A proposed tracked air-cushion vehicle weighs 195.71 kN (44,000 lb) and has eight lift pads, each of which is 4.27 m (14 ft) long and 1.3 m (4.25 ft) wide. The cushion is of peripheral jet type with jet thickness of 6.35 mm (0.25 in.) and the angle of the jet with respect to the horizontal is 50°. The clearance is 6.35 mm (0.25 in.) at equilibrium. If the vehicle is simplified to a single-degree-of-freedom system, estimate the equivalent stiffness of the air-cushion pads and the natural frequency of the vehicle in bounce about equilibrium position.

INDEX